CLIMATE CHANGE AND DISPLACEMENT

Environmental migration is not new. Nevertheless, the events and processes accompanying global climate change threaten to increase human movement both within states and across international borders. The Inter governmental Panel on Climate Change has predicted an increased frequency and severity of climate events such as storms, cyclones and hurricanes, as well as longer-term sea level rise and desertification, which will impact upon people's ability to survive in certain parts of the world.

This book brings together a variety of disciplinary perspectives on the phenomenon of climate-induced displacement. With chapters by leading scholars in their field, it collects in one place a rigorous, holistic analysis of the phenomenon, which can better inform academic understanding and policy development alike. Governments have not been prepared to take a leading role in developing responses to the issue, in large part due to the absence of strong theoretical and empirical frameworks from which sound policy can be constructed. The specialist expertise of the authors in this book means that each chapter identifies key issues that need to be considered in shaping domestic, regional and international responses, including the complex causes of movement, the conceptualisation of migration responses to climate change, the terminology that should be used to describe those who move, and attitudes to migration that may affect decisions to stay or leave. The book will help to facilitate the creation of principled, research-based responses, and will establish climate-induced displacement as an important aspect of both the climate change and global migration debates.

Climate Change and Displacement

Multidisciplinary Perspectives

Edited by Jane McAdam

·HART·
PUBLISHING

OXFORD AND PORTLAND, OREGON
2010

Published in the United Kingdom by Hart Publishing Ltd
16C Worcester Place, Oxford, OX1 2JW
Telephone: +44 (0)1865 517530
Fax: +44 (0)1865 510710
E-mail: mail@hartpub.co.uk
Website: http://www.hartpub.co.uk

Published in North America (US and Canada) by
Hart Publishing
c/o International Specialized Book Services
920 NE 58th Avenue, Suite 300
Portland, OR 97213-3786
USA
Tel: +1 503 287 3093 or toll-free: (1) 800 944 6190
Fax: +1 503 280 8832
E-mail: orders@isbs.com
Website: http://www.isbs.com

British Library Cataloguing in Publication Data
Data Available

ISBN: 978-1-84946-038-5

Typeset by Hope Services, Abingdon
Printed and bound in Great Britain by
CPI Antony Rowe, Wiltshire

ACKNOWLEDGEMENTS

The editor gratefully acknowledges the Australian Research Council for its financial support of this project, and the work of each of the contributors in compiling their chapters for this book. She also expresses her sincere thanks to Dr Emily Crawford and Trina Ng for their excellent research and editorial support; to colleagues at the Law Faculty, University of New South Wales and Lincoln College, University of Oxford for their interest and encouragement; and to Hart Publishing for their patience and professionalism. In particular, the editor wishes to thank Tony Whincup for permission to use his photograph of people collecting wood on the beach in Kiribati as the book's cover image.

CONTENTS

BIOGRAPHIES

Jon Barnett is a Reader in the Department of Resource Management and Geography at the University of Melbourne. He is a political geographer whose research investigates the impacts of and responses to environmental change on social systems. This includes research on climate change, environmental security, water and food. He has been conducting research on the social and institutional dimensions of vulnerability and adaptation to climate change since 2000. This has included field-based research in the South Pacific, China and Timor-Leste. Associate Professor Barnett is host convenor of the Australian research network on the social, economic and institutional dimensions of climate change, which is part of the National Climate Change Adaptation Research Facility. He has published three books and over 60 academic papers, and is on the editorial boards of *Global Environmental Change*, *Geography Compass* and *Wiley Interdisciplinary Reviews: Climate Change*.

Helen Berry is Associate Professor and Deputy Director (Research), Centre for Research and Action in Public Health at the University of Canberra. She also holds adjunct appointments as Associate Professor at both the Australian National University and the University of Newcastle, New South Wales. She is a psychiatric epidemiologist (MA, BSc, BAppPsych, PhD) with a particular interest in investigating the relationship between social capital and mental health, and their shared associations with contemporary issues in health and well-being. Recently, Associate Professor Berry has extended this work so as to place these research and policy issues in the context of climate change, particularly its impacts in rural and remote locations. Her work involves the use of advanced statistical modelling techniques to analyse representative datasets and evaluate mental health interventions. With a previous career in executive public and non-profit administration, she has a particular interest in the way in which research and public policy-making can work together. Associate Professor Berry leads collaborations on social capital, mental health and climate change with Australian government agencies, state and local government, and various universities, including in Vietnam.

Kathryn Bowen is a PhD candidate at the National Centre for Epidemiology and Population Health at the Australian National University in Canberra. She is studying the health risks of climate change and public health, with particular attention to the needs and processes relating to adaptation. She has an honours degree in psychology and an MSc in International Health. Since 2000, Kathryn has worked in health promotion, alcohol and drugs, mental health, HIV prevention and communicable disease surveillance. Her work has spanned research, education and programme development and management, both in Australia and overseas. Kathryn has travelled and worked in India, Cambodia, Vietnam, Switzerland, Germany and the United Kingdom. She is a co-founder of the Melbourne-based not-for-profit organisation, *Just Change*, which promotes equity through energy efficiency activities. Kathryn has recently been engaged by WHO and AusAID (Australia's national overseas aid agency) to conduct applied research on the strengthening of community and government capacity to adapt to the health effects of climate change in low-income settings, looking particularly at the intersection between public health governance, social justice, development and environmental sustainability.

John Campbell is Associate Professor in the Department of Geography, Tourism and Environmental Planning at the University of Waikato, New Zealand where he teaches courses on Resource Management, Pacific Island Geography, Disasters and Development and Human Dimensions of Environmental Change. His work is mostly in Pacific island countries and has focused on the human dimensions of disaster risk reduction and climate change adaptation. His most recent research has included a participatory investigation of a relocated village in Fiji and a regional survey of community relocation as a response to climatic variability and change, a study of traditional disaster reduction practices, the role of disaster relief, urban disaster vulnerabilities in Pacific island countries and problems confronting the Pacific region in building appropriate adaptation responses.

Stephen Castles is Research Professor of Sociology at the University of Sydney. He is also Associate Director of the International Migration Institute, University of Oxford, having been its Director and Professor of Migration and Refugee Studies until August 2009. From 2001 to 2006, he was Director of the Refugee Studies Centre at the University of Oxford. Between 1986 to 2000, he was Professor of Sociology and Director of the Centre for Multicultural Studies (1986–96) and then Director of the Centre for Asia Pacific Social Transformation Studies at the University of Wollongong in Australia. Professor Castles is a sociologist and political economist, and works on international migration dynamics, global governance, migration and development, and regional migration trends in Africa, Asia and Europe. His current research focuses on social transformation and international migration in the twenty-first century, with fieldwork in Australia, Ghana, Mexico and the Republic of Korea. He has been an advisor to the Australian and British governments, and has worked for the International Labour Organization, the International Organization for Migration, the European Union and other international bodies. From 1994 to 2001, Professor Castles helped establish and coordinate the UNESCO-MOST Asia Pacific Migration Research Network. His recent books include: *The Age of Migration: International Population Movements in the Modern World*, 4th edn (with Mark Miller; Basingstoke, Palgrave Macmillan,

2009); *Migration, Citizenship and the European Welfare State: A European Dilemma* (with Carl-Ulrik Schierup and Peo Hansen; Oxford, Oxford University Press, 2006); and an edited collection (with Raúl Delgado Wise) entitled *Migration and Development: Perspectives from the South* (Geneva, International Organization for Migration, 2008).

Lorraine Elliott is an Associate Professor and holds a Senior Fellowship in the Department of International Relations at the Australian National University. She has held appointments as Reader in International Relations at the University of Warwick in the United Kingdom, with visiting appointments at the University of Oxford (Balliol College); the Asia Research Centre at the London School of Economics and Political Science; the University of Keele; and the Institute for Environmental Studies at the Free University of Amsterdam. She is currently a Visiting Senior Fellow at the Centre for Non-Traditional Security at Nanyang Technological University, where she is lead researcher for a Macarthur-funded project on climate security, human security and social resilience. Associate Professor Elliott researches, publishes and teaches in the areas of global and regional environmental governance; non-traditional security, including climate security, human security and environmental security; transnational environmental crime; and Australian foreign policy (again with a focus on international environmental issues). She is the author of more than 70 book chapters and journal articles on these topics. Her publications also include books on Antarctic environmental politics, cosmopolitan militaries, and two editions of *The Global Politics of the Environment* (Basingstoke, Palgrave Macmillan, 1998 and 2004). She is currently working on a single-authored book on regional environmental governance under ASEAN and an edited book on comparative environmental regionalism. Associate Professor Elliott has held grants from the Australian Research Council, the Canadian government, the Royal Dutch Academy of Arts and Sciences and the United States Institute of Peace. She is a member of the Australian Committee of the Council for Security Cooperation Asia Pacific (CSCAP) and has recently been appointed to a three-year term on the Board of Directors of the Academic Council for the United Nations System (ACUNS).

Graeme Hugo is an Australian Research Council (ARC) Australian Professorial Fellow, Professor of the Department of Geographical and Environmental Studies and Director of the National Centre for Social Applications of Geographic Information Systems at the University of Adelaide. His research interests are in population issues in Australia and South East Asia, especially migration. His books include *Australia's Changing Population* (Melbourne, Oxford University Press, 1986); *The Demographic Dimension in Indonesian Development* (with TH Hull, VJ Hull and GW Jones; Singapore, Oxford University Press, 1987); *International Migration Statistics: Guidelines for Improving Data Collection Systems* (with AS Oberai, H Zlotnik and R Bilsborrow; Geneva, International Labour Office, 1997); *Worlds in Motion: Understanding International Migration at Century's End* (with

DS Massey, J Arango, A Kouaouci, A Pellegrino and JE Taylor; Oxford, Oxford University Press, 1998); several of the 1986, 1991 and 1996 census-based *Atlas of the Australian People Series* (Canberra, Australian Government Publishing Service); *Australian Immigration: A Survey of the Issues* (with M Wooden, R Holton and J Sloan; Canberra, Australian Government Publishing Service, 1990); *New Forms of Urbanisation: Beyond the Urban–Rural Dichotomy* (edited with T Champion; Aldershot, Ashgate, 2004); and *Australian Census Analytic Program: Australia's Most Recent Immigrants* (Canberra, Australian Bureau of Statistics, 2004). In 2002, Professor Hugo secured an ARC Federation Fellowship over five years for his research project, 'The new paradigm of international migration to and from Australia: Dimensions, causes and implications'. His recent research has focused on migration and development, environment and migration and migration policy. In 2009 he was awarded an ARC Australian Professorial Fellowship over five years for his research project 'Circular migration in Asia, the Pacific and Australia: Empirical, theoretical and policy dimensions'.

Walter Kälin is Professor of Constitutional and International Law at the Faculty of Law, University of Bern, Switzerland and a former Dean of the Faculty and Head of the Legal Department. Since 2004, he has been Representative of the United Nations Secretary-General on the Human Rights of Internally Displaced Persons. Between 2003 and 2008 he was a Member of the United Nations Human Rights Committee, and from 1991 to 1992 he was Special Rapporteur of the United Nations Commission on Human Rights on the Situation of Human Rights in Kuwait under Iraqi Occupation. Professor Kälin's research is in the areas of human rights law, refugee law and internal displacement, as well as Swiss constitutional law and the legal aspects of decentralisation. His most recent books include *The Law of International Human Rights Protection* (with Jörg Künzli; Oxford, Oxford University Press, 2009); *Guiding Principles on Internal Displacement: Annotations*, 2nd edn (Washington DC, American Society of International Law, 2008); *Grundrechte* (with Regina Kiener; Bern, Staempfli Publishers, 2007); and an edited collection with Rhodri Williams, Khalid Koser and Andrew Solomon entitled *Incorporating the Guiding Principles on Internal Displacement into Domestic Law: Issues and Challenges* (Washington DC, American Society of International Law, 2010).

Maryanne Loughry is a Sister of Mercy and the Associate Director, Jesuit Refugee Service Australia. Dr Loughry has been associated with the Jesuit Refugee Service since 1986 and through it worked in the Indochinese refugee camps in the Philippines (1988) and the Vietnamese Detention Centres in Hong Kong (1990, 1992–93) as a psychologist and trainer. Dr Loughry is a visiting research scholar at the Centre for Human Rights and International Justice, Boston College and the Refugee Studies Centre, University of Oxford. Prior to this she was the Pedro Arrupe tutor at the Refugee Studies Centre, University of Oxford for over seven years (1997–2004). Her doctoral work explored the impact of detention on unaccompanied Vietnamese children. Dr Loughry is a member of the Australian Government's Advisory Council for Immigration Services and Status Resolution and serves on several international boards, including the academic board of the Gaza Community Mental Health Programme (GCMHP) and the Governing Committee of the International Catholic Migration Committee (ICMC). She has conducted research and programme evaluation in numerous refugee and conflict settings, including Syria, Northern Uganda, Afghanistan, Kenya, Palestinian Territories, Kosovo, Indonesia and Timor-Leste. She has also conducted human-itarian trainings in Rwanda, Zimbabwe, Thailand, Kenya, Cambodia, Vietnam and the United Kingdom. Currently she is researching the psychosocial effects of climate-induced displacement in the Pacific.

Jane McAdam is an Associate Professor in the Faculty of Law at the University of New South Wales, Australia. She is the Director of Research in the School of Law and the Director of the International Refugee and Migration Law project at the Gilbert + Tobin Centre of Public Law. She is also a Research Associate at the University of Oxford's Refugee Studies Centre, and was the Director of its International Summer School in Forced Migration in 2008. She previously taught in the Faculty of Law at the University of Sydney and at Lincoln College at the University of Oxford, where she obtained her doctorate. Associate Professor McAdam holds two Australian Research Council Discovery Grants. The first sup-ports her research on 'Weathering Uncertainty: Climate Change "Refugees" and International Law', including field work in Kiribati, Tuvalu, Bangladesh and India; the second is a grant held with two historians to examine 'Immigration Restriction and the Racial State, c. 1880 to the Present'. She is the author of *Complementary Protection in International Refugee Law* (Oxford, Oxford University Press, 2007); *The Refugee in International Law*, 3rd edn (with GS Goodwin-Gill; Oxford, Oxford University Press, 2007); and the editor of *Forced Migration, Human Rights and Security* (Oxford, Hart Publishing, 2008). She is currently working on a mono-graph entitled *Climate Change, Displacement and International Law* (Oxford, Oxford University Press, forthcoming 2011). Associate Professor McAdam is the Associate Rapporteur of the Convention Refugee Status and Subsidiary Protection Working Party for the International Association of Refugee Law Judges; an adviser to the United Nations High Commissioner for Refugees on the legal aspects of cli-mate-related displacement; and has been a consultant to the Australian and British governments on migration issues.

Anthony McMichael is a Professor and an Australia Research Fellow at the National Centre for Epidemiology and Population Health, Australian National University, Canberra, where he heads the research programme on Environment, Climate and Health. He is a graduate in medicine (University of Adelaide), with a PhD in epidemiology (Monash University, Melbourne). From 1994 to 2001 he held the Chair of Epidemiology at the London School of Hygiene and Tropical Medicine. Over the past 15 years he has played a central role in the work of the

Intergovernmental Panel on Climate Change (IPCC) and the World Health Organization (WHO) in relation to the assessment of the health risks from climate change. In 2009 he assisted the governments of Vietnam and Cambodia in the (WHO-sponsored) assessment of health risks from climate change. In addition to his many published papers in this rapidly evolving topic area, his books include *Human Frontiers, Environments and Disease: Past Patterns, Uncertain Futures* (Cambridge, Cambridge University Press, 2001) and (with co-authors) *Climate Change and Human Health: Risks and Responses* (Geneva, World Health Organization, 2003).

Celia McMichael has a background in medical anthropology (MA, University of Edinburgh, and PhD, University of Melbourne) and in teaching public health (La Trobe University, Melbourne). She is currently a Research Fellow in the School of Social Sciences, La Trobe University, focusing on issues of refugee resettlement, health and well-being. She conducted her doctoral studies in the area of refugee resettlement, social capital and psychosocial well-being. She has carried out research in international health and development issues, including childhood diarrhoeal disease in Peru; gender, disaster and health in Sri Lanka; and indigenous women's health and cancer screening services in Queensland. From 2003–05, as a lecturer at La Trobe University, she developed and taught a course on evidence-based public health. She has also carried out fieldwork for the World Health Organization (Angola country office) in childhood immunisation (international polio eradication campaign). Dr McMichael has a particular interest in medical anthropology, qualitative research, social determinants of health inequities, international health and development, and forced migration and health.

Peter Penz is Professor Emeritus, Faculty of Environmental Studies, York University, Canada, and former Director of the University's Centre for Refugee Studies. He is senior author of *Displacement by Development: Ethics, Rights and Responsibilities* (with co-authors; Cambridge, Cambridge University Press, forthcoming), based on a two-team project he directed, in partnership with a unit at the Jawaharlal Nehru University in New Delhi. His previous publications include *Consumer Sovereignty and Human Interests* (Cambridge, Cambridge University Press, 1986); *The Real Poverty Report* (with co-authors; Edmonton, Hurtig, 1971), and the edited volumes *Political Ecology: Global and Local* (London, Routledge, 1998) and *Global Justice, Global Democracy* (Winnipeg, Fernwood, 1997). He has also published a monograph on structural unemployment, and chapters and articles on the ethics and conceptualisation of displacement by development; the ethics of asylum and of development assistance and conditionality; atrocities policing; state sovereignty and international justice; power and justice in international relations; land-rights mobilisation in India; and intra-state colonisation of tribal lands in Bangladesh and Indonesia. He has taught on a wide range of subjects, including project evaluation, environmental economics, environmental displacement, global environmental politics, theoretical perspectives on environment and society, socio-economic development, humanitarian crises and action, social policy, basic needs, political and social ethics, and social, environmental and global justice. He received his education in Germany (where he and his family had been displaced during WWII), East Pakistan, India, the University of British Columbia (economics, BA, MA) and the University of Oxford (DPhil). Before his academic career, he worked for six years for the federal government in Canada, including for the Special Senate Committee on Poverty (1969–71), from which he resigned to co-author a counter-report. International affiliations have been with the Centre for Development Studies in Thiruvananthapuram, Kerala, India, and the Network on Humanitarian Action, Universidad Deusto, Bilbao, Spain.

Michael Webber is Professorial Fellow in the Department of Resource Management and Geography at the University of Melbourne. He is an economic geographer whose research combines formal social theory and large-scale, survey-based empirical methods to identify how people's working lives are affected by international political and social processes. He has a subsidiary interest in environment and development. Professor Webber's recent research is about the economic and geographic transformation of modern China, the emergence of markets for water in China, the emergence of the global economy, the role of the state in industrial development in East Asia, and the restructuring of industries in Australia. He has published 13 books and over 100 academic papers. His research has also led him into consulting and pro bono activities on behalf of government departments, trade union and non-government organisations. He is a Fellow of the Academy of Social Sciences in Australia.

Roger Zetter is Director of the Refugee Studies Centre in the Department of International Development, University of Oxford, a position he has held since 2006. He has over 30 years' research, publication, teaching and consultancy experience in forced migration, refugee and humanitarian issues, with funding provided by the European Union, the United Kingdom Home Office, the Economic and Social Research Council, Oxfam, Housing Corporation, Swiss Agency for International Development, Brookings-Bern Project, various United Nations agencies (UNHCR, UNDP, UNFPA and UNHabitat), the International Organization for Migration, the Joseph Rowntree Foundation, and the Paul Hamlyn Foundation. From 1988 until 2001, he was Founding Editor of the *Journal of Refugee Studies*, published by Oxford University Press. Professor Zetter's research focuses on institutional and policy dimensions of the refugee regime and the impacts of humanitarian assistance on refugees and asylum seekers. His work includes all stages of the 'refugee cycle', from exile to reception and settlement policies, the experience of protracted exile and integration, repatriation and post-conflict reconstruction. He has directed large-scale research projects in Southern Africa and, more recently, in the EU and the UK, where his research has addressed the associational life of refugees and other migrants, issues of social cohesion and social capital and undocumented migration. Two papers on 'labelling' refugees in the *Journal of Refugee Studies* in 1991 and 2007 are among the most widely cited papers in the field of refugee studies. Currently he is investigating the scope of rights protection available to those displaced by the environmental impacts of climate change, with funding provided by the Swiss and Norwegian governments and the United Nations High Commissioner for Refugees. He co-authored a widely cited policy paper in 2008 (with C Boano and T Morris) entitled 'Environmentally Displaced People: Understanding Linkages between Environmental Change, Livelihoods and Forced Migration', Forced Migration Policy Briefing No 1 (Oxford, Refugee Studies Centre, 2008).

1

Introduction

JANE McADAM

I Background

Environmental migration is not a new phenomenon. Natural and human-induced environmental disasters and slow-onset degradation have displaced people in the past, and will continue to do so. However, global climate change threatens to significantly increase human movement, both within states and across international borders. The Intergovernmental Panel on Climate Change has predicted an increased frequency and severity of climate events such as storms, cyclones and hurricanes, as well as longer-term sea level rise and desertification, which will impact upon people's ability to live and maintain their livelihoods in certain parts of the world.[1] Around a fifth of the world's population lives in coastal areas affected by rising sea levels and natural disasters,[2] and there is a risk that some small island states, such as the Maldives, Tuvalu and Kiribati, could eventually be submerged altogether. Even though scientists cannot predict precisely *when* climate change may trigger displacement, or in what numbers people will move, it is clear that current international and national normative frameworks are ill-equipped to deal with it.

Predictions about how many people will be displaced 'are fraught with numerous methodological problems and caveats'.[3] This stems in part from the difficulties in accounting for unknown variables, such as exactly when the effects of climate change are likely to be felt most acutely, and 'the level of investment, planning and resources' that will be invested in trying to counter them.[4] Furthermore, one of the

---

[1] See, eg GC Hegerl et al, 'Understanding and Attributing Climate Change' in S Solomon et al (eds), *Climate Change 2007: The Physical Science Basis: Contribution of Working Group I to the Fourth Assessment Report of the Intergovernmental Panel on Climate Change* (Cambridge, Cambridge University Press, 2007); Intergovernmental Panel on Climate Change, *Climate Change 2007: Synthesis Report. Summary for Policymakers* (2007).

[2] Council of the European Union, Report from the Commission and the Secretary-General/High Representative to European Council on 'Climate Change and International Security' (Brussels, 3 March 2008) 3.

[3] F Biermann and I Boas, 'Preparing for a Warmer World: Towards a Global Governance System to Protect Climate Refugees', Global Governance Working Paper No 33 (November 2007) 9.

[4] N Stern, *The Economics of Climate Change: The Stern Review* (Cambridge, Cambridge University Press, 2007) 112.

most difficult variables to account for is human adaptive capacity, or 'resilience'.[5] As the refugee literature shows, it cannot always be anticipated when people will move in response to triggers like war or persecution. Some people flee instantly, some move later on, while others never move. The line between movement that is 'voluntary' and 'forced' is also very blurred, and people's decisions will involve a delicate mix of both elements in different proportions.

It is also difficult to disentangle the multiple causes for human movement, given the combined impacts of conflict, the environment and economic pressures.[6] Debates about the extent to which climate change intersects with and exacerbates underlying poverty, environmental degradation and unrest, and in turn impels migration, necessarily impact on the numerical estimates of displaced people.[7] As Castles has observed, the application of different methodologies by academics in this area has resulted in very different conclusions about the existence of 'environmental refugees'.[8]

Indeed, the fact that there is still no internationally agreed definition of what it means to be an environmental 'migrant', 'refugee' or 'displaced person' makes it difficult to systematically progress deliberations about appropriate multilateral legal and institutional responses. Questions of definition have governance implications because they inform the appropriate location of environmental migration institutionally—as an international, regional or local, developed and/or developing country concern/responsibility—as well as normatively—for example, within the existing refugee protection framework or under the UN Framework Convention on Climate Change.[9] Furthermore, there is a risk that a one-size-fits-all response could downplay the cultural and livelihood needs of displaced communities and local knowledge bases for adaptation.

II The Aims of this Book

Whereas scientists have been considering the impacts of climate change for many years, social scientists have come to the area relatively late. The idea behind the present book was to bring together the work of researchers from a variety of

[5] See JG Fritze et al, 'Hope, Despair and Transformation: Climate Change and the Promotion of Mental Health and Wellbeing' (2008) 2 *International Journal of Mental Health Systems* 13. Note, too, that historically, people moved in order to adapt to changing climatic patterns: eg SR Fischer, *A History of the Pacific Islands* (New York, Palgrave Macmillan, 2002) xvi, 37–38, 44. However, in earlier times, immigration controls did not hamper movement in the same way that they do today.

[6] Opening Statement by António Guterres, United Nations High Commissioner for Refugees (Geneva, 58th session of the Executive Committee of the High Commissioner's Programme, 1 October 2007).

[7] D Kniveton et al, *Climate Change and Migration: Improving Methodologies to Estimate Flows* (Geneva, IOM Migration Research Series No 33, 2008) 32.

[8] S Castles, 'Environmental Change and Forced Migration: Making Sense of the Debate', *New Issues in Refugee Research*, Working Paper No 70 (Geneva, UNHCR, 2002).

[9] United Nations Framework Convention on Climate Change (adopted 9 May 1992, entered into force 21 March 1993) 1771 UNTS 107.

disciplines—geography (political, economic and human) sociology, law, political economy, moral philosophy, public health, medical anthropology, epidemiology, psychiatric epidemiology, international relations and psychology—to see how the question of climate change and displacement is approached.

The past few years have seen an exponential growth in literature on climate change and human movement. It seems almost every discipline is, if it has not done so before, grappling with the ways in which climate change impacts on traditional frameworks of analysis, ways of understanding and future development. To what extent can existing categories, models, conceptions and responses simply be extended to address climate-related movement, and to what degree does this kind of migration present unique considerations and challenges?

Until now, and given the speed with which climate-induced migration/displacement has become a field of inquiry, much analysis has taken place in the online space: in reports by various international agencies and non-governmental organisations, and via academic research published relatively quickly in easily accessible web-based fora. The body of scholarly literature on the topic has also emerged, unsurprisingly, in discipline-specific journals, rather than compiled in a single place (although increasingly, journals are producing special issues on the topic). When this book was first proposed, there was nothing similar available. In the process of writing this book, however, an edited collection on human rights and climate change was published,[10] and another edited collection on climate change and migration is underway. Some of the same authors as appear in the present volume are featured in these other publications, which is testament to their expertise in the area.

This book is a first step in drawing together different disciplinary approaches on climate change and migration. It provides a multidisciplinary perspective on climate change and migration, rather than embarking on the next, and more difficult, step of true interdisciplinary research. That said, many of the authors already take a somewhat interdisciplinary approach, drawing on and speaking to the literature in other fields of inquiry. Some also combine theoretical and practical perspectives, informed by fieldwork in the Asia-Pacific region (Campbell, Hugo, Loughry, McAdam). The end product reveals that there is still a wide range of responses to the issue of climate change and displacement, and more dialogue is necessary. In part, this reveals the extent to which the phenomenon has already been conceptualised and examined in particular disciplinary areas, compared to areas where analysis is only just beginning.

While all the authors in this book acknowledge the real impact that climate change is having on some communities' ability to remain in their homes, the focal point of certain disciplines means that issues crucial to one are of little relevance for the purposes of another. For example, in areas like the law, terminology and language are fundamental. In law, the term 'refugee' has a precise meaning, and it is erroneous to speak of 'climate refugees'. By contrast, in the areas of health or

---

[10] S Humphreys (ed), Human Rights and Climate Change (Cambridge, Cambridge University Press, 2010).

moral philosophy, how people are labelled has little relevance to assessing health risks or the ethical response to human needs.

Governments have not been prepared to take a leading role on developing responses to the issue, in large part due to the absence of strong theoretical frameworks or empirical datasets from which sound policy can be developed. Responses need to be guided by considered, well-informed research, not by sensationalism, assumptions or fear. To oversimplify the causes of movement, misuse terminology, and not listen to the voices of affected populations obscures the multiplicity of factors that need n to be considered in any formal response. As some scholars have observed, it is essential to consider 'the socio-cultural-political-economic environment that communities exist in; the cognitive processes of the people experiencing the impact of climate change; the individual, household and community attitudes to migration and migration outcomes; and the type of climate stimulus that migration may be responding to'.[11] Understanding of this kind cannot come from a single discipline, but rather requires true interdisciplinarity.

III The Chapters

A number of geographers have been examining migration and the impact of environment or climate as a driver of movement for many decades. This is revealed in the breadth of scope of the chapters by Hugo, Barnett and Webber, and Campbell.

Graeme Hugo is a geographer well-known for his work on migration in the Asia-Pacific region. His chapter in this collection focuses on climate change 'hot spots' in the region which are likely to impinge upon population mobility. He argues that while it is incontestable that climate change will have a significant influence on migration this century, in most cases it is inaccurate to suggest that there is a direct 'cause and effect' between climate change and human movement. This is because people's vulnerability, resilience, resources and the general situation of their community will necessarily affect the extent to which climate change 'causes' movement. In addition, people's decisions about if and where to move are influenced by existing patterns of population mobility within their own community, and these can provide a good indication of where most movement is likely to occur. Finally, people may adapt *in situ* rather than moving at all. Forced relocation is a matter of last resort when other adaptation strategies have failed, rather than an automatic response to environmental degradation. An important policy implication of this is the need to examine how existing migration regimes might be adapted to better accommodate climate-related movement, rather than advocating a wholly new global regime.

Jon Barnett and Michael Webber, a political geographer and an economic geographer respectively, examine the role of migration as an adaptation strategy to

---

[11] Kniveton et al, *Climate Change and Migration*, above n 7, 57.

climate change. They highlight its potential to build financial, social and human capital, while noting that this positive view of migration as adaptation does not extend to situations of involuntary resettlement. They accordingly favour a policy approach that prioritises individual and community choice, respecting people's right to remain *or* to leave. Like Hugo, they observe that poverty and marginalisation are more significant determinants of migration outcomes than environmental change per se, although recognise it as an important proximate factor. They argue that adaptation would be assisted if aid and migration policies were coordinated.

John Campbell's chapter follows on well from Barnett and Webber, providing an excellent case study from the Pacific region of migration as adaptation. Campbell examines the indivisibility of the person–community–land bond in the Pacific in his analysis of community relocation as an adaptation strategy. His focus is on the importance of land within Pacific island communities, and the ramifications that moving away from land has on individuals and communities (dislocation, loss of homeland, disruption of culture, adjusting to a new lifestyle, diet and social norms, and so on). Most Pacific land is held under customary forms of tenure, and by and large cannot be owned in fee simple or as freehold. The relocation of communities not only breaks the link between the community and traditional land of those relocating, but may also disrupt the same links for the people into whose community they move.

Walter Kälin broadens out the discussion by considering how climate change and displacement should be understood conceptually. His chapter reflects both his scholarly expertise as an international law professor, and his practical experience as the Representative of the UN Secretary-General on the Human Rights of Internally Displaced Persons. Kälin sets out a conceptual roadmap on climate-induced displacement in order to suggest how international law and policy-makers might deal with the phenomenon. He examines a variety of climate change scenarios that may trigger population movements, the nature of these movements and who is affected, and the extent to which people are already protected by existing normative frameworks.

My own chapter isolates one of the scenarios presented by Kälin: whether those displaced from 'sinking' small island states should be classified as 'stateless persons'. To analyse this, the chapter examines whether the eventual submergence of small island states will result in the disappearance of these states as a matter of international law. Situated in a case study of the Pacific island states of Kiribati and Tuvalu, the chapter argues that the focus on loss of territory as the indicator of a state's disappearance may be misplaced, since states such as these will become uninhabitable long before they physically disappear. Accordingly, it is unclear whether their inhabitants would ever be recognised as 'stateless persons' under international law. The chapter also considers whether mechanisms like the 'government in exile' would enable a state to continue even when its territory is no longer habitable, and whether there would be advantages in pursuing alternatives to full statehood, such as becoming self-governing territories in free association with another state.

Roger Zetter, an expert in development and forced migration studies, examines the conceptual challenges raised by climate-induced migration. He considers how the relationship between climate change, the environment and migration is conceived; notions of forced versus non-forced movement; the 'labels' and the different geographies of displacement; and the moral justification for affording protection and attributing responsibility. He examines moral arguments that compel assistance for people displaced by climate change, such as humanitarianism and restorative justice. He argues that humanitarianism is a voluntary and virtuous act of giving, whereas restorative justice implies a substantial obligation to support measures to protect those who are most affected by climate change, such as the displaced and, potentially, those who remain. He notes, however, that regardless of which theory of justice is considered to be the more compelling, it may be impossible, both theoretically and practically, to protect or compensate people who have been forcibly displaced by climate change.

These arguments are extended by Peter Penz's chapter. Penz, a moral philosopher, asks: 'what are the ethical international responsibilities of states to those coerced or harmed by climate change impacts?'. He explores a range of moral reasons why states have responsibilities to assist, ranging from free movement responsibilities (requiring states to open their borders), to poverty alleviation responsibilities (requiring wealthier states to participate in significant global redistribution), to compensation responsibilities (requiring greenhouse gas-emitting states to accept responsibility for harm done and to provide compensation), to insurance responsibilities (requiring states to develop and participate in a global insurance scheme that pays compensation, with premiums payable according to each state's greenhouse gas emissions). The last of these is recommended by Penz as the most satisfactory formulation of international ethical responsibilities to those coerced or harmed by climate change, since it would provide compensation for adaptation, whether by migration or in situ adaptation.

Lorraine Elliott, a political scientist, explores the way security discourse has been utilised in the climate change and human movement debate. She provides a comprehensive survey of the securitisation of climate change and climate-related migration, both at the international level and in the Pacific region. She argues that claims about the security implications of climate migration are overstated and empirically and conceptually fraught. There is a paucity of evidence that climate-related movement will result in social unrest, conflict and regional instability. However, she suggests that a *human* security lens does provide a useful framework for addressing climate change and human movement, since *people* are most at risk from climate change and any instability, incapacity, social and economic stress that might occur. Human security focuses on adaptation as a security strategy that can potentially save lives, increase individual and community adaptive capacity, build societal resilience and reduce the chances of conflict.

The last part of the book is comprised of two health-focused chapters. Written from the perspectives of public health and psychology, they reveal how these disciplines are beginning to grapple with climate change. In particular, they examine the extent to which existing methodologies and responses can be applied to scenarios involving climate-related movement.

The chapter by Anthony McMichael, Celia McMichael, Helen Berry and Kathryn Bowen focuses on public health, drawing on the authors' combined experience in epidemiology (including psychiatric epidemiology), public health policy and psychology. They observe that the multifaceted relationship between climate change impacts and human health has been little studied to date and requires further research, documentation and evaluation of intervention policies. There is still no empirical base of evidence that would enable scenario-based quantitative modelling of how the impacts of climate change on health might trigger displacement, or the likely future health experiences of those displaced. They argue that the climate change–health–displacement relationship presents itself in three ways. First, they suggest that a change in people's actual health, or fears about health risks, may be a trigger for movement. Secondly, they argue that the experience of displacement (irrespective of its cause) typically increases the risks of various adverse health outcomes. Thirdly, they suggest that living in a new physical, social and cultural environment may have adverse health impacts on those who move, as well as the communities into which they move. Part of the reason why this might be a new area of inquiry for public health scholars is because how a person is categorised (migrant, refugee, and so on) is in many cases irrelevant for the purposes of characterising risk and prevalence of disease. For public health scholars, the real question is how climate change per se might affect the spread and incidence of disease, rather than how it will necessarily affect people displaced by climate change.

Maryanne Loughry's chapter examines how existing psychological frameworks might be used to assess the well-being and mental health prospects of communities facing natural hazards, an uncertain future and possible displacement on account of climate change. Drawing on her observations from the Pacific island of Kiribati, she considers how these approaches might best inform climate adaptation programmes so as to minimise the impact of climate change on people's well-being. She concludes that it is imperative to develop culturally appropriate mental health measures and services within affected populations, and introduce psychosocial interventions now so that fears presently expressed by communities about their potential displacement do not overwhelm their traditional capacity to cope with adversity. Loughry's chapter examines how psychology's understandings about human resilience and coping mechanisms might be extended to long-term studies of communities' adaptation responses to climate change.

Surveying the book as a whole, three general disciplinary approaches can be identified. First, there are disciplines like geography which focus on building up an empirical body of knowledge about the relationship between climate change and migration—documenting what is happening on the ground and what this means for those affected by it. Secondly, there are disciplines which focus on how this knowledge might help us to construct normative frameworks to shape legal and policy development (such as law, international relations and moral philosophy).

Thirdly, there are disciplines where climate change itself provides an important focus, but where the added dimension of movement may or may not be crucial to the analysis (such as public health and psychology).

In his 'Afterword', migration expert Stephen Castles reflects on all the book's contributions to assess the current state of debates about climate change and displacement. Tracing the evolution of the politics of the climate displacement phenomenon over the last 20 years, especially in light of the 2009 Copenhagen 'debacle', he synthesises some of the main aspects of the contemporary body of knowledge about the causes and consequences of climate-related movement. Drawing on the research presented in this collection, he identifies nine ideas that are gaining increasing recognition as warranting further research and intervention.

Perhaps what this book highlights most is the need for continuing interdisciplinary work on climate change and human movement. No single field of inquiry can adequately address all aspects of the phenomenon, and it is only by opening up a dialogue with all those with relevant expertise that a better understanding of the issues will be achieved.

2

Climate Change-Induced Mobility and the Existing Migration Regime in Asia and the Pacific

---

GRAEME HUGO

I Introduction

The relationship between environmental change and migration is complex[1] and has been of relevance throughout human history.[2] However, in much of the thinking about the potential impacts of twenty-first-century climate change on population movement, this has been ignored and the focus has been upon climate change *creating* population displacement. It is the argument of this chapter that the effects of impending climate change will be much more complex than this and mediated not only by the vulnerability, resilience, resources and situation of communities influenced by climate change but also by existing patterns of population mobility in those communities and the potential for other forms of adaptation. It cannot be contested that climate change will be a significant influence on migration, both internal and international, in the later decades of the twenty-first century. However, that impact will be of a simple 'climate change impact equals population displacement' type in only a limited number of cases. More commonly, climate change will be one of a number of elements impinging upon mobility and non-mobility.

The chapter begins with a brief consideration of areas in the Asia-Pacific region that are seen as being potential 'hot spots' of heightened climate change impact likely to impinge upon population mobility in those locations. While there is a considerable degree of uncertainty about the location, timing and severity of these climate change impacts, these are the areas where migration influences of climate

---

[1] GJ Hugo, 'Environmental Concerns and International Migration' (1996) 30 *International Migration Review* 105.

[2] HF Lee, L Fok and DD Zhang, 'Climatic Change and Chinese Population Growth Dynamics over the Last Millennium' (2008) 88 *Climatic Change* 131; J Wu and Z Wang, 'Agent-Based Simulation on the Evolution of Population Geography of China during the Past 2000 Years' (2008) 63 *ACTA Geographica SINICA* 185 (in Chinese).

change are likely to be most marked. The next section addresses the likely responses to these impacts and the potential role of population movement in such responses. While much of the debate focuses purely on forced population displacement as a result of environmental deterioration due to climate change,[3] it is argued that there will also be in situ adaptations as well as mobility adaptations. Forced resettlement must be seen as a last resort after other adaptation strategies have failed and resilience has been eroded, not as an automatic response to significant environmental deterioration. The chapter then summarises some of the major elements in knowledge of existing migration patterns in the hot spot areas which are relevant to understanding the likely effects of climate change impacts on future migration in those areas. Finally, it is argued that this approach of considering climate change as only one relatively new, albeit often important, element among a plethora of existing forces shaping mobility and non-mobility has important policy and planning implications. Among other things, it means that we should look at existing migration policy regimes to see how they can accommodate the influences of climate change impacts and how they can be modified to better cope with these trends. This approach contrasts with the dominant contemporary approach of attempting to establish a new global migration regime to accommodate 'climate-induced migrants'.[4]

II Environmental Change as a Cause of Migration

It is important to appreciate that the relationship between environmental change and migration is much more complex than the environmental deterioration equals population displacement nexus, which is often assumed. Figure 1 shows the complexity of interactions in the relationship between environmental change, migration and development. It is of fundamental importance to recognise that environmental change is usually not the only—or even most important—cause of migration in Asia and Pacific nations. It usually interacts with a range of other economic, social and demographic factors. This will also be the case where the environment is affected by climate change.

---

[3] Christian Aid, *Human Tide: The Real Migration Crisis* (May 2007); N Myers, 'Environmental Refugees: A Growing Phenomenon of the 21st Century' (2002) 357 *Philosophical Transactions of the Royal Society B* 609.

[4] S Humphreys, 'The Human Rights Dimension of Climate Change' (Oslo, HuriTalk Insight Series No 7, 2009); T Burton and D Hodgkinson, 'Climate Change Migrants and Unicorns: A Discussion Note on Conceptualising Climate Change Displaced People' (Draft, 2009) www.hodgkinsongroup.com/documents/PeopleDisplacedByClimateChange.pdf; F Biermann and I Boas, 'Preparing for a Warmer World: Towards a Global Governance System to Protect Climate Refugees', Global Governance Working Paper No 33 (November 2007).

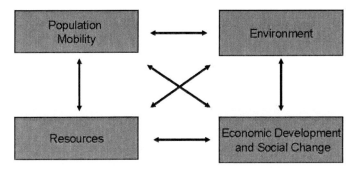

Figure 1: A complex interrelationship: migration, environment, resources and development

Stojanov has classified environmentally induced migrations according to the nature of their causes; his scheme is reproduced in Table 1.[5] Climate change can be involved in the first two types of migration. The distinction between rapid onset disasters and slow onset disasters is an important one in all environmentally induced migration, but especially when climate change is being discussed. It is the former which attracts most attention among policy-makers and researchers, while the latter is often neglected. There are a number of points that can be made about sudden impact natural disaster-induced migration:

Table 1: Principal Causes of Environmentally Induced Migration

Category	Natural Disasters	Cumulative (Slow-Onset) changes	Involuntarily-Caused and Industrial Accidents	Development Projects	Conflicts and Workforce
Particular Causes	Floods, earthquakes, volcanic eruptions, landslides, coastal storms, hurricanes, tsunamis	Land degradation, droughts, water deficiency, climate change, sea-level rise	Nuclear accidents, factory disasters, environmental pollution	Construction of rivers, dams and irrigation canals, mining natural resources, urbanisation	Biological workforce, intentional destruction of environment, conflicts due to natural resources

Source: R Stojanov, 'Environmental Factors of Migration' in R Stojanov and J Novasák (eds), *Development, Environment and Migration: Analysis of Linkages and Consequences* (Olomouc, Palacký University, 2008).

[5] R Stojanov, 'Environmental Factors of Migration' in R Stojanov and J Novasák (eds), *Development, Environment and Migration: Analysis of Linkages and Consequences* (Olomouc, Palacký University, 2008).

- The number of natural disasters is increasing significantly, as is the number of people affected by them.[6]
- These disasters occur disproportionately in less developed countries, because of the fact that many of these countries are located in more hazardous areas, more people live in vulnerable contexts in such countries, and those nations have less resources to ensure mitigation measures are in place.
- In areas influenced by environmental deterioration, the poor are disproportionately impacted by disasters because they lack the resources to adapt.

It is important to visualise the environment as a cause of migration along a continuum, as depicted in Figure 2. At the extremes we can conceive of people at one end moving voluntarily in response to environmental change, while at the other people are forced to flee from flooding or some other environmental disaster. In reality, however, there will be many moves where there are different levels of force exerted.

Figure 2: Environment as a cause of migration: forced versus unforced migration

It is important to recognise some of the key differences between forced and voluntary migrants, since this influences their ability to settle successfully at a destination. Table 2 lists some of these differences.

Table 2: Important Differences between Voluntary and Involuntary Migrants

Involuntary migrants:

- do not make preparations;
- maintain greater commitment to origin;
- are likely to be in a state of stress;
- are less likely to bring assets;
- are less likely to have connections at origin.

Renaud et al have differentiated between environmentally induced migrations according to the degree of force versus choice in the moves:

---

[6] Integrated Regional Information Networks (IRIN), *Disaster Reduction and the Human Cost of Disaster* (Nairobi, IRIN Web Special, 2005).

- 'Environmentally motivated' migrants are those who choose to move, and in their choice, environmental factors have a role.
- 'Environmentally forced' migrants are in situations where environmental change has destroyed, or is likely to destroy, their livelihood—they have no choice in having to move but some choice in the timing of the move.
- 'Environmental refugees' have no choice about either moving or the timing of the move.[7]

One of the key distinctions that needs to be made in considering the relationship between environmental change and migration is that between mobility as a strategy for *adapting* to the impacts, and as *displacement* when environmental deterioration becomes so extreme that people are forced to leave an area. Too often it is assumed that all environmentally induced movement is displacement migration. For some Pacific atoll countries, for example, the discourse on potential sea-level rises associated with climate change has been dominated by displacement migration as a response, to the extent that other forms of mitigation and adaptation have been neglected. This is especially the case in projecting the impact of climate change.[8] Population mobility as a response to environmental change can and does take many forms. Moreover, population mobility is often also one of several mitigation and adaptation strategies adopted by communities to cope with that change. It is essential then that environmentally induced population mobility be seen as:

(a) a wide array of mobility strategies and types, and not just displacement; and
(b) only one response among an array of potential mitigation and adaptation strategies.

The issue of migration as adaptation versus displacement is dependent on a timing factor. Migrating prior to a change in environmental condition that will make it impossible to remain in a place could be considered adaptation, whereas migrating when all viable options have been used up and it is not possible to remain in a place, is displacement. This distinction has been observed, for example, in studies of responses to various stages of famine.[9] Figure 3 shows a model of an initial response to perceptions of oncoming food shortages, which may be temporary migration or reallocation of some of the family's labour resources to areas outside of the region affected. However, this may give way to displacement on a temporary or permanent basis if the famine is prolonged and it becomes unsustainable to remain in the area. Of course, dramatic events such as a tsunami or flood may also make it unsustainable for people to remain in an area and may force displacement,

---

[7] F Renaud, JJ Bogardi, O Dun and K Warner, *Control, Adapt or Flee: How to Face Environmental Migration?* (UNU-EHS, InterSecTions No 5/2007, 2007).

[8] R Black, 'Environmental Refugees: Myth or Reality?', *New Issues in Refugee Research*, Working Paper No 34 (Geneva, UNHCR, 2001) 9.

[9] HG Bohle, T Cannon, G Hugo and FN Ibrahim (eds), *Famine and Food Security in Africa and Asia: Indigenous Response and External Intervention to Avoid Hunger* (Bayreuth, Bayreuther Geowissenschaftliche Arbeiten, 1991).

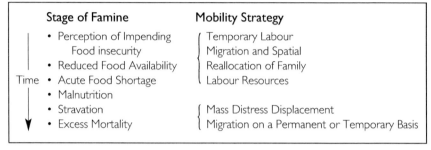

Stage of Famine	Mobility Strategy
• Perception of Impending Food insecurity • Reduced Food Availability • Acute Food Shortage • Malnutrition	Temporary Labour Migration and Spatial Reallocation of Family Labour Resources
• Stravation • Excess Mortality	Mass Distress Displacement Migration on a Permanent or Temporary Basis

Time (arrow pointing down)

Figure 3: A simple model of population mobility strategies associated with food insecurity and famine

Source: GJ Hugo, 'Changing Famine Coping Strategies under the Impact of Population Pressure and Urbanisation: The Case of Population Mobility' in HG Bohle, T Cannon, G Hugo and FN Ibrahim (eds), *Famine and Food Security in Africa and Asia: Indigenous Response and External Intervention to Avoid Hunger* (Bayreuth, Bayreuther Geowissenschaftliche Arbeiten, 1991).

at least on a temporary basis. Hence there will be clear differences in migration responses according to whether the impacts of climate change are of the sudden dramatic event type, or are slow onset changes.

In the literature on environment as a cause of migration, a key distinction is made between movement associated with the rapid onset of environmental disasters and that caused by the slower deterioration of the environment and a reduction in natural resources available to local populations. Table 3 provides some examples of the two types of environmental migration. Sudden disasters can be very destructive and may cause major population displacements, but these are usually temporary.[10] People displaced by disasters like the Asian Tsunami of 2004 mostly return and rebuild their community.[11] Indeed the influx of resources and the magnitude of the task of rebuilding can lead to a net in-migration because the reconstruction requires a larger workforce than is available in the local population.

Where the deterioration in the environment is more gradual, the migration response is more complex. A common coping mechanism to a decline in local productive resources in rural Asia and the Pacific is for families to deploy some of their labour to other labour markets, especially in cities but also, increasingly, internationally.[12] The remittances which they send back can help support the family members remaining at home. There also may be some permanent out-

[10] See W Kälin, 'Conceptualising Climate-Induced Displacement', in the present volume.

[11] F Laczko and E Collett, 'Assessing the Tsunami's Effects on Migration' (Feature Story for the Migration Information Source, April 2005), www.migrationinformation.org/feature/display.cfm?ID= 299. Such disasters can also lead to some of those displaced not returning to their devastated homes. For example, Hurricane Katrina in 2005 led to the displacement of almost the entire population of New Orleans. More than half of those displaced have chosen not to return, despite their former community having been reconstructed.

[12] See, eg Special Issue on 'Migrations and Family Relations in the Asia Pacific Region' (2002) 11 *Asian and Pacific Migration Journal.*

Table 3: **Types of environmentally induced migration**

Environmental Change	Examples	Mobility Response
Sudden, extreme events	—Tsunami —Flooding —Typhoon	—Large-scale but largely temporary displacement
Gradual, deterioration of environment	—Desertification —Dam construction	—Temporary, circular migration of family members to supplement local income generation —Gradual permanent out-migration of households

migration, perhaps preceded by a preliminary temporary migration. This out-migration can have the effect of reducing the pressure on resources in the origin, but also through remittances sent back can reduce the vulnerability of those left behind and increase community resilience. In both the temporary and permanent migration strategies it is usually the young adult population that is selectively involved, since they tend to be the group most able to be mobile and gain entry to outside labour markets.

The distinction between rapid onset disasters and low onset change in environmentally induced migration is applied to climate change scenarios by Piguet, who distinguishes between:

• migrations associated with real or perceived direct environmental hazards caused by climate change; and
• migrations associated with real or perceived access and utilisation of natural resources including land, water, soil or biological resources as a result of climate change.[13]

The changes to migration patterns might take various forms, but will principally involve an increase in the push forces that lead to out-migration pressures. The most relevant issues for migration directly related to climate change are:

• those associated with real or perceived direct environmental hazards; and
• those associated with real or perceived access and effective utilisation of natural resources, including land, water, soil or biological resources.[14]

Thus it will not just be the real or experienced hazards or depleted resource condition that leads to increasing emigration, but also changes in *perceptions* towards environmental risk or resource degradation.

Hence this section identifies four important distinctions which need to be recognised in considering environmental (including climate change) impacts on migration:

[13] E Piguet, 'Climate Change and Migration: A Synthesis' (Environment, Forced Migration and Social Vulnerability Conference, Bonn, 9–11 October 2008).
[14] ibid.

- dramatic sudden impacts versus slow onset change impacts;
- forced versus voluntary migration;
- moving as a result of perceived versus actual threats; and
- movement as forced displacement versus movement as adaptation to environmental impacts.

A fifth and important dimension which must be recognised in considering the impact of environmentally induced migration is that between linear and non-linear effects on migration.[15] Here the fundamental distinction is between situations where the environmentally induced movement is channelled along existing corridors of movement, and those where it creates new types and spatial patterns of movement. In the former case the mobility builds upon post and existing movement channels, while in the latter, new movement patterns are created. This raises a number of important issues. Could it be that in societies where migration is already well established, individuals and households are more likely to respond to environmental pressures by moving, compared to situations where mobility is not so well established? The theory of cumulative causation is regarded as a major element in the explanation of migration.[16] At the scale of households, communities, regions or ethnic groups, research has recognised that people are more likely to respond to economic or environmental pressures by adopting a mobility strategy if this is an established practice. Moreover, if it is an established practice, the uncertainties of migration are greatly reduced because people have family and friends who have successfully made such moves and who are established at potential destinations from which they can provide assistance in settlement and adjustment.

On the other hand, the onset (slow or immediate) of environmental pressures may provide the trigger for some individuals in households and communities to strike out in new directions. This may be influenced by assistance policies and programmes of growth and non-government organisations, but also may be spontaneously undertaken by individuals and groups acting on information which they have received about potential opportunities elsewhere, even though they have no family or acquaintances at the destination or have no direct experience of that destination. These 'pioneers' are often drawn selectively from the more entrepreneurial, risk-taking elements of the community, or they may be family members sent out by the family as an exploration to diversify the family's portfolio of income-earning opportunities. These pioneers can then be the 'anchors' for later chain migration from their communities of origin.

A sixth important dimension of environmentally induced migration is the fact that overwhelmingly it has involved migration *within* countries.[17] Very little

---

[15] GJ Hugo, DK Bardsley, Y Tan, V Sharma, M Williams and R Bedford, *Climate Change and Migration in the Asia-Pacific Region: Final Report to Asian Development Bank* (August 2009) 38–42.

[16] DS Massey, J Arango, G Hugo, Kouaouci, A Pellegrino and JE Taylor, 'Theories of International Migration: A Review and Appraisal' (1993) 19 *Population and Development Review* 431; DS Massey, J Arango, G Hugo, A Kouaouci, A Pellegrino and JE Taylor, *Worlds in Motion: Understanding International Migration at the End of the Millennium* (Oxford, Clarendon Press, 1998).

[17] Hugo, 'Environmental Concerns', above n 1; GJ Hugo, *Migration, Development and Environment* (Geneva, IOM Migration Research Series No 35, 2008).

international migration has resulted directly from environmental deterioration, although undoubtedly it has been a proximate or contributory factor. It is probable that the dominance of migration *within* countries will continue as environmental factors, including climate change, come to be of greater significance.

III Potential Hot Spots of Severe Climate Change Impacts in Asia and the Pacific

No region of the world is expected to be affected more by climate change than Asia and the Pacific. Preston et al have summarised the likely effects of climate change as follows:

• temperature increases of:

—0.5–2ºC by 2030, and
—1–7ºC by 2070
(greater in arid areas of Northern Pakistan, India and Western China);

• increasing rainfall especially in summer monsoon;
• greater monsoon variability;
• decline in winter rainfall in South and South East Asia;
• rise in global sea-level of:

—3–16 cm by 2030, and
—7–50 cm by 2070;

• more intense tropical cyclones; and
• changes in important modes of climate variability such as the El Nino Oscillation.[18]

A recent report has examined the available modelling of climate change in Asia and the Pacific in order to establish which areas in the region are anticipated to experience substantial impacts from:

• higher sea-levels and storm surges;
• increased intensity and frequency of cyclone activity;
• increased riparian flooding, especially due to glacier melt; and
• reduced intensity, frequency and reliability of rainfall in many low and moderate rainfall areas.[19]

[18] BL Preston, R Suppiah, I Macadam and J Bathols, *Climate Change in the Asia/Pacific Region: A Consultancy Report prepared for the Climate Change and Development Roundtable* (Australia, Commonwealth Science and Industry Research Organisation (CSIRO), 2006) 2.
[19] Hugo et al, *Climate Change and Migration*, above n 15, 142–43.

While there are some regions and countries in Asia and the Pacific where the anticipated climate change impacts will be favourable (such as New Zealand), the areas where the effects will be negative are more extensive and have much larger populations. Areas where climate change impacts are likely to be greatest in scope and intensity can be considered as 'hot spots', and these are places where the relationship between climate change and migration is likely to be most apparent. The study which delimited these hot spots identified four types of ecological locations in the Asia-Pacific region which are especially strongly represented.[20] These include:

• densely settled delta regions;
• low-lying coastal areas;
• low-lying atolls and coral islands;
• some river valleys; and
• semi-arid low-humidity areas.

The extent of vulnerability—or, conversely, resilience—of the people living in these areas is not only a function of the severity of climate change impact, but also of their socio-economic situation and the resources which they have to adapt to the impacts of environmental deterioration, the socio-cultural context, and the quality of governance and security of the region. Nevertheless, these five types of 'hot spot' are particularly at risk of experiencing severe impacts of climate change on their environments. Asia has some of the most densely settled delta regions of the world, with not only some of the world's most intensively cultivated areas but also some of the world's major megacities.[21] Moreover, these areas, especially the megacities, are experiencing rapid population growth as a result of in-migration, much of it from rural areas.[22] These intensively settled areas include the Mekong delta in southern Vietnam and eastern Cambodia, the Yangtze River delta around the Shanghai area, the Menam delta around Bangkok, and the Ganges delta in South Asia. These areas are especially vulnerable to the impacts of rising sea-levels, increased storm surges and riparian flooding, more so because they contain some of the poorest and least-resourced populations in Asia.

Table 4 shows some of Asia's largest cities and their average height above sea-level. It is apparent that several of these cities are vulnerable to a significant increase in sea-level and in the scale and frequency of storm surges. Several, like Shanghai, Bangkok and Ho Chi Minh City, are located in delta areas, while others are located in low-lying coastal areas. These cities have taken a distinctive form, involving extensive lateral spread enveloping nearby smaller-sized urban centres

[20] ibid, ch 4.
[21] Cities with 10 million or more inhabitants: United Nations Department of Economic and Social Affairs, Population Division, *World Urbanization Prospects: The 2007 Revision: Highlights* (New York, United Nations, 2008) 2.
[22] GW Jones, 'Urbanization Trends in Asia: The Conceptual and Definitional Challenges' in T Champion and G Hugo (eds), *New Forms of Urbanization: Beyond the Urban–Rural Dichotomy* (Aldershot, Ashgate, 2004).

and transforming the rural areas between them into a form of in situ urbanisation.[23] These cities are experiencing heavy in-migration and rapid population growth.[24] Moreover, they contain large poor populations which often reside in the areas most vulnerable to flooding. In the discussions about the impact of climate change on such cities, migration has not been put forward as a solution or adaptation mechanism. Overwhelmingly, there has been an emphasis on technological solutions, such as building dam walls, realigning and upgrading drainage and so on.[25] Clearly, however, there is a need to reconsider the nature of national settlement systems which currently focus on these megacities as the major location of investment and power—and they are, in fact, the most significant magnets to both internal and international migrants in the countries involved.

Table 4:   East Asia: Megacities Projected Population, 2005–25

	Average Height Above Sea-Level	Population ('000) 2005	2020	2025
Shanghai	4 m	14,053	18,456	19,412
Tianjin	4 m	7,040	8,745	9,248
Tokyo	5 m	35,327	36,399	36,400
Osaka	5 m	11,128	11,368	11,368
Guangzhou	5 m	8,425	11,218	11,835
Taipei	9 m	2,606	3,104	3,305
Nagoya	17 m	3,199	3,295	3,295

Source: United Nations Department of Economic and Social Affairs, Population Division, *World Urbanization Prospects: The 2007 Revision: Highlights* (New York, United Nations, 2008).

Most countries in the region which have a coastline are at some risk of climate change-induced flooding. In China, the north-east plains are vulnerable, as are the coastal cities such as Tianjin, Shanghai, Shenzhen, Guangzhou and Haikou. Other areas in North East Asia at risk of coastal flooding are coastal Seoul in South Korea and southern Honshu in Japan. In South Asia, sea-level rise poses a significant threat along the Bay of Bengal and the Arabian Sea, including the deltaic areas of the Ganges-Brahmaputra, the Mahanadi, Godavari, Krishna and the Indus Rivers.

---

[23] Y Zhu, 'Beyond Large-City-Centered Urbanization: *In situ* Transformation of Rural Areas in Fujian Province' (2002) 43 *Asia-Pacific Viewpoint* 9.

[24] Jones, 'Urbanization Trends in Asia', above n 22.

[25] See generally the following presentations from the Cities at Risk: Developing Adaptive Capacity for Climate Change in Asia's Coastal Megacities Conference, Chulalongkorn University, 26–28 February 2009, www.start.org/Program/cities_at_risk.html: A Snidvongs and NH Nhan, 'Scenario Modeling for Ho Chi Minh City: Future Climate Risk Communication Through Simulation and Visualization'; M Muto, 'ADB-JICA-WB Joint Study: Climate Change Impact and Adaptation in Asian Coastal Cities: Case of Metro Manila'; C Vitoolpanyakij, 'Coastal Cities and Adaptation to Climate Change; Bangkok Study'; SM Wahid, 'Adaptation in Action: Options and Strategies in Bangkok'.

In addition, Bangladesh, parts of India (such as West Bengal and coastal areas including Chennai and Mumbai) and southern Pakistan (coastal Karachi) are prone to significant coastal flooding. Bangladesh is at very high risk due not only to its low-lying nature but also because of a young, poor population heavily reliant upon agriculture. In South East Asia, too, sea-level rises and storm surges are of great concern in low-lying coastal areas, especially the delta areas of the Mekong, Red, Irrawaddy and Menam Rivers and the densely-settled urban centres such as Ho Chi Minh City, metropolitan Manila, Jakarta and Bangkok.

Low-lying islands and island states will be extremely vulnerable to sea-level rise, high-intensity cyclones and storm surges. In atolls, the salinisation of fragile fresh-water lenses by seawater intrusion threatens the livelihood of their populations. In some island states, such as Kiribati and Tuvalu, virtually the entire national space is vulnerable to flooding.

Reductions in rainfall across Central Asia, parts of India and Pakistan, Western China and significant areas in South East Asia and the Pacific also pose a significant threat. The large populations in these areas which rely upon agriculture for their livelihood are especially vulnerable, because the reduced rainfall will impact on agricultural productivity in many areas. For example, India's wheat production is anticipated to fall by 30 per cent by 2050.[26] In China, an anticipated fall in rice production is expected to be counterbalanced by an increase in wheat production.[27] In Central Asia, increasing desertification is a most serious climate change impact. The shrinking of the Aral Sea and its two most significant feeder rivers, the Amu Darya and the Syr Darya, is of concern.[28] Salinisation, inefficient water management practices, land degradation, heat stress, desertification and increasing aridity are crucial issues that are already influencing, and will continue to influence, out-migration on both permanent and temporary bases.

IV Mechanisms Linking Environmental Change and Migration

Adamo has argued that if precise measurement and (eventually) accurate forecasting of environmentally induced migration is to be achieved, there needs to be a better understanding of the mechanisms which link environmental stress and migration.[29] It is apparent that these mechanisms are complex. Only in extreme

---

[26] Hugo et al, *Climate Change and Migration*, above n 15.

[27] Asian Development Bank (ADB), *Building Climate Resilience in the Agricultural Sector of Asia and the Pacific* (Mandaluyong City, ADB, 2009).

[28] M Spoor, 'The Aral Seal Basin Crisis: Transition and Environment in Former Soviet Central Asia' (1998) 29 *Development and Change* 409.

[29] S Adamo, 'Addressing Environmentally Induced Population Displacements: A Delicate Task', Background Paper (Population-Research Network Cyberseminar on Environmentally Induced Population Displacements, 18–29 August 2008) 6.

cases do environmental factors operate on their own to shape population mobility. There are several elements to the complexity of the mechanisms linking migration to climate change. These include the fact that environmental forces are usually only one of several 'push' factors at the origin and 'pull' factors at the destination which impinge on individual decisions whether or not to migrate; these influences interact and are difficult to disentangle; and migration is only one of several responses and adaptations that individuals and groups can make in relation to environmental change.

The impact of environmental hazards is mediated not only by the severity of the hazard but by the community's resources to respond to that impact. Whether or not that will result in population mobility is also influenced by the availability of other responses and adaptations, and also the community's past experience in dealing with environmental hardship. Adamo also points out that people's subjective views and perceptions of hazards and of their own vulnerability are important: 'Individuals visualise and live risk according to past personal experience; present and past individual, household and community characteristics and the socio-economic, political and historical context in which they are embedded.'[30] All of these elements add extra complexity to the linkage between environmental impacts on the one hand, and population mobility on the other.

One of the important elements which will shape whether or not people are influenced by climate change or other environmental impacts to move is their past experience with population mobility and that of the community in which they live. Other things being equal, mobility is likely to be seen more as an option in communities with a history of movement and active migration networks. Moreover, in such contexts it is possible to think of there being a series of established channels or corridors of migration linking the origin area with one or more destinations. These corridors will be the channels that environmental change migrants are most likely to follow. One of the most universal findings in migration in the Asia-Pacific region is that the majority of movers are diverted to destinations to which family or friends have moved earlier.

Identifying these movement corridors for regions which are projected to experience severe climate change impacts is important. The World Bank, for example, identified the 30 largest corridors of international migration in 2005 according to the data which was available to it.[31] These are listed in Figure 4 on the following page; it will be noted that half of the largest corridors involve an Asia-Pacific country.

The impact of climate change on population mobility needs to be considered in the context of existing patterns and processes of population movement. This is because those influences operate, and will operate in the future, together with a range of other forces—economic, social, cultural and demographic—interacting to produce patterns of movement and non-movement. Moreover, existing patterns of movement—spatial flows, selectivity of particular groups, policies and

---

[30] ibid, 7.
[31] World Bank, *Migration and Remittances Factbook 2008* (Washington DC, World Bank, 2008) 6.

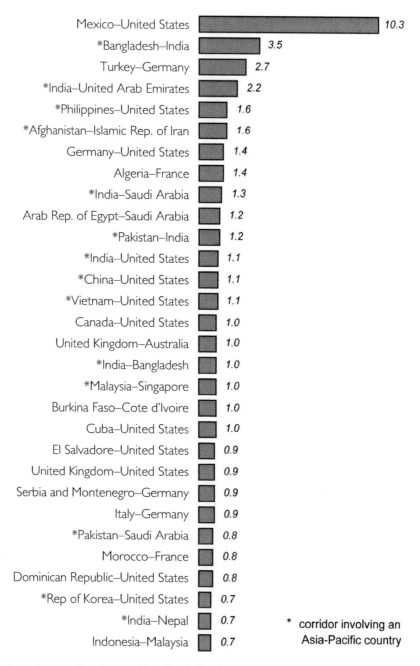

Figure 4: Top migration corridors (excluding former Soviet Union) (millions), 2005

Source: World Bank, *Migration and Remittances Factbook 2008* (Washington DC, World Bank, 2008).

so on—will also exert an effect on whether or not environmental changes cause movement and, if so, what form that movement takes.

The next section draws together a number of findings from existing migration research in the Asia-Pacific region which are likely to influence further patterns of climate change-induced mobility.

V Lessons from Existing Migration Research of Relevance for Climate Change-Induced Migration

As discussed above, there has been a tendency in the discourse on climate change impacts and migration to oversimplify what is in fact a complex relationship, and one which is surrounded by uncertainty. However, in anticipating the effects of climate change on mobility it is important to draw upon our understanding of existing patterns of mobility in the Asia-Pacific region. Accordingly, this section identifies, and briefly summarises, some of the lessons from the contemporary Asia-Pacific migration literature and their relevance for the potential impact of climate change effects on environmental deterioration. [32] The treatment will necessarily be brief and incomplete, but its objective is to illustrate the importance of viewing the impacts of climate change on migration through the prism of contemporary and post-migration experiences.

A Migration versus in situ Adjustment

While personal mobility has increased massively in Asia and the Pacific in recent decades,[33] it is important to remember that most people adjust to economic, social, demographic, political and environmental change *without* moving. Most adjustment to change occurs in situ. However, the assumption is often made that migration will be the only, or at least the predominant, response. Permanent migration may eventually be the ultimate result, but it is likely that a number of in situ adjustments will have been attempted prior to movement. It is important to recognise that only a minority of the populations to be impacted by climate change are likely to move. As Black has pointed out, 'although environmental degradation and catastrophe may be important factors in the decision to migrate, and issues of concern in their own right, their conceptualization as a primary cause of forced displacement is unhelpful and unsound intellectually and unnecessary in practical terms.'[34]

---

[32] For a more detailed summary, see Hugo et al, *Climate Change and Migration*, above n 15, ch 3.

[33] See GJ Hugo and S Young (eds), *Labour Mobility in the Asia-Pacific Region* (Singapore, Institute of Southeast Asian Studies, 2008).

[34] Black, 'Environmental Refugees', above n 8, 1.

To assume that all or most of the populations living in areas that seem likely to experience significant climate impacts will move is not only unrealistic and not justified by empirical knowledge of contemporary migration, but it can also be detrimental to developing effective adaptation policy in those areas. Connell points out in the context of Tuvalu and Kiribati (Pacific island nations that have been identified as being especially subject to inundation due to sea-level rise) that the option of resettlement has so heavily dominated the discourse on the impacts of climate change that it has been a barrier to a wider consideration of the full range of adaptation options.[35] Hence consideration of building up community resilience and potential in situ adaptation is being blocked by media, political and other commentators focusing only on displacement. It is important also to note that local communities often have a preference for in situ adjustment, rather than migration, and premature judgements can close off policies and programmes which might support these preferences.[36]

B The Role of Migration Networks

Migration research in Asia and the Pacific has long established that most population movement in the region is influenced by social networks. These networks are created when a pioneer migrant moves to a destination and, in so doing, gives his or her friends and relatives in the place of origin a piece of social capital in that destination which can be 'cashed in'—providing trusted information about opportunities in that destination, assistance in the moving process and an assurance of support upon arrival. Social network theory is one of the most powerful theories explaining the initiation and maintenance of migration streams in Asia and the Pacific. It explains why migrants are not drawn randomly from the origin and do not settle in the destination in such a way as to replicate the distribution of the total destination population. Networks proliferate with increased mobility which modern forms of transport have strengthened by facilitating more frequent and intimate contact between origin and destination. Massey et al have shown how networks can operate to influence migration, to some extent at least, independent of economic forces. They define migration networks as follows:

> Migrant networks are sets of interpersonal ties that connect migrants, former migrants and non migrants in origin and destination areas through tiers of kinship friendship, and shared community origin. They increase the likelihood of (international) movement because they lower the costs and risks of movement and increase the expected net retur'ns to migration. Network connections constitute a form of social capital that people can draw upon to gain access to foreign employment.[37]

[35] JC Connell, 'Climate Change: A New Security Challenge for the Atoll States of the South Pacific' (1993) 31 *Journal of Commonwealth and Comparative Politics* 173; JC Connell, 'Losing Ground? Tuvalu, the Greenhouse Effect and the Garbage Can' (2003) 44 *Asia Pacific Viewpoint* 89. See also the more recent work of J McAdam and M Loughry, 'We Aren't Refugees', *Inside Story* (30 June 2009), http://inside.org.au/we-arent-refugees/.

[36] McAdam and Loughry, 'We Aren't Refugees', above n 35.

[37] Massey et al, 'Theories of International Migration', above n 16, 438.

Migrant networks are fundamental to understanding much migration—internal and international—in Asia and the Pacific. Unlike the conventional stereotype of migrants arriving wide-eyed in alien new destinations not knowing anyone, most 'new' migrants move along trajectories well trodden by earlier generations of family and friends with whom they have kept contact, and from whom they receive information, help and assistance to adjust them to the destination.[38] Networks will be one of the major mechanisms which will ensure that mobility responses to the impact of climate change—both as a form of adaptation to the slow onset of change, and facilitating temporary and permanent displacement in response to sudden extreme events. The latter has been apparent, for example, in recent disasters such as the Asian Tsunami of 2004, when many of those displaced moved to houses of friends and relatives in areas not affected by the Tsunami disaster.[39] Similarly, in Hurricane Katrina in New Orleans in 2005, 24 per cent of those displaced had relocated to a different dwelling within the metropolitan area (among those surveyed in 2006).[40]

C Migration as a Mechanism for Households Coping with Change

There is a long history in Asia and the Pacific of migration being employed by families and households as a way of coping with reductions of income or production in the home area. In the past this was associated with the dominance of extended family structures and patriarchal power structures. The New Household Economics theory of migration has focused particular attention on the way in which households and families deploy family members to work elsewhere. This serves as a mechanism to reduce households' own vulnerability to reductions in their ability to earn a livelihood locally:

> Unlike individuals, households are in a position to control risks to their economic well-being by diversifying the allocation of household resources, such as family labour. While some family members can be assigned economic activities in the local economy, others may be sent to work in foreign labour markets where wages and employment conditions are negatively correlated or weakly correlated with those in the local area. In the event that local economic conditions deteriorate and activities there fail to bring in sufficient income, the household can rely on migrant remittances for support.[41]

In other work I have shown, for example, that during the Asian crisis of the late 1990s, many families in Indonesia sent female members to work in the Middle East

---

[38] GJ Hugo, 'Community and Village Ties, Village Norms and Village Networks in Migration Decision Making' in GF DeJong and RW Gardner (eds), *Migration Decision Making: Multidisciplinary Approaches to Microlevel Studies in Developed and Developing Countries* (New York, Pergamon, 1981).

[39] CL Gray, 'Tsunami-Induced Displacement in Sumatra, Indonesia' (XXVI IUSSP International Population Conference, Marrakech, 27 September–2 October 2009).

[40] N Sastry and J Gregory, 'Dislocation and Return of New Orleans Residents One Year after Hurricane Katrina' (XXVI IUSSP International Population Conference, Marrakech, 27 September–2 October 2009).

[41] Massey et al, 'Theories of International Migration', above n 16, 436.

in order to diversify the family's income sources. This helped them to cope with the loss of income resulting from job losses within Indonesia.[42]

This phenomenon has clear relevance to climate change impacts that may affect the abilities of families and households to earn a livelihood in their home areas. It is of particular significance to households that are dependent on agricultural production.

D Migration and Poverty

It is apparent that migration has played a role in reducing poverty in Asia and the Pacific, both among movers and their families as well as in communities of origin. However, a strong finding is that, in general, it is not the poorest of the poor who move.[43] The poor often lack the resources to be able to fund the risk of moving, and their information about, and networks to, potential destinations is often limited because they are less likely to have relatives and friends living elsewhere. The poor may not be able to adapt to anticipated environmental deterioration because they lack the means and/or resources to do so. Hence migration is less available to the poor as an adjustment mechanism to cope with climate change's impacts, and if it is to be made available to them there will need to be support and assistance provided to facilitate their migration.

The challenges for migration being a form of adaptation or response to the impacts of climate change for the poor are especially exacerbated in the case of international migration, as there are significant barriers to their movement in the Asia-Pacific region. While the barriers to entry of foreign highly skilled workers have been substantially reduced in recent years, those for low skilled groups have, if anything, been strengthened, so that many streams have become more selective, despite increasing evidence that international migration is a structurally important component of economies in the Asia-Pacific region.[44] Table 5 on the following page shows the substantial barriers to international migration. Indeed, the failure of most countries in the region to accept refugees recognised by the United Nations High Commissioner for Refugees for permanent settlement is indicative of their reluctance to consider settling forced migrants from other countries.

E Experience Regarding Forced Resettlement

While one of the arguments of this chapter is that there has been some exaggeration of potential forced displacement on account of climate change, the fact

---

[42] G Hugo, 'The Impact of the Crisis on Internal Population Movement in Indonesia' (2000) 36 *Bulletin of Indonesian Economic Studies* 115; G Hugo, 'The Crisis and International Population Movements in Indonesia' (2000) 9 *Asian and Pacific Migration Journal* 93.

[43] S Amin (ed), *Modern Migrations in Western Africa* (London, Oxford University Press, 1974); R Skeldon, 'Rural-to-Urban Migration and Its Implications for Poverty Alleviation' (1997) 12 *Asia-Pacific Population Journal* 3.

[44] Hugo and Young (eds), *Labour Mobility*, above n 33.

Table 5: Constraints on labour mobility in Asia and the Pacific

- Protection of national sovereignty.
- Fears of disturbing national homogeneity.
- Fears of driving down working conditions and salaries.
- Fears of migrants as the 'other'.
- Recency of migration's increased significance.
- Widespread negative characterisation of migrants by the media.
- Scapegoating of migrants.
- Refusal to accept mandated UNHCR refugees as permanent settlers.

Source: GJ Hugo and S Young (eds), *Labour Mobility in the Asia-Pacific Region* (Singapore, Institute of Southeast Asian Studies, 2008).

remains that such displacement will occur, albeit as a last resort after adaptation options have been exhausted. A crucial question which arises relates to the extent to which displacement caused by climate change impacts can be planned for, and operationalised, so that those families and communities forced to move are protected and their livelihoods maintained. In this context, there is considerable experience of resettlement within countries in the Asia-Pacific region, and it is crucial that it be drawn upon extensively in efforts to plan climate change-related resettlement. This experience with resettlement is derived from:

- planned agricultural resettlement programmes, which have sought to resettle people from densely settled parts of the national space to more lightly populated areas. Best known is the Indonesian transmigration programme,[45] but similar programmes have been adopted in Sri Lanka[46] and Malaysia;[47]
- resettlement, often on a temporary basis, due to the sudden impacts of natural disasters, such as the Asian Tsunami of 2004;[48]
- people displaced by conflict and resettled elsewhere within countries[49] and in other countries;[50]

---

[45] JM Hardjono, *Transmigration in Indonesia* (Kuala Lumpur, Oxford University Press, 1977).

[46] R Senaka-Arachchi, 'The Problems of Second Generation Settlers in Land Settlement Schemes: The Case of Sri Lanka' (unpublished PhD thesis, Population and Human Resources Program, Department of Geography, University of Adelaide, 1995).

[47] P Chan and H Richter, 'Land Settlement, Income and Population Redistribution in Peninsular Malaysia' in GW Jones and HV Richter (eds), *Population Resettlement Programs in Southeast Asia* (Canberra, Australian National University Development Studies Centre, 1981); LAP Gosling, 'The Demographic Implications of Agricultural Land Settlements: A Case Study of Malaysia's FELDA Schemes' in R Barlow (ed), *Case Studies in the Demographic Impact of Asian Development Projects* (Ann Arbor, University of Michigan Center for Research on Economic Development, 1982).

[48] United Nations High Commissioner for Refugees (UNHCR), *UNHCR Global Report 2006* (Geneva, UNHCR, 2006).

[49] GJ Hugo, 'Pengungsi: Indonesia's Internally Displaced Persons' (2002) 11 *Asian and Pacific Migration Journal* 297.

[50] UNHCR, *2008 Global Trends: Refugees, Asylum-Seekers, Returnees, Internally Displaced and Stateless Persons* (Geneva, UNHCR, 2009).

- people who have been resettled within countries because their home area was at high risk of destructive environmental events; and[51]
- planned resettlements associated with large-scale infrastructure projects, especially dam projects.[52] One of the largest cases is the Three Gorges Dam Project located in the lower reaches of the Yangtze River in China. The 17-year period of construction was to have been completed in 2011. The project has involved a displacement of more than 1.2 million people.[53]

Lessons must be drawn from this extensive experience in order to maximise the chances of climate change-related displacements having positive outcomes for those who are displaced. The overwhelming impression one gains from summarising the relevant literature, however, is that resettlement programmes have a poor record, often resulting in loss of income and well-being among those who move, as well as conflict with different ethnic groups in the destination.[54] Overwhelmingly, too, the experience of resettlement, with the exception of refugees, has involved migration *within* countries.

F Migration as a Gendered Process

One of the major developments in migration research in the Asia-Pacific region over the last decade has been recognition that migration is a profoundly gendered process.[55] There has been a faster increase in the mobility of women than of men, but overall there are similar proportions who move. Women dominate in several types of major movement, however, such as rural–urban migration, and in some key international labour migrations, such as that of domestic workers. The key point is that *patterns* of migration are not only often different between men and women, but so too are the *drivers* and *impacts* of migration. There is a complex relationship between the changing role and status of women in the region, on the one hand, and migration, on the other.[56] The implications of this for climate

---

[51] GRE Lucardie, 'The Geographical Mobility of the Makianese: Migratory Traditions and Resettlement Problems' in EKM Masinambow (ed), *Halmahera dan Raja Ampat sebagai Kesatuan Majemuk: Studi-studi terhadap suatu Daerah Transisi* (Jakarta, Lembaga Ilmu Pengetahuan Indonesia, 1983).

[52] MM Cernea, 'Internal Refugee Flows and Development-Induced Population Displacement' (1990) 3 *Journal of Refugee Studies* 4; MM Cernea and C McDowell (eds), *Risks and Reconstruction: Experience of Resettlers and Refugees* (Washington DC, World Bank, 2000).

[53] L Heming and P Rees, 'Population Displacement in the Three Gorges Reservoir Area of the Yangtze River, Central China: Relocation Policies and Migrant Views' (2000) 6 *International Journal of Population Geography* 439; Y Tan, *Resettlement in the Three Gorges Project* (Hong Kong, Hong Kong University Press, 2008).

[54] Cernea and McDowell (eds), *Risks and Reconstruction*, above n 52; G Hugo, 'Migration, Development and Environment' (Draft Paper for Research Workshop on *Migration and Environment: Developing a Research Agenda*, Munich, Germany, 16–18 April 2008).

[55] N Piper, 'Gender and Migration' (Paper prepared for the Policy and Research Programme of the Global Commission on International Migration, 2005).

[56] GJ Hugo, 'Migration and Women's Empowerment' in HB Presser and G Sen (eds), *Women's Empowerment and Demographic Processes: Moving Beyond Cairo* (Oxford, Oxford University Press, 2000).

change-related migration are not clear, but it is apparent that it is necessary to be gender sensitive not only in the investigation of mobility, but in any policy interventions relating to it.

G Migration and Development

While much of the environment and migration literature tends to see migration as problematical, there is an increasing body of work which suggests that migration can have beneficial impacts, both in origin and destination countries, within the right policy context. In fact, there has been what amounts to a paradigm shift in thinking on the migration–development relationship. In the past, 'brain drain' arguments focusing on migration reducing the stock of human capital in the country of origin were dominant, and the consensus was that migration had a net negative impact on development in origin areas. Following publications by key international agencies such as the World Bank,[57] United Nations,[58] International Labour Organization,[59] the United Kingdom Department of International Development[60] and the United States Agency for International Development (USAID),[61] however, there has been increased emphasis on the positive effects that migration can have on development in low-income countries and regions. This outcome results from the impact of remittances,[62] increased foreign direct investment due to migration,[63] knowledge transfer, and involvement of the diaspora in development activity at home and through temporary and permanent return migration.[64] In this way, it is argued that migration can deliver a triple win dividend, with positive outcomes not only for the migrant and his or her family, but also for the origin and destination countries. This does not mean, of course, that all migration produces such a positive income, as migrants can have both positive and negative effects. The key point, however, is that in the right policy

---

[57] World Bank, *Global Economic Prospects 2006: Economic Implications of Remittances and Migration* (Washington DC, World Bank, 2006); DF Terry and SR Wilson (eds), *Beyond Small Change: Making Migrant Remittances Count* (Washington DC, Inter-American Development Bank, 2005); D Ellerman, *Policy Research on Migration and Development* (Washington DC, World Bank Policy Research Working Paper No 3117, 2003).

[58] 'International Migration and Development: Report of the Secretary-General', UN GAOR 60th Session, UN Doc A/60/205 (8 August 2005).

[59] PL Martin, *Migration and Development: Toward Sustainable Solutions* (Geneva, International Institute for Labour Studies Discussion Paper No DPI53/2004, 2004).

[60] House of Commons International Development Committee (UK), *Migration and Development: How to Make Migration Work for Poverty Reduction* (London, The Stationery Office, 2004); Department for International Development (UK), 'Eliminating World Poverty: A Challenge for the 21st Century: White Paper on International Development' (Cm 3789, 1997).

[61] B Johnson and S Sedaca, *Diasporas, Emigrés and Development, Economic Linkages and Programmatic Response* (Washington DC, US Agency for International Development/Carana Corporation, 2004).

[62] D Ratha, 'Leveraging Remittances for Development' (Paper prepared for the Second Plenary Meeting of the Leading Group on Solidarity Levies to Fund Development, Oslo, 6–7 February 2007).

[63] DF Terry, 'Remittances as a Development Tool' in Terry and Wilson (eds), *Beyond Small Change*, above n 57.

[64] Report of the Secretary-General, above n 58.

context, migration can deliver a positive development dividend to origin communities. This should not be exaggerated, since sustainable development will only result from good governance, sound development, sensible policy and so on. Nevertheless, migration can make an important contribution to development in the countries of origin and in improving the lot of the migrants.

What does this mean for climate change-induced migration? In this context migration should not simply be viewed as an adjustment or coping mechanism. Migration can play an active role in building up resilience and adaptive capacity in areas affected by climate change through remittances and other diaspora influences. It also can materially improve the situation of the people moving, and their families. Getting the migration policy right in areas to be influenced by climate change, therefore, not only facilitates the survival of people living in those areas, but can positively encourage development in those areas and improve the situation of people living in them. Hence in climate change-affected areas, migration needs to be considered not only as a 'defensive' response, but also as an 'offensive' active intervention to encourage development.

VI Conclusion and Discussion

Understanding of the relationship between environmental changes and migration remains quite limited. This is partly a problem of information. In particular, migration data remains scarce and the understanding of the important drivers and impacts is also very weak. It can be concluded, however, that the role of the environment as a factor in migration, especially internal migration, has been underestimated. This is partly because of the proximate nature of the role of environment as a cause of migration.

There is still considerable debate in the migration literature regarding environment and migration. Lonergan and Swain argue that 'although the estimates and projections of environmental refugees are based almost entirely on anecdotal evidence and intuitive judgment, it is important not to trivialise the role environmental change and resource depletion may play in population movements.'[65]

This differs from Black who, in also recognising the weaknesses of the concept of 'environmental refugees', maintains that:

> although environmental degradation and catastrophe may be important factors in the decision to migrate, and issues of concern in their own right, their conceptualization as a primary cause of forced displacement is unhelpful and unsound intellectually and unnecessary in practical terms.[66]

---

[65] S Lonergan and A Swain, 'Environmental Degradation and Population Displacement' (1999) 2 *Aviso* (Global Environmental Change and Human Security Project, Oslo, 1999), www.gechs.org/aviso/02/.

[66] Black, 'Environmental Refugees', above n 8, 1.

Whichever side of the argument holds true in light of climate change remains uncertain, but almost certainly, the environment will have a greater influence on migration patterns in the future.

As the world seeks to develop a response to climate change through mitigation of the drivers of that change and adaptation to its impacts, migration will be important in the latter. However, there is a real danger that the migration response will be formulated by nation states and the international community with little recognition of existing migration patterns, processes and policies. An example of this tendency to see climate change-induced migration as a phenomenon which is different and totally separate from other forms of mobility are the current attempts to create a global regime on environmentally displaced persons. Burton and Hodgkinson have, for example, produced a draft treaty for people displaced by climate change.[67] There can be no doubt that provision for the protection of, and providing assistance to, climate change-forced migrants is a worthy and useful long and medium-term goal. In the short term, however, there would appear to be significant barriers to the formulation and widespread acceptance of such a regime for the following reasons:

- The considerable difficulty in identifying 'climate change'-forced migrants and separating them from other migrants and establishing their status;
- The reluctance of potential destination countries to agree to a new category of forced migrant and sign a convention similar to the 1951 Refugee Convention which would require them to provide international protection.[68] This reluctance has been fuelled by the pressure placed on the existing international protection regime. Figure 5 shows the large numbers seeking asylum under the refugee regime. It is politically very unlikely that destination countries will open up another category for those seeking asylum, at least in the short term;
- Countries of the Asia-Pacific region have not been among the most ready to sign key international migration instruments, as is evident from Table 6 which indicates the small number of countries in the region that have ratified the Refugee Convention; its Protocol and the Migrant Workers Convention.[69]
- The search for an international treaty on climate change-forced migrants which will be ratified by a large number of countries is a worthy and important enterprise.[70] Protecting the human rights of vulnerable groups that are impacted by climate change is being increasingly identified as an urgent priority,[71] and climate change-related migration is clearly important in this. Meanwhile, however,

---

[67] Burton and Hodgkinson, 'Climate Change Migrants and Unicorns', above n 4.

[68] Convention relating to the Status of Refugees (adopted 28 July 1951, entered into force 22 April 1954) 189 UNTS 137, read in conjunction with the Protocol relating to the Status of Refugees (adopted 31 January 1967, entered into force 4 October 1967) 606 UNTS 267.

[69] International Convention on the Protection of the Rights of All Migrant Workers and Members of Their Families (adopted 18 December 1990, entered into force 1 July 2003) 2220 UNTS 93.

[70] See W Kälin, 'Conceptualising Climate-Induced Displacement', and J McAdam, ' "Disappearing States", Statelessness and the Boundaries of International Law', in the present volume.

[71] Humphreys, 'The Human Rights Dimension of Climate Change', above n 4.

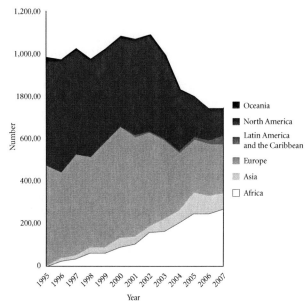

Figure 5: Asylum-seekers by region of asylum, 1995–2007

Source: UNHCR Statistics.

Table 6: Countries in Asia and the Pacific Which Have Ratified Key International Migration Instruments

• 1951 UN Convention on Refugees	
Afghanistan	Kyrgyzstan
Australia	New Zealand
Azerbaijan	Papua New Guinea
Cambodia	Philippines
China	Samoa
Fiji	Solomon Islands
Iran	Tajikistan
Japan	Timor-Leste
Kazakhstan	Turkmenistan
Korea, Republic of	Tuvalu

• 1992 ILO Convention on the Rights of Workers and Their Families	
Azerbaijan	Sri Lanka
Kyrgyzstan	Tajikistan
Philippines	Timor-Leste

Note: Bangladesh, Cambodia and Indonesia have signed, but not ratified, the Migrant Workers Convention

it is important to find ways in the short and medium-term to assist people who are (or who are likely to become) displaced, and such assistance is especially important from the major higher-income destination countries.

There are a number of strategies which need to be initiated. First among these is to accommodate climate change-related migration as far as possible *within existing international migration mechanisms*. This option has several advantages:

- it is immediately available to climate change-forced migrants, since the migration visa categories already exist;
- it overcomes the manifest suspicion of destination country governments and societies towards existing, let alone expanded, refugee categories;
- it obviates any need to set up new institutions, structures and mechanisms;
- many nations have a number of different categories for migration which provide a range of ways in which people displaced by climate change could be accommodated; and
- it would be possible to utilise existing migration networks (where they exist) to facilitate migration and to assist settlement at the destination.

A particular example of how such a system could be initiated is provided in Table 7 on the following page.

New Zealand has a range of permanent and temporary migration categories which, when taken together, could provide some corridors for Pacific Islanders forced to migrate as a result of climate change.[72] In countries like New Zealand and Australia, while the visa categories available are at present not necessarily easily available to climate change-forced migrants, they can be made so with relatively little change. Of course, making this feasible would require considerable cooperation, goodwill and commitment by governments administering the migration systems. However, the argument here is that such modification of existing channels of migration is a more achievable immediate objective than the introduction of a new migration regime.

Finally, temporary protection schemes may encounter less resistance among destination societies and governments than permanent resettlement options, yet provide an avenue to provide immediate protection, security and assistance to climate change-forced migrants. Table 8 on page 35 describes how such a scheme was activated in Australia to accept forced migrants displaced by conflict in Kosovo and Timor- Leste. The development of such schemes to cope with people displaced by sudden climate events, where they cannot all be protected within their own countries, needs consideration as part of a comprehensive response to coping with climate change-related movements, although ultimately these will need to be translated into durable solutions.

---

[72] G Hugo, P Callister and J Badkar, 'Demographic Change and International Labour Mobility in Australasia: Issues, Policies and Implications for Cooperation' in GJ Hugo and S Young (eds)), *Labour Mobility*, above n 33.

Table 7: Existing New Zealand migration categories which could accomodate climate change-forced migrants from the Pacific

---

Permanent Settlement: The New Zealand Immigration Program (NZIP)

- *Skilled Migrant Category:* migrants qualify by virtue of having a talent needed by the New Zealand economy. They sit a points assessment test.
- *Business Immigration Program:* Allows entry of migrants with proven business ability and investment capital.
- *Family Sponsored Stream:* Allows New Zealand resident immigrants to sponsor relatives to settle in New Zealand.
- *International Humanitarian Migration:* New Zealand is a signatory to the 1951 Refugee Convention and its 1967 Protocol.
- *Pacific Access Category:* Provides an annual quota of settlers selected from Tonga, Tuvalu, Kiribati and Fiji.
- *Western Samoan Quota Scheme:* Provides residence to 1,100 Western Samoan citizens annually conditional on their having definite employment in New Zealand, irrespective of skill and labour market needs.

Temporary Migration

- *Work Permit Scheme:* Allows New Zealand employers to recruit temporary workers from overseas to meet specific labour shortages that cannot be filled from within New Zealand. It is essential to have a job offer.
- *Recognised Seasonal Employer (RSE) Scheme:* Allows agricultural employers to bring in workers for an agricultural season. It is geared toward the Pacific, with employers able to recruit from eligible Pacific Island Forum Members: Federated States of Micronesia, Papua New Guinea, Kiribati, Nauru, Palau, the Republic of the Marshall Islands, Solomon Islands, Tonga, Tuvalu, Samoa and Vanuatu.

Source: GJ Hugo, P Callister and J Badkar, 'Demographic Change and International Labour Mobility in Australasia: Issues, Policies and Implications for Cooperation' in GJ Hugo and S Young (eds), *Labour Mobility in the Asia-Pacific Region* (Singapore, Institute of Southeast Asian Studies, 2008).

In summary, while work should continue towards the development of an international legal regime which provides for the recognition and protection of climate change-induced migrants, there is a need in the meantime to accommodate such migrants within existing migration mechanisms. This is imperative because it seems unlikely that a separate regime which will gain widespread acceptance by potential destination countries will be achieved in the short term.

In conclusion, it is necessary to embed thinking about migration induced by climate change in the context of the existing patterns and policies of migration. There can be no doubt that climate change will be an increasingly significant element driving migration as the twenty-first century progresses. However, understanding such migration, and developing appropriate policy responses, will be hampered if it is considered in isolation from the totality of migration.

Table 8: Australia's Temporary Safe Haven Visa Class (UJ)

This visa class was developed in 1999 to allow a fast and positive response to requests for humanitarian entry and temporary stay. They were places which were additional to the refugee/humanitarian program. The Department of Immigration and Multicultural Affairs developed two visa sub-classes:

- *448 Temporary Safe Haven:* Visas issued initially for three months and able to be extended until it became safe to go home.
- *449 Humanitarian Stay (Temporary):* Could be used anywhere in the world to grant entry and temporary stay to people displaced from their place of residence with no reasonable prospect of return, or who faced a strong likelihood of being displaced, and held grave fears for their personal safety.

These visas were activated for people displaced by conflict in Kosovo in Europe and East Timor in Asia. It involved cooperation of several government departments and the NGO sector.

Source: Department of Immigration and Multicultural Affairs (DIMA), *Annual Report 1998–99* (Canberra, DIMA, 1999).

3

Migration as Adaptation: Opportunities and Limits

JON BARNETT AND MICHAEL WEBBER

I Introduction

There is increasing concern about the implications of climate change for migration and about the ability of existing institutions to manage movements of people. Recent reports and media articles have focused for the most part on estimates of increases in the number of people exposed to environmental transformation as a result of climate change.[1] Dramatic reports about the risks of climate change and migration are at odds with the evidence about environmental change, migration and development. They rarely recognise that spontaneous and planned adaptations can reduce vulnerability to environmental change, much less that migration is itself a strategy to sustain livelihoods in the face of environmental and economic change. In many cases migration enhances the sustainable development of both sending and host areas.

For several decades, climate change has been identified as a potential driver of migration.[2] However, knowledge of the relative influence of environmental change on migration is limited,[3] in part because of the complexity of the concept of 'environmental migration'. Migration, in which environmental change may be a factor, can be a response to various sudden or slow-onset changes, may comprise movements over short or long distances and periods, and may involve small groups or entire communities. The causes and consequences of migration also

---

[1] Christian Aid, *Human Tide: The Real Migration Crisis*, (May 2007); KM Campbell et al, *The Age of Consequences: The Foreign Policy and National Security Implications of Global Climate Change* (Washington DC, Center for Strategic and International Studies, 2007); N Myers, 'Environmental Refugees: A Growing Phenomenon of the 21st Century' (2002) 357 *Philosophical Transactions of the Royal Society B* 609; RL Parry, 'The Last Tide Could Come at Any Time: Then These Islands at the End of the Earth Will Simply Vanish', *The Times* (21 December 2006), www.timesonline.co.uk/tol/news/world/article759319.ece.

[2] See, eg K Jacobsen, 'Livelihoods in Conflict: The Pursuit of Livelihoods by Refugees and the Impact on the Human Security of Host Communities' (2002) 40 *International Migration* 95.

[3] BR Döös, 'Can Large-Scale Environmental Migrations Be Predicted?' (1997) 7 *Global Environmental Change* 41.

depend on the social and ecological contexts from and to which people move,[4] and on the units of analysis (economies, social groups, households or individuals within households).[5]

This chapter examines the place of migration in adapting to climate change. It argues that in many ways migration can contribute positively to adaptation to climate change, notably through the way it can build financial, social and human capital. There are also policy measures that can enhance the contribution that migration can make to adaptation. However, this view of migration as a positive form of adaptation does not extend to involuntary resettlement, which may also arise in anticipation of or in response to climate change. In making this argument, we recognise that there is a continuum of migration decisions, with completely voluntary movements at one end and completely forced movements at the other.[6] The issue is best framed as maintaining the right to stay as well as the right to leave, allowing people to choose the response that best suits their needs and values.

We take as given that the social processes that create poverty and marginality are more important determinants of migration outcomes than environmental changes per se. For example, farmers in Australia, who experience climatic variability comparable to farmers in Northern Ethiopia, do not suffer hunger and do not resort to migration as a coping strategy in the same way as Northern Ethiopian farmers. Thus it could be argued that migrations triggered by drought in Northern Ethiopia are primarily driven by poverty and institutional failures, rather than by climatic variability.[7] In other words, migration may be an effect of environmental change (an outcome that migrants might rather have avoided) as well as an adaptation response (to avoid or adjust to an even more undesirable outcome). Therefore, reducing the likelihood of migration arising from climate change is largely within the control of people. However, without improved political and economic institutions to reduce poverty and marginality, environmental change will continue to be an important proximate factor in migration decisions.[8]

---

[4] C Locke, WN Adger and PM Kelly, 'Changing Places: Migration's Social and Environmental Consequences' (2000) 42 *Environment* 24.

[5] U Kothari, 'Staying Put and Staying Poor?' (2003) 15 *Journal of International Development* 645.

[6] G Hugo, 'Environmental Concerns and International Migration' (1996) 30 *International Migration Review* 105; G Hugo, 'Migration, Development and Environment' (Draft Paper for Research Workshop on *Migration and Environment: Developing a Research Agenda*, Munich, 16–18 April 2008).

[7] E Meze-Hausken, 'Migration Caused by Climate Change: How Vulnerable Are People in Dryland Areas? A Case-Study in Northern Ethiopia' (2000) 5 *Mitigation and Adaptation Strategies for Global Change* 379.

[8] On the relative weight of factors that affect decisions to migrate, see, eg S Amin, 'Migrations in Contemporary Africa: A Retrospective View' in J Baker and TA Aida (eds), *The Migration Experience in Africa* (Uppsala, Nordiska Afrikainstitutet, 1995); R Black, 'Environmental Refugees: Myth or Reality?', *New Issues in Refugee Research*, Working Paper No 34 (Geneva, UNHCR, 2001); ER Carr, 'Placing the Environment in Migration: Environment, Economy, and Power in Ghana's Central Region' (2005) 37 *Environment and Planning* 925; S Castles, 'Environmental Change and Forced Migration: Making Sense of the Debate', *New Issues in Refugee Research*, Working Paper No 70 (Geneva, UNHCR, 2002); WAV Clark, 'Environmentally Induced Migration and Conflict' (Berlin, German Advisory Council on Global Change (WBGU), 2007).

This chapter assumes a 2°C rise in global average temperature above pre-industrial levels, which the available literature indicates is inevitable and likely to have occurred by 2050.[9] Our conclusions and suggestions for accommodating migration to enhance adaptation apply up to this limit, both because this is now widely understood as the level beyond which climate change becomes 'dangerous', and because 40 years hence is already an extremely long time in which to frame policy.

II Environmental Change and Migration

We begin the argument by clarifying what we understand to be the range of relations between climate change and migration, in order to identify the likely patterns of movement.[10]

A Climate Change, Risk and Migration

Large-scale changes in climate are having, and will continue to have, significant effects on the ecosystem goods and services upon which humans rely (such as water suitable for drinking and growing food, fisheries, and forest products). People whose livelihoods depend most heavily on natural capital and who have the least financial resources are arguably those most vulnerable to the effects of climate change on the supply of ecosystem goods and services; their vulnerability is even more pronounced if they live in already degraded and variable environments.[11] Most of these people have proven strategies to cope with variability in resource stocks, often relying on social capital that enables the sharing of resources and labour, and migration (the benefits of which are discussed later in the chapter), though the effectiveness of those strategies may be undermined by changes in the frequency and magnitude of variations in resource stocks, coupled with long-term declines in mean conditions. However, it is not just resource-dependent, low-income rural people who are at risk: many people whose incomes depend on primary industries may also be affected, as may the urban poor, who might experience

[9] K Anderson and A Bows, 'Reframing the Climate Change Challenge in Light of Post-2000 Emissions Trends' (2008) 366 *Philosophical Transactions of the Royal Society A* 3863; Intergovernmental Panel on Climate Change (IPCC), *Climate Change 2007: Synthesis Report: Contribution of Working Groups I, II and III to the Fourth Assessment Report of the Intergovernmental Panel on Climate Change* (Geneva, IPCC, 2008); V Ramanathan and Y Feng, 'On Avoiding Dangerous Anthropogenic Interference with the Climate System: Formidable Challenges Ahead' (2008) 105 *Proceedings of the National Academy of Sciences of the United States of America* 14245.

[10] For details, see J Barnett and M Webber, 'Accommodating Migration to Promote Adaptation to Climate Change', Policy Brief for the Secretariat of the Swedish Commission on Climate Change and Development and the World Bank World Development Report 2010 Team (March 2009).

[11] N Leary et al, 'For Whom the Bell Tolls: Vulnerabilities in a Changing Climate: A Synthesis from the AIACC Project', Working Paper No 21 (Washington DC, AIACC, 2006).

increased health problems and rising prices of basic goods such as food and water.[12] The impacts and costs of climate change will fall disproportionately, and will be felt first and most acutely by the poorest people and the poorest countries.[13]

Migration is one way in which people can respond to climate risks.[14] Others may adapt without migrating. Yet others still may not adapt at all, so that their well-being declines.[15] Indeed, the number of people who cannot migrate in response to climate change (because they are poor, old, ill or face insurmountable barriers to movement) may far exceed the number that do, and there will be those who do not wish to move in any case; these people may pose a large, diffuse humanitarian problem. Nevertheless, climate-induced changes in environmental and social systems will affect people's perceptions of the risks and benefits associated with staying as compared to moving (either over short or long distances, or for short or long periods of time). If climate change exacerbates morbidity and mortality, reduces incomes and decreases access to important forms of natural capital, people may be more likely to choose to migrate to places that they perceive to offer a better life.

Disasters often lead to large-scale displacements of people, and this, in turn, can undermine development. However, people who move in response to disasters often return; most people seek to return to rebuild and continue living in familiar ways and places. Such movements are also typically short; relatively few people who are displaced by disasters cross an international border. The patterns of movement tend to follow social networks, as people move to stay with family and friends.[16]

On the other hand, slow-onset changes—such as desertification—undermine the contribution of natural capital to livelihoods, and if alternative sources of food and income are not available, people often choose to move either permanently[17] or for a short while. In response to slow-onset changes, households often take

---

[12] J Barnett and WN Adger, 'Climate Change, Human Security and Violent Conflict' (2007) 26 *Political Geography* 639.

[13] N Stern, *The Economics of Climate Change* (Cambridge, Cambridge University Press, 2006).

[14] Black, 'Environmental Refugees', above n 8; S Adamo, 'Addressing Environmentally Induced Population Displacements: A Delicate Task', Background Paper (Population-Research Network Cyberseminar on Environmentally Induced Population Displacements, 18–29 August 2008).

[15] Kothari, 'Staying Put and Staying Poor?', above n 5; M Loughry, 'Climate Change, Human Movement and the Promotion of Mental Health: What Have We Learnt from Earlier Global Stressors?', in the present volume.

[16] Black, 'Environmental Refugees', above n 8; Castles, 'Environmental Change and Forced Migration', above n 8; Hugo, 'Migration, Development and Environment', above n 6; S Lonergan, 'The Role of Environmental Degradation in Population Displacement' (1998) 4 *Environmental Change and Security Project Report* 5; SL Perch-Nielson, MB Bättig and D Imboden, 'Exploring the Link between Climate Change and Migration' (2008) 91 *Climatic Change* 375; E Piguet, 'Climate Change and Forced Migration', *New Issues in Refugee Research*, Research Paper No 153 (Geneva, UNHCR, 2008).

[17] For example, in the Sahel: A Afolayan and I Adelekan, 'The Role of Climatic Variations on Migration and Human Health in Africa' (1999) 18 *The Environmentalist* 213; S Davies, *Adaptable Livelihoods: Coping with Food Insecurity in the Malian Sahel* (Hampshire and London, Macmillan Press, 1996); T Hammer, 'Desertification and Migration: A Political Ecology of Environmental Migration in West Africa' in JD Unruh, MS Krol and N Kliot (eds), *Environmental Change and its Implications for Population Migration* (Dordrecht, Kluwer Academic Publishers, 2004).

migration decisions that involve selecting an individual to move to seek work. This strategy reduces the number of people that a household must support, creates an alternative income stream (remittances) and establishes connections that may help the migration of additional family members.[18] In times of extreme drought the rate of migration may decrease,[19] and the ratio of international to internal migrants falls because the income needed to finance movement declines.[20] There is also evidence that during slow-onset changes, the propensity to relocate is related to age (younger people tend to leave) and land holdings (those with secure access to better land are less prone to leave).[21] Attempts to support adaptation to sustain populations living in vulnerable areas, therefore, may need to entail adjustments in property rights regimes so that the distribution of resources across populations at risk is more equitable.

B Patterns of Movement

There are barriers to migration. Financial barriers include the costs of transport, housing on arrival and living expenses incurred while developing new income streams. Thus when people are too poor, they cannot afford to migrate; when they are rich, the financial benefits are few.[22] This fact implies that the poorest do not migrate, or only migrate short distances.[23] Most of the people who migrate in response to environmental changes are the lower middle classes, who have enough money to move, but not far.[24] There are information barriers to migration, including knowledge of where to go, how to get there, and ways to make a life upon arrival. There are also legal barriers associated with the ways states grant permission to enter and reside—and the conditions of entry and residence—that make it hard for

---

[18] O Stark, *The Migration of Labor* (Cambridge and Oxford, Basil Blackwell, 1991).

[19] S Findley, 'Does Drought Increase Migration? A Study of Migration from Rural Mali during the 1983–85 Droughts' (1994) 28 *International Migration Review* 539; K van der Geest and R de Jeu, 'Ghana' (2008) 31 *Forced Migration Review* 16.

[20] D Kniveton, K Schmidt-Verkerk, C Smith and R Black, *Climate Change and Migration: Improving Methodologies to Estimate Flows* (Geneva, IOM Migration Research Series No 33, 2008).

[21] EACH-FOR, 'Preliminary Findings from the EACH-FOR Project on Environmentally Induced Migration' (EACH-FOR Project Consortium, 2008), www.each-for.eu/documents/EACH-FOR_Preliminary_Findings_-_Final_Version.pdf; D Hutton and CE Haque, 'Human Vulnerability, Dislocation and Resettlement: Adaptation Processes of River-Bank Erosion-Induced Displacees in Bangladesh' (2004) 28 *Disasters* 41; Kothari, 'Staying Put and Staying Poor?', above n 5; R McLeman and B Smit, 'Migration as an Adaptation to Climate Change' (2006) 76 *Climatic Change* 31.

[22] N Nyberg-Sørensen, N Van Hear and P Engberg-Pedersen, 'Migration, Development and Conflict: State-of-the-Art Overview' in N Van Hear and N Nyberg-Sørensen (eds), *The Migration–Development Nexus* (Geneva, UN and IOM, 2003); H de Haas, 'International Migration, Remittances and Development: Myths and Facts' (2005) 26 *Third World Quarterly* 1269; H de Haas, 'The Complex Role of Migration in Shifting Rural Livelihoods: a Moroccan Case Study' in T van Naerssen, E Spaan and A Zoomers (eds), *Global Migration and Development* (London, Routledge, 2007); REB Lucas, 'Migration and Economic Development in Africa: A Review of Evidence' (2006) 15 *Journal of African Economies* 337.

[23] Amin, 'Migrations in Contemporary Africa', above n 8.

[24] C Krokfors, 'Poverty, Environmental Stress and Culture as Factors in African Migrations' in Baker and Aida (eds), *The Migration Experience in Africa*, above n 8; R Skeldon, 'Migration and Poverty' (2002) 17 *Asia Pacific Population Journal* 67.

migrants to move across international borders. Once migrants have established themselves in their new destinations, they help others within their social networks to overcome these information, financial and legal barriers.

Thus, migration is patterned. Flows of migrants point towards places where existing migrants have overcome the barriers to movement between places.[25] Most of the world's migrants move within their own countries, and most of them are economic migrants, moving from rural to urban areas in search of work. Nevertheless, each year about 10 million people are involuntarily resettled for development projects, about half of them for large dams.[26] Half of the world's international migrants originate from 20 countries: the largest number (21 per cent) comes from European countries (including the Russian Federation and Turkey) and another 11 per cent from South Asia.[27]

Climate change is likely to exacerbate existing migration patterns, rather than create entirely new flows. This means that a crude guide to the geography of future movements is present movements. These existing patterns, together with an understanding of the impacts of climate change on natural resources, lead us to identify four types of migration that may be affected by climate change.

i International and Internal Labour Migrants

It is probable that climate change will undermine the ability of people to finance long moves, and it is possible that climate change will reduce voluntary migration as it pushes some people into deeper poverty. Notwithstanding this, households at risk of climate change may deliberately and carefully pursue labour migration as an adaptation strategy. Labour migrants are typically young, single people who move in search of work. The decision to move is usually made by the household, and the move is enabled by savings and social networks. Thus labour migrants are generally seen to respond more to 'pull' factors than to 'push' factors. In this respect they are generally of lesser humanitarian concern than refugees, the internally displaced, and the forcibly displaced. Given this, it is reasonable to assume that labour migrants whose moves are partly stimulated by the need to adapt to climate change may for the most part not require humanitarian assistance. However, as we explain later, they nevertheless do require an environment that enables them to maximise the contributions they can make to the places they come from, as well as the places to which they have moved. Labour migration offers the best potential for harnessing the power of migration to promote adaptation to climate change.

---

[25] Lucas, 'Migration and Economic Development in Africa', above n 22; A de Haan, 'Livelihoods and Poverty: The Role of Migration: A Critical Review of the Migration Literature' (1999) 36 *Journal of Development Studies* 1; DS Massey and FG España, 'The Social Process of International Migration' (1987) 237 *Science* 733.

[26] MM Cernea and C McDowell, 'Introduction: Reconstructing Resettlers' and Refugees' Livelihoods' in MM Cernea and C McDowell (eds), *Risks and Reconstruction: Experience of Resettlers and Refugees* (Washington DC, World Bank, 2000); World Commission on Dams, *Dams and Development: A New Framework for Decision Making* (London, Earthscan, 2001).

[27] Development Research Centre on Migration, Globalisation and Poverty, 'Global Migrant Origin Database', www.migrationdrc.org/research/typesofmigration/global_migrant_origin_database.html.

ii Internal and International Displacement

Such displacement—in response to rapid-onset natural disasters—will be exacerbated by climate change.[28] Evidence suggests that these movements are likely to be over short distances, and those displaced are likely to wish to return.[29] Governments and the international community may need to increase their planning for disasters, as well as their capacity to support humanitarian needs and assist in the repatriation of displaced people.

iii Internal and International Permanent Migrants

Such migration is a consequence of stresses exacerbated by incremental changes and slow-onset disasters, such as drought. Migrants of this kind can be distinguished (at least in theory) from labour migrants in that their decisions to move are stimulated more by 'push' than pull factors, and movements are more likely to be made by families than individuals. While it is difficult to argue that people who have permanently moved from drought-affected areas in the Sahel and the Horn of Africa, for example, have moved primarily due to environmental reasons alone (poverty and conflict are also key variables), that many of these people remain in informal settlements and camps suggests that their decision to move was impelled rather than pulled.

iv Relocation of Communities

Resettlement of entire communities to reduce their exposure to climate change has been proposed by some commentators, and is widely implied in discussions about climate-induced migration.[30] This issue is discussed in greater detail later in this chapter. It suffices to say here that groups who are resettled arguably face the greatest risks to their livelihoods and human rights, and assisting them will challenge the international community.

III Migration and Adaptation

The capacity of a social system to respond to climate change to moderate or avoid its negative consequences depends on several factors: financial resources; governance (effectiveness and legitimacy); information (to anticipate climate risks, devise appropriate adaptations and learn from their implementation); social resources

---

[28] E Ferris, 'Making Sense of Climate Change, Natural Disasters, and Displacement: A Work in Progress' (Bern, Calcutta Research Group Winter Course, University of Bern, 14 December 2007).

[29] C Raleigh, L Jordan and I Salehyan, *Assessing the Impact of Climate Change on Migration and Conflict* (Washington DC, World Bank, 2008).

[30] See, eg S Byravan and SC Rajan, 'Providing New Homes for Climate Change Exiles' (2006) 6 *Climate Policy* 247.

(networking and bonding among people and groups so that social responses to climate change are cohesive, equitable and robust); infrastructure; and technology.[31] Although migration means that sending households and communities lose labour,[32] migration can make positive contributions to many of these determinants of adaptive capacity. In aggregate, migration seems to contribute positively to the capacity of those left behind to adapt to climate change and generally leads to net gains in wealth in receiving areas.[33] These findings are context-dependent, but they suggest that voluntary migration can enhance capacity to adapt to climate change.

Many of the financial benefits of migration for the adaptive capacity of communities of origin arise through remittances. Globally, the volume of remittances may be double that of Official Development Assistance,[34] and in many ways, far more reliable[35] (although there is debate about the durability of remittance transfers).[36] Remittances have many positive effects: smoothing consumption of basic needs such as food across seasons; sustaining access to basic needs in times of livelihood shocks; paying for the acquisition of human, social, physical and natural capital; and increasing demand and stimulating local production.[37] Families with labour migrants who remit incomes fare better during livelihood crises than those that do not.[38] Families with members living in developed countries tend to receive more remittances than do those with members working within the same country.[39] While the volume of resources sent home by poor migrants may be small, the relative contribution to household incomes and capital is large and so significantly increases adaptive capacity.[40]

---

[31] WN Adger et al, 'Assessment of Adaptation Practices, Options, Constraints and Capacity' in ML Parry et al (eds), *Climate Change 2007: Impacts, Adaptation and Vulnerability Contribution of Working Group II to the Fourth Assessment Report of the Intergovernmental Panel on Climate Change* (Cambridge, Cambridge University Press, 2007) ch 17.

[32] Kothari, 'Staying Put and Staying Poor?', above n 5.

[33] C Horst, 'Refugee Livelihoods: Continuity and Transformations' (2006) 25 *Refugee Survey Quarterly* 6; Skeldon, 'Migration and Poverty', above n 24; Kothari, 'Staying Put and Staying Poor?', above n 5; de Haan, 'Livelihoods and Poverty', above n 25; Nyberg-Sørensen et al, 'Migration, Development and Conflict', above n 22.

[34] Nyberg-Sørensen et al, 'Migration, Development and Conflict', above n 22.

[35] de Haas, 'International Migration', above n 22; REB Lucas, 'International Migration and Economic Development: Lessons from Low-Income Countries: Executive Summary' (Stockholm, Ministry for Foreign Affairs, 2005).

[36] LE Guarnizo, 'The Economics of Transnational Living' (2003) 37 *International Migration Review* 666; S Vertovec, 'Migrant Transnationalism and Modes of Transformation' (2004) 38 *International Migration Review* 970.

[37] A de Haan, 'Migrants, Livelihoods, and Rights: The Relevance of Migration in Development Policies', Social Development Department, Working Paper No 4 (London, Department for International Development, 2000); F Ellis, 'A Livelihoods Approach to Migration and Poverty Reduction: Paper Commissioned by the Department for International Development (DFID)' (London, Department for International Development, 2003).

[38] M Erza, 'Demographic Responses to Environmental Stress in the Drought- and Famine-Prone Areas of Northern Ethiopia' (2001) 7 *International Journal of Population Geography* 259.

[39] de Haas, 'The Complex Role of Migration', above n 22.

[40] de Haan, 'Migrants, Livelihoods, and Rights', above n 37; Lucas, 'Migration and Economic Development in Africa', above n 22.

When migrants are secure in their new destination and confident of being able to return if they leave temporarily, they tend to return regularly to their communities of origin. These returns can enhance the adaptive capacity of communities of origin by bringing understanding of the world and of climate change risks and responses, consolidating social networks, transmitting money and goods and transferring new skills. Returning migrants may also act as agents against corrupt practices or as advocates for peace.[41]

Migration also expands the social networks of households and communities, reducing the risks associated with short-term displacement in response to a crisis. Migration boosts incentives to pursue education (which is a determinant of success in moving) and so increases the educational attainment of sending populations.[42] Migration reduces per capita demands on resources in sending regions and can increase the acquisition of new technologies,[43] for migrants are often early adopters of information communication technology.[44]

Although the public and private sectors in many receiving countries fail to appreciate the benefits of labour migration,[45] labour migrants are generally hard-working, seeking to maximise incomes to finance a better life for themselves and their children, to send money to families at home, and to help new migrants overcome barriers to movement and settlement.[46] National and international assistance serves migrants' needs best when it supports migrants to maximise their opportunities, for example through secure access to land, micro-credit schemes and programmes to generate incomes for both migrant and host populations.[47] The ability and willingness of local and national governments to assist migrants are critical to maximising the benefits they can bring to host and destination areas, as well as minimising the costs that the migrants themselves experience. If local and national governments are unable to assist, their willingness to work with international agencies to fill capability gaps is important.

The literature on refugees and internally displaced persons (IDPs) supports these arguments. The entrepreneurial endeavour of such people makes them a potentially important resource that can enhance the capacity of host communities. They often bring resources with them, including their skills and labour, and use these to build livelihoods.[48] Like all migrants, refugees and IDPs are able to pursue the livelihood strategies that best suit their skills and values when their entitlements in the host community are maximised, and outcomes are most equitable when those entitlements are equal to those of their local hosts. When these

---

[41] Nyberg-Sørensen et al, 'Migration, Development and Conflict', above n 22.

[42] LT Katseli, REB Lucas and T Xenogiani, 'Effects of Migration on Sending Countries: What Do We Know?', OECD Development Centre, Working Paper No 250 (Paris, OECD, 2006).

[43] Kothari, 'Staying Put and Staying Poor?', above n 5.

[44] de Haas, 'International Migration', above n 22.

[45] Nyberg-Sørensen et al, 'Migration, Development and Conflict', above n 22.

[46] Skeldon, 'Migration and Poverty', above n 24.

[47] Jacobsen, 'Livelihoods in Conflict', above n 2.

[48] R Black, 'Refugee Migration and Local Economic Development in Eastern Zambia' (1994) 85 *Tijdschrift voor economische en sociale geografie* 249.

entitlements are maximised, displaced people can access labour markets and establish new businesses to grow their incomes, and they can borrow, save and remit money, and return to their communities of origin to help with development in those places.[49] Thus, the benefits of migrants to both their hosts and their places of origin are maximised when they have de jure or de facto citizenship, and policies that can achieve this status are desirable.[50] Much also depends on the labour market conditions and policy and institutional settings of receiving areas. If there are shortages of labour, migration makes a positive contribution to wealth creation and, by implication, adaptive capacity.[51] If migrants attract increases in official development assistance, that assists both them and the communities they move to, since it can lead to better social infrastructure, such as new schools and health care.[52] Where migrants find work and pay taxes, they contribute positively to growth and the provision of public goods. It is critical that the rate of growth in employment is commensurate with the increase in population, otherwise jobs can become scarce, which is blamed on migrants.

IV Maximising Benefits, Minimising Costs

Migration is, however, not without its costs. Migrants are often exploited, subjected to discrimination, denied basic rights and paid less than local counterparts.[53] People who have little choice but to move may lose their homes and sites that are important to them, as well as their jobs. Their communities and families may be broken up, their livelihoods disrupted, and so they may become poorer in absolute as well as relative (to their host population) terms. Yet, there is scope for careful and coordinated policies to minimise the potential costs and maximise the potential benefits arising from migration exacerbated by climate change.

A Labour Migrants

People who pursue labour migration partly in response to actual or perceived future climate change impacts at home may require assistance to minimise the costs to them of moving. This includes assistance with visas (if they cross a border), finding a job, finding housing, developing language skills, networking with

---

[49] Horst, 'Refugee Livelihoods', above n 33.

[50] Kothari, 'Staying Put and Staying Poor?', above n 5.

[51] Nyberg-Sørensen et al, 'Migration, Development and Conflict', above n 22.

[52] Black, 'Refugee Migration', above n 48.

[53] Afolayan and Adelekan, 'The Role of Climatic Variations', above n 17; R Hill, KJ Diener, S Miller and T White, 'IDP Livelihoods and Personal Security: Case Studies from Colombia and Sudan' (2006) 25 *Refugee Survey Quarterly* 40.

other migrants and understanding public services.[54] Public authorities should promote a positive image of migrants and should not allow them to become scapegoats for social and economic problems. These efforts will help maximise the benefits of migration to the host community, as they will speed up migrants' entry into the workforce and minimise the social frictions that may arise when migrants are disenfranchised.[55]

The benefits of labour migrants to their communities of origin can be maximised by reducing the costs of money transfers, for example by capping fees, encouraging multiple service providers and supporting governments and businesses in areas of origin to establish a service to receive money.[56] Citizenship and/or equal rights to work, social support and the freedom to move in and out of both the place/country of arrival and origin can facilitate freer movement of people, and so increase the benefits of this movement for the communities from which migrants originate.

There is scope to harmonise development and migration policies in developed countries to improve both the contribution of labour to growth in developed countries, and the contribution of migrants to the capacity to adapt to climate change in the places from which they move. Where there are shortages of unskilled labour, then developed countries could augment that labour supply by encouraging migration from communities which are vulnerable to climate change and which do not yet benefit from remittances. Where there are needs for semi-skilled labour, then developed countries could work with developing countries to invest in skills training in vulnerable communities, although care should be taken with respect to the social and cultural effects that can arise from changing the demographic structure of communities that have high rates of out-migration.

Such labour migration does mean that if those who leave have scarce skills and capabilities, the human capital deficits that arise can restrict adaptive capacity in the places of origin. Countries or regions that benefit from skilled international or internal migrants may offset these negative effects by facilitating temporary placements and investing in skills training in places of origin, maximising opportunities for remittance transfers, diversifying sources of skilled migrants and encouraging reverse migration. Information, transport and communications infrastructure to improve internal labour market mobility may also help balance supply and demand. Importing labour may also be possible if wages in areas of skills shortage are higher than in nearby countries.

---

[54] R Zetter, D Griffiths, N Sigona and M Hauser, 'Survey on Policy and Practice related to Refugee Integration: Report Commissioned by European Refugee Fund Community Actions 2001/2' (Oxford, Oxford Brookes University School of Planning, 2002).

[55] T Kuhlman, 'The Economic Integration of Refugees in Developing Countries: A Research Model' (1991) 4 *Journal of Refugee Studies* 1.

[56] Nyberg-Sørensen et al, 'Migration, Development and Conflict, above n 22; de Haas, 'International Migration', above n 22; Lucas, 'Migration and Economic Development in Africa', above n 22; A Hall, 'Globalized Livelihoods, International Migration and Challenges for Social Policy: The Case of Ecuador' (Paper presented at the New Frontiers of Social Policy Conference, Arusha, 12–15 December 2005).

B People Displaced by Extreme Events

Many of the people who will move temporarily in response to extreme events will have immediate humanitarian needs that create new demands on national governments and the international community. Those who move to places where they do not have established social networks that can support them are likely to require assistance with shelter, water and sanitation, food, and, in some cases, protection while they wait to return to their homes.

Meeting the needs of people displaced by natural disasters will be the responsibility of civil society, non-governmental organisations (NGOs), governments in the host country and bilateral and multilateral providers of humanitarian and development assistance. Much depends on their capacity and willingness to respond. The duration of that response will depend on how long it takes for disaster recovery efforts to convince people that it is safe to return home. It may therefore be in the interests of neighbouring countries to work cooperatively to implement disaster risk management strategies to reduce damage to property and livelihoods from extreme events, and to develop cooperative approaches to disaster recovery and repatriation of displaced peoples.

In some cases opportunistic actors may seize upon internal movements as a means to acquire the lands of those displaced.[57] Codifying and enforcing the property rights of the temporarily displaced is important, although such efforts may only be as effective as the governments that are responsible for them. There may therefore also be a role for the international community in assisting the displaced to secure their rights to property upon return.

Bilateral and multilateral providers of humanitarian and development assistance have the capacity to mobilise to meet the humanitarian needs of people displaced by extreme events when local institutions are unable or unwilling to do so. This capability has emerged out of the institutions established to safeguard the human rights and well-being of refugees under the aegis of the United Nations High Commissioner for Refugees (UNHCR)[58] and the 1951 Convention relating to the Status of Refugees.[59] However, refugees are a distinct category of migrant in a number of respects: they must have moved across an *international* border on account of a 'well-founded fear of being persecuted for reasons of race, religion, nationality, membership of a particular social group or political opinion', and be unable or unwilling to avail themselves of the protection of their country of origin. If these were the only criteria that mobilised an international response to a

---

[57] S Williams, 'Internally Displaced Persons and Property Rights in Cambodia' (2000) 19 *Refugee Survey Quarterly* 194.

[58] Statute of the Office of the United Nations High Commissioner for Refugees, UNGA Res 428 (V) (14 December 1950).

[59] Convention relating to the Status of Refugees (adopted 28 July 1951, entered into force 22 April 1954) 189 UNTS 137, read in conjunction with the Protocol relating to the Status of Refugees (adopted 31 January 1967, entered into force 4 October 1967) 606 UNTS 267 (together 'Refugee Convention').

humanitarian crisis in the future, there would seem to be little prospect of them safeguarding the rights of people displaced by climate change.[60]

Nevertheless, the international system can and does respond to humanitarian crises involving the displacement of people who are not refugees. Many of the same organisations that help to respond to refugee problems also respond to other humanitarian crises, including helping to meet basic and protection needs, and working with people and governments to aid in repatriation. This was most recently revealed in the response of bilateral and multilateral providers of humanitarian and development assistance after the Asian Tsunami in 2004.

Yet there is frequently inadequate funding for responses to humanitarian emergencies. Funding has often not been available when required, and has been given by donor governments according to their interests in certain regions.[61] Further, some donor countries prefer not to work within the United Nations (UN) system, creating duplication of services and inefficiencies. This has meant that there has been inadequate funding for emergencies in regions that are of little significance to the national interests of donors. To help address this problem, in 2006 the UN General Assembly established the UN Central Emergency Response Fund, which since its inception has disbursed over US$1 billion to assist people in 65 countries.

Coordinating the response of UN agencies, governments and local and international NGOs is necessary to maximise the effectiveness of emergency responses. This remains a persistent problem, even within the UN system where a collaborative approach to dealing with humanitarian crises has proven to be inadequate, despite improvements since 1991.[62] Much of the problem lies in the resistance of various agencies to centralised control in the field, and in the inconsistency between agencies in the nature and timeliness of their responses to emergencies of different kinds.[63] Many of these issues were revealed in the response to the Asian Tsunami in 2004. Despite significant mobilisation of resources from many countries and agencies, the basic needs of displaced people were compromised by difficulties in coordinating the delivery of the US$6.8 billion worth of assistance, and the activities of the 16 UN agencies, 18 Red Cross response teams, 160 or more international NGOs, hundreds of private and civil society groups, and 35 armed forces.[64]

A major problem in responding to the needs of the displaced is the willingness and capability of national governments to meet their own responsibilities with respect to human rights. Many of the current situations in which the governmental response is inadequate are those where conflict is the primary driver of displacement, and governments may lack the resources to protect people at risk and to provide humanitarian assistance. They may also choose not to do so, and to

---

[60] See J McAdam, 'From Economic Refugees to Climate Refugees?' (2009) 10 *Melbourne Journal of International Law* 579.

[61] United Nations High Commissioner for Refugees (UNHCR), *The State of the World's Refugees: Human Displacement in the New Millennium* (Oxford, Oxford University Press, 2006).

[62] ibid.

[63] ibid.

[64] ibid.

hamper the efforts of international agencies to assist, sometimes because the displaced may come from groups perceived to be opposing the government, and/or because humanitarian assistance and spaces can be used by armed groups in various ways to sustain their operations.[65]

There is debate about the desirability of extending the Refugee Convention to include other displaced people and/or the creation of new instruments to protect them.[66] For example, Williams argues for regionally oriented regimes to deal with migrant flows due to climate change which operate under the auspices of the UN Framework Convention on Climate Change.[67] Most commentators favour enhancing the UN system's existing frameworks for responding to humanitarian emergencies, such as the Guiding Principles on Internal Displacement developed a decade ago, which draw on principles of international human rights law, refugee law and humanitarian law to outline the rights of IDPs and the responsibilities of governments and humanitarian agencies to protect those rights.[68] While the Guiding Principles themselves are not a legally binding document, they have helped guide governmental action in relation to IDPs and are often used as a benchmark by governments, regional institutions, UN agencies and NGOs.[69]

C People Permanently Displaced

If people are to some degree forced to move in response to environmental changes driven by changes in climate, and this was an outcome they would rather have avoided, then such moves should be considered as impacts of climate change, and not adaptations.[70] Policies and programmes should therefore be developed to enable people to adapt in ways that do not entail permanent migration. The principle that people should have the 'right to stay home' is as important as the principle that they should be free to move if they choose.[71]

Adaptation efforts directed towards the most vulnerable communities must therefore be a priority if permanent migration is to be avoided. The specific nature of adaptation responses in any given location will depend critically on the nature of the social and ecological systems in which people live, and the needs, rights and

[65] J Goodhand and D Hulme, 'From Wars to Complex Political Emergencies: Understanding Conflict and Peace-Building in the New World Disorder' (1999) 20 *Third World Quarterly* 13; P Le Billon, 'The Political Economy of War: What Relief Agencies Need to Know', HPN Network Paper No 33 (London, Overseas Development Institute, 2000); M Duffield, *Global Governance and the New Wars: The Merging of Development and Security* (London, Zed Books, 2001).

[66] See R Zetter, 'Protecting People Displaced by Climate Change: Some Conceptual Challenges', in the present volume, 141.

[67] A Williams, 'Turning the Tide: Recognising Climate Change Refugees in International Law' (2008) 30 *Law and Policy* 502, referring to the UN Framework Convention on Climate Change (adopted 9 May 1992, entered into force 21 March 1993) 1771 UNTS 107 ('UNFCCC').

[68] Guiding Principles on Internal Displacement, UN Doc E/CN.4/1998/53/Add.2 (11 February 1998) ('Guiding Principles').

[69] UNHCR, *The State of the World's Refugees*, above n 61.

[70] C Mortreux and J Barnett, 'Climate Change, Migration and Adaptation in Funafuti, Tuvalu' (2009) 19 *Global Environmental Change* 105.

[71] D Bacon, 'The Right to Stay Home' (14 July 2008), www.truthout.org/article/the-right-stay-home.

values of people and communities.[72] Importantly, adaptation is more than merely avoiding climate risks, and must accommodate people's rights and aspirations for the future.[73] Adaptation responses are not universal; they must be determined through participatory processes, for which there are numerous guides.[74]

In so far as permanent migration may be triggered by a threshold event such as drought or a food crisis, well-timed and well-delivered disaster assistance can significantly offset migration. Effective responses to famines are those that seek to augment entitlements so that people in famine conditions do not lose assets and/or migrate, as these distress responses increase their vulnerability to subsequent famine events. There are many examples of systems that can successfully respond to food crises so that migration does not result, and there is a need to strengthen these where they exist and to replicate them where they do not.

The best, if approximate, guide to future migration flows is present flows due to the inhibiting effects of barriers to migration, which, once overcome, are followed by expanded flows, such that migration follows distinct temporal and spatial patterns. At present, the majority of the world's migrants move within their own countries, and the majority of international migrants move to neighbouring countries.[75] If efforts to avoid permanent migration exacerbated by climate change fail, then most of those people who move will be poor. They are therefore most likely to move within their own country, or to a neighbouring country, rather than over vast distances. In most cases, the countries that receive increased flows of permanent migrants will be developing countries whose ability to meet the needs of these migrants is limited. The international community must support these countries to meet the short-term humanitarian and longer-term settlement needs of migrants. Support can make the difference between increased security and sustainable livelihoods for migrants and people in host areas, on the one hand, and increasing conflict, poverty and environmental degradation, on the other.[76]

As with all migrants, the benefits of people who move permanently to places of origin and destination are maximised when they are entitled to the same freedoms and opportunities as people in the host community. Policies will be most successful when they support migrants to establish new livelihood strategies. When international agencies are involved in such efforts, partnering with organisations that understand the local social, economic and environmental context is critical.[77]

---

[72] J Barnett, 'The Effect of Aid on Capacity to Adapt to Climate Change: Insights from Niue' (2008) 60 *Political Science* 31.

[73] WN Adger et al, 'Adaptation to Climate Change in the Developing World' (2003) 3 *Progress in Development Studies* 179.

[74] R Few, K Brown and EL Tompkins, 'Public Participation and Climate Change Adaptation: Avoiding the Illusion of Inclusion' (2007) 7 *Climate Policy* 46; B Lim, E Spanger-Siegfried, I Burton, E Malone and S Huq (eds), *Adaptation Policy Frameworks for Climate Change: Developing Strategies, Policies and Measures* (Cambridge, Cambridge University Press, 2004); UNFCCC Secretariat, 'Compendium on Methods and Tools to Evaluate Impacts of, Vulnerability and Adaptation to, Climate Change' (Bonn, UNFCCC, 2005).

[75] See, eg Barnett and Webber, 'Accommodating Migration', above n 10.

[76] Nyberg-Sørensen et al, 'Migration, Development and Conflict', above n 22.

[77] Jacobsen, 'Livelihoods in Conflict', above n 2.

The ingredients required for successful re-establishment of livelihoods vary by location and group. In many cases, secure access to land is a critical factor.[78] It is important that local hosts are encouraged to see the benefits of new migrants and to provide them with the same rights and freedoms as local people. Services that can help migrants and host communities develop include short-term job creation to assist with immediate needs, micro-finance programmes, skills training, health care and agricultural extension.[79]

There may be a need to explore new migration regimes to respond to permanent displacement arising from climate change.[80] There are few precedents to guide this endeavour beyond the labour migration arrangements that have emerged among members of the European Union. Indeed, to a remarkable degree, regional agreements seeking to liberalise the movement of goods and capital do not address the movement of labour, and in so doing sustain asymmetries in the supply and demand of labour, and subsequent inequalities in returns to labour between countries.[81] To address this, many developing countries are seeking increased access to developed country labour markets under new trade liberalising agreements, such as the Economic Partnership Agreements being developed between the European Union and the African, Caribbean and Pacific countries. However, even if such nascent agreements result in increased labour mobility, they may not be equipped to accommodate demands for international migration arising from climate change (although they may contribute positively to adaptive capacity for all the reasons outlined in this chapter). There is, however, a precedent for deferral of removal in the case of natural disaster, in that some developed countries have deferred the deportation of illegal migrants to countries that have recently experienced a disaster, such as after the Asian Tsunami[82] and Hurricane Mitch.[83]

D Community Resettlement

It seems likely that beyond a 2°C rise in global average temperature, decision makers will need to plan for both spontaneous and planned community relocations. Nevertheless, despite some speculation in the media and environmental

---

[78] ibid.

[79] Hill et al, 'IDP Livelihoods and Personal Security', above n 53.

[80] D Smith and J Vivekananda, *A Climate of Conflict: The Links Between Climate Change, Peace and War* (London, International Alert, 2007). See also J McAdam and M Loughry, 'We Aren't Refugees', *Inside Story* (30 June 2009), http://inside.org.au/we-arent-refugees/.

[81] F Biermann and I Boas, 'Preparing for a Warmer World: Towards a Global Governance System to Protect Climate Refugees', Global Governance Working Paper No 33 (November 2007); UNHCR, *The State of the World's Refugees*, above n 61; K Warner et al, *Report: Human Security, Climate Change, and Environmentally Induced Migration* (United Nations University, Institute for Environment and Human Security Report, 30 June 2008).

[82] F Laczko and E Collett, 'Assessing the Tsunami's Effects on Migration' (Feature Story for the Migration Information Source, April 2005), http://www.migrationinformation.org/feature/display.cfm?ID=299.

[83] O Brown, *Migration and Climate Change* (Geneva, IOM Migration Research Series No 31, 2008).

community,[84] such relocations are unlikely to be necessary in the coming decades. Where they are, climate change is unlikely to be the principal driver. Indeed, in the near future there is a danger that powerful actors will use the excuse of reducing community exposure to climate change in order to conduct forced migrations, for political or economic gain.

Relocation of communities should be a strategy of last resort. The first reason for this is that even in the case of highly exposed populations, whose livelihoods are sensitive to climate and which have ostensibly low levels of adaptive capacity, such as those living on low-lying atolls, the full gamut of adaptation responses, and their barriers and limits, has not been adequately assessed.[85] People are reluctant to move from islands that sustain their material cultures, lifestyles and identities.[86] The second reason is that the empirical record of involuntary resettlement, which derives largely from resettlement for dams and environmental remediation,[87] points to the risks of landlessness, joblessness, homelessness, marginalisation, food insecurity, loss of access to common property resources, increased morbidity and community disarticulation. People lose resources, including their land and their knowledge of local farming conditions if they were farmers, and their local jobs if they were urban dwellers. Their communities are disrupted and their social networks broken, and their trust in social institutions such as government is reduced. Opportunities for corruption are created and much money is wasted on inefficient projects that are never likely to succeed.[88] In other words, the impacts of resettlement on communities imply that it leads to increased vulnerability to climate change. Therefore, moving communities in anticipation of climate change may precipitate vulnerability more than it avoids it.

If community relocation is absolutely unavoidable, then its social and political costs can be minimised by allowing adequate time for community consultation and planning. In this way, people can adjust to the idea of moving and do as much of the planning themselves as possible. Compensation for lost houses and assets is important, but that compensation should be paid at a level that is equal to the standard of housing and materials in the host community. Ensuring that the money and resources made available to assist communities to relocate is actually spent on those communities is important. Among other things, this means avoiding payments to intermediaries, and employing the people being moved to do whatever work their movement requires. Rebuilding the migrant community as a community is important, as it helps keep social capital intact. As with all forms of

---

[84] Byravan and Rajan, 'Providing New Homes', above n 30.

[85] WN Adger and J Barnett, 'Compensation for Climate Change Must Meet Needs' (2005) 436 *Nature* 328; J Barnett, 'Titanic States? Impacts and Responses to Climate Change in the Pacific Islands' (2005) 59 *Journal of International Affairs* 203.

[86] Mortreux and Barnett, 'Climate Change', above n 70.

[87] Cernea and McDowell (eds), *Risks and Reconstruction*, above n 26; MM Cernea, 'Risks, Safeguards and Reconstruction: A Model for Population Displacement and Resettlement' in ibid; World Commission on Dams, *Dams and Development*, above n 26.

[88] See, eg B McDonald, 'From Compensation to Development: Involuntary Resettlement in the People's Republic of China' (University of Melbourne, PhD thesis, 2006) analysing China's Three Gorges Project.

migration, encouraging the hosting population to be receptive to migrants and to respect their rights and freedoms is also important.

E Cross-Cutting Suggestions

There are a number of things that governments can do to minimise the costs and maximise the benefits of migration exacerbated by climate change. Principal among them is to reduce emissions of greenhouse gases. Stabilising greenhouse gas emissions to avoid 2°C of warming above pre-industrial levels may now be all but impossible, and therefore 'dangerous' climate change is almost certain to occur. However, deep cuts in emissions can minimise the danger—and the number of people whose movement would constitute an impact of climate change—and maximise the scope for more voluntary migration to contribute to adaptation.

There is a need to consider those who cannot or will not migrate, such as the elderly and the very poor, for whom the barriers to migration may be insurmountable. In so far as development tends to increase migration from an area (because it increases the capacity of people to afford to move), climate change might reverse this process because it may decrease the ability of people to pay for migration. In low-income areas, a lack of migration in response to environmental change may be an indicator of extreme vulnerability. Such communities should be priority recipients of programmes to assist them to adapt.

Secure entitlements to land and natural resources in places at risk seem to mitigate migration in response to environmental change. They also seem to minimise conflicts in areas to which migrants move, enhance the likelihood that such movements will not increase environmental degradation and help protect the rights of the temporarily displaced to lands they leave behind. This does not mean creating inalienable titles, but rather constructing a process that recognises and supports rights systems in whatever form they take, including customary and communal rights to property.[89]

Finally, it is important that information about changes in environments and livelihoods is collected on a regular basis, so that decision makers can respond to emerging problems in a timely manner. This is also true of migration, where there is a need to monitor population movements so that increases can be detected and responded to.

V Conclusions

Although the impacts of climate change will differ from place to place, as will the number of people exposed to them and migrating in response to them, it seems most

---

[89] S Mason and A Muller, *Linking Environment and Conflict Prevention: The Role of the United Nations* (Zurich, Centre for Security Studies and swisspeace, 2008).

likely that climate-induced migration in the near future will be almost exclusively a developing country problem, particularly for those countries already struggling to accommodate large numbers of internal and international migrants. A collaborative international effort is needed to monitor and respond effectively to changes in the livelihoods of people living in regions that are highly sensitive to climate change, as well as to population movements, particularly along existing migration routes. Targeting adaptation efforts at the most vulnerable populations, including migrants and potential migrants, is advisable from both a practical and an ethical perspective. Adaptation would be bolstered if aid and migration policies were coordinated.

Several policies can be pursued to ensure that migrants have the same entitlements as the people in their host communities, so as to maximise the chances of harmonious integration. Collaborative measures to clarify property rights among current and potential host populations are important. Education and other services should be provided, including schools and training packages, to encourage the development of skills that can support livelihoods. In cases where services are enhanced due to the presence of migrants, host populations should also have access to these services. Programmes implemented by states or donors that provide short-term employment for migrants can help them to establish new lives. The above actions, as well as promoting cultural awareness, contribute to efforts to build and broker peace between migrants and host populations.

To maximise the benefits of migration, particularly labour migration, positive measures that can be taken by states and donors include minimising transaction costs on remittances, facilitating the development of diaspora networks, and minimising, if not eliminating, barriers to return migration. Finally, migration agreements between one or more countries could be developed. It may be to the benefit of both the receiving and the migrating communities to introduce training in skills specifically required in developed countries.

In order to mitigate the negative impacts of migration as a result of disasters it is recommended that government commitments to the UN Central Emergency Response Fund be increased. Further, international humanitarian emergency response systems and mechanisms must be improved, including for instances where relief must be provided. In developing countries, investment in disaster-risk reduction should be undertaken. Finally, governments need to be made aware (and reminded) that it is their responsibility to protect the human rights of displaced people.

The extent to which climate change affects people and communities will depend in part on the extent to which these and other policy measures designed to improve adaptation are implemented. Perhaps most importantly, migration will work best as adaptation if people move voluntarily—in other words, where they are their own decision makers.

4

Climate-Induced Community Relocation in the Pacific: The Meaning and Importance of Land

JOHN CAMPBELL

I Introduction

In this chapter, the role of community relocation as an adaptation to climate change and variability is examined. In particular, the chapter addresses the importance of land to Pacific island communities, and the implications of this for those who may be forced to sever ties with it (in some extreme cases it is conceivable that land may even disappear). It also addresses the converse of this process—the implications for communities in Pacific island countries that may be required to provide resettlement areas to relocatees who have no traditional rights of access to that land.[1]

The Pacific Islands (see Figure 1) have been singled out as being among those places that may be rendered uninhabitable by the effects of climate change. In particular, it is anticipated by many that Pacific island communities may be among the vanguard of those who become environmentally forced relocatees.[2] Not all observers accept this view,[3] and while some leaders of atoll states earlier toyed with the notion of environmentally forced relocation (perhaps as a means of leverage to gain immigration access for their citizens in countries such as Australia and New Zealand),[4] many now reject such a response as unacceptable.[5] Nevertheless, the

---

[1] The term 'relocatee' is used in this chapter to refer to members of communities that are relocated as a group, as opposed to individual migrants. For a more detailed discussion of terminology, see section II below.

[2] See, eg N Myers, 'Environmental Refugees: A Growing Phenomenon of the 20th Century' (2002) 357 *Philosophical Transactions of the Royal Society B* 609; F Biermann and I Boas, 'Protecting Climate Refugees: The Case for a Global Protocol' (2008) 50 *Environment* 8.

[3] C Mortreux and J Barnett, 'Climate Change, Migration and Adaptation in Funafuti, Tuvalu' (2009) 19 *Global Environmental Change* 105.

[4] See Statement by the Hon Teleke P Lauti (Tuvalu) at COP 6 (The Hague, November 2000), cited in Climate Change Secretariat (UNFCCC), *Climate Change: Small Island Developing States* (Bonn, UNFCCC, 2005) 13.

[5] J McAdam and M Loughry, 'We Aren't Refugees', *Inside Story* (30 June 2009), http://inside.org.au/we-arent-refugees/.

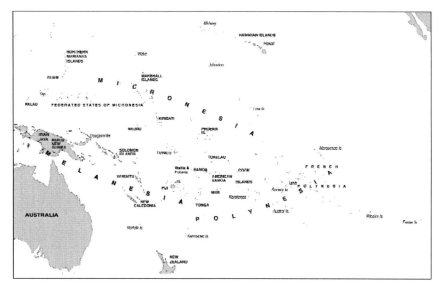

Figure 1: Map of the Pacific Islands region. Map drawn by Max Oulton.

habitability of many settlement sites and the sustainability of their inhabitants' livelihoods may well be placed at risk by the effects of global warming. In some cases this may require people to move to more environmentally secure locations.

II Community Relocation

There are a number of terms used in the context of environmental variability and change and the movement of people.[6] The term 'relocation' is often used in relation to a variety of these concepts. For the purposes of this chapter, it is important to distinguish community relocation from other concepts such as evacuation, displacement, migration and the so-called 'environmental refugee', although there is often some overlap in the meanings of these notions. Lieber uses the general term 'resettlement' to refer to 'a process by which a number of homogenous people from one locale come to live together in a different locale'.[7] Building on Lieber's definition, the term relocation is used in this chapter to refer to the permanent (or long-term) movement of a community (or a significant part of it) from one

---

[6] Biermann and Boas, 'Protecting Climate Refugees', above n 2; D Kniveton, K Schmidt-Verkerk, C Smith and R Black, *Climate Change and Migration: Improving Methodologies to Estimate Flows* (Geneva, IOM Migration Research Series No 33, 2008).

[7] MD Lieber (ed), *Exiles and Migrants in Oceania* (Honolulu, University of Hawaii Press, 1977) 343.

location to another, in which important characteristics of the original community, including its social structures, legal and political systems, cultural characteristics and worldviews, are retained: the community stays together at the destination in a social form that is similar to the community of origin. Community relocation, especially over long distances, may be considered as among the most radical forms of adaptation to climate change.

'Adaptation' has been defined by the Intergovernmental Panel on Climate Change (IPCC) as 'adjustment in natural or human systems in response to actual or expected climatic stimuli or their effects, which moderates harm or exploits beneficial opportunities'.[8] The IPCC acknowledges that adaptation may have costs, which include the 'costs of planning, preparing for, facilitating, and implementing *adaptation* measures, including transition costs'.[9] This implies that the costs of adaptation are finite and cease once the measure has been implemented. In this chapter I argue that community relocation cannot be achieved without long-term costs that may continue to be incurred over many generations. In the rural context of the Pacific Islands region, the relevant 'human systems' will be village communities, which may be seen as groups of people connected by kinship and linked by birthright and/or kinship to local land and sea resources.[10] Urban communities may also be impacted, but they are not considered in this chapter other than to note that most urban dwellers are migrants or the descendants of migrants, and therefore still have 'rights' to their ancestral homelands. The chapter seeks to identify some of the social costs of community relocation as an adaptive option. If a community is not able to re-establish itself in a new location, it may be considered to have failed to adapt successfully to change and variability. This is a distinct likelihood for the Pacific Islands region. Other forms of migration, which tend to be either individual or household-based, enable the possibility of individual people or households to be accommodated by host communities—an outcome that is much less likely for entire communities.

III Relocation as a Disaster-Reduction Measure

One of the most effective ways of reducing the impacts of extreme events is to avoid living in areas where they are common. In some jurisdictions (mostly in developed countries where land is held in fee simple and can be bought and sold), local government bodies encourage people living in hazardous sites to relocate through voluntary acquisition schemes, in which exposed properties are

---

[8] Intergovernmental Panel on Climate Change (IPCC), *Climate Change 2007: Impacts, Adaptation and Vulnerability: Contribution of Working Group II to the Fourth Assessment Report of the Intergovernmental Panel on Climate Change* (Cambridge, Cambridge University Press, 2008) 869.
[9] ibid.
[10] P Hunnam, *Lessons in Conservation for People and Projects in the Pacific Islands Region* (New York, United Nations Development Programme, 2002).

purchased (generally by the government), enabling the owners to purchase else-where in a safer place.[11] Moreover, in many such places, planning mechanisms exist that restrict subdivision and building on hazardous sites. Such approaches are viable in places where the dominant form of land ownership is through indi-vidual property rights. They are much more difficult to implement in places where property rights are not located in the marketplace but come under customary forms of tenure. In these settings, restricting land use on customary lands would place inequitable burdens on different communities, and those whose land is heavily exposed might find no alternatives for their settlements. The same consid-erations apply for communities that may find themselves increasingly exposed to the negative effects of climate change: coastal erosion and inundation, increased river flooding, and increased incidence of tropical cyclones and droughts.

There is no shortage of examples of Pacific island communities that have relo-cated to sites that are believed to be less exposed to natural extremes. Most com-monly, such movements are to nearby locations that lie within customary land boundaries. However, in pre-colonial times and probably well into the colonial era, it was not unusual for communities to move on to neighbouring lands with the acknowledgement of the original landowners. Usually this was achieved through customary forms of negotiation and exchange. Less common, but by no means totally unusual, were movements across greater distances.

IV The Meaning of Land in Pacific Islands

Land in Pacific island countries tends to have meanings to those who 'belong' to or are 'part of' it that are often difficult to encapsulate in English or other colonial languages. Land has multiple meanings in the majority of Pacific island countries, and in many cases cannot be separated from those who 'belong' to it (see Box 1). By and large, most Pacific land is not, and cannot be, owned in fee simple or as freehold. While it can be exchanged, this is nearly always only possible under tra-ditional arrangements. As Figure 2 shows, the great majority of land in the Pacific Islands region is held under customary forms of tenure, though these may differ from the arrangements that existed prior to contact and colonisation. Indeed, in those few countries where customary tenure accounts for less than 90 per cent of the land, 'public' forms of ownership make up the difference. By contrast, 'free-hold' land makes up less than 10 per cent of land in the region. Most countries experienced some alienation of land prior to colonial rule, following which remaining areas of traditionally tenured land often became protected or, in some

---

[11] RW Perry and MK Lindell, 'Principles for Managing Community Relocation as a Hazard Mitigation Measure' (1997) 5 *Journal of Contingencies and Crisis Management* 49; NJ Ericksen, *Creating Flood Disaster? New Zealand's Need for a New Approach to Urban Flood Hazard* (Wellington, Water and Soil Directorate, Ministry of Works and Development, 1986).

Box 1: Expressions of the importance of land

> Land to a ni-Vanuatu is what a mother is to a baby. It is with land that he defines his identity and it is with land that he maintains his spiritual strength. Ni-Vanuatu do allow others the use of their land, but they always retain the right of ownership.

The Hon Sethy Regenvanu, First Minister of Lands, quoted in HN van Trease, *The Politics of Land in Vanuatu: From Colony to Independence* (Suva, University of the South Pacific, 1987) xi.

> For example, in Cook Islands Maori, 'enua' means 'land, country, territory, after-birth': in Futuna (Wallace) 'fanua' means 'country, land, the people of a place'; in Tonga, 'fonua' means 'island, territory, estate, the people of the estate, placenta' and 'fonualoto', 'grave'. We can see that in some Polynesian languages, proto-fanua is both the people and the territory that nourishes them, as a placenta nourishes a baby.

W Pond, *The Land with All Woods and Water* (Waitangi Tribunal Rangahaua Whanui Series, Waitangi Tribunal, Wellington, 1997) 32, quoted in K Batibasaqa, J Overton, and P Horsley, '*Vanua*: Land, People and Culture in Fiji' in J Overton and R Scheyvens (eds), *Strategies for Sustainable Development: Experiences from the Pacific* (London, Zed Books, 1999) 100.

> The people of Nakorosule [a village in Fiji] cannot live without their physical embodiment in terms of their land, upon which survival of individuals and groups depends. It provides nourishment, shelter and protection, as well as a source of security and the material basis for identity and belonging. Land in this sense is thus an extension of the self; and conversely the people are an extension of the land.

A Ravuvu, *Development or Dependence: The Pattern of Change in a Fijian Village* (Suva, University of the South Pacific, 1988) 7.

> The land has even been viewed as possessing a sacred or spiritual quality, expressed in the mental attitudes of Marshallese when they think of the land as the very root of their worldly existence.

L Mason, 'Tenures from Subsistence to Star Wars' in RG Crocombe (ed), *Land Tenure in the Atolls: Cook Islands, Kiribati, Marshall Islands, Tokelau, Tuvalu* (Suva, University of the South Pacific, 1987) 4.

> For the people of Kapingamarangi Atoll, no other single concern seems to be as omnipresent and anxiety-provoking as their concern over land. No other single concern generates the intensity of interest and emotion as does land. People may insult one another, but the insults will be forgiven; tempers sometimes flare and end in fist fights, but others will intervene, and the opponents will apologize and forget the incident; marriages break up, but the wounds heal. But a land dispute is never forgotten, nor do the opponents forgive each other, nor is the matter ever really settled, even when the litigants are long deceased.

MD Lieber, 'Land Tenure on Kapingamarangi' in HP Lundsgaarde (ed), *Land Tenure in Oceania* (Honolulu, University Press of Hawaii, 1974) 70.

cases, were returned to the original owners after independence. Thus Fiji, for example, has about 8 per cent of its land under freehold ownership. Much of this is prime land 'purchased' or taken for plantations by early colonists and coastal land that is now valued for resort subdivisions.

Figure 2: Broad land ownership categories in the pacific islands region

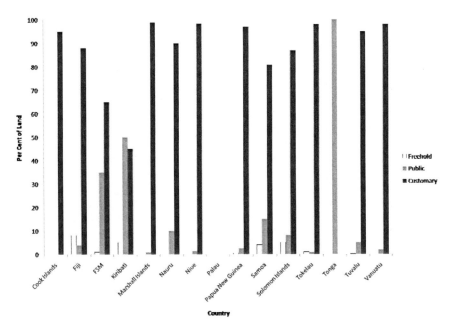

Source: Australian Agency for International Development (AusAID), *Making Land Work: Volume 1: Reconciling Customary Land and Development in the Pacific* (Canberra, Commonwealth of Australia, 2008) 4.

The nature of land 'boundaries' in Pacific island countries also needs to be considered, as relocation may involve crossing such borders. They exist in a variety of forms. The most highly codified system is in Fiji, where lands have been surveyed, boundaries established and the land registered according to *mataqali* (clan) membership, which for most children is registered at birth. In many other countries no such arrangements exist; boundaries may be flexible or fuzzy, and knowledge regarding them is transmitted orally. For many Pacific societies, particularly those on large land masses such as in Melanesia, landowners recognised a clear centre but their relationship to the land became increasingly vague with distance from it.[12]

---

[12] A Abramson, 'Bounding the Unbounded: Ancestral Land and Jural Relations in the Interior of Eastern Fiji' in A Abramson and D Theodossopoulos (eds), *Land, Law and Environment: Mythical Land, Legal Boundaries* (London, Pluto Press, 2000).

The forms of customary tenure vary across the region, ranging from arrangements for individual rights to land through to communal ownership. Despite this, the idea that people are intimately connected to their land was, and to a large extent remains, widespread, as indicated in Box 1. In many parts of Polynesia and Melanesia the linkage between land and placenta is strong, and is encapsulated in the New Zealand Maori term *whenua*, which refers to both the land and placenta. The placenta is returned to the ancestral land following birth, and for many, their final resting place is on the ancestral *whenua* as well.[13] Bonnemaison uses the notion of being rooted to the land to describe the linkage of ni-Vanuatu men to their land, although women (who were traditionally likely to marry outside of their birthplace) are metaphorically described as birds that may flee their home.[14] While men were able to leave their land, long absences and distances were not encouraged. However, in other parts of the region long-distance travelling was not uncommon and the region was characterised by a very large number of trading networks, some of which covered considerable distances.[15]

It is important here not to represent Pacific people and their communities as being somehow physically bonded by their location. Waiko outlines the movement of his village in north-eastern Papua New Guinea, named Tabara, which had a 'history of fusion, division and travel' that extended over 130 kilometres in distance.[16] Jolly points to the co existence of mobility and stability in many Pacific places and invokes the paradoxical notion of both roots and routes as important aspects of Pacific island lives.[17] But venturing on routes does not suggest the loss of roots, the perhaps less tangible, but nonetheless visceral, bonds that exist and connect people with their place. Many migrants, even long-term ones, still consider themselves to belong to their land, even if they are physically dislocated from it.[18]

Accordingly, while this chapter examines the role of land tenure, or the meaning of land, in Pacific island countries, it is important to add the cautionary note that the region cannot be easily generalised into a single representation of land, nor any other characteristic—it is remarkably heterogeneous. While the specifics vary considerably, there are nevertheless some commonalities regarding the

---

[13] A Mikaere, *The Balance Destroyed: Consequences for Māori Women of the Colonisation of Tikanga Māori* (Auckland, International Research Institute for Māori and Indigenous Education, 2003); N Simmonds, 'Mana Wahine Geographies: Spiritual, Spatial and Embodied Understandings of Paptūānuku' (unpublished Masters Thesis, Department of Geography, Tourism and Environmental Planning, University of Waikato, New Zealand, 2009).

[14] J Bonnemaison, 'The Tree and the Canoe: Roots and Mobility in Vanuatu Societies' (1985) 26 *Pacific Viewpoint* 30.

[15] E Hau'ofa, 'Our Sea of Islands' in E Waddell (ed), *In a New Oceania: Rediscovering Our Sea of Islands* (Suva, University of the South Pacific, 1993); GR Lewthwaite, 'Geographical Knowledge of the Pacific Peoples' in HR Friis (ed), *The Pacific Basin: A History of Its Geographical Exploration* (New York, American Geographical Society, 1967).

[16] JD Waiko, 'Na Binandere, Imo Averi? We Are Binandere, Who Are You?' (1985) 26 *Pacific Viewpoint* 9, 9 (Special Issue: Mobility and Identity in the Island Pacific).

[17] M Jolly, 'On the Edge: Deserts, Oceans, Islands' (2001) 13 *The Contemporary Pacific* 417.

[18] AD Ravuvu, *Development or Dependence: The Pattern of Change in a Fijian Village* (Suva, University of the South Pacific, 1988).

cultural links to land. The specific characteristics of the links may differ, but in a great many places they are very important in terms of identity, spirituality, culture and subsistence.

The effects of climate change upon the land, and the land's ability to sustain these myriad linkages, cannot be easily ignored. One of the outcomes may be that communities will have to move. Such climate-induced migration may have very serious implications, both for relocating communities and those who may have to make land available for them in their destinations. Above all, community relocation means that an important aspect of rootedness, having at least some people (kinfolk) there, sustaining the relationship with the land, or 'keeping the home fires burning', is lost. Secondly, where relocatees are moved to another place within their own country or elsewhere in the Pacific, the communal lands of other groups may need to be used. To leave one's roots is perhaps no more difficult than giving them up—in either case, there will be considerable loss: of cultural values, livelihoods, spirituality and identity. In the latter case, tensions may arise when people at the destinations feel aggrieved at having to give up land.

V Migration in and from Pacific Islands

As the discussion of roots and routes suggests, many Pacific island peoples have a great history of migration, and the ocean may be seen as a linking mechanism, a series of routes, rather than a barrier to mobility.[19] This may seem somewhat paradoxical given the strong ties to land outlined in the preceding sections. Following a symposium held in 1983 on the topic of population mobility, identity and politics, it was observed that 'if one theme overrode all the others . . . it was how the complex and deeply rooted meanings of land lay at the heart of islander identities and were in turn expressed through an astonishing diversity of movement behaviour'.[20]

The rootedness described by Bonnemaison helped explain the patterns of circular migration that were detected by early migration researchers in Pacific island countries (as well as Bonnemaison himself).[21] Migration has continued since these early studies, and for many Pacific island countries has expanded to international destinations such as Australia, New Zealand and California in the United States. For example, in the 2006 New Zealand census, the 'Pacific peoples' ethnic group included 265,000 people, an increase of 59 per cent since the 1991 census. Interestingly, 60 per cent of the 2006 Pacific island population was born in New Zealand. As well, Pacific urban centres are rapidly growing in size. Twenty-three per cent of the region's population is urban, and 10 out of 22 of the countries have

---

[19] Hau'ofa, 'Our Sea of Islands', above n 15.

[20] M Chapman, 'Introduction' (1985) 26 *Pacific Viewpoint* 1, 4 (Special Issue: Mobility and Identity in the Island Pacific).

[21] See, eg R Bedford, *New Hebridean Mobility: A Study of Circular Migration* (Canberra, Australian National University, 1973); Bonnemaison, 'The Tree and the Canoe', above n 14.

more than half their populations living in urban areas away from their villages and customary lands.[22] The rapid urbanisation of the majority of Pacific island countries, and the burgeoning populations of Pacific islanders in the Pacific rim, does not, however, necessarily imply that the important link to land is lost. In many cases it remains just as strong and is sustained by remittances and return visits of individuals and households, as well as family reunions—often including hundreds of people, often spanning three or more generations, many of whom are returning from their Pacific rim homes.[23] Just as migrants and their descendents provide remittances, the non-migrants sustain the link to the homelands by supplying traditional foods and other products from the land to their urban and international kin.

VI Likely Effects of Climate Change on Migration

So, against this backdrop of mobility, what are the implications of climate change effects on Pacific island migration patterns? The most significant effects of climate change include reductions in agricultural productivity; coral reef and mangrove degradation, and associated reduction of marine productivity; reductions in water quantity and quality, with associated impacts on agriculture and health; increases in the frequency and magnitude of some climatic events; and coastal erosion and inundation as a result of extreme events and sea-level rise. In some cases the very habitability of places will be compromised, and in many others the combination of economic and spatial marginality (which has increased since the days of colonisation and continues to do so in the post-colonial globalised world) and increasing environmental marginality may provide sufficient 'push' factors to cause significant migrant flows. A major question is: where will such people go?

There are a number of possibilities for relocation, as shown in Figure 3. The path of least resistance, where possible, will be for communities to relocate within their own land boundaries. The link to land need not be broken and the likelihood of tensions arising from landowners who may have to cede land is negated. This kind of relocation is not at all uncommon in the Pacific Islands region and examples may be found in a number of countries. In many cases, such relocations take place after devastating climatic extremes, such as tropical cyclones with their associated river flooding and storm surge. The typical movement is inland and up to higher elevations, though it has not been unusual for lateral relocations to take place (for example, along the coast or river), only for more devastation at a later date when more climatic extremes occur. An example is the inland village of

[22] Secretariat of the Pacific Community, *Pacific Island Populations 2008* (Noumea, Secretariat of the Pacific Community, 2008).

[23] R Bedford, 'Pasifika Mobility: Pathways, Circuits and Challenges in the 21st Century' in A Bisley (ed), *Pacific Interactions: Pasifika in New Zealand, New Zealand in Pasifika* (Wellington, Institute of Policy Studies, 2008).

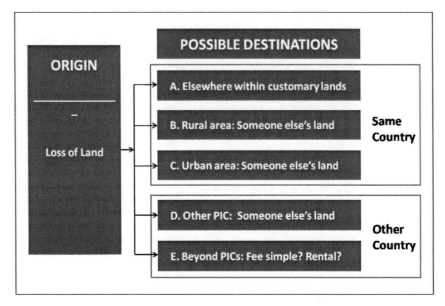

Figure 3: Options for relocation in and beyond Pacific island countries

Biausevu, located by the Biausevu River on the island of Viti Levu, in Fiji. The village occupied four different sites between 1881 and 1983, when it was finally established on a hill above the seemingly gentle river which was prone to flash flooding during tropical cyclones.[24]

Where such intra-communal shifts are not possible or feasible—the community may not have suitable options—resettlement elsewhere within the country may be required. This may range from being relocated on a neighbouring community's land, to a rural area some distance away, and even on another island. Such relocations are problematic because of the land issues discussed above. Even neighbouring communities guard their land jealously—it is 'part of' them and accordingly not something that can simply be given away or sold. Traditional means of exchange, where customary items of significant value (for example *tabua* or whale's teeth in Fiji), when presented to landowners may have enabled some relocation, are often now challenged by younger members of the 'host' or destination landowners who want evidence that legal transfer took place, even if it was generations ago when the relocation occurred.[25]

An alternative is relocation to an urban area. However, in most Pacific island towns and cities the same rules regarding land apply. While many of the early colonial administrative centres were established on relatively small areas of alienated

[24] J Campbell, 'International Relocation from Pacific Island Countries: Adaptation Failure?' (Environment, Forced Migration and Social Vulnerability Conference, Bonn, 9–11 October 2008).

[25] See, eg V Cagilaba, 'Fight or Flight? Resilience and Vulnerability in Rural Fiji' (unpublished Masters Thesis, University of Waikato, New Zealand, 2005).

land, they have since far outgrown their original dimensions, especially in the post-colonial era. While it is not uncommon to find settlements of people from the same island or village in urban areas, in most cases their situation is tenuous. Because all but a small proportion of land is communally owned, even in the towns, and especially in the peri-urban[26] areas where most urban growth is taking place, new migrants are forced to live in temporary arrangements (the landowners not being prepared to accept signs of permanent settlement). Squatter settlements in Oceania are typically neglected by urban and/or national government authorities, have low levels of infrastructure provision, high levels of unemployment and under-employment, and are often highly exposed to the possibility of extreme events, including flooding and tropical cyclones. Indeed the inhabitants of many existing squatter settlements, many of which are on low-lying swampy lands and unstable slopes, may well be adversely affected by climate change and also in need of relocation. Increasing the inflow from rural areas is likely only to increase the exposure and vulnerability of the communities in these locations.

The third set of migration options includes those incorporating international relocation. These are mostly foreshadowed in the academic and popular literature as being necessary for the inhabitants of countries that are entirely composed of atolls, in which there is no 'up' to go to. There are two sets of options. The first is to relocate to another Pacific island country where the environmental, social and cultural conditions are likely to be perhaps relatively close to the place of origin, and the social, cultural, spiritual and economic costs of relocation will not be too onerous. Again, the problem of land remains, and it is unlikely that communities from one Pacific island country will be happy to give up their land to newcomers in a way that enables the newcomers to maintain their social, cultural, political and economic ways.

The second international relocation option is to relocate the community outside the Pacific Islands region, most likely in New Zealand, Australia or the United States, the three metropolitan countries with strong links to the atoll states. The possibilities for international relocation outside the region (as opposed to other forms of migration) are extremely bleak. It is unlikely that any country, including those in the Pacific, would cede sovereignty over a part of their territory to a relocated group, and it is equally unlikely that a relocated group could sustain its 'way' in a foreign land that did not accept or understand many of their cultural beliefs or practices, including their bond to the land. Indeed, with the exception of relocation within communal lands, all other forms of relocation will be fraught, whether internal or international. This leaves the possibility of separate migration decisions by individuals or groups to a variety of destinations that will see community integrity weakened, if not badly damaged. Moreover, if the land is to become uninhabited, uninhabitable, or at worst non-existent, the critical people–land union may decline. Given the essential nature of this connection, it

---

[26] This term refers to areas that lie outside formal urban boundaries. Typically, such areas do not have access to urban services and infrastructure.

may be expected that social, cultural, emotional and spiritual impacts will emerge. The following two cases studies indicate some of the land-related issues that can arise as a result of community relocation.

VII In-Country Relocation: From the Carterets to Bougainville

An interesting case of possible environmentally, if not climatically, induced migration in the Pacific Islands is that of the attempted relocation of atoll dwellers from the Carteret Islands to the large plate boundary island of Bougainville in Papua New Guinea (see Figure 4 on the following page). The Carterets have been affected by unusually high (king) tides and experiencing considerable loss of coastal land. Singled out by the media in 2008 and 2009 as the world's first 'climate refugees',[27] the people of the Carteret Islands were engaged, in 2009, in a resettlement scheme at Tinputz, on the island of Bougainville. The Carterets are subsiding, although there seems to be no scientific certainty as to the cause. The area is tectonically unstable and this may be the reason, although the possibility of climate change-driven sea-level rise is a popular attribution. Irrespective of the causes of the subsidence relative to sea level, the Carterets provide much food for thought on the efficacy of relocation in Oceania. The case is not a new one: a group of colonial officials conducted a resource survey of the Carterets in 1964 and reported that 'erosion is a constant menace in these islands'.[28] Three years later a colonial officer visited the atoll and reported that the islands had lost hundreds of coconut palms and had been exposed to 'ruinous erosion'.[29] Population growth was adding to the stress on the atoll environment. By the late 1960s Carteret Islanders 'were reported to have a unanimous desire for resettlement as "heavy seas ... devastated gardens and there [was] an obvious shortage of food crops"'.[30]

The North Solomons Provincial Government in Papua New Guinea began to organise a resettlement scheme in 1979 and land was set aside for the establishment of a village, but the first group of 10 families from the Carterets did not arrive until 1984. As O'Collins reported, while some dislocation was expected, the transition proved more difficult than anticipated:

[27] A Morton, 'First Climate Refugees Start Move to New Island Home', *The Age* (29 July 2009), www.theage.com.au/national/first-climate-refugees-start-move-to-new-island-home-20090728-e06x.html; N MacFarquhar, 'Refugees Join List of Climate-Change Issues', *The New York Times* (28 May 2009), www.nytimes.com/2009/05/29/world/29refugees.html.

[28] HJ Redmond, J Curran and T Sweeney, 'Resources Survey, Carteret Islands, Bougainville District' (unpublished report to District Commissioner, Kieta, 1964) quoted in M O'Collins, 'Carteret Islanders at the Atolls Resettlement Scheme: A Response to Land Loss and Population Growth' in J Pernetta and P Hughes (eds), *Implications of Expected Climate Changes in the South Pacific Region: An Overview* (Nairobi, United Nations Environment Programme, 1990) 253.

[29] Quoted in O'Collins, above n 28, 253.

[30] ibid, 250 (Letter from KJ Hanrahan, Assistant District Commissioner to the District Commissioner at Sohano, Buka Island, 11 January 1968).

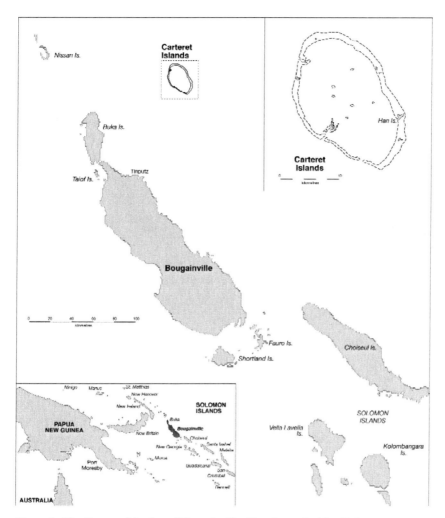

Figure 4: The Carteret Islands and Bougainville. Map drawn by Max Oulton.

The families and particularly those members engaged in clearing and establishing food gardens and in building houses, had to become used to many new food crops, new building materials and different techniques. Upon arrival the families had to accustom themselves to living under an iron roof, out of sight of the sea and surrounded by unfamiliar and rather frightening thick bush. . . . Children had to walk 6 km to school and this was a great distance for those who had no opportunity to walk any distance on their small atolls. Road traffic hazards, for those who had no experience of roads or vehicular traffic; fear of snakes for those who had no experience of walking on paths through thick bush; and the experience of being surrounded by tall trees, all required individual and community adjustment. ... Many women sat for long periods of time thinking about their island homes.[31]

[31] O'Collins, above n 28, 253.

By 1987, two of the original families had returned home. Others had adjusted relatively well, although there were concerns at delays in obtaining land on Bougainville for cocoa and copra production (their sole opportunity for cash production), and some worried that they would also lose their usufruct rights to the small and decreasing amounts of land left on the atoll. Moreover, there were serious concerns at the lack of support given to them to become self-sufficient.[32]

Little further information is available on the fate of these initial relocatees, and it is not clear what happened to the resettlement scheme. However, it was not long after this that Bougainville became involved in a prolonged and severe civil conflict (lasting from 1988 to 1997),[33] and in 1989 the people from the Carterets fled home.[34] A new group of relocatees has since reappeared, and these people have perhaps been reinvented in the news as the world's first 'climate refugees'. But given the reporting by O'Collins, we can see that this new wave is not the first group of environmentally induced relocatees, and this perhaps also casts doubt on whether or not the sole reason for their relocation is climate change, although it may well have an exacerbating effect. Nevertheless, the case study is instructive and we can also learn from the more recent scheme. Land was again to be made available, again on Bougainville, and an initial group of five male household heads moved to the new site in late April 2009.[35] But, like the 1980s attempt, success was hard to come by and by July 2009 it was reported that the men had returned:

> Three of these families complained that they were in frequent arguments with Tinputz landowners over land and that they were finding it difficult because they did not have gardens, sometimes no food and most of them no proper house.
>
> Earlier this year, acting administrator . . . told the *Post-Courier* that legal issues were hindering the efforts to resettle Carteret Islanders [and others from low-lying atolls] to Bougainville. He said that the Government's efforts on the resettlement exercise were being blocked as they were having trouble getting the legal rights to the land they needed.[36]

This article in Papua New Guinea's national press appeared three months to the day after the men arrived, indicating that the project had failed in a very short space of time. Moreover, it indicates the major difficulties likely to be encountered when relocating communities within Pacific island countries, when the relocation is on a different community's communal land. While most observers focus on the likely international relocation needs of atoll dwellers, internal relocation may be just as difficult, with the possibility of significant numbers of groups of internally displaced persons emerging. This issue has hardly been addressed in the discussion

---

[32] ibid, 267.

[33] P Reddy, 'Reconciliation in Bougainville: Civil War, Peacekeeping and Restorative Justice' (2008) 11 *Contemporary Justice Review* 117.

[34] U Rakova, 'How-to Guide for Environmental Refugees' (OurWorld 2.0, 16 June 2009).

[35] 'Carteret Islanders Become First Climate Refugees: PNG Relocates Families as Island Home Disappears', *Pacific Island Report* (4 May 2009), http://archives.pireport.org/archive/2009/may/05-04-09.htm, reporting a story from the *Papua New Guinea Post-Courier* (1 May 2009).

[36] T Vainerere, 'Climate Change Refugees Return to Bougainville Atolls', *New Guinea Post-Courier* (22 July 2009), http://lists.spc.int/pipermail/ppapd-fpocc_lists.spc.int/2009-July/000233.html.

of the implications of climate change in Pacific island countries. The second case study below looks at the possibilities for relocation within the region drawing on the experiences of the Banaban community, relocated from what is now Kiribati, to Rabi in Fiji.

VIII International Relocation: Banaba to Rabi

There have been three cases of international relocation of Pacific island communities, all involving atoll or raised limestone island communities (see Figure 5). The first of these is a Micronesian community from Banaba (now part of Kiribati), which was devastated by phosphate mining since its discovery in 1900 through to 1979. Most members of this community now live on Rabi island in northern Fiji. The second instance is a Polynesian community from Vaitupu (now part of Tuvalu) which resettled on Kioa island in northern Fiji. The island was purchased in 1946 and settlement began on 26 October 1947.[37] The final case is that of the Gilbertese (I-Kiribati) communities in Wagani and Gizo, Western Province, Solomon Islands.[38] This last group of relocatees was placed in areas where land quality was poor, and in many cases they did not have security of land tenure.[39] Despite these disadvantages for the migrants, the relocation has also been a source of tension in the destination communities, and 'while saying they were not hostile to the Gilbertese as such, Western [Province] leaders resented the fact that their province took all the burden of Gilbertese resettlement'.[40]

The focus here is on the first case, the relocation from Banaba to Rabi (see Figure 6). The transfer to Kioa from Vaitupu was a partial one, with a substantial and sustainable population remaining in the home island. This enabled the link to land to be sustained, as well as the assurance of a community 'keeping the home fires burning'. The relocation to the Solomon Islands was also partial, and no single communities were completely translocated. In comparison, the relocation from Banaba to Rabi was to all intents and purposes complete, although some 'caretakers' have returned to their home island, particularly since the 1970s. Accordingly, it gives us considerable insights into the likely effects of complete community relocation, should it be required as a result of climate change. This section is based on the work of a number of authors who have written about

---

[37] K-F Koch, *Logs in the Current of the Sea* (Canberra, Australian National University Press, 1978).

[38] KE Knudson, 'Making Sense: A Study of a Banaban Meeting' in Lieber (ed), *Exiles and Migrants in Oceania*, above n 7.

[39] J Fraenkel, 'Minority Rights in Fiji and the Solomon Islands: Reinforcing Constitutional Protections, Establishing Land Rights and Overcoming Poverty' (Paper prepared for United Nations Commission on Human Rights, Sub-Commission on Promotion and Protection of Human Rights, Working Group on Minorities) UN Doc E/CN.4/Sub.2/AC.5/2003/WP.5 (5 May 2003).

[40] R Premdas, J Steeves and P Larmour, 'The Western Breakaway Movement in the Solomon Islands' (1984) 7 *Pacific Studies* 34, 45.

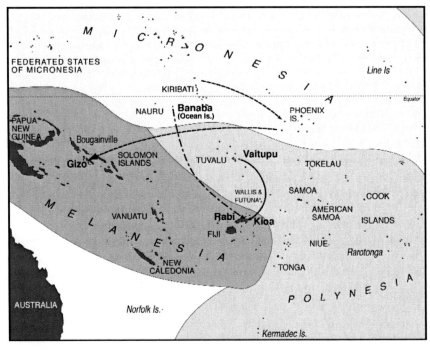

Figure 5: The 'international'-type relocations that took place during the colonial period under the colonial governance of the United Kingdom. The map shows the broad 'cultural regions' of Oceania and indicates that the three communities were relocated to quite distinct cultural milieux from their own. Map drawn by Max Oulton.

Banaba and Rabi.[41] Their work is summarised here as it is of considerable relevance to the issue of community relocation in Pacific island countries.

Banaba (also known as Ocean Island) is a raised limestone island lying close to the equator, a little less than 300 kilometres to the east of Nauru. Like Nauru, Banaba was covered by a thick layer of phosphate, and like Nauru this resource was mined aggressively, mostly to support the pastoral agricultural industries of New Zealand, Australia and the United Kingdom. Apart from some small

[41] W Kempf and E Hermann, 'Reconfigurations of Place and Ethnicity: Positionings, Performances and Politics of Relocated Banabans in Fiji' (2005) 75 *Oceania* 368; W Kempf, 'The Drama of Death as Narrative of Survival: Dance Theatre, Travelling and Thirdspace among the Banabans of Fiji' in T van Meijl and J Miedema (eds), *Shifting Images of Identity in the Pacific* (Leiden, KITLV Press, 2004); S King and K Sigrah, 'Legacy of a Miner's Daughter and Assessment of the Social Changes of the Banabans after Phospate Mining on Banaba' (Islands of the World VIII International Conference, 'Changing Islands: Changing Worlds', Kinmen Island (Quemoy), 1–7 November 2004); B Macdonald, *Cinderellas of the Empire: Towards a History of Kiribati and Tuvalu* (Suva, University of the South Pacific, 2001); MG Silverman, *Disconcerting Issue: Meaning and Struggle in a Resettled Pacific Community* (Chicago, University of Chicago Press, 1971); KM Teaiwa, 'Our Sea of Phosphate: The Diaspora of Ocean Island' in G Harvey and C Thompson (eds), *Indigenous Diasporas and Dislocations* (Aldershot, Ashgate, 2005).

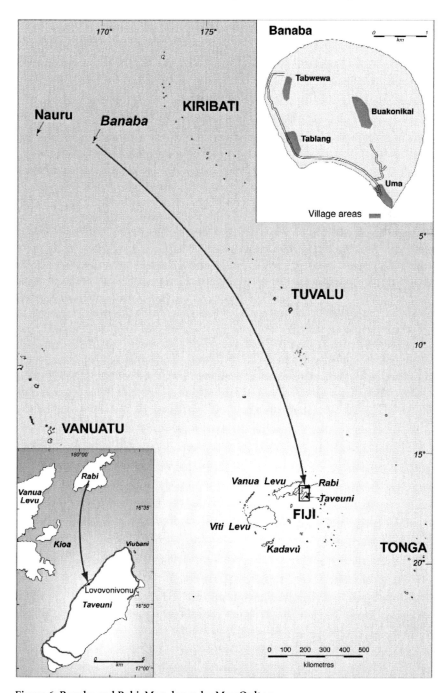

Figure 6: Banaba and Rabi. Map drawn by Max Oulton.

amounts remaining on Nauru, these deposits have been largely exhausted, with the populations of both islands left with little to show for the massive environmental degradation caused by the mining. The Nauru case is relatively well known. Millions of dollars placed in trust were lost in a series of investment failures.[42] Nevertheless, the people of Nauru remain on their island and are citizens of their own sovereign state.

The case of the Banabans unfolded quite differently. Initially, Banaba was too small to excite British interest, and it was excluded from the British colonial entity, the Gilbert and Ellice Islands Protectorate, which was formed in 1892.[43] However, with the identification of phosphate on the island in 1900 it was not long before Banaba was included in the Protectorate, by 1907 having become its headquarters, so important was the phosphate industry.[44] The island became a bustling and multicultural economy as the British Phosphate Corporation (BPC) extracted the valuable mineral. However, as the extraction continued, the utility of Banaba as a home for the Banabans was declining, and by 1940 the Protectorate government was encouraging the people to consider relocating to another site. This would also enable the BPC to intensify its mining activities. Islands in Fiji, such as Wakaya and Rabi, that had been alienated from their customary owners prior to colonisation, were considered for relocation purposes. While some Banabans were keen to move, others were less enthusiastic, and most were concerned that if they did, they would lose sovereignty over Banaba.[45] However, plans were put on hold in 1942 when Banaba was occupied by Japanese forces, shortly after the phosphate company staff and colonial officials abandoned the 'Protectorate'. The following year the Japanese removed many of the Banabans from their island to three other locations in Micronesia: Kosrae (now part of the Federated States of Micronesia), Nauru, and Tarawa (now the capital of Kiribati, the former Gilbert Islands). In addition, almost 350 Banabans and I-Kiribati perished on the island during its occupation.[46] After the war, Australian forces reclaimed Banaba and, ostensibly because of the extent of war damage, rather than repatriate the Banabans, the British colonial government resettled them on the island of Rabi in north-eastern Fiji. The relocatees were given two years to decide whether they would stay on Rabi or return. Such an arrangement would enable the phosphate company to continue mining unhindered by the needs and presence of a local population.[47] While the majority of Banabans were opposed to relocation, they eventually conceded as a result of compulsory land expropriations and concern that an alternative environment would be necessary to sustain future generations.[48]

Rabi was an island owned by Lever Brothers, the huge British soap company which owned and operated a number of coconut plantations around Melanesia in

---

[42] J Connell, 'Nauru: The First Failed Pacific State?' (2006) 95 *The Round Table* 47.

[43] MacDonald, *Cinderellas of the Empire*, above n 41, 94.

[44] Silverman, *Disconcerting Issue*, above n 41, 99.

[45] ibid, 148.

[46] RK Sigrah and SM King, *Te Rii Ni Banaba* (Suva, University of the South Pacific, 2001) 257.

[47] ibid, 258–59.

[48] Kempf, 'The Drama of Death as Narrative of Survival', above n 41, 162.

the first half of the twentieth century. Funds accumulated from phosphate royalties were used for the purchase, which was facilitated by the British colonial service in the form of the Western Pacific High Commission and the Governor of Fiji (one and the same person). The island had formerly been inhabited by Fijians, who were relocated in the village of Lovonivonu on the island of Taveuni to the south of Rabi in the pre-colonial era. Upon settling in Rabi, the Banabans set about reproducing a Banaban society in the new setting. A paradoxical condition ensued. Banabans set out to confirm both their status as the rightful inhabitants of Rabi, as well as retaining autonomy over Banaba (which was promised to them when the agreement to relocate to Rabi was settled). This proved to be less easily achieved than might have been expected. Their returns from royalties were much less than they anticipated, and at one point, the Gilbert and Ellice Islands Colony was receiving over 10 times the amount given to the Banabans.[49] By the end of the mining, the Banabans, while obtaining some payments for the phosphate, had received nothing in the order of royalties made available to the Nauru Trust Fund.

Seeking sovereignty for Banaba was a major way in which the link to the land could be sustained. It could also be used to leverage greater returns from the BPC in the mining era, and possibly as compensation in the future. In 1977, 100 young men, directed by their elders on Rabi, set up camp on Banaba while other representatives were taking legal action in London to have Banaba separated from the Gilbert and Ellice Island Colony.[50] Still more young people were sent to Banaba two years later, but on being informed that armed police might shoot to kill, the elders were forced to relent.[51] Meanwhile, the legal actions were to come to a head. They yielded relatively little joy for the Banabans, however, with the judge concluding that he was 'powerless to give . . . any relief', even though he considered that 'they have a raw deal'.[52] The finding did, however, assist in building political pressure in the United Kingdom and a A$10 million fund was established, although it took the Banabans four years before they would accept it.[53] When the last shipment of phosphate left Banaba, the machinery and plant was gifted to Kiribati, though from the perspective of King and Sigrah, this was merely a deft move to avoid spending millions of dollars in decommissioning plant and cleaning asbestos that had been used in some of the installations.[54] The island had been devastated, huge amounts of land removed and toxic waste left behind. The Banabans had no sovereign rights to the island, which became part of Kiribati upon its independence.

Anthropologist Martin Silverman wrote a detailed ethnology of Banaba/Rabi. He referred to the relationship between the people and the land of Banaba as one of mixed blood and mud—the two united and inseparable, as has been shown to

---

[49] Silverman, *Disconcerting Issue*, above n 41, 185.
[50] King and Sigrah, 'Legacy of a Miner's Daughter', above n 41, 950.
[51] ibid.
[52] ibid, 951.
[53] ibid.
[54] ibid.

be the case in many other Pacific island countries.[55] People and the land were mutually constituted: blood mixed with the land and the mud was contained in the tissue of the people. Upon moving to Rabi, the mud of Banaba retained its primacy in the identity of the people and numerous strategies emerged to retain this essential linkage. Katerina Teaiwa observes a much more visceral aspect to the mud–blood thesis developed by Silverman. For her, the situation is much more complex, since a great proportion of the land (the mud) of Banaba has been removed from the island and has become scattered around the world. While acknowledging the value of Silverman's work, Teaiwa observes that he describes the mud–blood linkage, especially the notion of land, as symbolic (perhaps more socially constructed), rather than as material or real. This would infer that the link between Banaba and Banabans living in Rabi does not have a tangible reality. Reducing the link to being symbolic, or socially constructed, largely undermines its importance to those involved in the actual relationship. The mining saw 20 million tonnes of land removed from the island. This equates to roughly a little less than 32,000 tonnes per hectare. For Teaiwa, this has important consequences for the indelible mud–blood relationship. Just where is the mud now located? Obviously, a huge amount has been taken away from Banaba, just like the population. Given this, how can the mud–blood union enable the people now resident in Rabi to bond to Banaba? To what extent is the visceral connection broken, and what are the implications of this for Banaban people living away from their land? She also raises another intriguing question, though outside the scope of this chapter: how much of Banaba is now spread over New Zealand and Australia? A moot point is raised as to the possibility that this may serve as a basis for a claim to settlement in New Zealand or Australia!

The intricacies aside, it is clear that the situation for the Banabans of Rabi is ambiguous and paradoxical, even after more than 60 years have passed since their removal from Banaba. Numerous strategies have been developed to sustain the linkage to the original homeland, but the visceral mud–blood linkage may be seen as under threat. Moreover, for the people of Rabi, the ambiguity lies not only in relation to their own homeland, but to their new one as well. Fraenkel reports that the 'Banabans remain one of Fiji's most disadvantaged and politically marginalised communities. Affirmative action programmes for indigenous Fijian and Rotuman communities in the aftermath of the 1987 and 2000 coups have not been targeted at Banaban peoples.'[56] Moreover, the original inhabitants of Rabi, who were displaced to the nearby island of Fiji, are seeking to reclaim their island.[57] Kempf and Herman argue that the assertion of Banaban identity not only preserves the linkage with the land of Banaba, but is also important for Banabans positioning themselves in the context of post-colonial Fiji, which is partly marked by strong nationalist movements and coups which have the potential to threaten

---

[55] Silverman, *Disconcerting Issue*, above n 41, 72–79.
[56] Fraenkel, 'Minority Rights in Fiji and the Solomon Islands', above n 39, 12.
[57] 'Relocated Fiji Villagers Want Rabi Island Back', *Pacific Island Report* (5 June 2007), http://archives.pireport.org/archive/2007/june/06%2D05%2D06.htm.

their security.[58] Clearly, the situation of these displaced people remains unsettled, both in terms of their dislocation from their original homeland and their security in their new island.

For climate migrants whose land no longer exists (either in its original state or through total inundation), Teaiwa's concerns have considerable resonance. How can this essential link exist if one of the elements no longer exists, or has been subjected to very high levels of environmental degradation? The case of Banaba/Rabi, then, should be of considerable relevance to those looking at community relocation in Pacific island countries as a response to climate change. The degradation of Banaba is not replicated in the other cases of long-distance intra-Pacific relocation. Climate change-induced degradation may be even more profound, and the implications for the relocatees even more devastating. Banaba has a 'caretaker' population physically sustaining the mud–blood union. Such arrangements may well also be the case for atolls that are facing inundation, coastal erosion or depletion, but in the end, under the most extreme scenarios, even that prospect may be rendered impossible.

All three of the international relocations discussed above took place in the context of colonialism, in particular the British colonial system in the Pacific, which included the Western Pacific High Commission (WPHC), responsible for Solomon Islands, New Hebrides (now Vanuatu), the Gilbert and Ellice Islands (now Kiribati and Tuvalu respectively) and the Colony of Fiji. The WPHC was based in Suva and at times the Governor of Fiji and the Western Pacific High Commissioner were the same individual. Movement of people among the colonies was orchestrated by the colonial services and did not require passports or contemporary protocols of residency, citizenship, visas and the like. Silverman noted a number of reasons why this is significant. Colonial administrations could make decisions about land and community locations with fewer constraints than is currently possible, where land is enshrined in laws established to protect customary land rights in the newly independent nations. Secondly, colonial administrations could easily move people across what are now international boundaries, as long as the territories were colonised by the same metropolitan power.[59]

While most Pacific island countries are now independent, as are all but one of the atoll countries (Tokelau), much can be learned from the colonial experiences. It is highly unlikely that it would be possible to transplant a community from one cultural and environmental setting to another in the contemporary Pacific. Where suitable land might become available (for instance, a freehold coconut plantation being sold, although they are no longer large in number), the descendants of the original inhabitants would most likely have priority in most countries in the region, if indeed the land was to be returned to customary ownership. Any community relocation that might take place could not be facilitated rapidly but would require

---

[58] Kempf and Hermann, 'Reconfigurations of Place and Ethnicity', above n 41, 369.
[59] MG Silverman, 'Introduction: Locating Relocation in Oceania' in Lieber (ed), *Exiles and Migrants in Oceania*, above n 7, 2–4.

a long period of negotiation—between sovereign states, between communities at both origin and destination and their respective governments, and ultimately between the relocating and recipient communities themselves. Large amounts of compensation might be required for both groups, given the losses they would incur. It is difficult to see rapid, if any, progress given the barriers, not the least of which is the embodiment of Pacific island people in their land.

Relocation outside the region, if possible, would most likely be to countries such as Australia, New Zealand and the United States, where land is held in fee simple and where the current political economy is capitalist and lifestyles are individualistic. In this sense, any form of population movement would be more likely to occur as migration, with original community characteristics being considerably transformed, if not completely destroyed.

IX Conclusions

The purpose of this chapter has been to illustrate the predicament of those Pacific island communities that may be faced with extreme climate change scenarios that render their homelands uninhabitable, or may even cause them to be inundated altogether. There have been numerous calls for countries such as New Zealand and Australia to make it possible for Pacific island communities to migrate to these two countries in particular. Such calls, while well meaning, fail to account for the extremely important losses that dislocation from the land will bring about. At the same time, many observers do not appreciate the difficulties for people who are displaced to find alternative sites in their own country, even where there are lands that are less likely to be exposed to the adverse effects of climate change. Internally relocated communities are likely to suffer great losses as well.

Migration and relocation may also have major effects upon the cultures of those who are forced to relocate. I am not arguing here that climate change will devastate some Pacific cultures. Culture is ever-changing, and the fluidity of cultures and social structures in the Pacific (as elsewhere) cannot be denied. It is possible after numerous generations that relocated people may find peace, no longer yearn for the land which was part of their ancestors, and build successful and prosperous lives in other environs. But, given the strength, tenacity and indivisibility of the person–community–land bond, relocation is bound to be disruptive for a considerable length of time over many generations. Moreover, relocation is not just about severing people from their land. It is also about drastic changes in lifestyle, economy, politics, legal systems and cultural norms. Diets will change and, in the most extreme cases, there will no longer be people at home to send the important foods to those who have migrated—whether it be varieties of taro and other root and tree crops, delicacies cooked in coconut cream, or the massive range of marine resources.

In the most extreme scenarios, Pacific communities forced to relocate as an entity (if they are lucky), or simply displaced as individuals and households, may find themselves placed in situations that are in some ways likely to be more hopeless than those faced by refugees, for the possibility of return may well be negligible. The land, once a visceral component of community and individual physicality and identity, may indeed become only a symbol of a former status.

5

Conceptualising Climate-Induced Displacement

WALTER KÄLIN*

I Introduction

Discussions about displacement, namely the involuntary movement of people, caused by the effects of climate change are sometimes marred by hasty conclusions: for some, affected persons are 'refugees'. Others do not hesitate to declare that populations living on islands threatened by submergence with rising sea levels will become 'stateless'. Still others see a direct relationship between the degree of global warming, the number of disasters causing displacement and the magnitude of the number of people affected by it. Thus, a maximalist school of thought expects hundreds of millions of people, even up to a billion, to be displaced as a consequence of climate change.[1] By contrast, a minimalist approach stresses that displacement is triggered by complex and multiple causes, among which climate change is just one, and predicts that the number of cases where displacement can be directly linked to the effects of climate change will be few.[2]

---

* This chapter is based on work done by the author in his capacity as Representative of the United Nations (UN) Secretary-General on the Human Rights of Internally Displaced Persons, but reflects his personal opinions only. See generally United Nations High Commissioner for Refugees (UNHCR), supported by the International Organization for Migration (IOM) and the Norwegian Refugee Council, 'Climate Change and Statelessness: An Overview' (Submission to the 6th Session of the Ad Hoc Working Group on Long-Term Cooperative Action (AWG-LCA 6) under the UN Framework Convention on Climate Change (UNFCCC), 1–12 June 2009, Bonn) (19 May 2009), http://unfccc.int/resource/docs/2009/smsn/igo/048.pdf.

[1] See, eg N Myers, 'Environmental Refugees in a Globally Warmed World' (1993) 43 *BioScience* 252, 257 where the author estimated that there would be 150 million displaced persons by 2050. Christian Aid estimates that, 'unless strong preventative action is taken, between now and 2050 climate change will push the number of displaced people globally to at least 1 billion': Christian Aid, *Human Tide: The Real Migration Crisis* (May 2007) 22.

[2] On these two schools of thought, see J Morrisey, 'Environmental Change and Forced Migration: A State of the Art Review' (Background Paper for the Environmental Change and Migration: Assessing the Evidence and Developing Norms for Response Workshop, Refugee Studies Centre, Oxford, 8–9 January 2009), http://www.rsc.ox.ac.uk/PDFs/Environmental%20Change%20and%20Forced%20Migration%20Review%20-%20Morrissey.pdf.

Overall, the phenomenon of people displaced by the effects of climate change is highly complex and in many ways little understood.[3] Nevertheless, there is growing evidence that at least the number of people affected by climate-related sudden-onset disasters is very substantial and likely to increase: the Norwegian Refugee Council's Internal Displacement Monitoring Centre and the United Nations (UN) Office for the Coordination of Humanitarian Affairs, for instance, found that in addition to 4.6 million people newly displaced within their own country by conflict, 'at least 36 million people were displaced by sudden-onset natural disasters in 2008. Of those, over 20 million were displaced by climate-related disasters, while almost 16 million were displaced by non-climate-related disasters'.[4] Thus, climate-related disasters, that is, those linked to windstorms, heavy rainfall and flooding, have become one of the primary causes of (often short-term) displacement, and their number is likely to grow. This raises the challenge of how to build the necessary financial, operational and legal capacities to respond to the specific protection and assistance needs of those displaced in the context of climate change. These challenges should be seen in the wider context of obligations that states are faced with in the context of climate change. They exist at three levels.

A Addressing the Cause: Mitigating Climate Change

States parties to the UN Framework Convention on Climate Change (UNFCCC) and its Kyoto Protocol have committed themselves to reducing the emission of greenhouse gases.[5] These mitigation measures aim to slow down and eventually stop climate change and its disastrous consequences. As such, they have an important preventive effect on displacement.

B Addressing the Effects: Reducing Risks Created by Climate Change and Vulnerabilities Caused by It

Climate change must be accepted to the degree it has developed so far: its environmental and human impacts are already felt today and will be felt in the future. This makes it necessary to take measures to reduce the adverse effects of climate change, such as by reducing the impact of natural hazards by mitigating vulnerabilities, enhancing resilience capacities and strengthening adaptation measures. The Hyogo Framework for Action: Building the Resilience of Nations and

---

[3] S Castles, 'Afterword: What Now? Climate Climate-Induced Displacement after Copenhagen', in the present volume.

[4] UN Office for the Coordination of Humanitarian Affairs, the Internal Displacement Monitoring Centre and the Norwegian Refugee Council, *Monitoring Disaster Displacement in the Context of Climate Change: Findings of a Study by the United Nations Office for the Coordination of Humanitarian Affairs and the Internal Displacement Monitoring Centre* (Geneva, 2009) 8–9.

[5] United Nations Framework Convention on Climate Change (adopted 9 May 1992, entered into force 21 March 1993) 1771 UNTS 107; Kyoto Protocol to the Framework Convention on Climate Change (adopted 11 December 1997, entered into force 16 February 2005).

Communities to Disasters,[6] adopted by the 2005 World Conference on Disaster Reduction, provides an important model that states should take into consideration. While legally non-binding, the Framework expresses the acknowledgment by states 'that efforts to reduce disaster risks must be systematically integrated into policies, plans and programmes for sustainable development and poverty reduction, and supported through bilateral, regional and international cooperation, including partnership',[7] and identifies priorities for action for the years 2005–15.[8] It is complemented by human rights obligations directly relevant to addressing displacement. Reduction of disaster risks and vulnerabilities, such as by setting up alarm and evacuation systems, has been described by the European Court of Human Rights as a human rights obligation.[9] If a disaster is foreseeable and the state is able to prevent ensuing threats to people's lives and property, then it must take appropriate action in conformity with its obligations under human rights law to protect life, privacy and property.[10]

C Addressing the Consequences: Protecting and Assisting Individuals Displaced by the Effects of Climate Change

Mitigation and ex ante adaptation measures are often insufficient to prevent individuals from becoming displaced or otherwise being affected by the negative consequences of climate change. Since the challenge of adaptation, properly understood, includes the need to adapt to the humanitarian consequences of climate change, adaptation measures must also cover protection of and assistance for the displaced. States hosting displaced people, as primary duty bearers, are bound by human rights law to respect (that is, refrain from interferences with) the rights of those affected, as well as to actively protect such rights and to take positive measures (necessary legislative and administrative steps) to enable displaced people to fully enjoy their rights.[11] From an operational perspective, protection can be understood as 'all activities aimed at ensuring full respect for the rights of the individual in accordance with the letter and the spirit of the relevant bodies of law

---

[6] Hyogo Framework for Action 2005–2015: Building the Resilience of Nations and Communities to Disasters (Hyogo, World Conference on Disaster Reduction, 18–22 January 2005) ('Hyogo Framework').

[7] ibid, para 4.

[8] The Hyogo Framework identifies the following priority actions: '1. Ensure that disaster risk reduction is a national and a local priority with a strong institutional basis for implementation. 2. Identify, assess and monitor disaster risks and enhance early warning. 3. Use knowledge, innovation and education to build a culture of safety and resilience at all levels. 4. Reduce the underlying risk factors. 5. Strengthen disaster preparedness for effective response at all levels': para 14.

[9] *Budayeva and Others v Russian Federation* (App Nos 15339/02, 21166/02, 20058/02, 11673/02 and 15343/02), European Court of Human Rights (20 March 2008).

[10] ibid, paras 128–37.

[11] With regard to Art 2 of the International Covenant on Civil and Political Rights (adopted 16 December 1966, entered into force 23 March 1976) 999 UNTS 171 ('ICCPR'), see UN Human Rights Committee, 'General Comment 31: The Nature of the General Legal Obligation Imposed on States Parties to the Covenant' (29 March 2004) UN Doc CCPR/C/21/Rev.1/Add.13, paras 6 and 7.

(i.e. human rights law, international humanitarian law and refugee law.'[12]

This chapter focuses on the issue of how best to conceptualise climate-induced displacement in order to develop appropriate legal and policy responses with which to address the third of these challenges. In this context, three non-controversial observations serve as a point of departure: (i) climate and climate change per se do not trigger the movement of people, but some of their effects, in particular sudden and slow-onset disasters, have the potential to do so; (ii) such movement may be voluntary, or it may be forced; and (iii) it may take place within a country or across international borders.

Based on these observations, this chapter addresses the following issues:

• What are the various climate change scenarios that trigger population movements?
• What is the nature of these movements and who is affected?
• To what extent are those affected protected by present normative frameworks, what are the normative gaps, and how can they be addressed? In particular, how should the case of people forcibly displaced across international borders be conceptualised? And should those displaced from 'sinking' small island states be classified as 'stateless persons'?

II Scenarios

Findings of the Intergovernmental Panel on Climate Change suggest that the main effects of global warming are related to water stress: some regions will be affected by a reduction of water availability, particularly in parts of the tropics, the Mediterranean and Middle Eastern regions and the southern tips of Africa and Latin America. By contrast, water availability may increase in parts of Eastern Africa, the Indian sub-continent, China and the northern latitudes. Due to rising sea levels, the densely populated 'mega-deltas', especially in Asia and Africa, as well as small, low-lying islands all over the world, are at the greatest risk from floods, storms, salinisation of groundwater and soils, coastal flooding and eventual submergence.[13]

In this context, the following typology of possible scenarios is proposed to distinguish situations requiring different legal and policy answers.

---

[12] Inter-Agency Standing Committee (IASC), 'Protection of Internally Displaced Persons', Committee Policy Paper Series No 2 (Geneva/New York, IASC, 2000) 2. This definition was originally agreed in the context of the International Committee of the Red Cross (ICRC) workshop process. See also ICRC, *Strengthening Protection in War: A Search for Professional Standards* (Geneva, ICRC, 2001) which also aptly describes in general terms what, under international law, is expected of states.

[13] Intergovernmental Panel on Climate Change (IPCC), *Climate Change 2007: Synthesis Report: Contribution of Working Groups I, II and III to the Fourth Assessment Report of the Intergovernmental Panel on Climate Change* (Geneva, IPCC, 2008).

(i) *Sudden-onset disasters*, such as flooding, windstorms (hurricanes/typhoons/cyclones) or mudslides caused by heavy rainfalls, can trigger large-scale displacement and incur huge economic costs. However, depending on recovery efforts, the ensuing displacement need not be long-term, and return will remain possible in most cases. While all of these disasters are climate-related, they are not necessarily an effect of global warming and the ensuing change of climate patterns. In fact, many hydro-meteorological disasters triggering displacement would occur regardless of climate change, and even where they are linked to climate change, such causality is difficult, if not impossible, to prove in a specific case. Furthermore, disasters such as volcanoes or earthquakes with similar impacts on people and on their movements are not linked to climate or to climate change,[14] but there is no reason why people displaced by those events should be treated any differently from those affected by climate impacts. Therefore, despite the current emphasis on climate change, it is conceptually sounder to look at sudden-onset disasters as a cause of displacement, and not to limit the focus to those triggered by global warming.

(ii) *Slow-onset environmental degradation* caused, inter alia, by rising sea levels, increased salinisation of groundwater and soil, long-term effects of recurrent flooding, thawing of permafrost, as well as droughts and desertification or other forms of reduced water availability, will see a dramatic decrease of water availability in some regions and recurrent flooding in others. This will impact upon economic opportunities and conditions of life will deteriorate in affected areas. Such deterioration may not necessarily cause displacement, but it may prompt people to consider 'voluntary' migration as a way to adapt to the changing environment and be a reason why people move to regions with better living conditions and income opportunities. However, if areas become uninhabitable over time because of further deterioration, finally leading to complete desertification, permanent flooding of coastal zones or similar situations, population movements will amount to forced displacement and become permanent.

(iii) So-called *'sinking' small island states* present a special case of slow-onset disasters. As a consequence of rising sea levels and their low-lying topology, such areas may become uninhabitable. In extreme cases, the remaining territory of affected states may no longer be able to accommodate their population, and such states may disappear entirely from the surface of the earth. When this happens, the population would become permanently displaced to other countries.

(iv) Governments may designate *areas as high-risk zones* too dangerous for human habitation on account of environmental dangers. Thus, people may (either with consent or against their will) be evacuated and displaced from

---

[14] In 2008, for example, the Sichuan earthquake alone displaced more than 15 million people (three-quarters of the number of people displaced by the 200 climate-related disasters occurring that year): see *Monitoring Disaster Displacement in the Context of Climate Change*, above n 4, 8–9.

their lands or, if they have already left, be prohibited from returning, or be relocated to safe areas. This could occur, for example, along rivers and coastal plains prone to flooding, but also in mountain regions affected by an increased risk of flooding or mudslides due to the thaw of permafrost. The difference between this situation and the case of sudden-onset disasters (scenario (i)) is that governmental action makes return impossible. Such cases will affect a relatively low number of people but raise particularly complex legal issues.

(v)   Finally, *unrest seriously disturbing public order, violence or even armed conflict* may be triggered, at least partially, by a decrease in essential resources due to climate change (such as water, arable land or grazing grounds). This is most likely to affect regions that have reduced water availability and cannot easily adapt due to poverty (for example, by switching to economic activities requiring less water). In such situations, there is little room for equitable sharing of the limited resources, making it difficult to reach peace agreements as long as resource scarcity continues.

III Nature of Movements and Affected People

These five scenarios can help to identify the character of the movement—whether it is forced or voluntary—and to describe those who move (are they migrants, internally displaced persons (IDPs), refugees, stateless persons or something else altogether?). They also help to assess whether, and to what extent, present international law is equipped and provides adequate normative frameworks to address the protection and assistance needs of such people. This is further discussed in Section IV.

A Sudden-Onset Disasters

i Internal Displacement

Hydro-meteorological disasters can trigger forced displacement inside a country or across borders. Experience shows that in most cases of sudden-onset disasters, the large majority (or even all) of those displaced remain inside their own country. Thus, they become IDPs and, as such, receive protection and assistance under human rights law and in accordance with the 1998 UN Guiding Principles on Internal Displacement,[15] as well as regional instruments such as the 2006 Protocol on the Protection and Assistance to Internally Displaced Persons[16] and the 2009

[15] Guiding Principles on Internal Displacement, UN Doc E/CN.4/1998/53/Add.2 (11 February 1998).
[16] Protocol on the Protection and Assistance to Internally Displaced Persons (adopted 15 December 2006, entered into force 21 June 2008) ('Great Lakes IDP Protocol'). This is a Protocol to the Pact on Peace, Security, Democracy and Development in the Great Lakes Region (adopted 15 December 2006, entered into force 21 June 2008).

African Union Convention for the Protection and Assistance of Internally Displaced Persons in Africa.[17]

The term 'internally displaced persons', according to the Guiding Principles on Internal Displacement, refers to 'persons or groups of persons who have been forced or obliged to flee or to leave their homes or places of habitual residence, in particular as a result of or in order to avoid the effects of . . . natural or human-made disasters, and who have not crossed an internationally recognized State border.' The two African instruments, which are binding upon states parties, contain the same definition.[18]

This notion of IDP is broad and sufficiently flexible to cover people evacuated or fleeing from their homes to escape the dangers of a sudden-onset disaster, or who are forced to leave in the disaster's aftermath because of the degree of destruction. The notion's particular strength lies in the fact that there is no need to determine whether or not the disaster was caused by the effects of climate change, or whether it was human-made or natural. Therefore, its application does not require a preliminary determination as to whether a specific disaster is linked to climate change.

ii Cross-Border Displacement

Sometimes, people displaced by sudden-onset disasters cross borders into other countries, such as when that is their only escape route or the protection and assistance capacities of their own country are exhausted. Others may opt to go abroad instead of staying within their own country simply because they hope for better protection and assistance there.

Such people do not lose the protection of human rights law, which states are obliged to respect in relation to *all* people within their territory or jurisdiction. However, international law, while under certain circumstances prohibiting rejection at the border,[19] does not provide any entitlements to be granted admission to or continued residence in a foreign country unless a person is a refugee or otherwise protected by the principle of *non-refoulement*.[20] The term 'refugee' refers to legal definitions in relevant international instruments: the 1951

---

[17] African Union Convention for the Protection and Assistance of Internally Displaced Persons in Africa (adopted 22 October 2009, not yet in force) ('Kampala Convention').

[18] Great Lakes IDP Protocol, Art 1(4); Kampala Convention, Art 1(k).

[19] See Convention relating to the Status of Refugees (adopted 28 July 1951, entered into force 22 April 1954) 189 UNTS 137, Art 33, which obliges states to examine claims of asylum seekers if rejection at the border would mean that they would have to return to their alleged country of origin. See GS Goodwin-Gill and J McAdam, *The Refugee in International Law*, 3rd edn (Oxford, Oxford University Press, 2007) 206ff.

[20] For example, on the basis of arbitrary deprivation of life, torture, or cruel, inhuman or degrading treatment or punishment. This is known as 'complementary' or 'subsidiary' protection: see, eg J McAdam, *Complementary Protection in International Refugee Law* (Oxford, Oxford University Press, 2007). For an analysis of its applicability in the climate change context, see J McAdam and B Saul, 'An Insecure Climate for Human Security? Climate-Induced Displacement and International Law' in A Edwards and C Ferstman (eds), *Human Security and Non-Citizens: Law, Policy and International Affairs* (Cambridge, Cambridge University Press, 2010) 378ff.

Convention relating to the Status of Refugees,[21] the 1969 OAU Convention,[22] and the 1984 Cartagena Declaration on Refugees.[23] Article 1A(2) of the 1951 Refugee Convention defines a 'refugee' as a person who:

> owing to well-founded fear of being persecuted for reasons of race, religion, nationality, membership of a particular social group or political opinion, is outside the country of his nationality and is unable or, owing to such fear, is unwilling to avail himself of the protection of that country; or who, not having a nationality and being outside the country of his former habitual residence as a result of such events, is unable or, owing to such fear, is unwilling to return to it.

Climate-induced displacement is neither covered by the wording and purpose of this definition, nor was it considered by the drafters of the treaty. Nonetheless, in situations where the victims of sudden-onset disasters flee abroad because their government has consciously withheld or obstructed assistance in order to punish or marginalise them on one of the five Convention grounds, such displaced people would qualify as refugees.[24] Such cases are likely to be few, and those forcibly displaced across borders by natural disasters are not usually persecuted for any of the relevant reasons listed in the definition. Furthermore, the definition of 'refugee', and refugee law as such, is based on the notion that someone who is persecuted 'is unwilling to avail himself of the protection of that country'—he or she has lost the protection of the government of his or her country of origin or habitual residence, a fact that destroys the bond of trust between the citizen and his or her country, which normally constitutes the fabric of modern societies.[25] It should not automatically be assumed that governments of countries affected by disasters are no longer able or willing to provide protection to their citizens.

The OAU Convention expands the notion of 'refugee' to include, inter alia, 'every person who, owing to . . . events seriously disturbing public order in either part or the whole of his country of origin or nationality, is compelled to leave his place of habitual residence in order to seek refuge in another place outside his country of origin or nationality'.[26] One could argue that sudden-onset disasters per se seriously disturb public order, but it is rather unlikely that the states concerned would be ready to accept such an expansion of the concept beyond its conventional meaning of public disturbances resulting in violence.[27] However, if a person sought refuge because of violence such as riots in the aftermath of a

---

[21] Read in conjunction with the Protocol relating to the Status of Refugees (adopted 31 January 1967, entered into force 4 October 1967) 606 UNTS 267 (together 'Refugee Convention').

[22] Organization of African Unity Convention Governing the Specific Aspects of Refugee Problems in Africa (adopted 10 September 1969, entered into force 20 June 1974) 1001 UNTS 45 ('OAU Convention').

[23] Cartagena Declaration on Refugees (22 November 1984) in Organization of American States, Annual Report of the Inter-American Commission on Human Rights (1984–85) OAS Doc OEA/Ser.L/V/II.66/doc.10, rev. 1, 190–93 ('Cartagena Declaration').

[24] See also J McAdam, 'From Economic Refugees to Climate Refugees?' (2009) 10 *Melbourne Journal of International Law* 579, 593.

[25] AE Shacknove, 'Who Is a Refugee?' (1985) 95 *Ethics* 274, 275.

[26] OAU Convention, Art 1(2).

[27] On this point, see A Edwards, 'Refugee Status Determination in Africa' (2006) 14 *African Journal of International and Comparative Law* 204, 225–27.

disaster, triggered by the government's unwillingness or inability to address certain consequences of the disaster or to provide the necessary assistance to the victims, then this instrument would apply. The same is true for the Cartagena Declaration, which also includes the criterion 'massive violation of human rights'.[28] Nevertheless, even in the regional contexts of Africa and Central America, cross-border displacement in the majority of climate-related cases will not be covered by refugee law.

This means that a normative gap exists with regard to most people displaced across borders in the aftermath of sudden-onset disasters, in particular with regard to admission, continued stay and protection against forcible return to the country of origin. In some cases, host governments have, for humanitarian reasons, allowed such persons to stay until they could return to their countries in safety and dignity,[29] but this practice has not been uniform. The status of these people remains unclear, and despite the applicability of human rights law, there is a risk that they may end up in a legal and operational limbo.

B Slow-Onset Disasters and Environmental Degradation

General deterioration of conditions of life and economic opportunities as a consequence of climate change may prompt people to look for better opportunities and living conditions in other parts of the country or abroad, before the areas in which they live become uninhabitable. Such people make use of their liberty to choose a new place of residence if they remain within their country,[30] and they become migrants if they go abroad. Their movement can be seen as a particular strategy to cope with and adapt to environmental and ensuing economic changes triggered by the effects of climate change.

There is no definition of 'migrant' in international law. The only definition that can be found in a universal treaty is that of a 'migrant worker', meaning 'a person who is to be engaged, is engaged or has been engaged in a remunerated activity in a State of which he or she is not a national'.[31] The International Organization for Migration uses a working definition of 'environmental migrants'[32] which is not, however, generally accepted.[33] Regardless of the terminology, people moving

---

[28] Cartagena Declaration, Art III(3).

[29] See section VI.B.ii below.

[30] ICCPR, Art 12.

[31] International Convention on the Protection of the Rights of All Migrant Workers and Members of their Families (adopted 18 December 1990, entered into force 1 July 2003) 2220 UNTS 93, Art 2(1).

[32] '**Environmental migrants** are persons or groups of persons who, for compelling reasons of sudden or progressive changes in the environment that adversely affect their lives or living conditions, are obliged to leave their habitual homes, or choose to do so, either temporarily or permanently, and who move either within their country or abroad': IOM, 'Discussion Note: Migration and the Environment' (1 November 2007) Doc MC/INF/288, para 6.

[33] IOM's definition includes IDPs as defined by the Guiding Principles on Internal Displacement, above n 15, and thus is not compatible with terminology accepted by the UN and regional organisations such as the African Union; see section IV.A below.

abroad by choice as part of their strategy to adapt to the effects of climate change are protected by general human rights law, as well as, where applicable, the specific guarantees provided to them by the International Convention on the Protection of the Rights of All Migrant Workers and Members of Their Families. However, such law does not give them any right to be admitted to another country.

If areas start to become uninhabitable because of complete desertification, salinisation of soil and groundwater or 'sinking' of coastal zones, movement may amount to forced displacement and become permanent, as inhabitants of such regions no longer have a choice except to leave—or, if they left earlier on a voluntary basis, to stay away permanently. If, in this latter case, people remain within their country, they are IDPs and fall, as outlined above, within the ambit of the Guiding Principles on Internal Displacement. If they go abroad, they have no protection other than that afforded by international human rights law; in particular, they have no right under international law to enter and remain in another country, and thus are dependent upon the generosity of host countries.

This scenario poses two particular challenges: (i) there are no criteria to determine where to draw the line between voluntary movement and forced displacement; and (ii) those forcibly displaced to other countries by the effects of climate change remain without specific protection as they do not, as outlined above, qualify as refugees or, in exceptional cases, for protection against forcible return under human rights law.[34] At the same time, as noted above, there is no legal definition of 'migrant' at the international level, and the notion of 'migrant workers' as defined by international law does not really fit, since even if such people find a job abroad, they are primarily in search of protection and assistance and their decision to leave is not just triggered by economic considerations.

C People Displaced from Small Island States[35]

The submersion and destruction of entire small island states, anticipated in some climate change scenarios, is likely to be gradual, if it happens at all. In the initial phases, this type of slow-onset disaster may encourage people, as part of individual or household adaptation strategies, to migrate to other islands belonging to the same country (where these exist) or abroad in search of better living conditions and prospects for the future. If they migrate to another country, they are protected generally by human rights law, including guarantees specifically protecting migrant workers and their families.[36]

Later, such movements may assume the character of forced displacement if areas of origin become uninhabitable or disappear entirely, or if the remaining

---

[34] On this protection, see section IV.B.ii.a.aa below.

[35] See J McAdam, ' "Disappearing States", Statelessness and the Boundaries of International Law', in the present volume.

[36] See, eg International Convention on the Protection of the Rights of All Migrant Workers and Members of their Families, above n 31.

territory is inadequate to accommodate the whole population. These scenarios would render return impossible, and the population would become permanently displaced to other countries. In this case, normative gaps exist for those who move abroad, leaving them in a legal limbo as (prima facie) they are neither migrant workers nor refugees. In particular, it is unclear whether provisions on statelessness would apply. The government of such countries may try to maintain a symbolic presence (such as on a built-up small island or platform), and their laws which, according to Article 1 of the Convention relating to the Status of Stateless Persons,[37] determine who their citizens are, may continue to be applied (for example to newly born children whose parents register them abroad at consulates of the country of origin).[38]

D Designation of High-Risk Zones Too Dangerous for Human Habitation

Governments may designate particular zones affected by disasters as too dangerous for human habitation. People who are evacuated from, or prohibited from returning to, such zones are IDPs, since they are forced to leave or stay away from their former homes. They cannot return but must be relocated to safe areas or be locally integrated in the areas to which they have been evacuated in a way that allows them to resume normal lives. Without such durable solutions, they remain in protracted displacement situations or may decide to spontaneously return to high risk zones because of a lack of viable alternatives, exposing them to risks to health, limb and even life. International human rights law, the Guiding Principles on Internal Displacement and analogous norms and guidelines on relocation in the context of development projects provide a sufficient normative framework for addressing these situations.[39]

Should people decide to leave their country because they reject relocation sites offered to them, or because their government does not provide them with sustainable solutions in accordance with relevant human rights standards, protection abroad will be limited to that offered by general human rights law, including provisions applicable to migrant workers. Their formal legal status will remain unclear, however, and they may not have a right to enter and remain in the country of refuge.

---

[37] Convention relating to the Status of Stateless Persons (adopted 28 September 1954, entered into force 6 June 1960) 360 UNTS 117.

[38] See section IV.B.C below.

[39] See 'Basic Principles and Guidelines on Development-Based Evictions and Displacement: Annex 1 of the Report of the Special Rapporteur on Adequate Housing as a Component of the Right to an Adequate Standard of Living' (18 May 2007) UN Doc A/HRC/4/18. See also 'Operational Policy 4.12: Involuntary Resettlement' in World Bank, *Operational Manual* (Washington DC, World Bank, 2001); Organization for Economic Cooperation and Development (OECD), *Guidelines on Aid and Environment: No 3: Guidelines for Aid Agencies on Involuntary Displacement and Resettlement in Development Projects* (Paris, OECD, 1992); Asian Development Bank, *Involuntary Resettlement* (August 1995).

E Climate Change-Induced Unrest, Violence and Armed Conflict

The effects of climate change, in particular dwindling resources, can contribute to social tensions, which in turn may degenerate into violent conflicts—for example, overly scarce vital resources, such as water or arable or grazing land, may trigger forced displacement. People who move within their own countries are IDPs. Those fleeing abroad may qualify as refugees protected by the Refugee Convention or regional refugee instruments, or be people in need of complementary forms of protection or temporary protection available for those fleeing armed conflict.[40] The available normative frameworks are the Guiding Principles on internal displacement, international humanitarian law, human rights law and refugee law. They provide a sufficient normative framework for addressing these situations since those affected are fleeing a breakdown of public order, violence, armed conflict or persecution, rather than the changes brought about by global warming per se.

IV Applicable Protection Frameworks

A Internally Displaced Persons

As the above analysis has shown, the following people qualify as IDPs: those forcibly displaced within their own country by sudden-onset disasters (scenario i); those whose place of origin has become uninhabitable as a consequence of a slow-onset disaster (scenario ii), or has been declared too dangerous for human habitation (scenario iv); and those who flee the dangers of climate-related violence and armed conflict (scenario v).

IDPs are protected by all human rights guarantees binding upon the state concerned because they remain citizens or residents of their own country and continue to be entitled to the full range of guarantees available to the general population. Human rights that are specifically relevant for the displaced are listed and further specified in the Guiding Principles on Internal Displacement. This important document covers all phases of displacement—protection from displacement, protection during displacement and protection during the return and recovery phase. They state, for instance, that forced evacuations in cases of disasters are prohibited 'unless the safety and health of those affected require' such measures (Principle 6), and that evacuations, if they become necessary, must be carried out

---

[40] In the European context, see, eg Council Directive (EC) 2004/83 on the Minimum Standards for the Qualification and Status of Third Country Nationals or Stateless Persons as Refugees or as Persons Who Otherwise Need International Protection and the Content of the Protection Granted [2004] OJ L304/12; Council Directive (EC) 2001/55 on Minimum Standards for Giving Temporary Protection in the Event of a Mass Influx of Displaced Persons and on Measures Promoting a Balance of Efforts between Member States in Receiving Such Persons and Bearing the Consequences Thereof [2001] OJ L212/12.

in a manner that does not violate 'the rights to life, dignity, liberty and security of those affected' (Principle 8). As regards protection during displacement, Principle 16 primarily addresses situations of armed conflict but also covers the needs of families separated by sudden-onset disasters, providing that '[a]ll internally displaced persons have the right to know the fate and whereabouts of missing relatives', and authorities concerned are obliged, in this regard, to 'endeavour to establish the fate and whereabouts of internally displaced persons reported missing, and cooperate with relevant international organisations engaged in this task. They shall inform the next of kin on the progress of the investigation and notify them of any result.' As regards humanitarian aid, IDPs have, at a minimum, the right to be provided with and have safe access to essential food and potable water, basic shelter and housing, appropriate clothing and essential medical services (Principle 18). Regarding the recovery phase, the Guiding Principles state the important principle that IDPs have the right to choose between voluntary return to their former homes, integrating where they have been displaced to, or moving to another part of the country (Principle 28). They also have the right to have their property that they left behind restituted to them (Principle 29).

The Guiding Principles, even though not a binding treaty, gain their authority from the fact that they reflect and are consistent with binding human rights law. Today, they are recognised by states as an 'important international framework for the protection of internally displaced persons'.[41] Several states have integrated them into their domestic law. In Africa, the Great Lakes IDP Protocol and the Kampala Convention specifically address displacement by natural disasters and reference the Guiding Principles.

An important tool for identifying and implementing the human rights of people affected by natural disasters, whether or not displaced, is the Operational Guidelines on Human Rights and Natural Disasters. These were adopted in June 2006 by the UN's Inter-Agency Standing Committee (IASC)—the coordinating body of the humanitarian agencies, including big international non-governmental organisations—in order to enhance the protection capacities of humanitarian actors.[42] They are based on the Guiding Principles but go beyond them insofar as they also cover non-displaced populations affected by natural disasters. They are a tool aimed at sensitising humanitarian workers to typical human rights challenges in such situations, and highlighting activities that should be undertaken to respond to such problems.

---

[41] '2005 World Summit Outcome', UNGA Res 60/1 (16 September 2005) para 132; 'Mandate of the Representative of the Secretary-General on the Human Rights of Internally Displaced Persons', Human Rights Council Res 6/32 (14 December 2006) para 5; 'Protection of and Assistance to Internally Displaced Persons', UNGA Res 62/153 (18 December 2007) para 10; 'Protection of and Assistance to Internally Displaced Persons', UNGA Res 64/162 (18 December 2009) para 10.

[42] They were initially developed by the Representative of the Secretary-General on the Human Rights of Internally Displaced Persons and submitted to the UN Human Rights Council in March 2007: see Human Rights Council, 'Operational Guidelines on Human Rights and Natural Disasters' (20 March 2007) UN Doc A/HRC/4/38/Add.1 ('Operational Guidelines'). A Field Manual suggesting practical steps for the implementation of the Operational Guidelines was published by the Brookings-Bern Project on Internal Displacement and disseminated in March 2008. After being tested in the field, the Operational Guidelines and Manual are currently being revised (May 2010).

Thus, for people forcibly displaced by the effects of climate change within their own country, the existing human rights framework codified in the Guiding Principles is sufficient. The challenge is to incorporate this framework into domestic law and to strengthen the capacities of national and local authorities to implement and apply it, including those responsible for disaster management, as well as communities at the grassroots level.

B People Displaced across International Borders

i *Refugees*

As outlined above, people displaced across international borders may qualify as refugees in some instances, particularly if the authorities refuse to assist and protect them on account of their race, religion, nationality, membership of a particular social group or political opinion in the context of disasters, violence or armed conflict triggered by the effects of climate change.[43] In such cases, the full protection of international and regional refugee law will apply.

Particularly important in this regard is the principle of *non-refoulement*. Article 33(1) of the Refugee Convention prohibits returning in any manner whatsoever a refugee 'to the frontiers of territories where his life or freedom would be threatened'. This prohibition is generally regarded as including rejection at the border and non-admission. While this prohibition does not provide a basis for permanent admission in another country, it obliges states at least to admit temporarily people fleeing dangers amounting to persecution. However, such protection deals with dangers emanating from agents of persecution and is not available to persons directly displaced by disasters.[44] As mentioned above,[45] in the two regions covered by the OAU Convention and the Cartagena Declaration, where events seriously disturbing public order may lead to refugee protection, the group of potential beneficiaries of such protection could be expanded by developing doctrine and guidance to states on the interpretation of this notion (but it remains open whether states would be ready to accept such an expansion of refugee protection).

ii *Other People*

The main challenge is to clarify, or even develop, the normative framework applicable to people crossing international borders in the wake of sudden-onset disasters (scenario i), as a consequence of slow-onset disasters (scenario ii), in the aftermath of the 'sinking' of small island states (scenario iii), or in the wake of designation of a place of origin as a high-risk zone that is too dangerous for human habitation (scenario iv). In these cases, different sets of issues need to be addressed.

---

[43] See section III.A.ii above.
[44] For a detailed examination of the application of refugee law in the climate change context, see McAdam, 'From Economic Refugees to Climate Refugees?', above n 24.
[45] See section III.A.ii above.

a Identifying People in Need of Protection Abroad

First, should those moving voluntarily and those forcibly displaced across borders be treated differently, not only with respect to assistance and protection while away from their homes, but also with respect to their possibility (or even right) to be admitted to other countries and remain there, at least temporarily, and how should the distinction between the two categories be drawn? The answer seems obvious: present international law, while recognising that all human beings are entitled to the full enjoyment of human rights, does in fact differentiate between people who move voluntarily and have no specific legal protection, and those forcibly displaced, for whom special normative regimes (refugee law, and the Guiding Principles on Internal Displacement) have been developed at least in some cases.

In general, state sovereignty in the area of admission and removal of foreigners is more limited where forced migrants are concerned, compared to the situation of people who migrate voluntarily. In the case of internal movement, the right to freedom of movement and choice of residence provides individuals with the possibility to go to other locations within their own country, regardless of whether or not they initially leave their place of residence voluntarily.[46] But the right to freedom of movement as such does not provide a right to be admitted to another state, even if forced movement was involved. While states should accept that voluntary migration may be part of individual adaptation strategies to respond to the negative effects of climate change and, depending on the circumstances, be facilitated as a contribution to adaptation in general,[47] international law, with the exception of refugee law and the principle of *non-refoulement* prohibiting under certain circumstances rejection at the border of the country of refuge,[48] provides no general entitlement to be admitted to another country.

Voluntary and forced movements often cannot be clearly distinguished in real life, but rather constitute two poles of a continuum, with a particularly grey area in the middle where elements of choice and coercion mingle.[49] However, because of its binary, bipolar nature,[50] law must always draw clear lines,[51] and must

---

[46] The relevant human rights guarantee, contained in ICCPR, Art 12, is not an absolute guarantee but, according to its para 3, can be subjected to restrictions 'which are provided by law, are necessary to protect national security, public order (ordre public), public health or morals or the rights and freedoms of others, and are consistent with the other rights recognized in the present Covenant.'

[47] See P Boncour, 'Keynote: "Migration and Climate Change: From Emergency to Adaptation"' (Keynote Speech at the 14th Conference of the Parties to UNFCCC: Side Event: Climate Change, Migration and Forced Displacement: The New Humanitarian Frontier?, 8 December 2008), www.iom.int/jahia/webdav/shared/shared/mainsite/activities/env_degradation/webcast.pdf.

[48] See Refugee Convention, Art 33(1), and the extension of the principle of *non-refoulement* in human rights law: E Lauterpacht and D Bethlehem, 'The Scope and Content of the Principle of *Non-Refoulement*: Opinion' in E Feller, V Türk and F Nicholson (eds), *Refugee Protection in International Law: UNHCR's Global Consultations on International Protection* (Cambridge, Cambridge University Press, 2003); McAdam, *Complementary Protection*, above n 20.

[49] See G Hugo, 'Climate Change-Induced Mobility and the Existing Migration Regime in Asia and the Pacific', in the present volume.

[50] See N Luhmann, *Law as a Social System* (Oxford, Oxford University Press, 2004) 173–210.

[51] For example, between 'legal' and 'illegal', 'guilty' and 'not guilty', 'refugee' and those not qualifying as such.

therefore necessarily qualify movement as either voluntary or forced. Thus, it is necessary to define the criteria relevant for distinguishing between those who voluntarily leave their homes or places of habitual residence because of the effects of climate change, and those who are forced to leave by such effects or—even if they left voluntarily in the first place—can no longer return and therefore should be entitled to protection abroad.

In order to draw this line, one could use a vulnerability analysis to assess when vulnerabilities have reached such a degree that a person is forced to leave his or her home. However, it would obviously be extremely complex to develop generic criteria on this basis and to apply them individually, in particular in situations of slow-onset disasters.

The author, while maintaining that, except in certain cases described above,[52] people displaced by certain effects of climate change are not normally refugees as defined by international law, suggests a different approach, one that takes inspiration from three elements of the refugee definition in Article 1A(2) of the Refugee Convention. These are: (i) being outside the country of origin, (ii) because of persecution on account of specific reasons (race, religion, nationality, membership of a particular social group or political opinion), and (iii) being unable or unwilling to avail oneself of the protection of one's country.

People displaced across borders by the effects of climate change obviously fulfil the first criterion of being outside the country of origin. It is also obvious that, except in the case of scenario (v) and some other cases that will be rather exceptional, such people are not refugees, because they do not fulfil the criterion of being persecuted on account of any of the relevant reasons. However, similar to persecution, the effects of climate change (such as windstorms, salinisation of groundwater and soils, and so on) as well as conditions in their aftermath (such as unavailability of adequate food, drinking water or health services after a sudden-onset disaster) may constitute serious threats to life, limb and health. In this broader sense, refugees and those displaced by the effects of climate change are faced with similar dangers, albeit for different reasons. The third criterion may also help to conceptualise solutions for these people. Exactly as we do for refugees, we should ask: under what circumstances should those displaced across borders by the effects of climate change not be expected to go back to their country of origin, and therefore remain in need of some form of surrogate international protection, whether temporary or permanent? In general, the answer will, as for refugees, depend on the elements of inability or unwillingness of the authorities in the country of origin or habitual residence to provide the necessary protection—and in the case of natural disasters, assistance to the people concerned. There is, however, a difference between the two situations: in the case of persecution, the prima facie assumption is that the authorities of the country of origin are unwilling to protect the person concerned. In the case of disasters, the assumption should be a continued willingness by these authorities to provide protection and assistance,

---

[52] See sections III.A.ii, III.E and IV.B.i above.

but in many cases it will be clear that the ability to do so is limited or even non-existent. Looking at it from the perspective of the people affected, the inability to obtain such protection and assistance must be the primary consideration in the context of climate-induced displacement.

Table 1: Comparison of refugees and persons displaced by climate change

Refugee as person in need of international protection.	*Person displaced across borders by the effects of climate change as person in need of international protection.*
Outside the country of origin or habitual residence.	Outside the country of origin or habitual residence.
Persecution, ie danger to life, limb or liberty, on account of race, religion, nationality, membership of a particular social group or political opinion.	Danger to life, limb or health as a consequence of the effects of climate change or the nature of the response, or the lack thereof, by competent authorities in the country of origin or habitual residence.
Unable or unwilling to avail oneself of the protection of the country of origin or habitual residence.	Unable or unwilling to avail oneself of the assistance and protection of the country of origin or habitual residence.

These criteria help to determine who should be admitted at the border of another state and allowed to remain, at least temporarily. It seems to be obvious that in the case of arrival at a border of a neighbouring country in the immediate aftermath of a natural disaster, those forced to flee should be initially admitted on the basis that their movement was forced at the moment of departure and they decided, to the best of their knowledge at the time of the disaster, that fleeing across a nearby border was the best option to reach safety.

The question whether such people can be obliged to return to their country of origin once the immediate danger is over is relevant and more complex. Here, the point of departure should not be the subjective motives of individuals or communities behind their decision to move, but rather whether, in light of the prevailing circumstances and the particular vulnerabilities of those concerned, it would be unreasonable, and thus inappropriate, to require them to return to their country of origin. This 'returnability' test helps to better identify those in need of international protection. It covers not only those who actually flee to another country, but also those whose initial movement was voluntary but who now cannot be expected to return because the situation has deteriorated to such an extent that return is no longer an option. Unlike the test used to determine who is an IDP, which focuses primarily on the forced nature of departure,[53] this test, like the one

---

[53] However, someone can be an IDP who left voluntarily but is later unable to return to his or her home, for example owing to the breaking out of an armed conflict: see W Kälin, *Guiding Principles on Internal Displacement: Annotations*, 2nd edn (Washington DC, American Society of International Law, 2008) 5.

to determine refugee status, emphasises the prognosis—whether it would be safe to return.

The returnability of the person concerned should be analysed on the basis of three elements: permissibility, feasibility (factual possibility) and reasonableness of return. This test only asks whether it is legally permissible, factually feasible and morally reasonable to oblige the person concerned to return to his or her country of origin or permanent residence. It does not automatically exclude the return of those who cannot go back to their homes and therefore would become IDPs. Rather, returnability would depend on the conditions such returnees would encounter, as outlined below.

aa Legal Impediments: The Criterion of Permissibility
There are certain cases where human rights law, by analogy to the refugee law principle of *non-refoulement*, provides that return is impermissible. The first example is the prohibition against returning someone to a situation when there are substantial grounds for believing that an individual would face a real risk of torture or cruel, inhuman or degrading treatment or punishment, or arbitrary deprivation of life. This prohibition was derived by the European Court of Human Rights[54] and the UN Human Rights Committee[55] from Article 3 of the European Convention on Human Rights and Article 7 of the ICCPR respectively, but has not yet been applied to disaster situations. The second example is the prohibition on collective expulsion, that is, the collective return of people that is not based on an individual assessment.[56]

bb Factual Impediments: The Criterion of Feasibility
Return may be factually impossible due to temporary technical or administrative impediments, such as when roads are cut off by floods or airports in the country of origin are closed. Return is also impossible for practical reasons if the country of origin refuses readmission for technical or legal reasons: during an emergency, a country may lack the capacity to absorb large return flows, or it may prevent readmission of persons whose travel documents or proof of citizenship was destroyed, lost or simply left behind when they left.

---

[54] See the long line of cases beginning with *Soering v United Kingdom* (1989) 11 EHRR 439, para 91, referring to the Convention for the Protection of Human Rights and Fundamental Freedoms (European Convention on Human Rights, as amended) (4 November 1950) ETS No 5 ('ECHR'), Art 3. See also *Chahal v United Kingdom* (1996) 23 EHRR 413, para 74.

[55] See, eg, UN Human Rights Committee, 'General Comment 20: Replaces General Comment 7 Concerning Torture or Cruel, Inhuman or Degrading Treatment or Punishment (Art 7)' (10 March 1992), para 9; *C v Australia*, Comm No 900/1999 (2002) UN Doc CCPR/C/76/D/900/1999, para 8.5; *Byahuranga v Denmark*, Comm No 1222/2003 (2004) UN Doc CCPR/C/82/D/1222/2003, para 11.3.

[56] This prohibition is implicit in ICCPR, Art 13 and explicit in the American Convention on Human Rights (adopted 22 November 1969, entered into force 18 July 1978) 1144 UNTS 123, Art 12(5); Arab Charter on Human Rights (adopted 22 May 2004, entered into force 15 March 2008), reprinted in (2005) 12 *International Human Rights Reports* 893, Art 26(2); Protocol No 4 to the ECHR (adopted 16 September 1963, entered into force 2 May 1968) ETS No 46, Art 4.

cc Humanitarian Impediments: The Criterion of Reasonableness

Even where return would be lawful and possible, people should not, on the basis of compassionate and humanitarian grounds, be expected to go back if the country of origin does not provide any assistance or protection, or if what is provided falls far below international standards of what would be considered adequate. The same is true where authorities do not provide the displaced with any kind of durable solutions that are in line with international standards and would allow them to resume normal lives, especially where areas of land have become (or have been declared) uninhabitable, and people's return to their homes is therefore no longer an option and they have been unable to find an acceptable alternative themselves. If the answer to one of these questions—is return *permissible?* is it *feasible?* can it *reasonably be required?*—is 'no', then individuals concerned should be regarded as victims of forced displacement in need of protection and assistance in another state. In such cases, they should be granted at least a temporary stay in the country where they have found refuge until the conditions for their return are fulfilled. Permanent solutions on the territory of other states must be found where either such vast parts of a country have become uninhabitable that it can no longer host its entire population, or in the particular circumstances of the individual case, return cannot reasonably be expected in the long term.

b Closing the Normative Gap

What is the best strategy to close the existing normative gap and provide protection to those who are forced to cross an international border due to the effects of climate change and cannot be returned (at least temporarily) because such measure would be either inadmissible under international human rights law, not feasible, or could not reasonably be expected from those displaced? Such protection regimes can be developed either at the domestic, regional or the international level.

Domestic laws may draw inspiration from existing provisions in some states addressing complementary (subsidiary) or temporary protection that provide for—or may be interpreted in such a way as to provide for—protection for people displaced by the effects of climate change and other environmental factors.[57] For example, the US Immigration and Nationality Act provides for the possibility of granting Temporary Protected Status (TPS) for nationals of a foreign state who are already in the US if (i) there has been an environmental disaster in the foreign state resulting in a substantial, but temporary, disruption of living conditions; (ii) the foreign state is unable, temporarily, to handle adequately the return of its own nationals; (iii) and the foreign state officially has requested such designation.[58] TPS was granted in the aftermath of the 1998 Hurricane Mitch that affected large

---

[57] See UNHCR, supported by IOM and the Norwegian Refugee Council, 'Climate Change and Statelessness: An Overview' (Submission to the 6th Session of the Ad Hoc Working Group on Long-Term Cooperative Action (AWG-LCA 6) under the UN Framework Convention on Climate Change (UNFCCC), 1–12 June 2009, Bonn) (19 May 2009), http://unfccc.int/resource/docs/2009/smsn/igo/048.pdf, 9–11.

[58] Immigration and Nationality Act, 8 USC § 244.

parts of Central America, but denied in the case of the devastating 2008 floods in Haiti. Finland's Aliens Act also provides temporary protection (for up to three years) in situations of mass displacement as a result of an environmental disaster.[59] The law also provides for a residence permit where a person cannot return to his or her home country or country of permanent residence because of an 'environmental disaster'.[60] A similar provision is contained in Sweden's Aliens Act.[61] The provisions in the Swiss asylum law dealing with subsidiary as well as temporary protection may be interpreted to cover climate-related scenarios, even though the law does not expressly mention natural or environmental disasters.[62]

Since these approaches are haphazard, discretionary and vary from one country to another, there is a clear need to go beyond domestic solutions to harmonise legal approaches. This is most likely to start at the *regional level*. In 2008, the Economic and Social Committee of the European Union suggested identifying areas where European law could play a useful part in adapting to the impacts of climate change.[63] EU law on the protection of forced migrants includes provisions on temporary and subsidiary protection that might be able to be interpreted as providing protection to those displaced cross-border by natural disasters. While the Temporary Protection Directive was designed to deal with the mass influx of people displaced by the effects of armed conflict or generalised violence, it cannot be excluded that it could also cover instances of mass influx due to the effects of climate change, since the definitional provision in art 2(c) is not exhaustive.[64]

Examples also exist in the area of internal displacement: the Great Lakes IDP Protocol covers people displaced by disasters. Article 3 obliges states 'to the extent possible, [to] mitigate the consequences of displacement caused by natural disasters and natural causes' and to 'establish and designate organs of Government responsible for disaster emergency preparedness, coordinating protection and assistance to internally displaced persons'. Furthermore, states must 'enact national legislation to domesticate the Guiding Principles fully and to provide a legal framework for their implementation within national legal systems' and, in this context, ensure that such legislation specifies the governmental organs responsible not only 'for providing protection and assistance to internally dis-

---

[59] Aliens Act 2004 (Finland) s 109.

[60] ibid, s 88.

[61] Aliens Act 2005 (Sweden) c 4, s 2.

[62] This was the conclusion of an inter-departmental roundtable discussion by the Swiss Ministry of Foreign Affairs on 13 January 2009, in which the author participated.

[63] Opinion of the European Economic and Social Committee on the 'Green Paper from the Commission to the Council, the European Parliament, the European Economic and Social Committee and the Committee of the Regions: Adapting to Climate Change in Europe—Options for EU Action' COM (2007) 354 final [2008] OJ C120/38, para 3.2.

[64] It refers to people displaced 'in particular', rather than 'only', by armed conflict etc. See V Kolmannskog and F Myrstad, 'Environmental Displacement in European Asylum Law' (2009) 11 *European Journal of Migration and Law* 313, 316ff. The UK Home Office stated in 2004 that '[t]he European temporary protection directive ... will enable all European Member States to act quickly and in a coordinated manner in the rare event that people from another country need to be offered temporary assistance because of armed conflict or natural disasters in their home country': 'UK Plans in Place to Protect Victims of Humanitarian Disasters' (Press Release, 20 December 2004).

placed persons' but also for 'disaster preparedness'.[65] The Kampala Convention obliges states to 'take measures to protect and assist persons who have been internally displaced due to natural or human-made disasters, including climate change', and provides that 'States Parties shall devise early warning systems, in the context of the continental early warning system, in areas of potential displacement, establish and implement disaster risk reduction strategies, emergency and disaster preparedness and management measures and, where necessary, provide immediate protection and assistance to internally displaced persons'.[66] These examples may provide inspiration for similar regional instruments on disaster-induced cross-border displacement.

C People Displaced from Submerged Small Island States

This leaves the case of the so-called 'sinking' small island states that may cease to exist. The question arises whether their populations will become stateless and should be treated as such under the Convention relating to the Status of Stateless Persons.[67] However, it remains to be seen whether those affected will really become 'stateless' as a matter of international law.

According to Article 1 of that treaty, the term 'stateless person' means 'a person who is not considered as a national by any State under the operation of its law'. Statelessness thus means being without a nationality, not without a state. Citizens of small island states do not become ipso facto stateless as long as there is some remaining part of the territory of their state and their government continues to exist. As highlighted by McAdam and Saul, the notion of 'statelessness' in international law 'is premised on the denial of nationality through the operation of the law of a particular State, rather than through the disappearance of a State altogether'.[68] Even where the whole territory of a country disappears, it is far from certain that its laws 'sink' with it.

In such cases, people from such states may become de facto stateless, but to treat them as de jure stateless persons would be problematic. While states, according to a traditional understanding, come into existence when they have a permanent population, a defined territory, a government and the capacity to enter into relations with other states,[69] they do not automatically disappear when one element falls away. Rather, in modern international law, there is, as has been stressed by Crawford, 'a strong presumption against the extinction of States once firmly established'.[70] In

---

[65] Great Lakes IDP Protocol, Arts 6(3) and 6(4)(c) respectively.

[66] Kampala Convention, Arts 5(4) and 4(2) respectively.

[67] See UNHCR, 'Climate Change and Statelessness', above n 57.

[68] McAdam and Saul, 'An Insecure Climate for Human Security?', above n 20, 374.

[69] Montevideo Convention on the Rights and Duties of States (adopted 26 December 1933, entered into force 26 December 1934) 165 LNTS 19, Art 1, which is said to represent the position under customary international law.

[70] J Crawford, *The Creation of States in International Law*, 2nd edn (Oxford, Clarendon Press, 2006) 715. On the extinction of states, see I Ziemele, 'States, Extinction of' in *Max Planck Encyclopedia of Public International Law* (Max Planck Institute for Comparative Public Law and International Law and Oxford University Press, 2009), www.mpepil.com.

the case of small island states, it is probable that their governments would try to retain at least a symbolic presence on their former lands, such as by building up a small island or surrounding it by dykes (even if that land would be too small or under-resourced to host any significant part of the population) and would continue to grant citizenship. Some states, such as the Maldives, have discussed the possibility of obtaining new territory where the state could continue to exist.[71] Such governments would therefore be unlikely to declare their extinction and withdraw their membership from the UN as long as they maintained a symbolic presence or continued to operate in exile.[72] It is also difficult to imagine that any other UN member state would want to tarnish its own reputation by being seen as lacking any compassion for the dire fate of such island states by asking for their exclusion from that or other international organisations.

Thus, it cannot be excluded that small island states will continue to exist as a legal entity as long as they possess a government and a population maintaining citizenship, even if their territory has disappeared and nobody is ready to formally terminate their statehood. International law would be flexible enough to provide for the continued existence of such states as non-territorial entities, as evidenced by the Sovereign Order of Malta, a subject of international law that continues to survive to this day, even though it lost its territorial base in Malta when Napoleon Bonaparte occupied the island on 12 June 1798.[73] All that is needed is a consensus by the international community in this regard.

The key issue, therefore, is not the question of statelessness, but rather how it can be ensured that citizens of submerged island states are admitted to other countries on a permanent basis where they can keep their nationality of origin, even if they or their descendants acquire the nationality of that country, and how their rights can be guaranteed in a way to avoid marginalisation. In this context, the question of the responsibility of the international community, in particular regarding relocation of whole communities, must be clarified as well. In other words, new law will be required if we are to avoid these populations becoming marginalised and disenfranchised inhabitants of their countries of refuge. The biggest challenge, however, concerns the issue of how to ensure that populations of affected small island states can continue to retain their identities as communities, and to exist as viable communities, even after the loss of most or all of their territory, an issue that goes beyond the scope of this contribution. Unfortunately, as of today, effective responses to this challenge seem to be non-existent.

---

[71] See, eg, 'Sinking Island's Nationals Seek New Home', *CNN* (11 November 2008), http://edition. cnn.com/2008/WORLD/asiapcf/11/11/maldives.president/index.html.

[72] State practice, as evidenced by the cases of Kuwait under Iraqi occupation 1990–91 or Somalia since 1991 until the creation of a (largely ineffective) Transitional Federal Government in 2004, does not readily assume extinction of a state because a government does not exist at a given moment or is in exile. See further McAdam, 'Disappearing States', above n 35.

[73] F Gazzoni, 'Malta, Order of' in *Max Planck Encyclopedia of Public International Law*, above n 70.

V Outlook

Displacement caused by the effects of climate change raises many complex issues that need to be addressed.[74] As a first step, it is important to reach a global consensus that displacement is an important aspect of adaptation, and that affected states need to be supported in their efforts to prevent climate change-induced displacement, address the protection and assistance needs of the displaced and find durable solutions for them. Taking into account the realities of present and future displacement caused by the effects of climate change, such adaptation efforts must complement any efforts to mitigate global warming. The 2009 UN Climate Change Conference in Copenhagen would have provided an opportunity to reach such consensus but, at the time of finalising this chapter, states parties to the UNFCCC had failed to negotiate and adopt any new legal framework to replace and further develop the present climate change regime. However, the issues discussed here are too pressing and important to be dropped from the climate change agenda and must be revisited in future rounds of negotiations.

---

[74] For a discussion of possible fora in which this might occur, see J McAdam, 'Environmental Migration Governance', *University of New South Wales Faculty of Law Research Series*, Working Paper No 1 (2009), http://law.bepress.com/unswwps/flrps09/art1.

6

'Disappearing States', Statelessness and the Boundaries of International Law

JANE McADAM*

'It is for the people to determine the destiny of the territory
and not the territory the destiny of the people.'[1]

I Introduction

The 'disappearing states' or 'sinking islands' phenomenon has become the 'canary in the coalmine'[2]—the litmus test for the dramatic impacts of climate change on human society. Predictions of whole countries disappearing Atlantis-style beneath the waves raise fascinating legal issues. As a purely academic exercise, pondering the dissolution of a state because of climate change rather than conflict, cession, merger or succession entails novel questions that go to the heart of legal rules on the creation and extinction of states. However, much of this deliberation is taking place in the abstract, such that the premises for why, when and how states might 'disappear', and the consequences of this, do not always sit comfortably with the empirical evidence.[3] There is therefore a risk that however academically stimulating and challenging these questions of extinction are, their practical relevance is undermined by some of the assumptions on which they are based. This, in turn, may lead to the adoption of well-intentioned but ultimately misguided policies.

This chapter is in part a response to the observation that a lack of specificity in climate migration research means that many of the normative and policy recommendations being made at the macro level are divorced from context.[4] Accordingly,

* I am grateful to the Australian Research Council for funding this research, and to Emily Crawford for her research assistance. Any errors or omissions remain my own.
[1] *Western Sahara Case (Advisory Opinion)* [1975] ICJ Rep 12, 122 (Separate Opinion of Judge Dillard).
[2] See Address by President Mohamed Nasheed (Maldives) to the United Nations General Assembly (UNGA) (21 September 2009), www.unmultimedia.org/tv/unifeed/d/13548.html.
[3] G Hugo, 'Climate Change-Induced Mobility and the Existing Migration Regime in Asia and the Pacific', in the present volume.
[4] J Barnett and M Webber, 'Migration as Adaptation: Opportunities and Limits', in the present volume.

it is anchored in a case study of the small Pacific island states of Kiribati and Tuvalu, which have become emblematic of the so-called 'sinking states' and 'climate refugee' phenomenon.[5]

The chapter argues that the focus on loss of territory as the indicator of a state's disappearance may be misplaced,[6] since small island states such as Kiribati and Tuvalu will become uninhabitable long before they physically disappear. In legal terms, the absence of population, rather than of territory, may provide the first signal that an entity no longer displays the full indicia of statehood (namely, a defined territory, a permanent population, an effective government, and the capacity to enter into relations with other states).

However, in the present context, the precise point at which a state loses its legal identity as a state is unclear. International law contemplates the formal dissolution of the state in cases of absorption (by another state), merger (with another state) and dissolution (with the emergence of successor states).[7] The potential extinction of a state because of climate change is markedly distinct, however, because the territory it abandons will not (cannot) be assumed by any other state. While the motivation behind this chapter is to determine the legal status of people displaced from 'disappearing states', its primary focus is on how and when such states would cease to exist, since this necessarily links to the ability to maintain nationality. In doing so, it examines mechanisms such as the government in exile as a means of enabling the state to continue even when the territory is uninhabitable, and briefly considers alternatives to full statehood, such as self-governance in free association with another state.

II Conceptual Problems: Macro versus Micro

One of the biggest drawbacks of much of the scholarship being generated on 'climate migration' is a tendency to treat climate-related movement as a single phenomenon that can be discussed in a general way. As Kälin's chapter highlights, a number of very different scenarios are captured within this rubric, and it is only through examining them separately, with attention to their distinctive and common features, that any meaningful policy or normative frameworks can be developed.[8]

    [5] See, eg J McAdam and M Loughry, 'We Aren't Refugees', *Inside Story* (30 June 2009), http://inside.org.au/we-arent-refugees/.
    [6] As Crawford observes, 'the substrate of the State is not property, it is the people of the State seen as a collective': J Crawford, *The Creation of States in International Law*, 2nd edn (Oxford, Oxford University Press, 2006) 717.
    [7] Succession can be described as a 'change in sovereignty over territory': MCR Craven, 'The Problem of State Succession and the Identity of States under International Law' (1998) 9 *European Journal of International Law* 142, 145.
    [8] W Kälin, 'Conceptualising Climate-Induced Displacement', in the present volume. Part of Kälin's chapter is an attempt to disaggregate these scenarios in order to develop appropriate institutional, legal and political responses to them.

While an overarching framework is helpful for identifying the range of climate impacts on human movement, the commonality of climate change as a driver is an insufficient rationale for grouping together a disparate array of displacement scenarios and proceeding to discuss policy responses in generic terms. Indeed, considerable conceptual confusion has arisen because of a lack of rigour and/or awareness in employing consistent terminology to describe those who move. Thus, despite an exponential expansion of the literature on environmental migration in the past few years, its 'cascading' or 'mainstreaming' effect has resulted in an over-simplification of the issues. As Barnett and Webber argue, we have in fact lost meaning because so much of the discussion lacks a real geo-social-political context.[9] This is problematic for the development of law and policy, because it risks being inappropriate and inaccurately targeted if it does not reflect understandings about the differences in nature, timeframe, distance, scale and permanence of potential movement.

The 'sinking island state' phenomenon is one such example. It is frequently raised in the media and scholarly literature,[10] but rarely analysed.[11] It has become emblematic of the most extreme impacts of climate change on human society, but is used haphazardly even by experts in the field.[12] In part, this may be because of the way that some small island states themselves have used the imagery of the drowning homeland to emphasise the impacts of climate change. Perhaps the most arresting example of this to date was an underwater Cabinet meeting held by the government of the Maldives in September 2009 to highlight its concerns about rising sea levels.[13] At a more formal level, in June 2009, the Pacific island states, with the support of a number of other countries, sponsored a UN General Assembly resolution on 'Climate Change and Its Possible Security Implications'.[14]

---

[9] Barnett and Webber, 'Migration as Adaptation', above n 4.

[10] See, eg J Bone and R Pagnamenta, 'We Are Sinking, Say Islanders, But There Is Still Time to Save the World', *The Times* (23 September 2009); R Callick, 'Don't Desert Us, Say Sinking Pacific Islands', *The Australian* (30 July 2009); R Colville, 'Vanishing Homelands', *Bangkok Post* (7 February 2008); C Lambert, 'That Sinking Feeling: What Would You Do If Your Country Was Disappearing under the Sea?' *The Times* (18 March 2009); J Lateu, 'That Sinking Feeling: Climate Refugees Receive Funds to Leave Islands', *New Internationalist* (March 2008); N Schmidle, 'Wanted: A New Home for My Country', *The New York Times* (10 May 2009); C Sherborne, 'Sinking Sandbanks', *The Monthly* (March 2009).

[11] For an exception, see C Farbotko, 'Representing Climate Change Space: Islographs of Tuvalu' (unpublished PhD thesis, University of Tasmania, School of Geography and Environmental Studies, 2008); C Farbotko, 'Tuvalu and Climate Change: Constructions of Environmental Displacement in the *Sydney Morning Herald*' (2005) 87B(4) *Geografiska Annaler* 279. For some helpful international law scholarship, focusing in particular on law of the sea issues, see R Rayfuse, 'W(h)ither Tuvalu? International Law and Disappearing States', *University of New South Wales Faculty of Law Research Series*, Working Paper No 9 (2009) 8, http://law.bepress.com/unswwps/flrps09/art9/; AHA Soons, 'The Effects of a Rising Sea Level on Maritime Limits and Boundaries' (1990) 37 *Netherlands International Law Review* 207; D Freestone and J Pethick, 'Sea Level Rise and Maritime Boundaries: International Implications of Impacts and Responses' in GH Blake (ed), *Maritime Boundaries* (London, Routledge, 1994).

[12] At a recent conference in Geneva, one distinguished academic referred to the 'tens of millions of people who will sink from their islands'. The remark went uncontested despite the fact that the island states at risk do not have combined populations of anything near this magnitude.

[13] See, eg 'Maldives Cabinet Makes a Splash', BBC News (17 October 2009), http://news.bbc.co.uk/2/hi/8311838.stm.

[14] UNGA Res 63/281 (3 June 2009). On climate change as an existential threat, see L Elliott, 'Climate Migration and Climate Migrants: What Threat, Whose Security?', in the present volume.

During debate, delegates referred to the unprecedented 'real possibility' of 'the disappearance of whole nations',[15] and the resolution's 'pursuit of greater guarantees of our territorial integrity'.[16] The President of the Federated States of Micronesia stressed the impact of climate change on 'our own security and territorial integrity, and on our very existence as inhabitants of very small and vulnerable island nations.'[17] The President of Vanuatu noted the risk that

> 'some of our Pacific colleague nations will be submerged. If such a tragedy should happen, then the United Nations and its members will have failed in their first and most basic duty to a Member and its innocent people, as stated in Article 1 of the Charter of the United Nations.'[18]

Arguing along the same lines, the President of Nauru expressed the expectation that 'the Security Council will review particularly sensitive issues such as the implications of the loss of land and resources and the displacement of people for sovereignty and international legal rights.'[19]

III The Nature of Disappearance

Though some states themselves use the 'disappearing islands' imagery to dramatic effect, the empirical evidence suggests that a simple 'climate change' cause and effect is not so straightforward, and motivations for movement even less so. That is not to say that climate change is not having real impacts on small island states; it is. But the Atlantis-style predictions that have captivated the imagination of some are unlikely to materialise as the means by which states cease to exist.

While 'defined territory' is one criterion of statehood, and although territory ultimately may disappear as a result of rising sea levels, it is more probable that the other indicia of statehood—a permanent population, an effective government, and the capacity to enter into relations with other states—will have been challenged prior to this occurrence. For low-lying islands such as Tuvalu and Kiribati, insufficient fresh water, as the water lens shrinks, has been cited as the most probable trigger for rendering these countries uninhabitable in the longer term.[20] Climate change threatens to reduce habitable land in other ways as well, including through coastal erosion and increased salinisation of the soil. This will impact upon agricultural capacity and, in turn, is likely to lead to greater urbanisation (as

---

[15] UNGA 63rd session, 9th plenary meeting (25 September 2008) UN Doc A/63/PV.9, Mr Chin (Palau).

[16] ibid, Mr Litokwa Tomeing (President of the Marshall Islands).

[17] UNGA 63rd session, 10th plenary meeting (25 September 2008) UN Doc A/63/PV.10, Mr Emanuel Mori (President of the Federated States of Micronesia).

[18] UNGA 63rd session, 11th plenary meeting (26 September 2008) UN Doc A/63/PV.11, Mr Kalkot Matas Kelekele (President of the Republic of Vanuatu).

[19] UNGA 63rd session, 9th plenary meeting (25 September 2008) UN Doc A/63/PV.9, Mr Marcus Stephen (President of the Republic of Nauru).

[20] See, eg N Mimura et al, 'Small Islands' in ML Parry et al (eds), *Climate Change 2007: Impacts, Adaptation and Vulnerability: Contribution of Working Group II to the Fourth Assessment Report of the Intergovernmental Panel on Climate Change* (Cambridge, Cambridge University Press, 2007).

people move from the outer islands) and increased pressure on an already poor labour market. There are also negative health consequences as people become increasingly reliant on imported processed foods. It is therefore likely that long before the land disappears, the bulk of the population will have moved.

Movement away from island states such as Tuvalu and Kiribati, like the nature of the climate process itself, is likely to be slow and gradual, although climatic events such as cyclones or king tides may, in the interim, trigger more sudden, but probably temporary (and internal) moves.[21] Migration is, and has long been, a natural human adaptation strategy to environmental variability. As Bedford notes, it is a normal response.[22] But whereas Pacific islanders could once freely move to other islands in times of resource scarcity or climate change,[23] the legal (and sometimes physical) barriers to entry imposed by states today considerably restrict freedom of movement. Accordingly, a key policy objective of both the Tuvaluan and Kiribati governments is to enhance existing migration options to developed countries in the region, primarily Australia and New Zealand,[24] thereby building up 'pockets' of their communities abroad.[25]

The discussion about 'sinking islands' is premised on the assumption that at some point, the territories of states such as Kiribati and Tuvalu will disappear—either completely, or to the point that they can no longer sustain permanent populations. Though international law contemplates the disappearance of states, it does so within the context of state succession. The conventional ways in which a state can become extinct—through voluntary absorption by another state, merger with another state, extinction by dissolution (voluntary or involuntary)[26]—all presuppose that a successor state begins to exist on, or assumes control over, the territory of the previous state. Indeed, the two treaties on state succession define this as 'the replacement of one State by another in the responsibility for the international relations of territory'.[27] There is never simply a void. As Marek observed in her leading work on the identity and continuity of states, a state's extinction entails a succession and prevents any further continuity of that state; a 'miraculous resurrection' is impossible.[28]

---

[21] The Red Cross in Tuvalu said that only four families have moved in response to flooding from king tides, and this was temporary: author's interview with Red Cross representative, Tuvalu (27 May 2009). Most movement after the Samoan tsunami in 2009 was internal.

[22] R Bedford, 'Environmentally-Induced Migration within the Context of Existing Migration Patterns' (Climate Change and Migration in the South Pacific Region: Policy Perspectives Conference, Wellington, 9–10 July 2009).

[23] See SR Fischer, *A History of the Pacific Islands* (Basingstoke, Palgrave, 2002) ch 1, on ancient Pacific mobility.

[24] Author's interview with Anote Tong, President of Kiribati (12 May 2009); Bedford, 'Environmentally-Induced Migration', above n 22.

[25] Author's interviews with Anote Tong, President of Kiribati (12 May 2009), and David Lambourne, Solicitor-General of Kiribati (8 May 2009).

[26] See generally Crawford, *The Creation of States in International Law*, above n 6, ch 17.

[27] Vienna Convention on Succession of States in Respect of Treaties (adopted 23 August 1978, entered into force 6 November 1996) 1946 UNTS 3, Art 2(1)(b); Vienna Convention on Succession of States in Respect of State Property, Archives and Debts (adopted 8 April 1983, not yet in force), Art 2(1)(a).

[28] K Marek, *Identity and Continuity of States in Public International Law* (Geneva, Librairie E Droz, 1954) 5–6, referred to in Crawford, *The Creation of States in International Law*, above n 6, 669. But see the case of Syria: 690.

In the present context, unless the territory of Tuvalu or Kiribati were ceded to another state, the normal rules on state succession would not apply. For this reason, this chapter turns its attention to the *creation* of states, to determine at what point the absence of certain criteria of statehood might lead other states (and the international community, through international organisations) to deny a state's continued existence.

IV What is a 'State'?

Whether or not a state exists is a 'mixed question of law and fact'.[29] The absence of a formal international law definition of a 'state' might be explained by the fact that questions about an entity's nature only tend to arise in borderline cases, as well as by the tendency of states to preserve as much freedom of action as possible with respect to new states.[30] Logically, this might also be said to apply in reverse, to enable states themselves to determine when an entity's loss of the indicia of statehood should indicate the end of that state. Crawford queries whether the rules determining statehood 'have been kept so uncertain or open to manipulation as not to provide any standards at all.'[31]

The classic formulation of statehood is contained in Article 1 of the 1933 Montevideo Convention on the Rights and Duties of States,[32] which is generally regarded as reflecting customary international law. The four elements of statehood are: a defined territory, a permanent population, an effective government, and the capacity to enter into relations with other states. While all four criteria would seemingly need to be present for a state to come into existence, the lack of all four may not mean the end of a state. This is because of the strong presumption of continuity of existing states,[33] which may account for the fact that since the establishment of the United Nations Charter in 1945, there have been very few cases of

---

[29] H Waldock, 'General Course on Public International Law' (1962) 106 *Recueil des Cours de l'Académie de Droit International* 5, 146, cited in Crawford, *The Creation of States in International Law*, above n 6, 5.

[30] Crawford, *The Creation of States in International Law*, above n 6, 45; see also 40.

[31] ibid, 45. Crawford notes that, at times, states have treated as states entities that do not come within the accepted definition of the term, such as the Holy See (1870–1929), British India (1919–47), and the United Nations (UN) membership of Byelorussia and Ukraine.

[32] Montevideo Convention on the Rights and Duties of States (adopted 26 December 1933, entered into force 26 December 1934) 165 LNTS 19.

[33] Crawford says international law is 'based on this assumption': *The Creation of States in International Law*, above n 6, 715, 701. He says: 'there is a strong presumption against the extinction of States once firmly established': 715. See generally references referred to there: Marek, *Identity and Continuity of States in Public International Law*, above n 28, 548; O Schachter, 'State Succession: The Once and Future Law' (1993) 33 *Virginia Journal of International Law* 253, 258–60; R Mushkat, 'Hong Kong and Succession of Treaties' (1997) 46 *International and Comparative Law Quarterly* 181, 183–87; M Koskenniemi, 'The Wonderful Artificiality of States' (1994) 88 *Proceedings of the American Society of International Law* 22.

extinction of states and virtually none of involuntary extinction.[34] It is also significant that so-called 'failed states' have continued to be recognised as states even during the period when they were objectively failing.[35] As Craven observes, an analysis of state practice reveals that 'in many cases the issue is not simply one of determining the existence of the state, but rather the degree of identity and extent of continuity.'[36]

The next section briefly highlights the key elements of each criterion of statehood to tease out possible implications for the 'sinking island' scenario.

A Defined Territory

Crawford writes: 'Evidently, States are territorial entities.'[37] But do they need to remain so in order to preserve their legal status? Certainly, there is no minimum amount of territory that needs to be held, and loss of some territory at least should not affect the legal status of the entity, since it is not necessary for a state to have precisely defined boundaries.[38] The requirement is only that 'the right to be a State is dependent at least in the first instance upon the exercise of full governmental powers with respect to some area of territory.'[39] Such territory does not have to be contiguous, and '[l]ittle bits of States can be enclaved within other States.'[40]

---

[34] Crawford, *The Creation of States in International Law*, above n 6, 715.

[35] D Thürer, 'The "Failed State" and International Law' (1999) 81 *International Review of the Red Cross* 731. Crawford argues, however, that the notion of a 'failed state' involves some conceptual confusion, and that many cited cases of 'failed states' are in fact crises of government or governance, rather than about the extinction of the state in question: *The Creation of States in International Law*, above n 6, 721–22. If a 'failed state' describes 'a situation where the structure, authority (legitimate power), law, and political order have fallen apart and must be reconstituted in some form, old or new', the very notion of 'reconstitution' suggests that a reformulation of the state is possible, *qua* state, rather than as some other kind of entity: IW Zartman, 'Introduction: Posing the Problem of State Collapse' in IW Zartman (ed), *Collapsed States: The Disintegration and Restoration of Legitimate Authority* (Boulder, Lynne Rienner Publishers, 1995) 1, cited in Crawford, *The Creation of States in International Law*, above n 6, 720.

[36] Craven, 'The Problem of State Succession', above n 7, 160. He goes on to state: 'What this means is that emphasis should not be so much upon the existence of "external" rules of succession that allow for the "transference" of rights and duties from one subject to another, but rather upon determining the extent to which legal continuity should follow from elements of material (social, cultural or political) identity.'

[37] Crawford, *The Creation of States in International Law*, above n 6, 46.

[38] See, eg *Deutsche Continental Gas-Gesellschaft v Polish State* (1929) 5 AD 11, 15, in which the German–Polish Mixed Arbitral Tribunal observed that it is sufficient that 'territory has a sufficient consistency, even though its boundaries have not yet been accurately delimited'.

[39] Crawford, *The Creation of States in International Law*, above n 6, 46.

[40] ibid, 47, referring to *Case concerning Sovereignty over Certain Frontier Land (Belgium/Netherlands)* [1959] ICJ Rep 1959, 209, 212–13; 229; *Case concerning Right of Passage over Indian Territory (Portugal v India)* [1960] ICJ Rep 1960, 6, 27. However, as a practical matter, there have been situations in the past where states have refused to recognise as states territories that are highly fragmented. For instance, the United Kingdom argued that 'the fragmentation of the territory of Bophuthatswana within South Africa, the pattern of the population and the economic dependence on South Africa more than justify our refusal to recognise Bophuthatswana': Minister of State, Foreign and Commonwealth Office, Hansard HC vol 105 col 100 (12 November 1986), cited in Crawford, *The Creation of States in International Law*, above n 6, 47.

The link between statehood and territory is crucial, and inherent in possession of territory (as an indicator of statehood) is exclusive control over it.[41] Crawford therefore frames the territorial requirement of statehood as 'a constituent of government and independence', rather than as a separate criterion.[42] While Lowe argues that the concept of a state 'is rooted in the concept of control of territory', this is arguably more about ensuring that the criterion of independence is met rather than about the territory per se, since such control is 'to ensure that activities within its borders are not regulated by any other State'.[43] Jessup argued that the rationale for a state needing to possess territory was that 'one cannot contemplate a State as a kind of disembodied spirit . . . [T]here must be some portion of the earth's surface which its people inhabit and over which its Government exercises authority.'[44]

And yet, as will be examined below, states can continue to function even when their governments operate from outside the national territory. The mechanism of the government in exile has enabled governments to function extraterritorially, although this has always been contemplated as temporary and exceptional. Furthermore, it is premised on the continued existence of a permanent population on the state's territory (although the government in exile also retains jurisdiction over nationals abroad as well). Indeed, the general requirement that states have 'a certain coherent territory effectively governed'[45] assumes that there remains a population on that territory to be governed.

B Permanent Population

Just as international law does not require a state's territory to be a minimum size, nor is there a minimum population requirement.[46] Indeed, Tuvalu is the second smallest state by population (after the Vatican). The notion of a 'permanent' population simply means that it cannot be transitory. For present purposes, the

---

[41] Crawford, *The Creation of States in International Law*, above n 6, 48. 'The only requirement is that the State must consist of a certain coherent territory effectively governed': ibid, 52. See section VII below on leased land.

[42] ibid, 52.

[43] V Lowe, *International Law* (Oxford, Oxford University Press, 2007) 138.

[44] US Ambassador Jessup, UNSCOR 383rd meeting (2 December 1948), 11, cited in Crawford, *The Creation of States in International Law*, above n 6, 48. Yet, in the context of belligerent occupation, Grant writes: 'Territory is not necessary to statehood, at least after statehood has been established . . . [it] appears to be the case that once an entity has established itself in international society as a state, it does not lose statehood by losing its territory or effective control over that territory': TD Grant, 'Defining Statehood: The Montevideo Convention and its Discontents' (1999) 37 *Columbia Journal of Transnational Law* 403, 435.

[45] Crawford, *The Creation of States in International Law*, above n 6, 52.

[46] On this point, see TM Franck and PL Hoffman, 'The Right of Self-Determination in Very Small Places' (1976) 8 *New York University Journal of International Law and Politics* 331, 383: 'infinitesimal smallness has never been seen as a reason to deny self-determination to a population.' On the position of the Vatican, see JC Duursma, *Fragmentation and the International Relations of Micro-States: Self-Determination and Statehood* (Cambridge, Cambridge University Press, 1996) 374, 411–12.

relevant question is whether a state ceases to meet this criterion of statehood when a large proportion—or all—of its population lives outside the state's territory.

There are already a number of Pacific countries with very large populations outside their territory, and yet this does not affect their ability to continue to function as states. For example, 56.9 per cent of Samoans and 46 per cent of Tongans live outside their own country.[47] Thus, the proportion of population living on the territory does not seem to be determinative of the population criterion for statehood. But if an exodus of population is accompanied by, or premised on, the imminent or eventual loss of territory, then does it assume a different significance? If no population remains on the territory, can the state continue to exist by retaining its own outpost on the territory (as is being contemplated in Kiribati) or elsewhere (as a government in exile or on territory that another state permits it to use)? This links to the next section: at what point does a government cease to function?

C Government

The existence of an effective government satisfies another requirement of statehood: independence. Crawford distinguishes between these two criteria as follows: 'government is treated as the exercise of authority with respect to persons and property within the territory of the State; whereas independence is treated as the exercise, or the right to exercise, such authority with respect to other States.'[48] He regards government as the most important criterion of statehood, 'since all the others depend upon it',[49] but notes that in practice its application may be much more complex (since it will be in borderline cases that its identification and scope will be tested).

States may nonetheless choose to recognise an entity as a state even where it is doubtful that the full signs of statehood exist. For example, in 1960 Congo was widely recognised as a state and was accepted as a UN member without dissent, even though it lacked an effective government.[50] Crawford concludes that this was because the requirement of government may be less stringent than thought, and, importantly, that it has two aspects: 'the actual exercise of authority, and the right or title to exercise that authority.'[51] In that case, the conferral of independence by the former colonial power Belgium meant that there was no state against which the recognition of Congo could be unlawful, and the assumption followed that where

---

[47] See table in CW Stahl and RT Appleyard, *Migration and Development in the Pacific Islands: Lessons from the New Zealand Experience* (Canberra, AusAID, April 2007) 7, which draws on census information from Australia (2001), New Zealand (2001) and the US (2000) to show the population at home and the population abroad of Pacific island countries.

[48] Crawford, *The Creation of States in International Law*, above n 6, 55. With respect to 'territory', it refers in this sense 'to the extent of governmental power exercised, or capable of being exercised, with respect to some territory and population. *Territorial sovereignty is not ownership of but governing power with respect to territory*': 56 (emphasis added).

[49] ibid, 56.

[50] ibid, 56ff.

[51] ibid, 57.

a former sovereign grants full independence, the new state has the right to govern its territory.

The case of secession is different because the seceding state has to establish its adverse claim, which includes demonstrating effective and stable exercise of governmental powers.[52] Indeed, this may explain why the presumption of continuity is so strong. First, premature recognition of another state could be seen as unlawful interference in the domestic affairs of the original state, which itself might undermine international stability.[53] Secondly, and related to the first point, there would otherwise be a void in international relations in which states would 'find it difficult or impossible to continue many mutually advantageous economic, administrative and technical relations with other nations'.[54]

Arguably, the case of 'disappearing islands' is more akin to the former, in that there is no competing claim and the presumption of continuity will apply until states no longer recognise the government (which may be in exile).[55] At the margins, the notion of continuity becomes quite subjective: '[i]n many instances the claim to continuity made by the State concerned will be determinative; other States will be content to defer to the position taken.'[56]

D Capacity to Enter into Relations with Other States

The capacity to enter into relations with other states is a conflation of the requirements of government and independence. It is, accordingly, a consequence, rather than a criterion, of statehood.[57] Crawford regards independence (sometimes also called 'sovereignty'[58]) as the central criterion for statehood, since it is the right to exercise 'in regard to a portion of the globe . . . to the exclusion of any other State, the functions of a State.'[59] It has two main elements: a separate existence within

[52] ibid, 58. See also at 59, drawing on C Warbrick, 'Recognition of States: Recent European Practice' in MD Evans (ed), *Aspects of Statehood and Institutionalism in Contemporary Europe* (Aldershot, Dartmouth Press, 1997) 14–16.

[53] On which, see Schachter, 'State Succession', above n 33, 259.

[54] International Law Association, 'Interim Report of the Committee on the Succession of New States to the Treaties and Certain Other Obligations of Their Successors', Annex E to *International Law Association Report of the Fifty-Second Conference* (1966) 584, cited in Mushkat, 'Hong Kong and Succession of Treaties', above n 33, 183. As Craven notes, 'states are not willing to jeopardize legal relations with an entity where there is clearly no successor state': 'The Problem of State Succession', above n 7, 159.

[55] On the other hand, the absence of any other state staking a claim over the territory may make it easier for states to deny its continuity, since there is no adverse claim (and thus no risk of premature recognition which could constitute interference in the state's domestic affairs).

[56] Crawford, *The Creation of States in International Law*, above n 6, 668, referring also to R Mullerson, 'The Continuity and Succession of States, by reference to the Former USSR and Yugoslavia' (1993) 42 *International and Comparative Law Quarterly* 473, 477; B Stern, 'La succession d'Etats' (1996) 262 *Recueil des Cours de l'Académie de Droit International* 9, 82–86; W Czaplinski, 'La continuité, l'identité et la succession d'Etats—évaluation de cas récents' (1993) 26 *Revue Belge de Droit International* 374, 391–92.

[57] Crawford, *The Creation of States in International Law*, above n 6, 61.

[58] ibid, 89. Crawford says that 'it is better to use the term "independence" to denote the prerequisite for statehood and "sovereignty" the legal incident.'

reasonably coherent borders, and not being subject to the authority of any other state.[60]

It is important to distinguish between independence as an 'initial qualification' for statehood, and its role for a state's 'continued existence'.[61] Crucially, for present purposes, the strong presumption of continuity of existing states means that other states may continue to treat it as such, despite a lack of effectiveness[62] or even a 'very extensive loss of actual authority'.[63] As Thürer notes in the context of so-called 'failed states':

> Even when States have collapsed, their borders and legal personality have not been called in question. Such 'fictitious' States have not lost their membership of international organizations and, on the whole, their diplomatic relations have remained intact. Though they are unable to enter into new treaty obligations, the international law treaties they have concluded remain in force.[64]

Similarly, when a government operates in exile, the state continues to exist but its governmental functions are (the assumption is, temporarily) unable to be performed from within its own territory. Since the principle of territorial sovereignty means that a government may only act as a government in exile with the consent (express or implied) of the state in which it is located,[65] the powers of such a government are necessarily more circumscribed than when it operates within its own territory. For example, in cases concerning the scope of jurisdiction of the courts of governments in exile within Britain during the 1940s, it was observed that 'the sovereignty of any State is unrestricted on its own territory only, while on foreign territory it naturally yields to the sovereignty of the foreign State',[66] and 'this jurisdiction [of Dutch service courts] is only possible so far as it is authorised by the British legislature and can only be exercised in accordance with the statutory provisions referred to and subject to the conditions and safeguards specified by statute'.[67] However, provided the government in exile's functions are not interfered with, or controlled by, the host state (or any other), its independence is preserved.

---

[59] *Island of Palmas Case (United States of America v The Netherlands)* (1928) 2 RIAA 829, 838.

[60] Crawford, *The Creation of States in International Law*, above n 6, 66 (fn omitted).

[61] ibid, 63.

[62] ibid. The examples Crawford has in mind are unlawful invasion or annexation of a state.

[63] ibid, 89.

[64] Thürer, 'The "Failed State"', above n 35, 752.

[65] See further S Talmon, *Recognition of Governments in International Law: With Particular Reference to Governments in Exile* (Oxford, Oxford University Press, 1998) 215ff. The host state can determine the extent to which the courts of the government in exile may exercise jurisdiction: 217.

[66] *Allied Forces (Czechoslovak) Case* (1941–42) 10 AD No 31, 123, 124, cited in Talmon, *Recognition of Governments in International Law*, above n 65, 217.

[67] *Amand v Home Secretary and Minister of Defence of Royal Netherlands Government* [1943] AC 147, 159 (Lord Wright), cited in Talmon, *Recognition of Governments in International Law*, above n 65, 217. However, the host state cannot prescribe how that jurisdiction is to be exercised: 218.

V Governments in Exile

There is a strong presumption in international law that states continue to exist even if there is a period without a government (or an effective one).[68] This shows the distinction between the 'state' and 'government', on which the legal position of the government in exile depends.[69] It might also suggest that states are willing to tolerate a hiatus between the loss of indicia of statehood and acknowledgement that a state has ceased to exist.

The term 'government in exile' does not denote a special status or subject of international law, but rather reflects the domicile of a government (namely, 'the depository of a State's sovereignty and its representative organ in international relations').[70] History is replete with examples of governments being able to operate in exile in the territory of other states.[71] The institution is most common in the case of belligerent occupation or illegal annexation. Traditionally, it has operated on the assumption that it is a time-bound mechanism which enables a government to operate outside its territory until it once again becomes possible for that government to reassert its control in its own territory.

The fact that governments can operate in exile suggests that the existence of territory, while essential to the original constitution of that entity as a state, is not integral to the exercise of certain governmental functions. As the French Foreign Minister wrote in 1814: 'A sovereign whose States are conquered . . . by the conquest only loses *de facto* possession and consequently retains the right to do everything that does not require that possession.'[72] Though a government's absence from its state does not automatically suspend or terminate existing treaties,[73] if it has to operate in exile then certain treaties may be terminated (or suspended) for reasons such as impossibility of performance or a fundamental change of circumstances.[74]

Functions that governments have continued to perform in exile include treaty-making, maintaining diplomatic relations, and conferring immunities, privileges and jurisdiction over nationals.[75] In particular, the exercise of diplomatic protection has included providing consular representation, lodging protests, arranging deportations of nationals, concluding amnesty agreements and providing

---

[68] Crawford, *The Creation of States in International Law*, above n 6, 34.

[69] ibid, 34 (fn omitted).

[70] Talmon, *Recognition of Governments in International Law*, above n 65, 16 (citation omitted).

[71] See ibid.

[72] CM de Talleyrand-Périgord, *Mémoires du prince de Talleyrand* (Paris, Calmann Levy, 1891) vol ii, 214–54, cited in ibid, 174.

[73] Talmon, *Recognition of Governments in International Law*, above n 65, 136; see also *Valk v Kokes* (1950) 17 ILR 114, 358.

[74] See Vienna Convention on the Law of Treaties (adopted 23 May 1969, entered into force 27 January 1980) 1155 UNTS 331, Arts 61(1), 62; Talmon, *Recognition of Governments in International Law*, above n 65, 136ff.

[75] Talmon, *Recognition of Governments in International Law*, above n 65, 15; see further 146–49.

passports and identity documents to prevent nationals from being treated as stateless persons.[76] This last function is of particular relevance to the climate-displacement context. In this regard, however, it is interesting to note that such documents have also been validly issued or extended by authorities in exile recognised in a lesser capacity than a government.[77]

The government in exile idea is premised on there still being an identifiable population over which the government has jurisdiction. In the conventional case, the majority of those people will continue to reside in the state's territory, from which the government is temporarily severed. In the 'disappearing state' scenario, the need for the government to operate in exile is premised on the uninhabitability of the state's territory, at least for the majority of the population. Accordingly, given that the bulk of the population will be residing in other sovereign states, they will be subject to the laws and jurisdiction of those states. The role of the home state therefore becomes the same as the jurisdiction that any state can exercise with respect to its nationals abroad (predominantly diplomatic protection). Once people begin to acquire dual nationality, the presumption of diplomatic protection may gradually favour the state in which the person resides (on the assumption that this is where nationality is more 'effective').[78] Over time, the function of the government in exile will wane. In particular, if the government in exile over time merged with the organs of the host state, especially if done voluntarily,[79] then this would normally result in the first state's extinction (provided 'there is no other perceived international interest in asserting the continuity of the State').[80]

As Kälin notes in his contribution to this volume, it is unlikely that small island states will readily relinquish their claims to statehood.[81] State practice suggests that the international community would be willing to continue to accept maintenance of the status quo (recognition of on-going statehood) even when the facts no longer seem to support the state's existence. Furthermore, the point at which a

[76] ibid, 204–5 and citations there. The state's 'personal sovereignty over its nationals' can protect them and their interests abroad: see generally 202–3. On the possible withdrawal of consular protection, see Hansard HC vol 353 cols 229–30 (8 November 1939), cited at 203.

[77] Talmon, *Recognition of Governments in International Law*, above n 65, 205. See further JF Engers, 'The United Nations Travel and Identity Document for Namibians' (1971) 65 *American Journal of International Law* 571; (1968) 4 *Revue Belge de Droit International* 293–94 (discussing Belgium's acceptance of travel documents issued by unrecognised governments in exile). For example, during the Second World War the US recognised the French Committee of National Liberation (CFLN) not as the government of France, but 'as functioning within specific limitations during the war', namely 'as administering those French overseas territories which acknowledge its authority': see Talmon, *Recognition of Governments in International Law*, above n 65, 25, referring to a statement by the US on 26 August 1943.

[78] In dual nationality cases, the contemporary approach, based on the rule of real and effective nationality, is to 'search for "stronger factual ties between the person concerned and one of the States whose nationality is involved"', involving consideration of 'all relevant factors, including habitual residence, center of interests, family ties, participation in public life and other evidence of attachment': *Islamic Republic of Iran v United States of America*, Case No A-18 (1984) 5 Iran–US CTR 251, 25.

[79] For example, if a self-governing colony reverts to imperial rule: see Crawford, *The Creation of States in International Law*, above n 6, 701.

[80] ibid, and citations there.

[81] Kälin, 'Conceptualising Climate-Induced Displacement', above n 8.

state such as Tuvalu or Kiribati could be said to have finally ceased to exist would depend not just on isolated acts of non-recognition by individual states, but their cumulative effect.[82] In this regard, we are looking for 'a general acceptance by the international community as a whole that the situation has been resolved', rather than any particular length of time passing.[83] Accordingly, '[a] State is not necessarily extinguished by substantial changes in territory, population or government, or even, in some cases, by a combination of all three.'[84] Indeed, its legal identity may be preserved to a degree even if it becomes a protectorate with some international legal personality.[85]

VI Statelessness?

If the state does cease to exist, then what is the legal status of its (prior) population? In the absence of having acquired a new nationality, could its people be considered 'stateless' as a matter of international law?

Even when a state becomes extinct according to conventional international law, the resultant legal status of the population on the territory is unclear.[86] There is no general right to nationality in customary international law, although there is certainly 'a strong presumption in favor of the prevention of statelessness in any change of nationality, including in a state succession.'[87] Although Article 15 of the Universal Declaration of Human Rights contains a right to nationality, it lacks a correlative duty on the state to confer nationality.[88] Indeed, the absence of a right to nationality in the International Covenant on Civil and Political Rights has been ascribed to the complexity of the issue and states' inability to agree on its inclusion in the treaty.[89]

---

[82] Crawford, *The Creation of States in International Law*, above n 6, 704–5. See also Talmon, *Recognition of Governments in International Law*, above n 65, 174ff.

[83] Crawford, *The Creation of States in International Law*, above n 6, 704.

[84] ibid, 700.

[85] ibid, 700–1. See section VIII below on self-governing territories.

[86] See generally P Weis, *Nationality and Statelessness in International Law*, 2nd rev edn (Alphen aan den Rijn, Sijthoff and Noordhoff International Publishers,1979) 135ff.

[87] JL Blackman, 'State Successions and Statelessness: The Emerging Right to an Effective Nationality under International Law' (1998) 19 *Michigan Journal of International Law* 1141, 1183.

[88] Universal Declaration of Human Rights (adopted 10 December 1948), UNGA Res 217A (III) ('UDHR').

[89] JMM Chan, 'The Right to a Nationality as a Human Right: The Current Trend Towards Recognition' (1991) 12 *Human Rights Law Journal* 1, 4–5. The only ICCPR provision relating to the right to a nationality is Article 24 on a child's right to acquire a nationality: International Covenant on Civil and Political Rights (adopted 16 December 1966, entered into force 23 March 1976) 999 UNTS 171 ('ICCPR'). See also the views of Hernández-Truyol and Hawk, who propose a 'deterritorialized, relational, and identity-based' citizenship based 'not on the nation's view of the individual, but rather the individual's view of themselves': BE Hernández-Truyol and M Hawk, 'Traveling the Boundaries of Statelessness: Global Passports and Citizenship' (2005) 52 *Cleveland State Law Review* 97, 111. See also the notion of 'pragmatic citizenship' suggested in E Mavroudi, 'Palestinians and Pragmatic Citizenship: Negotiating Relationships between Citizenship and National Identity in Diaspora' (2008) 39 *Geoforum* 307, 309: 'The assumption that there is a naturalised and potentially exclusive relationship between

The closest one comes to locating such a duty is the 'negative duty' arising under the statelessness treaties.[90]

While treaty law aims to prevent the inhabitants of an existing state from becoming stateless when a new state emerges on that territory,[91] there is divergent practice on whether nationality automatically changes or whether further provision has to be made by the new state for that to occur.[92] Crawford believes that the better view, in line with the decision of the Permanent Court of International Justice in the *Question concerning the Acquisition of Polish Nationality*, is that, subject to any stipulation to the contrary, people habitually resident in the territory of the new state acquire its nationality, for all international purposes, and lose their former nationality, although the new state may choose to delimit further who it will regard as its nationals.[93] While the issue of state succession does not apply to the Kiribati or Tuvalu context, the relevant point here is that existing international law lacks uniform practice in satisfactorily resolving the issue of nationality when one state ceases to exist. Though poorly ratified, the 1961 Convention on Reduction of Statelessness obliges states to ensure that any transfer of territory does not render people stateless.[94]

Perhaps unsurprisingly, the two international treaties on statelessness do not envisage the eventuality of literal, physical statelessness.[95] In any event, the legal definition of 'statelessness' is carefully and deliberately circumscribed to apply only to de jure statelessness—premised on the denial of nationality through the operation of the law of a particular state.[96] It does not even extend to the situation of de facto statelessness—where a person formally has a nationality, but which is ineffective in practice, although the drafters of the 1961 Convention adopted a resolution, appended to the Final Act of that treaty, stating that 'persons who are

territory, national identity and citizenship, whereby national identity is neatly located in a clearly demarcated and bounded nation-state can be seen as problematic.'

[90] Blackman, 'State Successions and Statelessness', above n 87, 1176. See, in particular, the Convention on the Reduction of Statelessness (adopted 30 August 1961, entered into force 13 December 1975) 989 UNTS 175 ('1961 Convention'), Arts 1(1), 1(3), 1(4), 4 and 10.

[91] 1961 Convention, especially Arts 8–10; International Law Commission's (ILC's) Draft Articles on Nationality of Natural Persons in Relation to the Succession of States, annexed to UNGA Res 55/153 (12 December 2000).

[92] Crawford, *The Creation of States in International Law*, above n 6, 52–53; Contrast the views of I Brownlie, 'The Relations of Nationality in Public International Law' (1963) 39 *British Year Book of International Law* 284, 320; DP O'Connell, *State Succession in Municipal Law and International Law*, vol 1 (Cambridge, Cambridge University Press, 1967), 497–528. See *AB v MB* (1951) 17 ILR 110, which refers to the 'absurd result of a State without nationals'.

[93] Crawford, *The Creation of States in International Law*, above n 6, 53, referring to *Questions concerning the Acquisition of Polish Nationality* (Advisory Opinion) PCIJ Series B No 7 (1923) 15; see also N Berman, '"But the Alternative is Despair": European Nationalism and the Modernist Renewal of International Law' (1993) 106 *Harvard Law Review* 1792, 1834–42.

[94] 1961 Convention, Art 10. See also the ILC's Draft Articles on Nationality, above n 91, Art 1 of which contains a 'right to nationality'; Art 4 requires states to take measures to prevent statelessness as a consequence of succession.

[95] Convention relating to the Status of Stateless Persons (adopted 28 September 1954, entered into force 6 June 1960) 360 UNTS 117 ('1954 Convention'); 1961 Convention.

[96] 1954 Convention, Art 1(1): 'For the purpose of this Convention, the term "stateless person" means a person who is not considered as a national by any State under the operation of its law.'

stateless de facto should as far as possible be treated as stateless de jure to enable them to acquire an effective nationality'. Thus, the instruments' tight juridical focus leaves little scope for arguing for a broader interpretation that would encompass people whose state is at risk, or in the process, of disappearing (unless, of course, the state formally withdrew nationality and through that act brought them within the legal concept of statelessness).

However, UNHCR's institutional mandate to prevent and reduce statelessness encompasses de facto statelessness as well.[97] In the 'sinking state' context, UNHCR has argued that even if the international community were to continue to acknowledge a state's on-going existence, despite signs that it no longer met the full indicia of statehood, its population could be regarded as de facto stateless. This view is based on the many practical constraints that the government would face in such a scenario, which would mean that 'their populations would be likely to find themselves largely in a situation that would be similar to if not the same as if statehood had ceased.'[98] From an institutional perspective, UNHCR is empowered to engage with states about preventing statelessness and therefore advocating on behalf of affected populations. In this regard, it has suggested that multilateral comprehensive agreements would facilitate planned and orderly movement to other states, and that the early introduction of educational and other measures to prepare people for displacement could not only increase their resilience and adaptability once they move, but also while they remain on their islands.[99]

Furthermore, although the 1954 Convention did not include de facto stateless persons within the definitional provision, its drafting history reveals a general sympathy towards their plight. Indeed, the drafters recognised that many de facto stateless persons were in the same position as de jure stateless persons, because despite legally being nationals of a particular state, they could not derive any benefits from it. However, the drafters wanted to avoid granting benefits to people who simply renounced their nationality for personal convenience. It was therefore proposed that the definition would include a provision enabling states to extend protection to 'any person living outside his own country who, for reasons recognised

---

[97] See, eg UNGA Res 50/152 (9 February 1996), reiterated in UNGA Res 61/137 (25 January 2007), UNGA Res 62/124 (24 January 2008), UNGA Res 63/148 (27 January 2009). The work of the United Nations High Commissioner for Refugees (UNHCR) extends in some cases to situations of de facto statelessness, such as in trying to get 'States to cooperate in the establishment of identity and nationality status of victims of trafficking, many of whom, especially women and children, are rendered effectively stateless due to an inability to establish such status, so as to facilitate appropriate solutions to their situations, respecting the internationally recognized human rights of the victims': Executive Committee of the High Commissioner's Programme, 'Statelessness: Prevention and Reduction of Statelessness and Protection of Stateless Persons' (14 February 2006) UN Doc EC/57/SC/CRP.6, para 7. See also UNGA Res 50/152 (9 February 1996) paras 14–15; UNGA Res 3274 (XXIX) (10 December 1974); UNGA Res 31/36 (30 November 1976).

[98] UNHCR, supported by the International Organization for Migration and the Norwegian Refugee Council, 'Climate Change and Statelessness: An Overview' (Submission to the 6th Session of the Ad Hoc Working Group on Long-Term Cooperative Action (AWG-LCA 6) under the UN Framework Convention on Climate Change (UNFCCC), 1–12 June 2009, Bonn) (19 May 2009), http://unfccc.int/resource/docs/2009/smsn/igo/048.pdf, 2.

[99] ibid, 3.

as valid by the state in which he is a resident, has renounced the protection of the state, of which he is, or was, a national', but this was ultimately reworded slightly and moved to the non-binding Final Act.[100]

In the case of Tuvalu and Kiribati, at a certain point the objective evidence will make clear that continued habitation in those territories is imminently impossible. In keeping with the object and purpose of the treaty, and the recommendation in the Final Act of the 1961 Convention that de facto stateless persons be treated in the same way as de jure stateless persons, one might argue that the benefits of the Convention should be extended to them. However, the Convention only binds states that have ratified it, and only in relation to stateless persons within their territory. Few states even have a status determination procedure to identify stateless persons, by contrast to refugees. Accordingly, its practical application may be limited. Attention would therefore be better focused on states' duty to prevent statelessness,[101] as outlined by UNHCR in the present context:

> To prevent temporary statelessness, acquisition of an effective nationality should be foreseen prior to the dissolution of the affected State. Dual nationality may therefore need to be permitted at least for a transitional period. As well, a waiver may be required of formal requirements for renunciation or acquisition of nationality which might be difficult to fulfil for affected populations. Such arrangements would need to provide *inter alia* for the right of residence, military obligations, health care, pensions and other social security benefits. Citizens of affected States that might have been displaced earlier, possibly to third States not party to the agreement, may also need to be considered.[102]

VII Relocation

As a matter of principle, there is nothing in international law that would prevent the reconstitution of a state such as Kiribati or Tuvalu within an existing state, such as Australia (although the political likelihood of this happening today seems

---

[100] See generally N Robinson, 'Convention relating to the Status of Stateless Persons: Its History and Interpretation' (commentary by Nehemiah Robinson, Institute of Jewish Affairs, World Jewish Congress, 1955, reprinted by UNHCR, 1997), commentary on Art 1. The British delegate also argued that the Refugee Convention already covered de facto stateless persons who were unable or unwilling to access the protection of their government, and that opening the 1954 Convention to all de facto stateless persons would be tantamount to granting them benefits from which they were excluded as refugees: see Robinson, referring to SR.3, 2–3.

[101] UNHCR argues that the prevention of statelessness is a corollary of the right to a nationality: 'Climate Change and Statelessness', above n 98, 2. That right is contained in its broadest form in the UDHR, Art 15; and in relation to children in the ICCPR, Art 24(3); Convention on the Rights of the Child (adopted 20 November 1989, entered into force 2 September 1990) 1577 UNTS 3, Art 7; International Convention on the Protection of the Rights of All Migrant Workers and Members of Their Families (adopted 18 December 1990, entered into force 1 July 2003) 2220 UNTS 93, Art 29. See also Convention on the Elimination of All Forms of Discrimination against Women (adopted 18 December 1979, entered into force 3 September 1981) 1249 UNTS 13, Art 9; International Convention on the Elimination of All Forms of Racial Discrimination (adopted 7 March 1966, entered into force 4 January 1969) 660 UNTS 195, Art 5(d)(iii); 1961 Convention on the Reduction of Statelessness.

[102] UNHCR, 'Climate Change and Statelessness', above n 98, 3.

remote).[103] Theoretically, too, it would be possible for one state to 'lease' territory from another, although one might query the extent to which power could then be freely exercised in a manner sufficient to meet the other requirements of statehood in such a case: while a state might be afforded jurisdiction over that territory, it would not be unencumbered by the 'landlord' state's territorial jurisdiction unless expressly obtained from the previous sovereign.[104]

A related issue, and one perennially discussed in the 'sinking state' context, is the *en masse* relocation of a state's population to another country. Both Kiribati and Tuvalu have raised this on occasion with Australia and New Zealand,[105] but most recently, and most vocally, it has been embraced by the President of the Maldives who, on coming to office, boldly stated that he was seeking to purchase land in India or Australia to which to relocate his nation.[106] Subsequently, although it is unclear whether this was in direct response, the Indonesian Maritime Minister announced that Indonesia was considering renting out some of its 17,500 islands to 'climate change refugees'.[107]

---

[103] The right to self-determination does not operate so as to give the inhabitants of these states a right to claim land in other states.

[104] UNHCR, 'Climate Change and Statelessness', above n 98, 3; see also R Higgins, *The Development of International Law through the Political Organs of the United Nations* (London, Oxford University Press, 1963) 24. Note that the case of New Iceland in Canada was not a state within a state, as has sometimes been suggested: see, eg Steina Sommerville (nee Stefansson) in *The Interlake News* in 1946, who dubbed New Iceland 'The Twelve Year Republic'; Rayfuse, 'W(h)ither Tuvalu?', above n 11; UN Secretary-General, 'Climate Change and Its Possible Security Ramifications: Report of the Secretary-General' (11 September 2009) UN Doc A/64/350, 21. It was created as an Icelandic 'reserve' by Canadian Order-in-Council No 875 of 8 October 1875 to provide land to Icelandic immigrants who had left considerable environmental degradation (in part from volcanic eruptions) and poverty at home, and was ultimately dissolved by Order-in-Council No 2306 of 9 October 1897. This process of creation and dissolution alone indicates that it was not a sovereign equal of Canada, and historians have consistently emphasised that the settlers had no intention of creating an Icelandic colony: WJ Lindal, *The Icelanders in Canada* (Winnipeg/Ottawa, National Publishers, 1967) 135. This is reflected in an address given on the occasion of the Canadian Governor-General's visit to New Iceland on 14 September 1877: 'We have gathered under the flag of our new land, and as British subjects . . . We accept gladly our new way of life as British subjects with the opportunity to acquire all the freedom and rights which pertain thereto. As British subjects, we desire that these rights be granted to us, and we are firmly resolved to preserve them. We are prepared to do our share in the maintenance of public order, and in the defense of our country, to perform the duties which England expects of every citizen': Address by Friðjón Friðriksson, cited in N Gerrard, ' "A Matter of Honour": The Constitution of New Iceland: Then and Now' (Building a New Relationship Conference, University of Manitoba, 27 October 2000), www.sagapublications.com/articles.html.

[105] See, eg Senate Foreign Affairs, Defence and Trade Committee, *A Pacific Engaged: Australia's Relations with Papua New Guinea and the Island States of the South-West Pacific* (Canberra, Commonwealth of Australia, 2003) para 6.78; author's interviews with Anote Tong, President of Kiribati (12 May 2009); Sir Kamuta Latasi, Speaker of the Tuvaluan Parliament (and former Prime Minister) (27 May 2009). See also B Crouch, 'Tiny Tuvalu in Save Us Plea over Rising Seas', *Sunday Mail* (5 October 2008), www.news.com.au/adelaidenow/story/0,22606,24440703-5006301,00.html.

[106] R Ramesh, 'Paradise Almost Lost: Maldives Seek to Buy a New Homeland', *The Guardian* (10 November 2008), www.guardian.co.uk/environment/2008/nov/10/maldives-climate-change>.

[107] 'Indonesian Islands for Rent', *The Straits Times* (6 May 2009), www.straitstimes.com/Breaking%2BNews/SE%2BAsia/Story/STIStory_373069.html; 'Indonesia Offers Pacific Climate Refugees Island Rental', *Pacific Beat*, Radio Australia (3 June 2009), www.radioaustralia.net.au/pacbeat/stories/200906/s2588395.htm (citing Secretary-General of the Maritime Affairs Ministry, Dr Syamsul Maarif); see also S Holland, 'Indonesia's Rent-an-Island Answer to Climate Change', *ABC News* (3 June 2009), /www.abc.net.au/news/stories/2009/06/03/2588165.htm.

There is much more to relocation than simply securing territory, however. Those who move need to know that they can remain and re-enter the new country, enjoy work rights and health rights there, have access to social security if necessary, be able to maintain their culture and traditions,[108] and also what the status of children born there would be. The acquisition of land alone does not secure immigration or citizenship rights, but is simply a private property transaction.[109] Unless individuals personally acquire such rights (and in some cases, even if they do but retain dual nationality[110]), there is little in international law that would prevent a host country from expelling them should it wish to do so, provided there is another country obliged to admit them. This poses an on-going risk as long as the home state continues to exist. Even if the latter does 'disappear', its relocated citizens would not automatically have the same rights as the nationals of their host country. It is only with formal cession of land at the state-to-state level that one state acquires the lawful international title to it and nationals can move to that area as part of their own national territory. The likelihood of this happening today is remote.[111] Thus, if *en masse* relocation to another country is to be considered as a permanent solution, then issues other than land alone need to be considered in order to provide security for the future.[112]

Even when such legal issues are resolved, relocation may still not be a popular option. As the following example from the Pacific region illustrates, concerns about the maintenance of identity, culture, social practices and land tenure are very real to those whose movement is proposed, and these may not be readily understood by outsiders. This, in turn, may lead to misunderstandings

[108] See, eg 'Report of the Office of the United Nations High Commissioner for Human Rights on the Relationship between Climate Change and Human Rights' (15 January 2009) UN Doc A/HCR/10/61, 17–18; Economic and Social Council, Commission on Human Rights (Sub-Commission on the Promotion and Protection of Human Rights), 'Prevention of Discrimination: Prevention of Discrimination and Protection of Indigenous Peoples' (Expanded working paper by Françoise Hampson on the Human Rights Situation of Indigenous Peoples in States and Other Territories Threatened with Extinction for Environmental Reasons) (16 June 2005), UN Doc E/CN.4/Sub.2/2005/28; S Humphreys (ed), *Human Rights and Climate Change* (Cambridge, Cambridge University Press, 2010).

[109] Examples include the purchase of Rabi island in Fiji by the Banabans (from Kiribati) and the purchase of Kioa island in Fiji by the Vaitupu people of Tuvalu. As Crawford notes in *The Creation of States in International Law*, above n 6, 717, 'the persistent analogy of territorial sovereignty to ownership of real property is misguided', indicating the vastly different functions that state links to territory serve.

[110] For example, Britain can revoke citizenship from nationals (albeit in limited circumstances) if doing so would not render them stateless: British Nationality Act 1981 (as amended in 2002 and 2006), s 40.

[111] Although following the 2010 Haitain earthquake, the African Union was reported to be considering a proposal to create a new state for them in Africa, citing 'a sense of duty and memory and solidarity' given that Haitians are descendants of African slaves: 'African Union to Consider "Land for Haitians" Plan' (31 January 2010), www.reuters.com/assets/print?aid=USTRE60U0IV20100131. Arguably, this is a special case based on historical links.

[112] Furthermore, as Campbell discusses, the ability of states to give away land in itself may raise serious human rights considerations for those already inhabiting (or with claims to) that land: J Campbell, 'Climate-Induced Community Relocation in the Pacific: The Meaning and Importance of Land', in the present volume.

and misguided policies, which can have negative long-term, inter-generational effects.[113]

In the 1960s, as a result of the immense environmental destruction caused by phosphate mining, it was proposed that the population of Nauru be resettled in Australia.[114] Sites were originally investigated in and around Papua New Guinea but they did not meet the three necessary requirements: 'employment opportunities enabling Nauruans to maintain their standard of living; a community which would accept the Nauruans; and willingness and readiness on the part of the Nauruans to mix with the existing people.'[115] On 12 October 1960, the partner governments of Australia, New Zealand and the United Kingdom agreed to offer permanent residence and citizenship in those countries to any Nauruans willing 'to transfer to those countries and . . . likely to be able to adapt themselves to life there'.[116] While Australian government documents state that '[i]t was envisaged that the transfer should take place gradually over a period of 30 or more years and that some material assistance to that end would be given',[117] the Nauruan view was that '[i]t was never envisaged that all Nauruans would take up the offer. Many would stay, and it was understood that Nauru would always remain a spiritual home for those resettled.'[118]

The resettlement offer was rejected by the Nauru Local Government Council on the basis that the very nature of the scheme 'would lead to the assimilation of the Nauruans into the metropolitan communities where they settled'.[119] The Nauruans instead requested an island of their own in a temperate zone, and in 1963 Australia offered them Curtis Island (near Gladstone, Queensland). The Nauruans were to be given freehold title; pastoral, agricultural, fishing and commercial activities were to be established; and 'and the entire costs of resettlement including housing and community services such as electricity, water and sewerage etc would be met out of funds provided by the Governments of Australia, New Zealand and the United Kingdom. It was estimated that the cost would be in the region of 10 million pounds.'[120] While Australia made clear that 'Australian sovereignty would not be surrendered over any mainland or island location',[121] those resettled would 'be enabled to manage their own local administration and to make domestic laws or regulations applicable to

---

[113] See ibid.

[114] Nauru had been a British mandate territory administered on behalf of the League of Nations. In 1919, Australia, the United Kingdom and New Zealand entered into an agreement to jointly control the administration of Nauru, predominantly to facilitate phosphate mining. When the UN's international trusteeship system succeeded the League's mandate system, it became a trust territory of Australia, New Zealand and the United Kingdom (the 'partner governments').

[115] *Case concerning Phosphate Lands in Nauru (Nauru v Australia)* (International Court of Justice) (Preliminary Objections of the Government of Australia) vol 1 (December 1990), para 60.

[116] ibid, para 61, citing Annex 4.

[117] ibid, para 61.

[118] *Case concerning Phosphate Lands in Nauru (Nauru v Australia)* (International Court of Justice) (Written Statement of Nauru), para 19.

[119] Preliminary Objections of the Government of Australia, above n 115, para 61.

[120] ibid, para 63, citing statement by the Australian Minister for Territories (20 August 1964).

[121] ibid, para 62.

their own community', subject to their acceptance of 'the privileges and responsibilities of Australian citizenship'.[122]

Nauru again rejected the offer, deeming these political arrangements unsatisfactory. The Nauruan representatives feared that they would not be able to maintain their distinct identity and would be 'assimilated without trace into the Australian landscape':[123]

> Your terms insisted on our becoming Australians with all that citizenship entails, whereas we wish to remain as a Nauruan people in the fullest sense of the term even if we were resettled on Curtis Island. To owe allegiance to ourselves does not mean that we are coming to your shores to do you harm or become the means whereby harm will be done to you through us. We have tried to assure you of this from the beginning. Your reply has been to the effect that we cannot give such an assurance as future Nauruan leaders and people may not think the same as we do.[124]

Nauruan and Australian perspectives on the issue of relocation reveal quite different approaches as to why it failed. Nauru claimed that resettlement in Australia was offered as a quick-fix solution that would cost the Australians far less than rehabilitating the land.[125] It saw it as 'an attempt to break up the Nauruan identity and their strong personal and spiritual relationship with the island',[126] ignoring Nauruan land tenure laws and 'the right of the Nauruan people at international law to permanent sovereignty over their natural wealth and resources.'[127] The Nauruans maintained that they were never 'seeking full sovereign independence' over Curtis Island, but that 'anything which did not preserve and maintain [their] separate identity was quite unacceptable.'[128] By contrast, the Australian government believed it was making 'a genuine and generous attempt to meet the wishes of the Nauruan people',[129] and regarded the sovereignty issue as the sticking point in negotiations.

---

[122] Trusteeship Council Official Records, 13th session (May/June 1963) UN Doc T/SR.l203-1224, 6, cited in *Case concerning Phosphate Lands in Nauru (Nauru v Australia)* (International Court of Justice) (Memorial of the Republic of Nauru) vol 1 (April 1990), para 169.

[123] Nauru Memorial, above n 122, para 171.

[124] Nauru Talks 1964, 1–2, Annexes, vol 3, Annex 1, cited in ibid.

[125] Written Statement of Nauru, above n 118, para 22. See also para 18: 'Resettlement was simply a *quid pro quo* for depriving the Nauruan community of suitable and productive living space as a consequence of the devastation of their land *(cf,* Nauru *Memorial,* para. 177). It was also, perhaps, a way of avoiding the issue of rehabilitation.'

[126] ibid, para 20.

[127] ibid, para 74.

[128] 'Statement by Hammer DeRoburt, OBE, GCMG, MP, Head Chief, Nauru Local Government Council', Appendix 1 to Nauru Memorial, above n 122, para 21. The issue resurfaced in 2003, when the Australian Foreign Minister, Alexander Downer, was reported as saying that he was considering the resettlement of all Nauruans in Australia, or giving them a vacant island to move to. This was dismissed by the President of Nauru, who again said it would undermine Nauru's identity and culture: K Marks, 'Australia Moots Radical Future for Bankrupt Nauru', *The Independent* (20 December 2003), www.independent.co.uk/news/world/australasia/australia-moots-radical-future-for-bankrupt-nauru-577190.html: 'Mr Downer said Canberra was "very concerned" about the situation in the tiny island state, which is bankrupt and widely regarded as having no viable future. ... He later played down the idea of giving Australian passports to Nauruans and resettling them, observing that other Pacific nations might expect similar treatment.'

[129] UNGA Official Records, 18th Session, 4th Committee, 1513th Meeting (12 December 1963) UN Doc A/C.4/SR.1513, 565, para 4, cited in Nauru Memorial, above n 122, para 170.

Cultural misunderstandings about the importance of land and cultural identity remain at the heart of discussions today about relocating entire Pacific communities in response to climate impacts. While some suggestions to relocate communities are no doubt well-intentioned, there are significant implications of doing so from a top-down approach. As Campbell notes, the effects of dislocation from home can last for generations, and can have significant ramifications for the maintenance and enjoyment of cultural and social rights by resettled communities.[130]

VIII Self-Governing Alternative

Relocation does not, of itself, necessarily preclude claims that the state continues to exist, especially if some of the original population remains in the home state.[131] Indeed, one of the ideas proposed by the President of Kiribati is the establishment of a small government outpost on the state's only high ground, Banaba Island, so as to retain the state and its control over resources, such as those generated by its extensive exclusive economic zone (EEZ).

A more radical alternative, however, would see the deliberate, earlier dissolution of the independent, sovereign state, but with the aim of preserving the 'nation'—as an identifiable national, linguistic and cultural community—for longer.[132] For many Tuvaluans and I-Kiribati, the issues of key importance to them are the retention of 'home'—land, community, identity—rather than preserving the political entity of the state itself.[133] Indeed, a claim to self-determination does not necessarily involve a claim to statehood and secession.[134]

There are a number of ways in which a move away from fully-fledged statehood to a self-governing alternative could be undertaken. For present purposes, the option considered is one based on a well-established model within the Pacific: self-governance in free association with another state. The rationale behind this model is to respect 'the individuality and the cultural characteristics of the territory and its peoples' and give the associated territory 'the right to determine its internal constitution without outside interference',[135] while certain functions (such as

---

[130] Campbell, 'Climate-Induced Community Relocation in the Pacific', above n 112.

[131] Indeed, as Nauru observed about its own negotiations with Australia: 'But Nauru would, at that point, still have remained under Trusteeship. Resettlement would not have granted to Australia or the British Phosphate Commissioners any further title to the land than that which they could claim under the Trusteeship. By the act of resettlement, Nauru was not to be annexed to Australia. As a self-determination unit, the Nauruan community could still seek control in Nauru both politically, through independence, and economically, in respect of the phosphate industry': Written Statement of Nauru, above n 118, para 18.

[132] See generally J Crawford (ed), *The Rights of Peoples* (Oxford, Clarendon Press, 1988).

[133] Author's interview with Tebao Awerika, Ministry of Foreign Affairs in Kiribati (12 May 2009).

[134] I Brownlie, 'The Rights of Peoples in Modern International Law' in Crawford (ed), *The Rights of Peoples*, above n 132, 6.

[135] UNGA Res 1541 (XV) (15 December 1960), Principle VII.

defence) are carried out by another state. Crawford describes association as 'one of the more significant possibilities of self-government communities (especially island communities) that are too small to be economically and politically viable standing alone.'[136] It is also familiar in the Pacific context, being the relationship of the Cook Islands and Niue vis-à-vis New Zealand.[137]

That there is no single concept of self-governance is borne out in the different approaches of Niue and the Cook Islands.[138] The Cook Islands has continually stressed its independence,[139] while Niue has resisted being treated like an independent state[140] (indeed the constitution of Niue commits New Zealand to provide it with 'necessary economic and administrative assistance'). Nonetheless, both are separate administrative entities within the realm of New Zealand—their governments have full executive powers and their parliaments can make their own laws. By agreement, Niueans and Cook Islanders hold New Zealand citizenship (and do not have additional Niuean or Cook Islands citizenship) and can freely enter, live and work in New Zealand (and thus also Australia).[141]

There are historical reasons for this relationship.[142] Given the absence of such strong historical ties with Kiribati and Tuvalu, it is questionable whether New Zealand or Australia would be willing to enter into a similar free association relationship with them. Alternatives such as federation[143] or incorporation[144] might be perceived as more attractive, given the economic benefits that could be gained

---

[136] Crawford, *The Creation of States in International Law*, above n 6, 626.

[137] Crawford writes that the Cook Islands and Niue 'are not States but have some separate international status by virtue of the relevant association agreements': ibid, 492.

[138] The status of associated territories depends on the specific arrangements made, and their implementation: ibid, 632.

[139] 2001 Joint Centenary Declaration of the Principles of the Relationship between the Cook Islands and New Zealand.

[140] See A Quentin-Baxter, 'Niue's Relationship of Free Association with New Zealand' (1999) 30 *Victoria University of Wellington Law Review* 589, 593.

[141] See Cook Islands Constitution Act 1964 (NZ); Niue Constitution Act 1974 (NZ); Constitution of the Cook Islands (Schedule to the Cook Islands Constitution Act); Constitution of Niue (Schedule 2 of the Niue Constitution Act). The 1973 Trans-Tasman Travel Arrangement permits New Zealand citizens to visit, live and work in Australia, and vice versa.

[142] The Cook Islands and Niue are former British protectorates which were annexed as dependent territories by New Zealand at the turn of the twentieth century. Through acts of self-determination overseen by the UN, in 1965 and 1974 respectively their populations chose to become self-governing territories in free association with New Zealand, which is a status distinct from full independence: see respectively UNGA Res 2064 (XX) (16 December 1965); UNGA Res 3285 (XXIX) (13 December 1974).

[143] A federal state is 'a sole person in the eyes of international law': Montevideo Convention on the Rights and Duties of States, Art 2. Federation is not discussed here, since it would require the dissolution of Kiribati or Tuvalu as a state. As a system of political organisation in which a state is comprised of different national groups, Brownlie regards federalism as 'probably better able than any other system to provide a regime of stable autonomy which provides group freedoms within a wider political cosmos and keeps the principle of nationality in line with ideas of mutuality and genuine coexistence of peoples': Brownlie, 'The Rights of Peoples in Modern International Law', above n 134, 6. See further Crawford, *The Creation of States in International Law*, above n 6, 483–89.

[144] This is the basis on which the Cocos (Keeling) Islands joined Australia. Principle IX of the Annex to UNGA Res 1541 (XV) (15 December 1960) assumes that the people of the state that integrates into another should be treated as equal citizens of the integrating state, accorded full citizenship rights and freedom of movement: see Crawford, *The Creation of States in International Law*, above n 6, 624.

by merger, such as control over the extensive EEZs of Kiribati and Tuvalu.[145] In any event, the political likelihood of the Tuvaluan and I-Kiribati populations determining by referendum to move to a self-governance model, let alone to dissolve the state altogether through merger, seems remote in light of how recently independence was obtained.[146]

IX Conclusion: The Boundaries of States, the Boundaries of Law

State practice suggests that there is likely to be a presumption of a state's continuity for some time, even as the legal indicia of statehood begin to wane. However, at some future point this may cease as the objective characteristics of statehood start to recede,[147] and states, unilaterally or collectively, may gradually withdraw their recognition of an entity as a state.[148]

International legal personality is not confined to states, and other entities, such as international organisations, groupings of states, Taiwan and the Sovereign Order of Malta, operate to differing degrees at the international level. While they do not have the same extensive 'full' powers of states to act, they have certain functional powers that enable them to operate at the international level.[149]

If Tuvalu and Kiribati were at some point regarded as having acquired a different kind of international legal personality, other than as a state, then (in the absence

---

[145] See Soons, 'The Effects of a Rising Sea Level', above n 11. Rayfuse, 'W(h)ither Tuvalu?', above n 11, 11 has suggested that conditions of merger could include a requirement that any revenue generated from these territorial acquisitions be placed into a trust fund to pay for the resettlement of the merging state's population (including on-going costs that might normally be borne by the state, such as pensions, although it should be noted that there is very little social security in Kiribati or Tuvalu).

[146] Author's interview with David Lambourne, Solicitor-General of Kiribati (8 May 2009); Tebao Awerika, Ministry of Foreign Affairs in Kiribati (12 May 2009).

[147] Rayfuse, 'W(h)ither Tuvalu?', above n 11, 13 writes: 'in an international community still based on the Westphalian notion of states, it may not be appropriate or realistic to envisage the permanent establishment and continuing existence of deterritorialised states *ad infinitum*. Rather, it may be useful to view this status as transitional, lasting perhaps one generation (30 yrs) or one human lifetime (100 yrs), by which time it is likely that much else in the international legal regime, including the existing law of the sea regime, will have to be reconsidered and reconfigured, in any event.'

[148] Although the better view is that recognition is declaratory, rather than constitutive, of statehood, it is acknowledged that 'the present state of the law makes it possible that different states should act on different views of the application of the law to the same state of facts': DJ Harris, *Cases and Materials on International Law*, 6th edn (London, Sweet and Maxwell, 2004) 145.

[149] It is not certain that small island states such as Kiribati and Tuvalu would ever fall into this category, only because states sometimes continue to recognise statehood even when its criteria 'are only marginally (if at all) complied with': Crawford, *The Creation of States in International Law*, above n 6, 223. This is the case with the state of the Vatican City. The strength and influence of its government, the Holy See, compensates for its very small territory and lack of a permanent population, in the same way that in certain 'failed states', the existence of territory and people compensate for the virtual absence of a government: Crawford, 223. The question is whether, in the absence of a permanent population within a diminishing territory, other states would be prepared to continue to recognise Tuvalu and Kiribati as on-going states or not.

of acquisition of a new nationality) their former nationals could be said to meet the definition of a 'stateless person' in Article 1 of the 1954 Convention relating to the Status of Stateless Persons: people 'not considered as a national by any State under the operation of its law'. This is because in international law, when a state ceases to exist, so does nationality of that state.[150] States parties to the 1954 Convention would thus be obliged to afford former nationals the rights contained within it, including 'as far as possible facilitat[ing] the[ir] assimilation and naturalization'.[151] While this would finally bring those displaced within an existing legal category, it is far from adequate as a means of addressing potential displacement from small island states. It is reactive, rather than proactive; it requires people to leave their homes and be present in the territory of a state party to the Convention in order to claim its benefits; and, in the absence of any status determination procedure for stateless persons, there is no clear means by which those benefits could be accessed.

While there is no simple legal 'solution' to the 'disappearing states' phenomenon and the status of those displaced, it is important to be aware of the human rights implications of certain mooted alternatives, in particular with respect to (and for) individual and community decision-making and choices. Historical examples from the Pacific show that relocation *en masse*, while theoretically a means of maintaining cultural integrity, has been fraught with difficulties in practice and risks being seen as a top-down 'solution' that strips individuals and communities of agency. By contrast, self-governance in free association with another state is an option that would preserve a degree of autonomy and sense of 'nation' and culture for some time, but it is questionable whether this move away from full statehood would presently appeal to recently independent states such as Kiribati and Tuvalu, and, moreover, to potential partner states like Australia and New Zealand.

Paradoxically, planned and staggered migration over time—the solution favoured by Pacific islanders if in situ adaptation to climate change is not possible—may ultimately start to erode longer-term claims to continued sovereignty and statehood, since the state's 'disappearance' may begin once the bulk of the permanent population has moved abroad and obtained a legal status in a new country (either through naturalisation or by being born a citizen there). Additionally, though the 'population' criterion of statehood does not require that a majority of nationals live within the state's territory, a substantial loss of population would start to erode the effectiveness of the state's government as its economic base declined. However, it seems to be the option that will offer individuals and households the most choice about when to move, and which will afford them the opportunity to establish 'pockets' of their communities abroad which others can join over time. It also enables potential host states to better plan for inward-movement and develop culturally sensitive policies towards those migrants, rather than trying to spontaneously accommodate people who do not easily fit existing legal categories.

---

[150] As Weis, *Nationality and Statelessness in International Law*, above n 86, 136 notes: 'In the case of universal succession, the predecessor State is extinguished and its nationality ceases to exist. All persons who were nationals of the predecessor State cease to be such.'

[151] 1954 Convention, Art 32.

7

Protecting People Displaced by Climate Change: Some Conceptual Challenges

ROGER ZETTER

I Introduction

Migration, and especially forced displacement, places substantial pressure on the ways in which the human rights of people on the move might be safeguarded. Recognising these special claims, a substantial body of international and domestic law and norms has been developed over the last six decades to protect the human, civil, political and social rights of different migrant categories—such as refugees, internally displaced persons (IDPs), and those who are trafficked. There is growing awareness that climate change will have significant displacement impacts: rising sea levels will potentially force large numbers to migrate, while desertification will also have migratory impacts (although these are less clear-cut). With increasing concern about environmental migration resulting from climate change, the question arises whether the rights of those who are displaced might also demand specific forms of legal protection. This chapter addresses the conceptual challenges which this question raises, specifically in relation to climate change-induced migration.

The chapter is divided into two main parts. First, the chapter sets the context by briefly narrating the recent history of legal and normative frameworks of rights protection for different categories of migrants that has unfolded in the international domain over the last few decades. Conclusions are drawn on the general principles and how they might inform the case of people displaced by climate change. In the second, and main, part the chapter explores the conceptual challenges that arise in extending to migrants, who are displaced by climate change, the principles of rights protection that exist for these other designated categories of displaced people. Presenting first the opportunities, but also the conceptual limitations, of applying existing legal instruments and frameworks, the analysis then reveals broader challenges: these concern issues of causality and the extent to which climate change 'forces' displacement and, using the discourse of moral philosophy, the conceptual challenge in determining the locus of accountability and responsibility for protection. Consideration is also given to the rights of the much larger number of people who seem likely to be affected by climate change but who do not, or cannot, migrate. Low-income and developing countries constitute the focus of the discussion because this is where the migratory impacts of climate change are likely to be most severe and the resources for mitigation, adaptation and protection most constrained.

Concern about the migratory impacts of climate change has been long-standing, and rights protection is one of many social, political and economic challenges posed by this newly perceived form of migration—new in the sense of recognising the anthropogenic drivers of climate change which induce migration. An Inter-Agency Standing Committee (IASC) Working Paper observed that: 'Neither the UN Framework Convention on Climate Change, nor its Kyoto Protocol, includes any provisions concerning specific assistance or protection for those who will be directly affected by the effects of climate change.'[1] Whether these instruments can appropriately address protection needs is widely debated. The focus of this chapter is on the substantial lacuna in responding to the *rights-based implications*, pointed out by the IASC (and reports of other international agencies and advocacy groups),[2] a lacuna all the more pressing after the failure to reach agreement to address the fundamentals of climate change impacts, including migration, at Copenhagen in December 2009.

II Setting the Context: Involuntary Migration and Rights Protection

Rights-based concerns are driven by the need to offer protection to people whose livelihoods will be depleted or destroyed by the climate-induced environmental changes which impel them to migrate. The starting point to explore the issue of rights protection is the 1948 Universal Declaration of Human Rights (UDHR).[3] Providing a general, and non-binding, framework to promote and protect human rights, including those of migrants (although these are largely implicit in the UDHR), the UDHR's aspirations have been found to be inadequate to deal with specific conditions and different categories of migrant peoples. In particular, they have been deemed insufficient to protect migrants who are perceived to be 'forcibly' displaced rather than those who move voluntarily. Thus, over the last 60 years the

---

[1] Inter-Agency Standing Committee (IASC), 'Climate Change, Migration and Displacement: Who Will Be Affected?' (Working paper submitted by the informal group on Migration/Displacement and Climate Change of the IASC, 31 October 2008), http://unfccc.int/resource/docs/2008/smsn/igo/022.pdf.

[2] In terms of advocacy for the link between climate change and human rights, see, eg International Council on Human Rights Policy, *Climate Change and Human Rights: A Rough Guide* (Versoix, International Council on Human Rights Policy, 2008). Likewise, the UN Human Rights Council passed a resolution in 2009 on 'Human Rights and Climate Change', Human Rights Council Res 10/4 (25 March 2009).

[3] Universal Declaration of Human Rights (adopted 10 December 1948) UNGA Res 217A (III).

international community has responded by developing a 'portfolio' of protection instruments in international law, through treaties and other normative frameworks, to tackle the perceived threats to the human rights of a diverse range of social groups whose migration is determined to be involuntary. These initiatives have been elaborated and further developed through regional and domestic instruments, such that the protection of the rights of displaced people, especially where migration is 'forced' rather than voluntary, is now well established, both as a concept and through legal instruments and norms. Whereas this aspect is covered in more detail in the chapter by Walter Kälin, the aim of the present chapter is to provide an overview of the instruments, with a view to concluding with some general principles which underpin the conceptual discussion which follows in the next section.

At the core of this framework are the 1951 Convention relating to the Status of Refugees and its 1967 Protocol,[4] which deal with the protection of refugees: those with a well-founded fear of persecution on account of their race, religion, nationality, political opinion or membership of a particular social group. In two regional contexts, the refugee definition has been elaborated upon to extend protection to additional groups of people. The two principal regional instruments—the Organization of African Unity (OAU) Convention and the Cartagena Declaration—in addition to protecting Convention refugees, adopt a broader interpretation of the causes for people fleeing and thus their protection needs.[5] Given the widespread use of the term 'environmental refugees' to describe those displaced by climate change and other environmental hazards, the Refugee Convention and related instruments merit particular investigation, conducted in the next section.

The refugee instruments mentioned above apply to people who have crossed an international border. By contrast, the 1998 Guiding Principles on Internal Displacement, which are themselves non-binding but draw on binding principles of refugee, human rights and international humanitarian law, set out principles of protection for certain forced migrants who are internally displaced. The Guiding Principles are elaborated by other frameworks, such as the IASC Operational Guidelines and National Guidelines.[6] In 2009, in an innovative regional application of the Guiding Principles, the African Union (the renamed OAU) innovatively adopted a treaty on internal displacement.[7] Significantly, the Guiding Principles

[4] Convention relating to the Status of Refugees (adopted 28 July 1951, entered into force 22 April 1954) 189 UNTS 137, read in conjunction with the Protocol relating to the Status of Refugees (adopted 31 January 1967, entered into force 4 October 1967) 606 UNTS 267 (together 'Refugee Convention').

[5] Organization of African Unity Convention Governing the Specific Aspects of Refugee Problems in Africa (adopted 10 September 1969, entered into force 20 June 1974) 1001 UNTS 45; Cartagena Declaration on Refugees (22 November 1984) in Organization of American States in Annual Report of the Inter-American Commission on Human Rights (1984–85) OAS Doc OEA/Ser.L/V/II.66/doc.10, rev. 1, 190–93.

[6] *Protecting Persons Affected by Natural Disasters: IASC Operational Guidelines on Human Rights and Natural Disasters* (Washington DC, Brookings-Bern Project on Internal Displacement, 2006); Brookings-Bern, *Protecting Internally Displaced Persons: A Manual for Law and Policy Makers*, (Washington DC, Brookings-Bern Project on Internal Displacement, 2008); W Kälin, 'Conceptualising Climate-Induced Displacement', in the present volume.

[7] African Union Convention for the Protection and Assistance of Internally Displaced Persons in Africa (adopted 22 October 2009, not yet in force) ('Kampala Convention').

extend to include those displaced by disasters and conflict.[8] This broader interpretation of forced displacement, and the fact that probably most of those displaced by climate change will remain in their own countries, suggest that the potential to extend the Guiding Principles further to include those displaced by climate change also merits further investigation, which is provided in the main part of the chapter.

The provisions of the 1954 Convention relating to Stateless Persons, the 1961 Convention on the Reduction of Statelessness, as well as the 1990 International Convention on the Protection of the Rights of All Migrant Workers and Members of Their Families, provide examples of protection instruments for other specific categories of migrants whose potential vulnerability places the defence of their rights at risk.[9] As regards the former, statelessness may well apply to the inhabitants of island states that may eventually disappear with rising sea levels.[10]

Concern for the rights of indigenous and mobile peoples, whose livelihoods and cultural identity are increasingly impacted by involuntary or forced displacement, has resulted in the elaboration of principles for enhanced protection such as the 1991 ILO Convention 169 on the Rights of Indigenous People and the 2002 Dana Declaration on Mobile Peoples and Conservation,[11] which together provided the momentum for the 2007 UN Declaration on the Rights of Indigenous Peoples.[12] These instruments have extended protection norms to yet another specific category of migrant. In this case, though, it is in the more general sense of measures to conserve attributes of culture and livelihood which national governments, in countries where mobile peoples reside or migrate, are recommended to adopt. While exemplifying the general argument of this section—that the international community increasingly designates different categories of involuntary migrants for different forms of protection—it also serves to remind us that forced displacement can cause devastating loss of livelihood which will certainly be a major attribute of climate change-induced displacement.

Another category of forcibly displaced people is those whose land and property is acquired because of development carried out by governments and public sector agencies.[13] The right of eminent domain and compensation exists in most coun-

---

[8] Guiding Principles on Internal Displacement, UN Doc E/CN.4/1998/53/Add.2 (11 February 1998).

[9] See respectively, Convention relating to the Status of Stateless Persons (adopted 28 September 1954, entered into force 6 June 1960) 360 UNTS 117; Convention on the Reduction of Statelessness (adopted 30 August 1961, entered into force 13 December 1975) 989 UNTS 175; International Convention on the Protection of the Rights of All Migrant Workers and Members of Their Families (adopted 18 December 1990, entered into force 1 July 2003) 2220 UNTS 93.

[10] See J McAdam, ' "Disappearing States", Statelessness and the Boundaries of International Law', in the present volume.

[11] Convention concerning Indigenous and Tribal Peoples in Independent Countries (ILO No 169), 72 *ILO Official Bulletin* 59 (adopted 27 June 1989, entered into force 5 September 1991). The 2002 Dana Declaration on Mobile Peoples and Conservation (www.danadeclaration.org/) is not legally binding but has been a valuable advocacy tool in highlighting the vulnerability of mobile peoples.

[12] United Nations Declaration on the Rights of Indigenous Peoples (adopted 13 September 2007), UNGA Res A/RES/61/295.

[13] MM Cernea and C McDowell (eds), *Risks and Reconstruction: Experiences of Resettlers and Refugees* (Washington DC, World Bank, 2000); C de Wet (ed), *Development-Induced Displacement:*

tries. But in the developing world, the rights of resettlement as a form of property restitution for those displaced by development, for example by large public-sector government projects such as infrastructure and dam construction, has historically been poorly safeguarded. More recently, policy and practice has attempted to anticipate, and thus compensate, to some degree, the projected negative impacts on livelihoods and the destruction of the socio-economic fabric of communities caused by large-scale development projects. International treaties specifically relating to development-induced displacement do not exist, however. Instead, over the last two decades or so, a framework of norms has been developed, largely pioneered by the World Bank and taken up by other donors. The analytical tools of 'development-induced displacement and resettlement' (DIDR) and the Impoverishment Risks and Recovery (IRR) model seek to provide a comprehensive framework for the appraisal of losses and the implementation of resettlement policies and instruments for those directly and permanently displaced by large-scale development projects in both rural and urban areas. Introducing the right of resettlement, through these initiatives, has considerable relevance in the present context since, although the cause of displacement is quite different, the resettlement needs of those displaced by climate change will present major logistical and political challenges for governments and donors, for which the DIDR and IRR models may offer some experience.

For the most part, all the instruments and norms mentioned above are reactive, dealing not with the root causes and 'drivers' of migration but with the consequences for people who have been forcibly displaced. By contrast, conventions dealing with human trafficking (another designated category of forced migrant), a matter of increasing international concern, are more proactive, in that their primary objective is to prevent the process of involuntary migration perpetrated by human trafficking and traffickers, as well as dealing with the victims of trafficking. The adoption in 2000 of the Palermo Protocols to the UN Convention against Transnational Organized Crime illustrates this shift of emphasis to the factors driving involuntary migration (the traffickers), as much as the migrant victims of it.[14] Clearly, it is a false premise to compare the involuntary migration of trafficking with that of people compelled to move because of the impacts of climate change. Nevertheless, the general relevance of this point in the present context is that the UN Framework Convention on Climate Change also attempted to deal proactively with root causes—through mitigation and adaptation—as much as the consequences for individuals.[15] For the time being there will be no extension of the

Problems, Policies and People (New York, Berghahn Books, 2006); C McDowell (ed), *Understanding Impoverishment: The Consequences of Development-Induced Displacement* (Oxford, Berghahn Books, 1996).

[14] Protocol to Prevent, Suppress and Punish Trafficking in Persons, Especially Women and Children (adopted 15 November 2000, entered into force 25 December 2003) UNGA Res 55/25; Protocol against the Smuggling of Migrants by Land, Sea and Air (adopted 15 November 2000, entered into force 28 January 2004) UNGA Res 55/25.

[15] United Nations Framework Convention on Climate Change (adopted 9 May 1992, entered into force 21 March 1993) 1771 UNTS 107 ('UNFCCC').

UNFCCC, post-Copenhagen, let alone more specific action with respect to migration. Yet, the principle of a proactive engagement with the root causes of involuntary migration is established and may provide a platform for future developments.

Finally, there are additional international human rights instruments concerned with other social groups, although not specifically related to migrants. Nevertheless, they provide additional forms of protection by virtue of the fact that they apply to all human beings and could be invoked to provide added rights protection for people facing involuntary migration caused by climate change. Here, specialised instruments such as the 1989 Convention on the Rights of the Child and the 1979 Convention on the Elimination of All Forms of Discrimination against Women sit alongside the more general human rights treaties, such as the 1966 International Convenant on Civil and Political Rights and the 1966 International Covenant on Economic, Social and Cultural Rights.[16]

Taking stock of all these legal instruments, five conclusions can be drawn. First, human rights protection in the context of involuntary displacement is a longstanding, accepted and, indeed, an expanding concept which is embedded in the responsibilities of states and other international actors. In theory, therefore, a plausible argument could be made to extend this notion to those who are involuntarily displaced by climate change.

Secondly, existing protection 'machinery' does not, in general, deal with the drivers of displacement.[17] To do so would frequently question the role of state actors and thus impinge on issues of sovereignty. Rather, it deals with the consequences, in terms of specific, affected groups that are deemed to have been forcibly displaced. This issue is of particular relevance in attributing a migratory 'force' to changing climatic conditions, the so-called environmental drivers, which will be discussed in detail in the next section.

Thirdly, many of the human rights instruments discussed so far are designed to deal with the consequences of rapid-onset, extreme events, such as conflicts and disasters, where the causes which lead to displacement are relatively clear. By contrast, the salient characteristic of many climate-induced changes to environmental conditions, which may then precipitate migration, is their slow onset. As we shall see, this poses significant challenges in trying to attribute causation.

Fourthly, loss of livelihood attributable to involuntary displacement and the right to some form of restitution through resettlement is a significant, if relatively rare, feature of the protection discourse. Yet it will be an issue of immense significance in the case of displacement caused by climate change.

Finally, lying behind these frameworks of rights protection is the concern that forced migration should not diminish the human agency of the migrants. Indeed,

---

[16] Convention on the Rights of the Child (adopted 20 November 1989, entered into force 2 September 1990) 1577 UNTS 3; Convention on the Elimination of All Forms of Discrimination against Women (adopted 18 December 1979, entered into force 3 September 1981) 1249 UNTS 13; International Covenant on Civil and Political Rights (adopted 16 December 1966, entered into force 23 March 1976) 999 UNTS 171; International Covenant on Economic, Social and Cultural Rights (adopted 16 December 1966, entered into force 3 January 1976) 993 UNTS 3.

[17] The exception here is the case of trafficking, discussed above.

contemporary migration theory, even in the case of manifestly forced migrants, argues that human agency can play a central role in the migration process.[18] Again, this conclusion has significant implications when we turn to consider the case of migrants displaced by climate change.

It is within this context that the call to consider the protection of people's rights in relation to climate-induced displacement is now a pressing issue. Among the significant dimensions of this challenge, two predominate: the global nature of climate change, and thus the volume and spatial distribution of the migration which this might produce; and the fact that human agency is unquestionably at the centre of climate change and, therefore, the migratory outcomes.

III The Conceptual Challenges

The issue of what forms of protection currently exist for environmentally displaced people and, perhaps more importantly, what norms and instruments might be needed to deal with the potential migratory consequences, has begun to inform the climate change agenda in a variety of fora and has become the concern of a number of international actors.[19] But beyond acknowledging the problem, there has been little systematic inquiry into either the conceptual challenges this migration poses or the norms and legal frameworks that might be appropriate to address the protection challenges.[20]

With these considerations in mind, the chapter now turns to its core concern. This is to confront four conceptual challenges which underlie any attempt to develop rights-based protection for people displaced by the effects of climate change.

A Climate Change, Environmental Change and Migration: The Issue of Causality

The evidence that climate change can generate vulnerable, and potentially mobile, populations focuses attention on trying to identify the volume, socio-economic categories and distribution of people who might be displaced. Accordingly, developing

---

[18] S Castles, 'Towards a Sociology of Forced Migration and Social Transformation' (2003) 37 *Sociology* 13.

[19] See, eg IASC, *Humanitarian Action and Climate Change* (IASC Principals Meeting, Geneva, April 2008); IASC, 'Climate Change, Migration and Displacement', above n 1; O Brown, *Migration and Climate Change* (Geneva, IOM Migration Research Series No 31, 2008); European Council, 'Climate Change and International Security' (Paper from the High Representative and the European Commission to the European Council, Brussels, 14 March 2008) S113/08; Christian Aid, *Human Tide: The Real Migration Crisis* (May 2007); VO Kolmannskog, *Future Floods of Refugees: A Comment on Climate Change, Conflict and Forced Migration* (Oslo, Norwegian Refugee Council, 2008).

[20] Kälin, above n 6.

viable protection solutions to their insecurity requires the identification of links between climate change, subsequent changes to environmental conditions and the propensity to migrate.

There are substantial conceptual and empirical problems in identifying this cause–effect link, and the extent to which the linkage is direct. There is some difficulty in isolating climate change impacts from other environmental impacts that might cause migration but in which climate change is not a factor (for example in some cases of land degradation). We should be cautious in attributing every negative environmental condition to climate change.

Even where climate change plays a part in environmental change, empirical evidence points to the difficulty of disaggregating changes to environmental conditions from the underlying socio-economic and political processes which might produce migration. Not only do these processes themselves produce changes to the environment, but through their differential generation of vulnerability they also mediate the potential for a migratory response.[21] Thus, the decision to migrate has to be situated in this complex array of variables where the direct impacts of changing environmental conditions on economic livelihoods may be less significant than subsequent indirect impacts and broader social forces.[22]

A secondary consideration, if indeed a causal link can be established between climate change and involuntary displacement, is the time period over which change takes place, the extent to which it is progressive and thus the nature of the migratory process. For example, there is substantial evidence to show that communities adapt to relatively short-term variations in climatic conditions, such as drought, through periodic but temporary migration. But if we consider climate change in terms of irreversible, slow-onset change over an extended period, then this has rather different implications for the volume and permanency of migration, and thus the objectives and form of protection measures.

These concerns apply particularly to slow-onset desertification. However, with respect to the impact of rising sea levels, establishing causality between climate change, rising sea levels and migration is less problematic than in the case of desertification.[23] Rather, the challenge here lies in predicting the time period over which

---

[21] J Belcher and F Bates, 'Aftermath of Natural Disasters: Coping through Residential Mobility' (1983) 7 *Disasters* 118; M de Bruijn and H van Dijk, 'Changing Population Mobility in West Africa: Fulbe Pastoralists in Central and South Mali' (2003) 102 *African Affairs* 285; K Hampshire and S Randall, 'Seasonal Labour Migration Strategies in the Sahel: Coping with Poverty or Optimising Security?' (1999) 5 *International Journal of Population Geography* 367.

[22] Hampshire and Randall, 'Seasonal Labour Migration Strategies in the Sahel', above n 21.

[23] Current understanding of global warming indicates that a 2°C rise in average global temperatures by 2100 will lead to a 1.4 metre sea level rise. A one metre rise will put over 145 million people at risk. The estimated global population in low-elevation coastal zones is 634 million: see G McGranahan, A Balk and B Anderson, 'The Rising Tides: Assessing the Risks of Climate Change and Human Settlements in Low Elevation Coastal Zones' in J Bicknell, D Dodman and D Satterthwaite (eds), *Adapting Cities to Climate Change: Understanding and Addressing the Development Challenges* (London, Earthscan, 2009). Low-elevation coastal zones are defined as land up to 10 metres above sea level. This is substantially higher than the Intergovernmental Panel on Climate Change's 1990 prediction that sea levels would rise by 39 centimetres by 2080, and gives some indication of the scale of population which might be affected, especially by rising sea levels, flooding and storm surges (especially if the ice caps

rising sea levels will have an impact. Even in the case of rising sea levels, current evidence on migration is muted.[24]

Thus, while it could be suggested that climate change impacts should be distinguished from other processes of environmental change, it is clear that the interrelatedness of climate change, general changes in environmental conditions and socio-economic factors which underpin decisions to migrate, make it particularly challenging to invoke some form of legal protection for the rights of people who migrate because of negative changes to their environments solely induced by climate change. Significantly, many authors do not specifically identify climate-induced change in their definitions of what they term environmental migrants,[25] invoking instead depletion of environmental conditions. The International Organization for Migration (IOM) defines 'environmental migrants' as 'persons or [a] group of persons who, for compelling reasons of sudden or progressive changes in the environment that adversely affect their lives or living conditions, are obliged to leave their habitual homes, or choose to do so, either temporarily or permanently, and who move either within their country or abroad'.[26] In an otherwise nuanced definition, even here the IOM only implicitly refers to climate change, by using the classic distinction which climate change experts make between rapid and slow-onset environmental change.

The intention of this discussion is not to downplay the importance of climate change in inducing or compelling the decision to migrate. Instead, it is necessary to appreciate that whilst climate change may be one, albeit highly significant, variable which produces involuntary migration, this must be set within a wider context of social, economic and political factors, as well as other changes to environmental conditions, that underpin the reasons why people migrate.[27]

The complex role which climate-induced change plays in the migration process does not diminish the claim for human rights protection. However, it poses challenging circumstances for the design and application of such protection.

melt at a faster rate than predicted in 1990): Intergovernmental Panel on Climate Change, *First Assessment Report: Scientific Assessment of Climate Change: Report of Working Group I* (Cambridge, Cambridge University Press, 1990).

[24] See J McAdam and M Loughry, 'We Aren't Refugees', *Inside Story* (30 June 2009), http://inside.org.au/we-arent-refugees/.

[25] N Myers, 'Environmental Refugees: An Emergent Security Issue' (Paper presented to 13th Economic Forum, Prague, 23–27 May 2005), www.osce.org/documents/eea/2005/05/14488_en.pdf; A Lopez, 'The Protection of Environmentally-Displaced Persons in International Law' (2007) 37 *Environmental Law Review* 365.

[26] IOM, 'Expert Seminar: Migration and the Environment' (Geneva, International Dialogue on Migration No 10, 2008).

[27] Research evidence confirms multi-causal explanations of migration over the mono-causal impact of changing environmental conditions: see, eg S Castles, 'Environmental Change and Forced Migration: Making Sense of the Debate', *New Issues in Refugee Research*, Working Paper No 70 (Geneva, UNHCR, 2002); S Lonergan, 'The Role of Environmental Degradation in Population Displacement' (1998) 4 *Environmental Change and Security Program Report* 5; S Lee, *Environment Matters: Conflict, Refugees and International Relations* (Tokyo, World Human Development Institute Press, 2001); C Boano, R Zetter and T Morris, 'Environmentally Displaced People: Understanding the Linkages between Environmental Change, Livelihoods and Forced Migration', Forced Migration Policy Briefing No 1 (Oxford, Refugee Studies Centre, 2008).

Given these difficulties in determining causality, it may be more prudent to adapt existing norms and instruments for protecting migrants, and shape them to incorporate the emerging rights-based challenges posed by climate change. In this way, the problem of agreeing a particular set of causal relationships between climate change, environmental change and migration can be side-stepped, but without diminishing the main objective, which is to protect rights.

B 'Forced' Migration and Climate Change

Can climate change and its environmental impacts be considered to force migration? Is there an existential threat posed by displacement induced by climate change? This question is significant because many of the protection norms and instruments for other migrant categories discussed in the first part of this chapter (such as refugees, the internally displaced and trafficked people) are predicated on notions of force and involuntariness. Indeed, much of the protection apparatus draws its meaning precisely from the fact that it is designed to tackle the abuse or loss or rights brought about by forcible displacement and, ultimately, an existential threat.

Despite the evidence of multi-causality discussed above, there is still a perception amongst some policy-makers and humanitarian actors which asserts that environmental factors 'force' migration. Perhaps disingenuously, some humanitarian agencies have also used this argument, or at least labels such as 'environmental refugee', to denote what they claim to be the irreversible force of changing environmental conditions in precipitating migration.[28] There are situations where climate change will indeed have irreversible impacts on livelihoods, irrespective of socio-economic differences, such that a large volume (or even the total population) of an area will be forced to migrate, if not in the near future then within the next few decades. Rising sea levels, the inundation of small island states, as well as extreme hydro-meteorological hazard events are cases where connections can be made between climate change and migration, links which (at least in the longer term) will exist irrespective of pre-existing socio-economic or environmental conditions.

However, the particular difficulty in making a conclusive argument for forced displacement is that, aside from increasing episodic events, climate change is mainly generating slow-onset, incremental environmental degradation.[29] In these circumstances, and with so many intervening variables, it is less easy to argue that climate change 'compels' or 'forces' displacement. Distinguishing between force and choice is not clear-cut and, in any case, migration cannot be divorced from

---

[28] See, eg Christian Aid, *Human Tide*, above n 19; Kolmannskog, *Future Floods of Refugees*, above n 19; Environmental Justice Foundation, *No Place Like Home: Where Next for Climate Refugees?* (London, Environmental Justice Foundation, 2009).

[29] The arguments in this chapter are mainly based on the impact of changing climate *processes*, rather than climate *events*. Nonetheless, as I have suggested above, even in the case of climate events— the so-called extreme hydro-meteorological events—it is only in the longer term that compulsion will play a part in permanent population displacement.

complex historic and contemporary circumstances, as has been argued above. The challenge here, in developing the machinery of rights protection, lies in distinguishing between who is 'forced', *uniquely*, by changing climatic (and/or environmental conditions), which is the claim made by Myers and others, as opposed to a *combination* of decisive factors including climate and environmental change, which is the argument made by authors such as Black and Castles.[30]

C What Instruments Might Protect People Displaced by Climate Change?

A third conceptual challenge arises with the need to consider the types of norms and legal instruments which might be used to protect the human and other rights of people displaced as a result of climate change. Given the lack of motivation or consensus now, or in the foreseeable future, for a new treaty to provide special forms of protection, recourse to extant instruments discussed in Section II of this chapter may prove to be the only solution.[31] But here we face the challenge of what instruments are available and, more significantly, how applicable they are, since this will be contingent on how we label those displaced by climate change and the different spatial patterns of displacement, whether internal or international.[32]

Populist use of the label 'environmental refugees' echoes the perception of *forced* displacement. Some claim that the 1951 Refugee Convention could (or should) be extended to embrace this newly termed category.[33] Indeed, to highlight this idea even further, a research group in France has drafted a convention on the international status of environmentally displaced persons.[34]

This proposal is problematic for a number of reasons. Climatic and other environmental changes are not persecutory—crucial to the Convention definition—nor do they occur for reason of one of the five Convention grounds.[35] While

---

[30] R Black, 'Environmental Refugees: Myth or Reality?', *New Issues in Refugee Research*, Working Paper No 34 (Geneva, UNHCR, 2001); Castles, 'Environmental Change', above n 27; Myers, 'Environmental Refugees', above n 25.

[31] The failure of the Copenhagen conference to agree binding commitments to mitigate climate change, let alone very modest proposals to address migration issues, is symptomatic of this reluctance.

[32] See further J McAdam, 'Environmental Migration Governance', *University of New South Wales Faculty of Law Research Series*, Working Paper No 1 (2009), http://law.bepress.com/unswwps/flrps09/art1.

[33] Kolmannskog, *Future Floods of Refugees*, above n 19; Christian Aid, *Human Tide*, above n 19; Republic of Maldives Ministry of Environment, Energy and Water, *Report on the First Meeting on Protocol on Environmental Refugees: Recognition of Environmental Refugees in the 1951 Convention and 1967 Protocol relating to the Status of Refugees* (Male, 14–15 August 2006) cited in F Biermann and I Boas, 'Protecting Climate Refugees: The Case for a Global Protocol', *Environment* (November–December 2008), www.environmentmagazine.org/Archives/Back%20Issues/November-December%202008/Biermann-Boas-full.html.

[34] Draft Convention on the International Status of Environmentally-Displaced Persons (CRIDEAU and CRDP, Faculty of Law and Economic Science, University of Limoges) (2008) 4 *Revue Européene de Droit de l'Environnement* 375.

[35] See further J McAdam, 'From Economic Refugees to Climate Refugees?' (2009) 10 *Melbourne Journal of International Law* 579.

predictions of the number of migrants who will be displaced by climate change are highly disputed,[36] a not unreasonable assumption is that the majority of those displaced by the impacts of climate change are unlikely to cross international borders—a third crucial condition on which refugee status is predicated.[37] Fourthly, migration induced by climate change or other environmental factors, even if forced, does not involve state actors—another element of the Convention definition—as opposed to a more general global responsibility for global warming which has caused climate change. Fifthly, the Refugee Convention envisages return home as one of the three durable solutions. This may only rarely, if at all, be possible in the climate-induced displacement context, where rising sea levels and desertification may ultimately preclude this solution. Finally, in an era of resistance towards and deterrence of refugees, seeking to expand the scope of the Refugee Convention to 'climate' or 'environmental refugees' might diminish still further states' responsibilities to protect those who have manifestly fled persecution and implicitly conflict.[38] Furthermore, it seems plausible that with increasing claims, states may be even more inclined to engage in increasingly restrictive interpretations of the Convention, and/or to engage in more extensive non-arrival policies to limit their Convention obligations. That said, several have tentatively begun to make provision for temporary protection of environmental migrants, discussed below.

While persecution is the defining element of refugee status, forced displacement and exile are frequently linked to conflict. Following this contention, the question arises whether conflict over the increasing scarcity of natural resources caused by climate change may lead to exile. Whereas in the 1990s the argument was accepted that scarcity of environmental resources contributed to violent conflicts within states,[39] from a more recent examination of over 30 recent cases of refugee crises, evidence is muted on the environmental resource depletion–conflict–migration nexus.[40] Nevertheless, the fact remains that many of the countries which are likely to be most affected by climate change are also those which have fragile govern-

---

[36] Boano et al, 'Environmentally Displaced People', above n 27.

[37] See generally F Laczko and C Aghazarm (eds), *Migration, Environment and Climate Change: Assessing the Evidence* (Geneva, IOM, 2009).

[38] See generally Castles, above n 27, 10; D Keane, 'The Environmental Causes and Consequences of Migration: A Search for the Meaning of "Environmental Refugees"' (2004) 16 *Georgetown International Environmental Law Review* 209; A Suhrke, 'Environmental Degradation and Population Flows' (1994) 47 *Journal of International Affairs* 437, 492; R Zetter, 'More Labels, Fewer Refugees: Making and Remaking the Refugee Label in an Era of Globalisation' (2007) 20 *Journal of Refugee Studies* 172.

[39] T Homer-Dixon 'On the Threshold: Environmental Changes as Causes of Violent Conflict' (1991) 16(2) *International Security* 76; T Homer-Dixon and V Percival, *Environmental Scarcity and Violent Conflict: Briefing Book* (Toronto, American Association for the Advancement of Science, 1996).

[40] R Reuveny, 'Climate Change-Induced Migration and Violent Conflict' (2007) 26 *Political Geography* 656. Recent evidence from Kenya, though acknowledging the complexity of the relationship, asserts a correlation between the scarcity of natural resources resulting from drought and violent conflict: Conservation Development Centre (CDC), International Institute for Sustainable Development and Saferworld, *Climate Change and Conflict: Lessons From Community Conservancies in Northern Kenya* (Conflict-Sensitive Approaches Report, 2009).

ments and governance. In the present context, issues of security and stability in relation to declining resources therefore cannot be ignored.[41]

Given these conclusions with respect to the Refugee Convention, the conceptual case for adapting the Guiding Principles on Internal Displacement is more compelling,[42] not least because many (and perhaps the majority) of those who are displaced by the impacts of climate change on their environments and livelihoods will remain in their own country. They will therefore fall within the responsibility of their own state to ensure that their human rights are respected in accordance with that state's international and domestic obligations.

The wider interpretation of displacement embodied in the Guiding Principles also opens up a potentially more productive case for their application to the situation of climate change displacement. Here, the issues raised are definitional and operational as much as conceptual. One of the advantages of the Guiding Principles is their recognition of protection needs deriving from the impacts of natural disasters and conflict. While rapid-onset climate change, such as the increased intensity and frequency of extreme weather events, readily fits within the disaster framework, the conception of slow-onset climate change as a disaster has yet to be fully accepted.[43]

Recognition that displacement may be permanent as well as temporary, and thus require resettlement, and also that there are different stages of displacement, are subsequent developments of the Guiding Principles.[44] These developments offer additional scope for protecting the rights and addressing the needs of those who will be displaced by climate change.

Notwithstanding the role which the Guiding Principles might play, there are at least two potential protection gaps. First, they would not cover the displacement of people from island states predicted to eventually disappear with rising sea levels. Their displacement is finite: they will not be able to migrate to higher land or adjoining countries. And although they will be literally 'landless', the question that arises is whether they will be stateless as a matter of law: they will still possess a nationality, and they will be citizens of a state, albeit one that no longer exists. In these circumstances, can the legal and normative protection and rights-based frameworks of the statelessness conventions be extended to this new category?[45]

A second protection gap relates to climate change migrants who cross an international border. They are not IDPs, nor (in the absence of other criteria) are they

---

[41] D Smith and J Vivekananda, *Climate Change, Conflict and Fragility: Understanding the Linkages, Shaping Responses* (London, International Alert, 2009).

[42] IASC, 'Climate Change, Migration and Displacement', above n 1; Kälin, 'Conceptualising Climate-Induced Displacement', above n 6.

[43] See typology developed by W Kälin, 'The Climate Change–Displacement Nexus' (Speech delivered at United Nations Economic and Social Council Panel on Disaster Risk Reduction and Preparedness: Addressing the Humanitarian Consequences of Natural Disasters, New York, 16 July 2008), www.brookings.edu/speeches/2008/0716_climate_change_kalin. aspx; Kälin, 'Conceptualising Climate-Induced Displacement', above n 6.

[44] Brookings-Bern, *Protecting Internally Displaced Persons*, above n 6.

[45] See McAdam, above n 10 for analysis of these questions.

stateless or refugees. They have little, if any, recourse to protection. In such circumstances, finding a remedy depends largely on there being domestic legislation in place in a particular country. For example, countries such as Finland and Sweden have recently adopted immigration provisions that extend subsidiary or temporary protection to certain types of environmentally displaced people, although they do not expressly apply to those displaced by climate change.[46] Nevertheless, this initiative perhaps opens the door to exploring the ways in which other newly conceived categories of involuntary migrants, such as those displaced by climate change, might also be offered some limited forms of protection.

Operationally, too, doubts remain about the capacity of those countries most impacted to be able to implement the Guiding Principles. Weak governance and civil society structures, a lack of resources and, sometimes, a lack of political will, militate against the effective deployment of the Guiding Principles. Strengthening institutional capacity is, therefore, an urgent priority.

D Humanitarian or Restorative Justice?

It can be argued that the impacts of climate change place a moral obligation on society to provide some form of protection for people whose lives are made vulnerable by such change, such as migrants who try to overcome their vulnerability by moving away from the conditions which cause it. Awareness that climate change impacts are irreversible has reinforced these arguments, shifting the focus of protection *to* the needs of the people themselves and *away* from the focus on protecting the environment per se (the latter having dominated the sustainability discourse in recent decades). This significant refocusing of the policy-making discourse raises a third set of conceptual and policy-making challenges: what is the moral imperative for providing protection, what is the locus of such protection, and how should it be discharged?[47]

The moral reasoning for protection rests on two contrasting theories of justice.[48] One argument highlights the *humanitarian* motivation for protecting people who are impacted by climate change: this borrows from mainstream understandings of protection since 1951. The other, and equally compellingly, argument rests on claims for *restorative* justice, which rests on the rationale that some form of compensation is necessary where involuntary displacement, loss of livelihoods and resettlement occur (discussed in the context of DIDR and IRR in the previous section). Both the humanitarian and the restorative positions are underpinned by more recent arguments which cite security concerns as the rationale for providing

---

[46] Aliens Act 2004 (Finland) s 109; Aliens Act 2005 (Sweden) c 4, s 2.

[47] See generally M Conisbee and A Simms, *Environmental Refugees: The Case for Recognition* (London, New Economics Foundation, 2003); D Bell, 'Environmental Refugees: What Rights? Which Duties?' (2004) 10 *Res Publica* 135; Lopez, 'The Protection of Environmentally-Displaced Persons', above n 25.

[48] See P Penz, 'International Ethical Responsibilities to "Climate Change Refugees"', in the present volume.

protection in order to address the links between migration and climate change.[49] These contrasting theories of justice hold significant implications for the locus of responsibility for protection and, by extension, the capacity and the tools to deliver protection.

Evidence for the *humanitarian* case is premised on the notion that displacement is 'forced' by the impacts of environmental change, such as those caused by global warming, combined with the sense that the migrants are vulnerable victims whose actual, or potential, livelihood impoverishment calls for humanitarian action. Moreover, depleted environmental conditions, as a result of climate change, are buttressed by wider 'humanitarian' issues, such as the prevailing conditions of livelihood vulnerability, poverty and 'failed development', as well as fragile governance structures which struggle to protect social, economic and civil rights. These matters fit squarely within the humanitarian domain.

As we have seen, some of the premises on which this migration discourse is based are increasingly challenged. Nevertheless, even if the causal link between climate change and migration remains unproven, there is some empirical evidence from environmental change literature that migrants have tended to be involuntary, and that, moreover, they have tended to be among the more socially and economically marginalised people in their home and host societies.[50] These conditions resonate with the humanitarian case for protection. But, at the same time, they undermine claims for the agency of those who are displaced, while reinforcing the palliative rather than developmental support which still infuses so much humanitarian policy and practice in the more conventional situations of refugee assistance and disaster relief and recovery.

If the case for protection is indeed a 'humanitarian' imperative, then it follows that states are the main duty-bearers, rather than protection being a global obligation. This position replicates the current locus of refugee and IDP protection. Following this line of reasoning, and again replicating the contemporary humanitarian architecture, we would expect the duty to be supported by external, international humanitarian actors.

The fact that those countries most susceptible to the migratory impacts of climate change are the least responsible for the causes of global warming reinforces this conclusion, and segues to the second line of moral reasoning, which poses the challenge of duty-bearers rather differently. Here, the case for a theory of justice is premised on claims for *restorative* justice. This reasoning contends, first of all, that climate change is a global problem and thus the moral burden to address it falls on global society. Secondly, and more specifically, these burdens differ from those

---

[49] KM Campbell (ed), *Climatic Cataclysm: The Foreign Policy and National Security Implications of Climate Change* (Washington DC, Brookings Institution, 2008). See also L Elliott, 'Climate Migration and Climate Migrants: What Threat, Whose Security?', in the present volume.

[50] WN Adger, 'Institutional Adaptation to Environmental Risk under the Transition in Vietnam' (2000) 90 *Annals of the Association of American Geographer* 738; WN Adger, 'Vulnerability' (2006) 16 *Global Environmental Change* 268; SE Findley, 'Does Drought Increase Migration? A Study of Migration from Rural Mali during the 1983–1985 Drought' (1994) 28 *International Migration Review* 539; de Bruijn and van Dyke, 'Changing Population Mobility in West Africa', above n 21.

that exist for other groups of migrants, such as refugees and IDPs, where more local factors are perceived to generate these types of forced migrant. By contrast, the case for restorative justice argues that those countries primarily responsible for causing the global phenomenon of climate change have the main duty and responsibility to develop and finance protection of the rights of those (countries and people, including those who are involuntarily displaced) who are least responsible. This line of reasoning—echoing as it does the North–South burden-sharing refugee assistance arguments of earlier eras—is given added impetus because it is the countries which are least responsible that will suffer the severest impacts, including population displacement.[51] Ironically, the same countries which bear the heaviest responsibility also have the greatest capacity to reduce their own vulnerability, through policies of mitigation and adaptation.

Thus, discharging restorative justice provides a second and rather different argument to support the case for developing protection norms and frameworks. In parallel to the humanitarian argument, the case is contingent on many factors. Not the least of these is the highly politicised issue of whether developed countries are seriously prepared to adopt this responsibility: the evidence to date on emission controls, mitigation and the failure of Copenhagen indicate a poor prognosis. In addition, while an argument based on 'grounds of responsibility' constitutes a morally compelling line of reasoning and could, indeed, both reduce the propensity to migrate and compensate those who do, it will not prevent migration. Indeed, the legacy effect and the irreversibility of climate change, at least for several decades, suggest that substantial population displacement will still occur. In this respect, and while not detracting from rights-based protection measures that directly address the needs of actual and potential migrants, invoking restorative justice is not a substitute for, or an alternative to, mitigation measures and the reduction of carbon emissions.

Despite the impact which climate change will have on migration, even taking the oft-cited but widely disputed figure of 200 million people,[52] the majority of those who are, and will be, affected will not migrate. Different social groups[53]—for example the old, the young, the asset-less and those living in extreme poverty—may lack the resources or be unwilling to migrate in response to the diminution of their environmental resources and livelihoods. Thus, if displacement is to be minimised, then an equally powerful case can be made for extending the argument of restorative justice to those who remain by developing protection norms and instruments to support mitigation and adaptation. This issue is considered below.

These two positions imply different levels of responsibility. Restorative justice in relation to the impacts of climate change indicates a substantial duty and an

---

[51] Conisbee and Simms, *Environmental Refugees*, above n 47; Bell, 'Environmental Refugees', above n 47; International Council on Human Rights Policy, *Climate Change and Human Rights*, above n 2.

[52] See, eg Myers, 'Environmental Refugees', above n 25; also cited by N Stern, *The Economics of Climate Change: The Stern Review* (Cambridge, Cambridge University Press, 2007).

[53] M Pelling and S High, 'Understanding Adaptation: What Can Social Capital Offer Assessments of Adaptive Capacity?' (2005) 15 *Global Environmental Change* 308.

obligation to support measures to protect those who are most impacted, such as the displaced and, potentially, those who remain. This obligation arises because the anthropogenic causes of climate change are clear. By contrast, for the humanitarian case, the notion of the 'humanitarian imperative' implies the same level of moral obligation. However, while moral claims are still present, humanitarianism remains a voluntary and virtuous act of giving, lacking the same level of obligation and accountability.

The argument now shifts to exploring in more detail the locus of responsibility, and, more particularly, the capacities of different actors to provide the protection instruments. From the perspective of migrants themselves, addressing their protection and assistance needs is best conducted at regional, national and local levels. Accordingly, there is a powerful case for ensuring that the adaptation or the development of norms and legal instruments also resides at these levels. Such a view reinforces the current situation where the rights-protection apparatus for both voluntary and involuntary migrants is a duty discharged largely at the national level. By default, as well, the lack of effective international agreement to mitigate climate change, or to create an international treaty body to mediate responsibilities, inevitably reinforces the role of national governments (and international organisations) to protect those displaced by the impacts of climate change on their local environments.

However, this still begs the question: how is the apparatus to be financed, given that the most affected countries are neither mainly responsible for causing climate change and displacement, nor able to resource the implementation of such measures? From the perspective of climate change as a global issue, the locus of responsibility for funding the protection apparatus lies with the developed, carbon-producing countries. In this sense, the principle of restorative justice is the direct responsibility of developing countries: they cannot derogate their responsibility for 'humanitarian' justice, burden-sharing and capacity-building, and they should be expected to discharge their responsibilities by resourcing international and regional protection mechanisms. However, the design and the implementation of the measures needed to mediate migration outcomes and to avert the impacts of climate change must reside at the local level.

Irrespective of which theory of justice is the more compelling, it may be impossible, both theoretically and practically, to protect or compensate people who have been forcibly displaced.[54] The paradigms of resilience, adaptation and sustainability offer one way forward, but effectively mobilising them would require fundamental changes in the way development assistance is provided. More prosaically, experience from the IRR model used to resettle people displaced by development also offers some technical solutions which could be applied to climate change-displaced populations. Here a major challenge would be the scaling up from the thousands displaced by a single location-specific development project, to the hundreds of thousands, if not millions, of people displaced from many different locations by climate change.

---

[54] See Penz, 'International Ethical Responsibilities', above n 48.

The experience of carbon trading points to many of the difficulties which would arise in mobilising a North–South burden-sharing and compensation framework of rights protection and meeting the 'costs' of migration. Indeed, proposals were made, but not taken up, in Copenhagen for a new international environmental migration fund that could provide the financial basis for measures to deal with the impacts of migration from climate change.[55] In some respects this would have extended the poorly-implemented Global Environmental Facility for funding adaptation measures under Article 4 of the UNFCCC. Hence the impetus may well shift back to supporting mitigation measures, such as reducing carbon emissions, to prevent displacement from occurring.[56] On the other hand, to include the issue of migration and rights protection in any international agreement on climate change has the danger of reducing the treatment of affected people to the level of a tradable currency like carbon credits. States might willingly pay to resettle people in order to keep emitting, which would also undermine sustainable mitigation and adaptation measures.

As if to underpin this line of reasoning, which shifts the focus of debate from protection back to mitigation and compensation, there are the security concerns, sometimes tendentiously invoked, in relation to potentially large-scale, inter-regional migration.[57] Despite the lack of empirical evidence to support the large numbers of predicted climate change and other environmental migrants, securitising climate-related migration is nevertheless on the agenda. States' fears that they will be unable to prevent the entry of migrants fleeing such change reinforces the saliency of policies in developed countries to reduce carbon emissions, in the belief that this will reduce the potential for large-scale displacement and the resulting threats to future global security.[58]

IV Conclusions

Climate change substantially influences the way we conceptualise rights protection. This chapter has examined how society's responsibility for protecting the rights of people experiencing some of the most severe impacts of climate change—namely involuntary migration—might be discharged. While at an abstract level a case can be made for affording some form of protection for groups made vulnerable because of migration, this is conceptually problematic.

[55] German Advisory Council on Global Change, *Climate Change as a Security Risk* (London and Sterling, Earthscan, 2008).

[56] Bell, 'Environmental Refugees', above n 47.

[57] Smith and Vivekananda, *Climate Change, Conflict and Fragility*, above n 41. See also CDC et al, *Climate Change and Conflict*, above n 40; Elliott, 'Climate Migration and Climate Migrants' above n 49.

[58] G Baechler, 'Environmental Degradation in the South as a Cause of Armed Conflict' in A Carius and K Lietzmann (eds), *Environmental Change and Security: A European Perspective* (Berlin, Springer, 1999); Reuveny, 'Climate Change-Induced Migration', above n 40; R Reuveny, 'Ecomigration and Violent Conflict: Case Studies and Public Policy Implications'(2008) 36 *Human Ecology* 1.

The chapter has defined this problem in four ways: the manner in which the relationship between climate change, the environment and migration is conceived; the notions of force; the 'labels' and the different geographies of displacement; and the moral justification for affording protection and attributing responsibility. For these reasons, the concern to isolate climate change as a separate driver of migration, rather than as part of a multi-causal nexus of events and processes, limits the way in which these protection needs might be conceptualised because it promotes the claim for a separate category of protection which, as we have seen, is hard to sustain.

Accordingly, these conceptual challenges will be best met through an adaptive approach which builds on the current framework of norms and instruments, in particular the Guiding Principles on Internal Displacement. Retaining the existing locus of the norms and instruments of rights protection that apply in other fields will be much more feasible than developing a new architecture of rights protection. This strategy resonates with the reluctance of states to negotiate new treaties.

However, this strategy is contingent on acceptance that rights protection, in the context of climate change-induced migration, is a global responsibility. This means finding new modalities of sharing the burden of protection between the North and the South, and between sovereign state interests and international frameworks, while always ensuring that people themselves are the focus of protection. Inevitably, those countries and regions most impacted by climate-induced migration have weak governance and civil society structures and are least able, or willing, to protect human rights and security. While the need for protection is clear, the capacity for providing it remains a challenge.

It is also important to recognise that a balance must be struck between protecting the rights of those who move, and protecting the rights of the much larger number who will not migrate but whose environments and livelihoods will be adversely impacted. They may be just as vulnerable precisely because they lack the resources to migrate. Although not the subject of this chapter, protecting the social, economic, human and civil rights of the non-migrants is just as necessary and poses similar conceptual challenges.

A preoccupation with the need to protect assumes that rights will be lost and livelihoods diminished, and that migrants are the passive victims of forces outside their control. This reductionist perspective may mislead us into thinking that migration is the implicit failure of households to adapt. Migration is sometimes a positive strategy by households seeking to diversify risk and reduce vulnerability, rather than a last resort in times of extreme livelihood vulnerability.[59] Protecting the rights of migrants to deploy their agency should be as much an objective of rights protection as the need to safeguard vulnerable people.

---

[59] F Berkes and D Jolly, 'Adapting to Climate Change: Social-Ecological Resilience in a Canadian Western Arctic Community' (2001) 5(2) *Conservation Ecology* 18; K Hussein and J Nelson, 'Sustainable Livelihoods and Livelihood Diversification', Working Paper No 69 (Brighton, Institute of Development Studies, 1998).

Despite the conceptual challenges, upholding and enhancing international and national human rights obligations must play a crucial role in the global response to the displacement effects of climate change. A rights-based approach to protection provides both the means of addressing some of the challenges of migration, as well as averting some of the migratory outcomes. However, environmental change does not undermine rights and security in isolation from the broader conditions of poor governance and poverty. Accordingly, the inclusion of environmental displacement impacts should be located in the wider policy discourse on protection, rights and security.

8

International Ethical Responsibilities to 'Climate Change Refugees'

PETER PENZ*

I Introduction

The purpose of this chapter is to analyse international ethical responsibilities towards those who have been referred to as 'climate change refugees'. To do this, a set of questions is posed. What do we mean by 'climate change refugees'? If this refers to a particular form of forced migrant, is coercion what distinguishes this group from those who are subject to the same pressures but stay? Are the latter not equally subject to coercion? Is coercion the crucial concept here, or is it the simpler concept of harm? Coming then to the central question, what are the international ethical responsibilities of states with respect to those coerced or harmed by climate change impacts? The strategy in this chapter is to find a conception of such responsibilities with appeal across a wide section of ethical perspectives. The chapter explores various articulations of responsibilities, ranging from free movement responsibilities that require states to open their borders, to poverty alleviation responsibilities that require richer states to participate in significant global redistribution, to compensation responsibilities that require greenhouse gas-emitting states to accept responsibility for harm done and to provide compensation, and finally to insurance responsibilities that require states to develop and participate in a global insurance scheme that pays compensation, while collecting premiums in accordance with each state's greenhouse gas emissions. The last of these is recommended as the most satisfactory formulation of international ethical responsibilities to those coerced or harmed by climate change, providing compensation for adaptation, whether by migration or in situ adaptation.

* I thank (i) the Erasmus Mundus programme of the European Union and the Network on Humanitarian Action unit at Universidad Deusto, Bilbao, Spain, for a research stay that allowed me to resume research on this topic; (ii) York University's Social Sciences and Humanities Research Council fund and the Research Committee of the Faculty of Environmental Studies for financing my attendance at the 12th conference of the International Association for the Study of Forced Migration, University of Nicosia, Cyprus, 28 June–2 July 2009, where I was able to present an earlier version of this paper; and (iii) Jennifer McMahon for very diligent and effective research assistance.

II 'Climate Change Refugees'

A term that has emerged in journalistic and civil society circles is 'climate change refugees'. It is a useful point of departure for clarifying the basis for the subsequent discussion of ethical international responsibilities towards those displaced by climate change. It is recognised here that this is a descriptive, not a legal, term. In international law, a 'refugee' is someone who has crossed an international border and has a well-founded fear of persecution.[1] While this definition is now widely accepted, it does not necessarily conform with everyday language use, where the term 'refugees' often refers to people who flee for reasons other than persecution, and even to people who do not cross international borders.[2] I therefore use the term 'refugees' broadly, and acknowledge the much narrower legal definition provided by the Refugee Convention by referring to 'Convention refugees'. The latter has the strong imprint of the conditions and concerns of the 1940s. Since then, these have changed considerably, though not such as to obviate the need for the category of Convention refugees. 'Climate change refugees', on the other hand, do not have a legal status in international law. As a non-legal, or perhaps pre-legal, definition, the term can be taken to refer to those who are forced to move due to the effects of climate change.

That the term 'climate change refugees' is not acceptable to some of those who face the prospect of being displaced by climate change will be set aside for now, for the following reasons.[3] First, it will be shown that to analyse this term conceptually turns out to be productive. Secondly, the crucial concept for international responsibility turns out not to be that of displacement by climate change, but a broader one that refers to all those harmed by climate change. Thirdly, an obvious alternative term, such as 'climate change displaced people', can easily become equally stigmatised, just as 'displaced persons' or 'DPs' was shortly after the Second World War. Finally, more important than avoiding terms that are being stigmatised or given meanings that truncate the complex set of characteristics of the status is, I believe, to challenge such stigmatisation or truncation and insist that victimhood and agency are not mutually exclusive. As a matter of fact, victims such as refugees often have to be exceptional agents, in that they have to make major and often sudden decisions about migration (timing, what to sell, with whom, by what route, by what mode of travel, where to and so on), and they have to be tough, resilient and flexible in carrying out such decisions in conditions of

---

[1] Convention relating to the Status of Refugees (adopted 28 July 1951, entered into force 22 April 1954) 189 UNTS 137, read in conjunction with the Protocol relating to the Status of Refugees (adopted 31 January 1967, entered into force 4 October 1967) 606 UNTS 267 (together 'Refugee Convention').

[2] For example, the German label '*Flüchtling*' was applied to Germans who fled the advancing Red Army at the end of the Second World War and to those evicted from territory transferred to Poland and the Soviet Union at that time.

[3] See further J McAdam and M Loughry, 'We Aren't Refugees', *Inside Story* (30 June 2009), http://inside.org.au/we-arent-refugees/.

danger and adversity. It should not be accepted that refugees are mere passive victims, regardless of how they are displaced.

What distinguishes refugees in general from a wider category of migrants is that they are *forced* to move. That means that there can be war refugees, famine refugees, development refugees and possibly poverty refugees. 'Climate change refugees', then, is simply another category of forced migrant, although there may be overlaps with the others. What is crucial is to clarify what it means to be *forced* to move.

I have argued elsewhere that coercion with respect to migration due to certain pressures by socio-economic development can take three forms.[4] One is direct compulsion, such as evictions, compulsory evacuations and deportations. A second form consists of threats. Convention refugees who flee persecution escape from certain dangers, as do those who flee war, famine, disease and so on. Finally, people can be forced to move by being deprived of necessities and to such an extent that staying is an unreasonable option. If a family's house and crop have been burned down by someone determined to grab that property, that may be sufficient to force the family to leave. No further threat may be needed. Forced migration can thus take the form of compulsion, threat or harm. This conception of forced migration or displacement was developed in relation to socio-economic development, which is largely driven by human intentions, although it does involve unintended side effects.[5]

When it comes to climate change, the whole process of climate change and its effects is a massive, unintended 'side effect'. The above conceptualisation can still be maintained. Most of the impacts of climate change fall under actual harm sufficient to force people to move. People may also move in anticipation of such harm, or the expectation of future recurrence of harm already experienced. In such cases, they move in the face of a certain threat, although an environmental rather than directly human threat. They may also be compelled to move by authorities determined to reduce their exposure to harm. The prohibition by the Sri Lankan government of the reconstruction of houses close to the seashore, following the devastating Indian Ocean Tsunami of 2004, is a relevant example, albeit one relating to an undersea geological event, rather than an atmospheric event.[6]

However, more important for the following discussion is that this conceptualisation of forced migration also serves to make a point crucial to the following argument, namely that the distinction between those who move and those who do

---

[4] P Penz, 'Displacement by Development and Moral Responsibility: A Theoretical Treatment' in F Crépeau et al (eds), *Forced Migration and Global Processes: A View From Refugee Studies* (Lanham, Lexington Books, 2006) 73.

[5] For a more expansive, land-clearance definition of displacement which includes in 'displacement for development' those who leave as a result of uncoerced negotiations, making such displacement voluntary, see P Penz, J Drydyk and P Bose, *Displacement by Development: Ethics, Rights and Responsibilities* (Cambridge, Cambridge University Press, forthcoming 2010).

[6] B Khazai, JC Ingram, G Franco and C Rumbaitis-del Rio, 'Post-Disaster Recovery Dilemmas: Challenges in Balancing Short-Term and Long-Term Needs for Vulnerability Reduction' (2006) 9 *Environmental Science and Policy* 607, 607–8.

not may be overdrawn, at least for the identification of international responsibilities. Two people may experience the same harm from environmental processes that can be attributed to climate change, yet one moves and the other does not. They are subject to the same coercion to move, but one resists it and the other does not. Does the (forced) migration of the latter make a difference to ethical international responsibilities?

III Migration or in situ Adaptation?

Before raising later in this chapter the question whether the countries that are the primary emitters of greenhouse gases have an obligation to admit climate change refugees, I will ask what the needs are of those harmed by climate change. Is their need to migrate to the countries that are primarily responsible for climate change, as arguments for opening the doors of the highly industrialised countries to climate-change refugees imply, or are their needs more diverse?

Of course, one need is the prevention of climate change impacts in the first place. This can consist of primary or secondary prevention. Primary prevention involves the prevention or minimisation of climate change itself, through the reduction of greenhouse gas pollution or through geo-engineering projects that compensate for such pollution, such as by reflecting back a fraction of solar radiation or increasing the capacity to absord greenhouse gases (for example, the carbon-sink capacity of oceans). Secondary prevention is a second line of defence, which prevents or minimises the harm arising from climate change through such things as the construction of dykes and cyclone shelters to deal with an increasing incidence of storms combined with a rise in the sea level, the development of early warning systems, and reservoir, cistern and irrigation projects to counteract aridification. The focus here is on adaptation rather than mitigation. Secondary prevention is part of adaptation. Also part of adaptation, however, is increasing the capacity of affected countries to respond to climate-driven disasters that are not prevented, both by rescuing people and by subsequently rebuilding their homes and livelihoods.

As described, such efforts do not involve migration. However, both preventive adaptation (secondary prevention) and disaster responses may involve migration. That is to say, people may move (or be moved by state authorities) to prevent exposure to disaster, or they may move (or be moved) following a devastation. Movement may also be temporary until reconstruction has reached a certain stage of livability, or it may be permanent. Temporary moves will usually be within countries and typically not far from the place of origin. Permanent migration, however, can vary greatly in distance, depending on where alternative opportunities for home and livelihood are available. Much migration can be expected to be fairly local, such as to the closest city, or further away but still within the country of nationality. Even when border-crossing is involved, it may be within a particular region, such as South East Asia. Not only the distance of migration, but the very choice whether to move or to stay in the original location (or return to it after a temporary move), will depend on alternative opportunities. If the best opportunities are far away (for example, across the Sahara and the Mediterranean) and the resources to migrate and overcome the obstacles involved are available, then that may well be the preferred choice of those affected by climate change. And with a worst-case scenario, such as described in *Climate Wars*,[7] the loss of opportunities may be so radical and widespread in the region that long-distance migration may be the only reasonable option.

Worst-case scenarios aside, long-distance migration is not likely to be the best option for adaptation, especially when first-line responsibility for adaptation is assumed by the states of those harmed by climate change. In choosing the best adaptation option, the costs and benefits (broadly defined) of migrating have to be compared with the costs and benefits of staying or returning and engaging in in situ adaptation. In either case, the need is for covering the costs of adaptation. That applies to individuals as well as states.

IV International Ethical Responsibilities

The management of climate change occurs in the context of international relations. The central principle that governs this system is that of state sovereignty. The external aspect of state sovereignty requires non-interference in other countries. It means in the first instance that cross-border arrangements are determined or governed by consensual relations among states. This principle of sovereignty is integral to international law. International law, however, is also the repository for commitments that states make to each other and which then become binding. Such commitments constitute the corpus of international law.

International law with respect to climate change has primarily focused on mitigation. Little has been developed with respect to adaptation. What is to guide the development of law in this gap? Moreover, if the principle of state sovereignty and other elements in current international law hinder such development, what is to be the basis of a challenge to them? The law can be likened to a stew created from the ingredients of ethical considerations and the process of power politics. While power politics will necessarily shape new law, the lead should be taken by ethical considerations concerning justice. The focus of this chapter is therefore on ethical considerations that should guide the development of international law with respect to global climate change, specifically with respect to adaptation, and migration as a form of adaptation. This is not to say that legal argumentation cannot go beyond what the law currently allows or provides for. Indeed, a case for free

---

[7] G Dyer, *Climate Wars* (Toronto, Random House, 2008).

movement across borders from a legal perspective is made, for example, by Juss.[8]
In this chapter, however, I will focus on arguments made in political theory and
philosophy. Moreover, the focus in this short treatment is on the mainstream discourse in political theory and philosophy on global justice.[9]

The literature relevant here is that on global justice. Contending schools of
thought are represented in it, and different classifications have been employed.
The one that is most relevant here is that which distinguishes between (i) sceptical
realism, (ii) internationalism and (iii) cosmopolitanism.

Sceptical realism stems from the traditionally hegemonic perspective in international relations. It holds that there is no scope for ethics and considerations of
justice in inter-state relations: might is right. The reason given is that there is no
effective enforcement of ethical norms in the state system, and states are left to rely
on themselves to pursue their interests. The absence of an overarching authority,
and the consequent need for self-reliance, mean that states exist in a highly insecure environment, and their security has to come first and thus displaces all
opportunity for ethical considerations. In fact, realists draw the conclusion that
the one ethical consequence is that state leaders have a responsibility not to compromise the interests of their country by pursuing norms of international ethics,
apart from those that also happen to serve the national interest. I will not draw on
this perspective but will simply mention two criticisms as my reasons for doing so.
One criticism is that the empirical claim that the state system involves such a high
level of insecurity that there is no room for ethical considerations without serious
damage to one's country is highly dubious. While there is no doubt that there is a
substantial national interest factor in states' foreign policies, including with
respect to climate change, it would be difficult to explain the whole range of countries' foreign policies, including development assistance and the reduction of
greenhouse gas emissions, strictly in terms of what will maximally serve the
national interest. The second criticism concerns the conception of ethics. Just
because ethical considerations are not backed by effective enforcement does not
negate them in their function of evaluating the status quo and guiding reform. For
these reasons, sceptical realism will be left aside.

A perspective that offers a critique of realism, but maintains its focus on relations among states, is internationalism.[10] Its critique of realism targets the international amoralism of the latter, by focusing on and affirming agreed normative
principles of international order—especially the principle of state sovereignty, but
also other norms of inter-state relations explicitly agreed on through international
treaties, inter governmental institutions, as well as implicitly in the form of inter-
state practice. I am here conflating two perspectives that would normally be

    [8] SS Juss, *International Migration and Global Justice* (Hampshire, Ashgate Publishing, 2006).

    [9] For that reason, relevant literature, such as Jordan and Düvell, which combines political economy
with political philosophy, is not engaged with here. It should be noted, however, that their comparison
of 'nationalist', 'globalist', 'federalist' and 'ethical' perspectives is of potential interest: see B Jordan and
F Düvell, *Migration: The Boundaries of Equality and Justice* (Cambridge, Polity Press, 2003).

    [10] N Dower, *World Ethics: The New Agenda*, 2nd edn (Edinburgh, Edinburgh University Press,
2007) 21.

distinguished, but in the following discussion of international responsibilities this distinction is not important and there is therefore no point in emphasising it. Nevertheless, for the sake of clarity, it needs to be noted that it covers both the 'morality of states'[11] or 'the "society of states" approach',[12] on the one hand, and nationalist ethics, on the other.[13] The former focuses on ethical relations between states. With respect to the latter, it is important to set aside conventional notions of 'nationalism', which tend to adopt a realist position towards international responsibilities. 'Nationalist ethics' in international relations, by contrast, has come to refer to a position more akin to the morality of states. However, instead of focusing on states and their relations among each other, it treats states as instruments of peoples or 'nations', and ethical responsibilities across borders as, in the first instance, referring to relations between nations. Given that the following discussion attends to the relations of states to their own citizenry in only two or three instances, this distinction is not material here.

The third important perspective on global justice is cosmopolitanism. It holds that there are not only relevant ethical values in the international sphere, but that these go beyond merely values regarding the relations between states; rather they consist of ethical relations between people around the world. The relevant moral community is humanity as a whole, and strong cosmopolitanism holds that whatever ethical obligations are recognised within countries should be applied globally. Borders therefore are not fundamental moral demarcation lines, and states are instrumental to the worldwide moral obligations of their citizens. This perspective is important because it informs the starting point for international responsibilities outlined below.

The methodological strategy in this chapter is to explore different conceptions of international responsibilities in terms of internationalism and cosmopolitanism, giving preference to those conceptions of responsibilities that can muster support across both rather than just one. From this vantage point, which is as much political as ethical, a conception of responsibilities recognised by perspectives beyond cosmopolitanism is deemed superior.

The following discussion goes through a sequence of steps, each of which considers a type of responsibility that is potentially applicable to climate change refugees. I begin with what I refer to as 'free movement responsibilities'. This locates the issue of climate-induced displacement within the free movement debate. One argument that has been made against border controls for people is that the right to free movement is a quite basic right of human beings.[14] If such a

---

[11] CR Beitz, *Political Theory and International Relations* (Princeton, Princeton University Press, 1979) 67–123.

[12] S Caney, *Justice Beyond Borders: A Global Political Theory* (Oxford, Oxford University Press, 2005) 10–13.

[13] ibid, 13–15.

[14] This has been argued from a liberal egalitarian perspective by Carens and Goodin, and from a libertarian perspective by Steiner. The argument is not that the right to free movement, including across borders, is indefeasible, but only that normal conditions do not provide reasons to override it: in B Barry and RE Goodin (eds), *Free Movement: Ethical Issues in the Transnational Migration of People*

right stands up to critical scrutiny, it then creates a free movement responsibility for others, including states. The right and responsibility do not apply to climate change refugees exclusively, but they certainly include them. Climate change refugees thus have the right to move out of harm's way, and others, including states, have the responsibility to let them do so.

The next type of responsibility to be considered is what I term 'poverty alleviation responsibilities', which locates climate-induced displacement in the debate about global poverty. Poverty alleviation responsibilities arise from what Pogge has referred to as the 'radical inequality' that gives rise to the acute global poverty we are witnessing.[15] Again, this does not apply exclusively to climate change refugees, but includes them, in two ways. One is that the poor are more prone to being displaced by environmental disasters than those with the resources to avoid or limit such hazards.[16] The other is that those displaced by climate change are typically impoverished in the process. This holds whether those affected flee or not, as it does for the next type of responsibility.

'Compensation responsibilities' are those that arise from one party harming another and incurring responsibilities to the latter as a result. While this kind of responsibility can apply to many kinds of harm, harm from climate change applies specifically to those affected by it, and the responsibilities are thus specifically towards them.

Finally, partly to improve the chances that justifiable responsibilities are actually met, and partly to deal with certain difficulties in the justification and realisation of compensation responsibilities, I add the category of 'insurance responsibilities'. These refer to responsibilities to set up and participate in a global insurance scheme that meets the costs of climate change adaptation.

V Free Movement Responsibilities

The purpose of starting with free movement responsibilities is to locate the climate change issue within the debate about free movement across borders. However, advocacy of free movement remains politically marginal and the rationale for it intellectually contentious.[17] Moreover, it will be shown that free movement

---

and of Money (University Park, The Pennsylvania State University Press, 1992). In that volume, see JH Carens, 'Migration and Morality: A Liberal Egalitarian Perspective', 25; RE Goodin, 'If People Were Money . . .', 7–9; and H Steiner, 'Libertarianism and the Transnational Migration of People', 93–94.

[15] T Pogge, *World Poverty and Human Rights* (Cambridge, Polity Press, 2002) 197–99; T Pogge, 'Real World Justice' in G Brock and D Moellendorf (eds), *Current Debates in Global Justice* (Dordrecht, Springer, 2005) 37.

[16] B Wisner, P Blaikie, T Cannon and I Davis, *At Risk: Natural Hazards, People's Vulnerability, and Disasters*, 2nd edn (London, Routledge, 2004).

[17] The compendium of perspectives by Barry and Goodin (eds), *Free Movement*, above n 14, covered liberal egalitarian, libertarian, Marxist, natural law and international relations realist perspectives, but also brought out at least as much the opposing positions on free movement within these perspectives as among them.

responsibilities would not be adequate to address international responsibilities with respect to climate change and the adaptation option of migration.

The most basic argument for the right to free movement is that, if liberty is to mean anything, it must be that, in addition to security in their sphere of privacy (the home), people can come and go as they believe will serve their interests.[18] Carens has argued that liberal egalitarianism

'entails a deep commitment to freedom of movement as both an important liberty in itself and a prerequisite to other freedoms. Thus the presumption is for free migration and anyone who would defend restrictions faces a heavy burden of proof [in terms of liberty and equality].'[19]

As this position includes crossing borders, it encounters Miller's criticism which is that, even in a liberal society that emphasises freedom, free movement is not an absolute and unconstrained right; rather, it simply needs to be sufficient to meet people's basic interests and usually free movement within countries meets this requirement.[20] Of course, when it comes to low-lying island and archipelago states, like the Maldives, there simply may not be enough room within the state territory to move everyone out of harm's way, so that sufficiency with respect to freedom of movement may actually require crossing borders. Whether this applies also to much more populous delta states such as Bangladesh, Egypt and Vietnam is not clear.[21] Thus, even when the *general* argument for freedom of movement does not encompass border-crossing, the case of displacement by climate change may create a *specific* instance of free movement obligations to permit a particular category of people to move beyond their national territory.

Apart from a basic liberty right to free movement, which is not to be confined by state borders, two further arguments have been made for free movement: one in terms of a basic right to exit a country, implying a corresponding right to enter other states; and the other in terms of a right to freedom of association, including with people on the other side of borders. The symmetry claim in the first argument has been challenged on the ground that associations that have no right to stop someone from leaving do not thereby have an obligation to admit anyone who wishes to

[18] Carens, 'Migration and Morality', above n 14; Goodin, 'If People Were Money . . .', above n 14.

[19] Carens, 'Migration and Morality', above n 14, 25. In his earlier classic article, Carens had not so much taken this particular position as argued that the right to free movement derives from various political theories, specifically libertarianism, utilitarianism and Rawlsian contract theory. As employed by Carens, these are all taken to end up in a cosmopolitan frame. See JH Carens, 'Aliens and Citizens: The Case for Open Borders' (1987) 49 *Review of Politics* 251.

[20] D Miller, *National Responsibility and Global Justice* (Oxford, Oxford University Press, 2007) 204–8.

[21] A 2007 World Bank study of displacement by a rise in sea level indicated that a one metre rise would affect Vietnam to a significant extent, while affecting only one per cent of land in Bangladesh: see S Dasgupta, B Laplante, C Meisner, D Wheeler and J Yan, 'The Impact of Sea Level Rise on Developing Countries: A Comparative Analysis', Policy Research Working Paper No 4136 (Washington DC, World Bank, 2007) However, while Bangladesh has relatively little scope for relocation, Vietnam contains highlands that could offer room for internal migration. How severe climate change ultimately becomes will, in the end, determine how much pressure will be placed on cross-border migration.

enter.[22] A response to the free association claim has been that part of free association is the right not to associate with particular individuals and, more importantly, both inclusion and exclusion arguments based on freedom of association acquire strength only when vital interests are involved, as in intimate associations.[23] That constitutes a case for a right to family reunification rather than for open borders. Carens has also offered two further arguments for free movement. One is that the principle of equality of opportunity requires free movement. The other is that free movement reduces global inequalities.[24] These arguments, however, will be considered in the next section under poverty alleviation responsibilities.

The above arguments for free movement all come from a cosmopolitan framework. However, support for and opposition to unqualified freedom of movement that includes border crossing does not simply coincide with the division of schools of thought in international political theory between cosmopolitanism and its rivals. Criticism also comes from within the cosmopolitan camp. Thus Brian Barry has argued that uncontrolled immigration would not create an overall better world relative to the world that could be created by a substantial transfer of resources to countries whose poverty is driving migration.[25] In particular, cosmopolitans can be as concerned about community protection and self-determination worldwide as about free movement. This in itself is not to say that the latter is in the end unjustifiable, but merely that it is highly contentious. Introducing climate change displacement can add specific admission claims to current Convention refugee claims, but does little to strengthen the controversial argument for free international movement.

At least as important for this ethical analysis as the contentiousness of free movement rights and responsibilities is the inadequacy of free movement to respond to the impacts of climate change and their displacement pressures. As was mentioned previously, cross-border migration is only one adaptation option. The alternatives are migration within countries, and staying at home and engaging in in situ adaptation, whether that is in response to sudden disasters (rebuilding and protective measures) or gradual environmental deterioration (responding to aridification or increasingly irregular rainfall by irrigation and water storage). Simply offering free movement as a way out is to heavily tilt adaptation towards the international migration option. That may not accord with the preferences of the affected population and is likely to be inefficient from a global perspective. It will also be argued below that it is unjust. I therefore turn to an approach to international responsibilities that does not tilt adaptation in favour of migration; namely poverty alleviation.

[22] B Barry, 'The Quest for Consistency: A Sceptical View' in Barry and Goodin (eds), *Free Movement*, above n 14, 283–85.

[23] Miller, *National Responsibility*, above n 20, 209–13.

[24] Carens, 'Migration and Morality', above n 14, 26–28.

[25] Barry, 'The Quest for Consistency', above n 22, 179–83.

VI Poverty Alleviation Responsibilities

What I have in mind with 'poverty alleviation responsibilities' are two kinds of responsibility that could be dealt with separately, but for the sake of simplicity are addressed under a single term. One kind of responsibility is to reduce ethically unacceptable global inequalities. The other is to reduce ethically unacceptable deprivation worldwide. The two are, in fact, drawn together by Pogge's concept of 'radical inequality'. Pogge used it to describe a situation where the poor are very badly off in both absolute and relative terms, but where, although the deprivation is inescapable and affects all aspects of life, it is avoidable, in that alternative institutional arrangements could prevent such deprivation without 'the better-off . . . becoming badly off themselves.'[26]

Climate change refugees can benefit from such responsibilities in two ways. One is that, on the whole, displacement by climate change is likely to affect the poor. It is characteristic of the poor that they do not have the resources to locate themselves in low-risk areas, nor to provide themselves with means to get out of harm's way early.[27] The other way is that those displaced by climate change will normally be impoverished by the process, and many are likely to end up in dire poverty unless compensatory action is taken. Obligations of the global rich to the global poor will thus help both those prone to displacement by climate change, and those actually so displaced. Two points, though, need to be added. First, those harmed by climate change without being impelled or able to move are equally entitled to assistance. Secondly, poverty alleviation responsibilities apply to deprivation in general, whether or not it is caused by climate change. Poverty connected with radical inequality is thus the decisive criterion for such responsibilities, not displacement or climate change.

What is the basis of poverty alleviation responsibilities? Several bases are possible, and I will merely mention four: (i) equality of opportunity as a central principle of liberalism; (ii) the diminishing-marginal-utility argument in utilitarianism that supports strongly egalitarian redistribution; (iii) duties of beneficence under Kantian deontology; and (iv) the difference principle in Rawlsian contract theory which requires institutions to maximise the conditions for the worst-off (once basic liberties are assured). When it comes to global poverty, the crucial question with respect to each of these is whether it applies globally, and not merely within each country. Advocacy of such cosmopolitan applications has come, for example, from Carens for the equal opportunity argument,[28] from Singer for the utilitarian argument,[29] from O'Neill for the Kantian argument,[30] and from Beitz, Pogge and

---

[26] Pogge, 'Real World Justice', above n 15, 37.

[27] Wisner et al, *At Risk*, above n 16, ch 3.

[28] Carens, 'Migration and Morality', above n 14.

[29] P Singer, *Practical Ethics*, 2nd edn (Cambridge, Cambridge University Press, 1993) ch 8.

[30] O O'Neill, *Faces of Hunger: An Essay on Poverty, Justice and Development* (London, HarperCollins, 1986) ch 7.

Moellendorf for the contract-theory argument.[31] This cosmopolitan extension has been challenged for each of them (and in the case of contract theory, the challenge came from Rawls himself). They therefore cannot be presented as some kind of philosophical consensus.

I will neither dismiss such cosmopolitan applications of poverty alleviation responsibilities nor put much weight on them in this discussion of climate change refugees, because my primary concern is with responsibilities that arise from doing harm. I therefore acknowledge the importance of such arguments, together with that of the rough convergence of such arguments regarding international action—namely to reduce global inequality and poverty—but will follow Pogge's argumentative strategy of moving on to the claims based on harm.[32] I do so for two reasons: (i) the hope that this is a more persuasive argument, thus agreeing with Pogge; and (ii) the more consensual basis that climate change provides for such obligations than Pogge's radical inequality argument.

VII Compensation Responsibilities

A focus on harm and its implications for justice becomes particularly important since the cosmopolitan distributive justice argument regarding worldwide deprivation has not been successful so far in shaping international practices and institutions. The meagre amounts of humanitarian and development assistance, relative to the extent of deprivation and the affluence of donor countries, do not come close to the amounts that various forms of this argument require. Consequently, I follow Pogge's strategy of turning from arguments framed as positive duties or responsibilities (in terms of what the globally privileged owe the globally disadvantaged) to negative responsibilities (in terms of avoiding harm and, when it is inflicted, providing compensation for it).[33] With respect to climate change, the 'harm' is the damaging consequences of climate change.

Where this harm is not avoided, compensation is required. The principle of compensation for harm has very wide acceptance across societies and political and legal systems. Does it also apply internationally? For cosmopolitans, the relevant scope of responsibilities is the world population. There will be no difference in responsibilities to those harmed whether they are compatriots or people living on the other side of the planet. That position does not hold for internationalists, to whom sovereignty and borders remain important. From their perspective, what is to be noted about the principle of state sovereignty is that it was designed to make

[31] See respectively Beitz, *Political Theory*, above n 11, 127–53; Pogge, *World Poverty and Human Rights*, above n 15, 197–99; Pogge, 'Real World Justice', above n 15, 104–8; D Moellendorf, *Cosmopolitan Justice* (Boulder, Westview Press, 2002) ch 4.

[32] Pogge, *World Poverty and Human Rights*, above n 15; Pogge, 'Real World Justice', above n 15.

[33] Pogge, *World Poverty and Human Rights*, above n 15, 197–98; Pogge, 'Real World Justice', above n 15, 34–36.

harm across borders unacceptable. It is true that it does not specifically refer to environmental harm, and certainly not harm through changes to the atmosphere and consequent changes to the global ecosystem, but this is a feature of the conditions and knowledge of the times, when the principle of sovereignty was formulated and rearticulated and the central concern to the international community was war (whether the seventeenth century's Thirty Years War, the Napoleonic Wars or the Second World War). While war has certainly not disappeared as a threat to humanity, climate change has come to match it as a major worldwide threat. This is not only because of the broad range of impacts, and the possibility of particularly severe impacts, as well as of cascading ecological effects, such as reduced reflection of solar radiation due to shrinking icesheets, but also the danger of climate-change-induced environmental conflicts leading to war.[34] To the extent that sovereignty remains a useful protective norm, protection against harm to countries through alteration of the global commons is required for the self-determination and self-government of countries. The right to non-interference, which is the external aspect of sovereignty, therefore now needs to cover human-caused invasion by destructive environmental processes. Climate change thus constitutes a violation of an environmentally redefined conception of sovereignty. This should hold at least for those to whom sovereignty remains a fundamental norm of international ethics.

Such harm across borders, while as invisible as the harm that Pogge asserts with respect to global poverty, is conceptually more straightforward and, I believe, closer to acceptance than Pogge's argument. Pogge's argument involves a certain complexity, in the form of arguing that there are alternative global social orders possible, each with its distinctive global distribution. Using a Rawlsian conception of justice that requires a social order that does as well as possible for the worst-off in the world, Pogge argues that the de facto selection of our current social order harms the deprived by the extent to which this makes their deprivation greater than it would be under a social order that conformed with Rawlsian justice.[35] Given that huge numbers are afflicted by severe deprivation as a result, and that millions more die than need to, Pogge concludes that the injustice ethically constitutes a crime against humanity.[36] The possibility of famines and the likelihood of extreme storms may well lead to a similar conclusion with respect to climate change. The difference in the argument of harm in the form of massive poverty and in the harm argument about climate change lies in the different kinds of reference standards involved. Pogge's poverty argument has as its reference standard a morally ideal (although, at least in principle, feasible) order; harm consists of the shortfall in the conditions of the poor under the actual order relative to their conditions under this ideal order. In the case of climate change, a much simpler

---

[34] N Stern, *The Economics of Climate Change: The Stern Review* (Cambridge, Cambridge University Press, 2007) ch 3; G Dyer, *War*, rev edn (Toronto, Random House, 2004) 423; Dyer, *Climate Wars*, above n 7, ch 1.
[35] Pogge, 'Real World Justice', above n 15, 42.
[36] ibid, 33; Pogge, *World Poverty and Human Rights*, above n 15, 24–25.

standard is available. It is that of the current status quo or the status quo ante in relation to climate change. The conception of harm is thus less contentious.

With respect to the question of in situ adaptation, on the one hand, or migration, on the other, in line with the earlier argument on this above, restitution simply requires the restoration of living conditions equivalent to those before the damaging climate change events. Whether that is best accomplished by international migration or not is a separate question. When it comes to preventive adaptation, the costs of protection against damage need to be covered. Only when in situ adaptation is impossible or exorbitantly expensive is migration a preferable adaptation option.

Compensation for harm (or 'damages') is central to tort law. For that reason, the philosophy of tort law will be used as the frame in which to identify difficulties in applying the harm principle to climate change.[37] This means largely moving from distributive justice, implicit in the preceding analysis, to corrective justice, which now defines tort law.[38] At the same time, the corrective justice approach has distributive justice implications in the case of climate change, in that it affects the distributive justice of the burden of paying for the costs of climate change. But distributive justice with respect to this particular burden is more limited than justice with respect to the overall distribution of global income and resources. Applying corrective justice to identify difficulties in applying the harm principle to compensation here serves the purpose of making a case for converting compensation responsibilities into insurance responsibilities.

Rather than treating as seriously problematic the question whether it is states or people that are legitimate plaintiffs, and whether it is states or emitters that are appropriate holders of responsibility, the following simplification is adopted. Under internationalist ethics, states represent individuals and entities within their jurisdiction. Under cosmopolitanism, that generally remains the case, even though states are treated as much more instrumental than under many forms of internationalism. Accordingly, the focus of the following discussion will be on state-to-state relations, with the understanding that a further set of relations is then involved between states and those under their jurisdiction, whether they are producers of injury or victims of such injury. Only later in the chapter will this latter set of relations surface again with respect to supervision and accountability.

One question that might be raised is what culpability those who have caused climate change have for consequent harm when they did not intend it. For tort law this is not an issue. Harm does not have to be intended for it to be considered

---

[37] Although tort law as such is generally not applied across borders, Verheyen has identified the no harm rule in international environmental law as a primary rule in customary international law: R Verheyen, *Climate Change Damage and International Law: Prevention, Duties and State Responsibility* (Leiden, Martinus Nijhoff Publishers, 2005) 223–24, ch 4.

[38] Some decades ago, utilitarianism was deemed to be the philosophical bedrock of tort law, with the legal provisions constituting instruments serving the social goal of maximising human well-being. Utilitarianism also derives its conception of distributive justice from this aggregative goal: see B Zipursky, 'Philosophy of Tort Law' in MP Golding and WA Admundson (eds), *The Blackwell Guide to the Philosophy of Law and Legal Theory* (Oxford, Wiley-Blackwell, 2005) 128–29.

tortious and thus requiring compensation. As a matter of fact, much of tort law deals with accidental harm. Climate change, which can be considered a colossal, planetary accident, in this respect fits well into the tort law framework. What has been contested in tort law, however, is whether it is negligence that makes the harming party liable or whether, by virtue of the principle of 'strict liability', it is mere causation that makes the harming party responsible. Underlying these two principles of liability are two different conceptions of harm, one based on causation (strict liability) and the other on behaviour that is not only harmful, but also constitutes wrong-doing (negligence).[39]

Is the behaviour of those who have caused and continue to cause climate change negligent? Here a distinction has to be made between those who caused climate change in the past (before the phenomenon of the greenhouse effect and the human contribution to its intensification were known), and the more recent past, present and future, following its recognition. Earlier contributors cannot be deemed to be negligent because of the lack of knowledge of the consequent changes and risks to people. At what point they should be treated as negligent, given the period of contention over anthropogenic climate change and the difficulty of making rapid changes to economic systems to reduce greenhouse gases, is not clear. As far as the present and future are concerned, there is also uncertainty in applying the negligence criterion. How rapid does the conversion from a high-to-low-carbon economy have to be, for a country not to be liable for negligence? Does a country's persistence in greenhouse-gas-emitting industrialisation and consumption until poverty has been reduced to some acceptable level, or until the country has sufficiently reduced the gap between itself and the industrially advanced countries, constitute negligence? This lack of morally intuitive clarity is one argument against applying the negligence criterion.

Moreover, although within tort law the move towards strict liability based on causation alone was reversed after the third quarter of the twentieth century,[40] in this case there is a strong argument for the application of strict liability for the following reasons. Even if the damaging behaviour should not be deemed negligent, it has typically benefited the party with causal responsibility. Greenhouse gas emissions have facilitated industrialisation and consumption unimpeded by relevant restraints; this benefits industrialised and consuming countries.[41] Of course, benefiting from greenhouse-gas-emitting activities applies to all countries, but not equally. What distinguishes them is that some have been and continue to be net beneficiaries of this process and, now that consequent climate change is manifesting itself, there will be net losers. These are countries not as far along in their industri-

---

[39] J Feinberg, *Harm to Others: The Moral Limits of the Criminal Law* (New York, Oxford University Press, 1984) 33–36.

[40] Zipursky, 'Philosophy of Tort Law', above n 38, 125–26. But there are still strict liability regimes in some countries for various things.

[41] It is true that, with alternative technology, similar benefits that do not entail high levels of greenhouse gas emissions are possible. However, the technology developed until recently involved a trade-off between low emissions and high levels of production and consumption.

alisation and consumption levels to obtain such benefits. The damage to them will exceed the benefits obtained. What is more, they will not have attained the level of affluence that enables them to finance preventive, protective and restorative adaptation. Such differential impacts of the benefits and damage from incidentally injurious activities violates fundamental fairness and invokes corrective justice for the impacts caused rather than mere negligence.

Stemming from the preceding argument, an alternative to the application of the mere causal criterion of strict liability is the introduction of a further principle, which can be called the *benefit criterion* of responsibility and liability. Rather than rely on the generalisation that all countries that engage in greenhouse-gas-producing industrialisation and consumption benefit and treat it as an empirical *assumption*, the benefit criterion could be made the relevant test for liability. A greenhouse gas emitter is liable *if* the emitter benefits. The reason for this criterion would be that to allow the harming party, even when not behaving negligently, to benefit from actions that harm others offends rudimentary notions of fairness.[42]

Applying the benefit criterion or the causal criterion strictly, however, runs into certain difficulties. Determining what benefits were derived from atmosphere-damaging activities would be technically challenging. To distinguish what proportion of economic growth is due to production and consumption unrestrained by controls on greenhouse gas emissions requires comparing an actual growth trajectory with a hypothetical one. Crucial assumptions would have to be made about what would have occurred under a regime of controls on greenhouse gases that was consistent with the absorption of such gases without climate change. A just distribution of such controls would first have to be determined. Even given such a distribution, an analysis of hypothetical effects would require a range of assumptions that is likely to vary among experts. Applying the benefit criterion strictly, to determine liability, does not seem promising.

The causal criterion does not fare better with respect to getting agreement on how it is to be applied. Although there is now a reasonable consensus in the scientific community about the fact of anthropogenic climate change, and we now have a basis for attributing causal responsibility on the basis of the extent of greenhouse gas emissions, the consensus is likely to fall apart when it comes to the specifics of the consequences. First of all, there is great uncertainty about the magnitude of the aggregative impact on the atmosphere and oceans in terms of warming. Then there are regional effects, such as the shrinking of the very big icesheets of Antarctica and Greenland, shifts in particular ocean currents and changes to regional precipitation patterns. Finally, the damaging effects on particular countries have to be assessed. Can particular events and developments, such as the 2004 Hurricane Katrina in Louisiana or the much more deadly 2008 Cyclone Nargis in

---

[42] Whether the benefit criterion could replace the causal criterion, or should be combined with it, to determine liability is an interesting question. The former would mean that even those who benefit incidentally from the harming activity, even though they themselves cannot be deemed to be causal agents in it, are still liable. Should their gains also be called upon to pay for the harm done? In light of the next argument, this question will not be further pursued here.

the Irrawaddy Delta of Myanmar, or the aridification of the Darfur region which is causally implicated in the brutal and devastating war there, be wholly attributed to greenhouse gas emissions? Even if there were consensus on such detailed causal links, these can only be specified in probabilistic terms.

The next difficulty in applying the causal criterion with or without the benefit criterion is that it is onerous for the poorest, most vulnerable and often very small countries, such as small island states, to pursue compensation for climate change damage on a case-by-case basis if the model of tort law were to be made applicable in international law. It is true that there is the model of class-action suits so that harmed parties can combine as plaintiffs. But even this model does not fit readily the case of climate change, where all countries are greenhouse gas emitters and all countries suffer damages, with the central issue being the differentials in emissions and damages. Given that in any case a new institutional structure is required to accommodate such compensation initiatives, combined with the other difficulties mentioned for tort-law-modelled compensation, the next section will explore a somewhat different approach, one based on a model of social insurance. It still involves corrective justice, but side-steps some of the complications arising from the tort law model.

VIII Insurance Responsibilities

Beginning in 1884 in Germany, some of the more industrialised countries adopted a form of social insurance that replaced tort liability in the workplace. Instead of workers injured on the job being left, often in impoverished conditions, to sue employers for unsafe conditions and having to demonstrate that they themselves had not been negligent, an insurance system was inserted between the workers and their employers. Compensation to workers on a no-fault basis means that disentangling complicated webs of causal links is avoided; workers are paid simply on the basis of their illness or disability being shown to be work-related. On the other side, employers are freed of their liability, instead paying premiums into the insurance system.[43] The more sophisticated systems adjust these premiums to the rate of workplace injuries and illnesses, so that companies with riskier workplaces pay higher premiums than those with statistically demonstrated safer workplaces. This kind of substitution of an insurance model for a tort model for damage by climate change will be explored in this section.

Global climate change insurance would be an inter-state system providing compensation to affected states for climate-related damage. The periodic payouts would need to be predicted to determine the requisite funds and thus the level of

---

[43] For an extensive justification of this institutional arrangement in terms of ethical responsibilities, see RE Goodin, 'Social Welfare as a Collective Social Responsibility' in D Schmidtz and RE Goodin, *Social Welfare and Individual Responsibility: For and Against* (Cambridge, Cambridge University Press, 1998).

premiums that each state would have to pay to the scheme. Given the great disparities in per capita greenhouse gas emissions, these premiums would be assessed on the basis of such emissions. An initial fund could be established on the basis of an assessment of past emissions. Levies for this initial fund would need to be determined on the basis of a formula that took the following considerations into account: (i) the global ecosystem's absorptive capacity (atmosphere, oceans, forests) already used up by the past emissions of particular countries; and (ii) the period of ignorance about climate change (the negligence criterion), counterbalanced by the benefits obtained from relatively unrestrained emissions during this earlier period (the benefit criterion, applied broadly rather than in detail, possibly using the level and growth of production and consumption).

The payouts should be for the costs of various kinds of adaptation to deal with climate change damage. Relative to workers' compensation, this is complicated by the fact that adaptation is not only reactive to specific harmful events, in the form of rescue operations and rebuilding after destructive sudden-onset disasters, but is also preventive and thus anticipatory. Moreover, slow-onset or gradual disasters, such as creeping desertification and rising sea levels, require action to be anticipatory as well as reactive. Determining to what extent preventive adaptation is warranted will inevitably involve considerable discretion. Inserting insurance staff with appropriate expertise and professional impartiality between claimant states and payer states will serve to contain conflict over such discretion.

What to treat as attributable to climate change and what to treat as due to other causes does remain a significant issue. However, here an additional point can be brought to bear to make this less critical in terms of compensation payouts. Even in the absence of climate change, there is a strong case to be made for global insurance against natural or environmental disasters. It is simply a way of transferring the risk of a large loss or cost from an agent not strong enough to readily absorb such a set-back, to an agent that diversifies such risk through the participation of many agents. For the insured agent, it is an exchange of a certain small loss (the premium) for the avoidance of the risk of a big loss. Such broader insurance would be globally efficient as well as just (by avoiding undeserved set-backs). Without getting side-tracked to insurance for non-anthropogenic disasters, such as earthquakes, volcanic eruptions and tsunamis, I will limit the point here to simply saying that, to the extent that global climate change insurance ends up covering adaptation to events that are not really due to climate change, this will mean that an element of such broader insurance ends up being encompassed. It certainly does not impair global efficiency or justice. It also means that, when in doubt, we should err on the side of inclusion rather than exclusion of disastrous events and compensation for them. What is crucial for the argument here is that it makes the distinction between climate-change-caused damage and other kinds of damage less critical.

This insurance approach has the crucial advantageous features of the tort-based approach, while avoiding some of the difficulties of it. It provides for corrective justice and compensation to climate-change-harmed countries at least as well as the tort-based approach. In both cases there are compensatory payouts and there is third-party adjudication. Both approaches also involve substantial incentives for climate change mitigation—the tort-based approach with the prospect of having to pay damages, and the insurance approach by fixing premiums in accordance with the level of greenhouse gas emissions.[44] The advantage of the insurance approach is the avoidance of expensive litigation and the complicated assessment of complex causal links. Such avoidance of costs contributes to global efficiency. It also avoids the injustice that can result from states with limited resources having to incur additional costs to finance litigation under the tort model and risking losing, thus possibly forgoing the pursuit of justified compensation.

The social insurance approach is conceptually different from adaptation schemes, including funding, that have been emerging within the Kyoto framework.[45] One form of adaptation funding, such as for National Adaptation Programmes of Action (NAPAs) for the poorest countries, seems to be grounded in the same basis as development assistance: it is funding voluntarily provided by donor countries in response to need and promising adaptation schemes. It does not establish a clear right to such funding as compensation for harm done or risk imposed. More recently, a new Adaptation Fund has been initiated, with funding from proceeds from the Clean Development Mechanism. In this case, adaptation funding is incidental to climate change mitigation and again seems to depend on discretionary assessment of need and adaptation proposals. Similarly, proposals that the Exclusive Economic Zone of coastal states, such as Kiribati, be counted as carbon offset to establish adaptation funding entitlements also make such funding incidental to mitigation incentives, rather than grounding it clearly in compensation for endangerment or outright damage.[46]

While the social insurance approach to adaptation is intended to clearly represent corrective justice, it is not without its complications. For one thing, the ground-rules for a global insurance scheme with respect to the kinds of damage and preventive adaptation to be covered will be subject to dispute and multilateral negotiation; but the ethical argument here (in the preceding paragraph) is that there are good reasons for erring on the expansive side, namely the efficiency and justice of insurance protection against disastrous events in general. Another prob-

---

[44] Of course, like any incentive approach, it only deters and does not prohibit emissions that drive climate change. Whether the emission disincentive of the assessed insurance premiums would be sufficient for mitigation or not is beyond the scope of this chapter.

[45] It should be noted that climate change damage to individuals and countries is peripheral to both the United Nations Framework Convention on Climate Change and its Kyoto Protocol: United Nations Framework Convention on Climate Change (adopted 9 May 1992, entered into force 21 March 1993) 1771 UNTS 107; Kyoto Protocol to the Framework Convention on Climate Change (adopted 11 December 1997, entered into force 16 February 2005). These are essentially concerned with minimising climate change. See Verheyen, *Climate Change Damage and International Law*, above n 37, 134–35.

[46] L Allison, 'Climate Change Adaptation: The Case of Kiribati', Participatory Development Working Paper No 09/01 (Canberra, Australian National University Master of Applied Anthropology and Participatory Development (MAAPD) Program, 2009), http://rspas.anu.edu.au/maapd/papers/; BI McNeil, 'Oceanic Implications for Climate Change Policy' (2006) 9 *Environmental Science and Policy* 595, 603.

lem is 'moral hazard', the incentive to forgo protective action provided by the prospect of compensation when damage occurs. This involves in part the relations between states and their citizenry, which feature further complications. As a matter of fact, responsible states will not expose their people to avoidable hazards, even in the face of prospective compensation. Moreover, if the global insurance agency pays for preventive and protective measures, that incentive is substantially reduced. A third problem is that a global insurance scheme could create incentives for corruption on the part of irresponsible governments. And that does potentially create a dilemma in a system of sovereign states. However, international agreements, treaties and institutional memberships by states include conditions that involve a certain compromise with sovereignty. While it is sovereign states that agree to enter such arrangements, they enter them with all the conditions that they involve and these constrain future actions by such states.[47] Given the increasingly accepted doctrine of sovereignty as responsibility, in addition to the older one of sovereignty as right, it is not inappropriate for participation in the global insurance scheme to require accountability of how funds are spent and how closely they conform to the objective of genuine adaptation measures that save lives and livelihoods. Such accountability and correlative monitoring by the global insurance agency could deter not only corruption, but also avert major incompetence. Avoiding the latter may well mean that some funds may be required for building up local and at times national capacity to design and implement appropriate adaptation projects. Of course, with such conditionalities (intra-national conditions for entitlement to adaptation funding), justifiable though they are, it is important that, unlike in the Bretton Woods institutions, decision-making power is not tilted towards states that are net payers into the system, but rather that there is equal representation for those entitled to net compensation (that is, their receipts will be greater than their premiums).

Insurance pay-outs can be for various kinds of adaptation. One of these is migration. Setting cross-border migration aside for the moment, all adaptation projects, including migration, can be assessed and approved on the basis of appropriate analyses that take account of harm, risks, costs and benefits. Funds may go not only to migrants themselves, but to migrant-receiving communities for their accommodation. In some cases, resettlement projects may be required and these then need to meet the kinds of standards that have been articulated for such projects.[48] If displacement by climate change is to be accommodated by urbanisation, compensation funds may need to go into expanding urban infrastructure to absorb additional people moving into cities without making conditions worse. If cross-

---

[47] At the time of writing, the Copenhagen climate change negotiations were still under way. The US insistence on transparency and verification with respect to emissions at these negotiations reflects this position.

[48] United Nations Environment Programme (UNEP), *Dams and Development: Relevant Practices for Improved Decision Making* (Nairobi, UNEP, 2007); MM Cernea, 'Theoretical Issues in Defining Compensation for Displacement' in MM Cernea and HM Mathur (eds), *Can Compensation Prevent Impoverishment? Reforming Resettlement through Investments and Benefit-Sharing* (New Delhi, Oxford University Press, 2008); Penz et al, *Displacement by Development*, above n 5.

border migration turns out to be the best option, then funds may need to go to receiving states, both as an incentive to accept migrants and as compensation for expenses incurred in accommodating and integrating them.

Commercial insurance for climate-related risks is another adaptation. It has been noted that commercial insurance has begun to reflect climate risks.[49] While it protects the insured at least against certain monetary losses, such protection also means increased premiums that vulnerable individuals and owners of vulnerable assets have to pay. What commercial insurance thus does, or will be doing, is to bring forward from the future to the present anticipated risks and turn them into current monetary harm in the form of increased premiums for those requiring insurance. This means that part of what global *social* insurance needs to do is to compensate (presumably via states) individuals and enterprises for climate-driven increases in insurance premiums.

While there is a clear incentive for states that will be net beneficiaries of compensation to join the insurance system, the opposite will be the case for prospective net payers of compensation. Ideally, climate change insurance would be compulsory, like workers' compensation insurance. But in the system of sovereign states, there is no enforcing authority that can compel states to join and submit to such a system. However, the discussion here is not about what will in the end compel states to enter such an insurance system. That requires a whole other treatment involving conceivable future scenarios. Instead, the discussion here is about ethical responsibilities. The move from compensation responsibilities to insurance responsibilities therefore means that not only do states whose contributions to climate change exceed the damage they might suffer from it have a responsibility to pay compensation, but, given the advantages of an insurance approach, they have the responsibility to initiate, join and contribute to the just design of a global climate change insurance scheme.

IX Conclusion

The final focus on insurance responsibilities, based on a global climate change insurance scheme, is the outcome of an analysis that started with the concept of 'climate change refugees'. While inconsistent with the conception of refugees in international law, the term was used to focus on the conceptual analysis of forced migration. The coercive element that was brought out as a result was shown to apply also to those who are harmed but resist migration. This led into a discussion of migration in relation to adaptation to harmful climate change impacts, where

---

[49] N Stern, *The Global Deal: Climate Change and The Creation of a New Era of Progress and Prosperity* (New York, Public Affairs, 2009) 66–67, 99, 130, 135; E Mills, 'Synergisms between Climate Change Mitigation and Adaptation: An Insurance Perspective' (2007) 12 *Mitigation and Adaptation Strategies for Global Change* 809, 819.

migration was treated as merely one adaptation option. Cross-border migration was viewed as a rather extreme adaptation option, with intra-national migration and in situ adaptation being at least as important as cross-border migration. Even within cross-border migration, intra-regional migration to adjacent or other neighbouring countries is much more likely, and a more cost-effective adaptation option, for the vast majority of those displaced by climate change impacts than long-distance migration to countries that permanently integrate Convention refugees.

From there the chapter moved to a consideration of states' international responsibilities in relation to the displacement impacts of climate change. The focus was on ethical rather than legal responsibilities, with the former showing the way for the appropriate development of the latter. Four conceivable types of international ethical responsibility were analysed, with the aim of identifying a conception of state responsibility that would be persuasive not only for cosmopolitan theorists of normative international relations, but also internationalists.

The first step was to focus on climate-related displacement to reinforce a certain cosmopolitan argument for a right to free movement, and for states to respect this movement by removing border controls for people. However, it was argued that this displacement by climate change does little to make the general argument for free movement less controversial and, in any case, is insufficient in this context. It is insufficient because harm is also suffered by those who do not move, and their entitlements are ignored by a free movement regime. The second type of international responsibility discussed, the alleviation of global poverty, has similar weaknesses if it is based on a strictly egalitarian argument. Instead of focusing on migrants, it focuses on the deprived. But deprivation by climate change is treated as simply part of deprivation in general. The general egalitarian argument for the alleviation of global deprivation remains controversial and neglects the particular entitlements of those deprived by climate change.

The chapter's focus then shifted from positive responsibilities to improve the conditions of the deprived to the negative obligation not to harm and, when harm has been done, the remedial obligation to provide compensation. Harm-based responsibilities are much more readily accepted by those committed to internationalist rather than cosmopolitan ethics. Moreover, applying the harm principle to climate change is more straightforward than Pogge's argument about harm to the global poor, because the reference standard for climate-related harm is merely the status quo ante, while for the latter it is fully fledged distributive justice. Tort law and corrective justice models were then explored in relation to injury by climate change to identify difficulties that might arise from compensation for climate-related harm. Although an argument was made for a causal interpretation of compensation responsibilities, in light of benefits that accrue to greenhouse gas emitters, rather than a negligence interpretation, the complexity of causal links in the case of climate change was recognised as a difficulty. To address this set of difficulties, a shift from compensation responsibilities to insurance responsibilities was made. An insurance system that ensures compensation without requiring detailed demonstration of causal responsibility, while determining premiums in accordance with states' greenhouse gas emissions, was argued to have the crucial advantages of the tort model underlying compensation responsibilities, while avoiding the difficulty of detailed causal determination. Erring in including non-anthropogenic injury was argued not to be a great concern, on the ground that incidentally insuring for non-anthropogenic disasters would not be a bad thing. Accountability for the use of compensation for adaptation was treated as important and justified in terms of qualifications to sovereignty. The concluding point was that, although there may be no incentive for net payer states to join such an insurance scheme, they have ethical responsibilities to develop such a scheme and participate in it.

Finally, stepping beyond the ethical responsibility approach of this chapter, it can be briefly noted that there are possible pressures for the eventual adoption of an arrangement such as that proposed. One could be a quid-pro-quo negotiating position by developing countries that need to be brought into a climate change regime but that are unwilling to join without protection against climate harm. Another is advocacy by the climate justice movement in developed countries. And then there are possible developments in international law, such as the application to climate change of the no harm rule and the law on state responsibility.[50] Prospective pressures such as these raise the hope that a just climate regime is not merely an ethical fantasy, but a beacon that can guide changing reality.

---

[50] Verheyen, *Climate Change Damage and International Law*, above n 37, ch 5.

9

Climate Migration and Climate Migrants: What Threat, Whose Security?

LORRAINE ELLIOTT

I Introduction

The proposition that climate change will or could generate international security concerns has become prominent in public discourse over the last few years. Building on a much longer tradition of debates and contentions about 'environmental security', various think tanks, government agencies and non-governmental organisations (NGOs) have produced reports on climate change, conflict and national security that argue, among other things, that migration can be a major risk factor in the chain of effects that link climate change and violent conflict.[1] Given the Pacific region's high degree of vulnerability to climate change, the issue of climate-change induced migration is an important environmental, social and political challenge for the region's peoples and governments.[2] The question is whether this is also a security issue and, if so, for whom?

This chapter explores the ways in which climate change and climate migration have been securitised, first in the general (global) context, and then in the Pacific more specifically. In theoretical terms, securitisation involves claims by authoritative actors that a problem constitutes a threat to a significant referent object, usually (in a Realist problématique) the state. The most orthodox of the

---

[1] D Smith and J Vivekananda, *A Climate of Conflict: The Links between Climate Change, Peace and War* (London, International Alert, 2007) 16.

[2] While the term 'climate refugees' has become part of the popular lexicon, it remains controversial. The usual objection is that it runs the risk of undermining the legal meaning of 'refugee' in the Convention relating to the Status of Refugees (adopted 28 July 1951, entered into force 22 April 1954) 189 UNTS 137, read together with the Protocol relating to the Status of Refugees (adopted 31 January 1967, entered into force 4 October 1967) 606 UNTS 267. The term used by the International Organization for Migration (IOM) is 'environmental migrants', defined as 'persons or groups of persons who, for compelling reasons of sudden or progressive changes in the environment that adversely affect their lives or living conditions, are obliged to leave their habitual homes, or choose to do so, either temporarily or permanently, and who move either within their country or abroad': IOM, 'Discussion Note: Migration and the Environment', (1 November 2007) Doc MC/INF/288, para 6. See further R Zetter, 'Protecting People Displaced by Climate Change: Some Conceptual Challenges', in the present volume.

climate–migration–security analyses are informed by efforts to explore whether climate change will be a factor in the 'traditional indicators of insecurity—violent conflict and the outbreak of war'.[3] According to the theory of successful securitisation advanced by the Copenhagen School, the discursive concern is not whether a referent object is *actually* threatened, such that its continued existence in its present form is brought into doubt, but whether problems are conceptualised or presented in those terms by actors who are in an authoritative position to do so, most commonly 'political leaders, bureaucracies, governments, lobbyists and pressure groups'.[4] While the focus on the speech act and the way in which language is used suggests that security is socially constructed through discursive claims—'something is [constructed as] a security problem when *elites* [the securitising actors] declare it to be so', as Ole Wæver puts it[5]—in practice, much of the security/securitised discourse also involves claims about the *actual* security consequences that are anticipated to arise from particular 'threats'.[6] This is because successful securitisation requires not just that something is declared to be a security threat, but that the relevant audience, which could be other elites or the wider public, also accepts any claims for emergency or extraordinary measures that might follow.[7] Securitising elites therefore need to make some kind of case to persuade the relevant audience of the veracity of their claims.

Claims about climate and environmental security, and about the security implications of climate migration, are, however, both empirically and conceptually fraught. As other chapters in this volume have demonstrated, confident predictions about the likely extent of climate-induced migration in the Pacific and elsewhere often derive from rather crude methodologies that rely on extrapolation from historical events or on assumptions about 'single agent causality'.[8] Convincing evidence that climate migration, if and/or when it does occur, will result in social unrest, conflict and regional instability is similarly sparse. What is more certain is that both the climate change impacts that might impel people to move, and the consequences of migrating, are human security issues and should be addressed as such.

The chapter begins with an overview and critique of claims in the security literature about the challenges to international security that can or might arise from climate change and climate-induced migration. What is frequently missing from this literature is a concern with human security which, in the form articulated by the United Nations Development Programme in 1994, was intended to offer an

---

[3] P Diehl, 'Environmental Conflict: An Introduction' (1998) 35 *Journal of Peace Research* 275.

[4] B Buzan, O Wæver and J de Wilde, *Security: A New Framework for Analysis* (Boulder, Lynne Rienner Publishers, 2008) 40–41.

[5] O Wæver, 'Securitization and Desecuritization' in RD Lipschutz (ed), *On Security* (New York, Columbia University Press, 1995) 55 (emphasis added).

[6] The concept of the 'speech act' in securitisation theory draws on linguistic theory to convey the idea that what one says—about security in this case—has a performative component; see also Buzan et al (eds), *Security*, above n 4.

[7] Buzan et al (eds), *Security*, above n 4.

[8] WAV Clark, *Environmentally Induced Migration and Conflict* (Berlin, German Advisory Council on Global Change (WBGU), 2007) 15.

antidote to models of security that focused on challenges to and conflicts between states. In the second part of the chapter, I turn to a specific investigation of the securitisation of, and the security challenges that arise from, climate change in the Pacific and the role of migration in those debates. In the Pacific context, the apparent incommensurability of securitisation as a statist practice and human security as a critical non-statist practice starts to break down. It is difficult to separate the security or vulnerability of people from existential threats to states. Yet, it is the human security emphasis on adaptation and social resilience that provide security strategies that can address both.

II Environmental Security, Climate Security: A Brief Overview

As part of a move to examine security in what are usually referred to as 'non-traditional' terms, 'environmental security' and, more recently, 'climate security' seemed to offer new answers to the questions, 'security for whom, and from what?'. The background to this broadening and deepening of what it means to be secure, and what might constitute a threat, is well known and need only detain us briefly here. The context was provided by the political changes that accompanied the winding-down and then the end of the Cold War, and by the growing impact of globalisation in its economic, political, social and environmental manifestations. In the face of asymmetric and networked non-state threats, intra-state conflict and state failure, and extremes of wealth, poverty and disadvantage, academics and policy-makers alike were impelled to re-examine what it meant to be secure. Security came to be defined variously as protection against existential threats, freedom from fear and harm, and human survival.[9]

The most dystopian views are echoed in Robert Kaplan's claims that environmental degradation would be 'the national security issue of the early twenty-first century'. Kaplan argued that:

> the political and strategic impact of surging populations, spreading disease, deforestation and soil erosion, water depletion . . . and, possibly, rising sea levels in critical, overcrowded regions like the Nile Delta and Bangladesh—developments that will prompt mass migrations and, in turn, incite group conflicts—will be the core foreign policy challenge from which most others will ultimately emanate.[10]

---

[9] See, eg the Environmental Change and Security Program at the Woodrow Wilson International Center in Washington DC; the International Human Dimensions Programme on Global Environmental Change, which is sponsored by the International Council of Scientific Unions, the International Social Science Council and the United Nations University; the Institute for International Cooperative Environmental Research, which works closely with the North Atlantic Treaty Organization (NATO) on environmental protection and security issues; and Green Cross International, founded by former Soviet leader Mikhail Gorbachev.

[10] R Kaplan, 'The Coming Anarchy' (1994) 273 *The Atlantic Monthly* 58.

Somewhat more moderate concerns about the impact of environmental degradation on security, and particularly the likelihood of instability and conflict, were expressed in a series of high-profile public statements about international peace and security in a post-Cold War era. Boutros Boutros-Ghali's 1992 *Agenda for Peace*, for example, suggested that ecological damage might be a new risk for stability.[11] In the same year, a communiqué from the first ever UN Security Council Summit of Heads of State and Government declared that 'non-military forms of instability in . . . the ecological field have become threats to peace and security'.[12] In 1994, US Secretary of State Warren Christopher identified environmental degradation (along with terrorism and nuclear proliferation) as a key issue of strategic importance for American and international security.[13] In its revised *Strategic Concept*, NATO also rehearsed the proposition that 'security and stability have . . . environmental elements as well as the indispensable defence dimensions'.[14]

These themes became somewhat commonplace in the articulation of threats for the new century. UN Secretary-General Kofi Annan reported to the General Assembly in his Millennium Report that the degradation and even possible destruction of the planet's ability to provide life-sustaining services was a fundamental global challenge to the security of current and future generations.[15] The Report warned of a real risk that 'resource depletion [and] severe forms of environmental degradation [could] increase social and political tensions in unpredictable but potentially dangerous ways'.[16] The introduction of a human dimension to environmental security was echoed by US Secretary of State Colin Powell in a speech just before the 2002 World Summit on Sustainable Development. In identifying sustainable development as a 'security imperative', he argued that 'destruction of the environment' (along with poverty) was a 'destroyer of people, of societies, of nations, a cause of instability . . . that can destabilize countries, and even destabilize entire regions'.[17] These concerns were taken up once more by the 2004 report of the UN Secretary-General's High-Level Panel on Threats, Challenges and Change,

[11] United Nations (UN) Secretary-General, 'An Agenda for Peace: Preventive Diplomacy, Peacemaking and Peace-Keeping', Report of the Secretary-General Pursuant to the Statement adopted by the Summit Meeting of the Security Council on 31 January 1992, UN Doc A/47/277–S/24111 (17 June 1992), para 12.

[12] UN Security Council (UNSC), 'Note by the President of the Security Council' (31 January 1992) UN Doc S/23500, 3.

[13] C Timura, '"Environmental Conflict" and the Social Life of Environmental Security Discourse' (2001) 74 *Anthropological Quarterly* 104.

[14] NATO, 'The Alliance's Strategic Concept approved by the Heads of State and Government participating in the Meeting of the North Atlantic Council in Washington DC' (Press Release NAC-S(99)65, 24 April 1999) para 25.

[15] UN Secretary-General, *We the Peoples: The Role of the United Nations in the 21st Century* (New York, United Nations, 2000) (also known as the 'Millennium Report') 55–65.

[16] ibid, 44.

[17] C Powell, 'Making Sustainable Development Work: Governance, Finance and Public–Private Cooperation' (Remarks at State Department Conference, Meridian International Center, Washington DC, 12 July 2002).

which proclaimed that the 'biggest security threats . . . extend to environmental degradation'.[18]

Governments, international organisations and NGOs have increasingly directed their attention to climate change as a security issue and a likely source of conflict.[19] Climate change is most likely to be presented as a threat multiplier, overstretching societies' adaptive capacities and creating or exacerbating political instability and violence. This is an updated version of predictions made by scholars in the late 1980s and early 1990s that environmental degradation could contribute to instability, the 'disruption of legitimised and authoritative social relations'[20] and 'civil turmoil and outright violence'.[21] In the more extreme versions, the stresses associated with climate change, including migration, are implicated in political radicalisation, extremism and 'conditions that will extend the war on terror'.[22] The security referent that is identified as existentially vulnerable to the impact of climate wars and climate conflict includes not just the state, but also regions and the international system of global governance.

In March 2007, the new UN Secretary-General Ban Ki-moon anticipated that in coming decades, climate-related changes in the environment and 'the resulting upheavals—from droughts to inundated coastal areas to loss of arable lands—are likely to become a major driver of war and conflict'.[23] Earlier that year, the Board of the *Bulletin of Atomic Scientists* concluded that 'global warming poses a dire threat to human civilisation that is second only to nuclear weapons' (and moved the hands of its doomsday clock from seven, to five, minutes to midnight in consequence).[24] In the same month, the UK Ministry of Defence's *Strategic Trends* identified climate change, a shifting environment and an increased demand for natural resources (such as food, water and energy) as challenges to stability that would create new sources of insecurity and tension.[25] In April 2007, the Military Advisory Board of the Center for Naval Analysis in the US released a widely cited report arguing that climate change constituted a significant threat to US national security interests.[26] The UN Security Council also held its first, and somewhat

[18] UN Secretary-General, *A More Secure World: Our Shared Responsibility: Report of the High-Level Panel on Threats, Challenges and Change*, (New York, United Nations, 2004) 1.

[19] The short discussion here focuses mainly on reports from within defence and security agencies and think tanks. There have also been a number of reports on climate and conflict, or climate and security, produced by NGOs, scientific organisations and public policy think tanks.

[20] TF Homer-Dixon, 'On the Threshold: Environmental Changes as Causes of Acute Conflict' (1991) 16 *International Security* 76, 78.

[21] N Myers, 'Environment and Security' (1989) 74 *Foreign Policy* 24.

[22] CNA Corporation (CNA), *National Security and the Threat of Climate Change* (Alexandria VA, CNA Corporation, 2007) 17.

[23] UN Secretary-General, 'Address to the United Nations International School—United Nations Conference on "Global Warming: Confronting the Crisis"' (1 March 2007), www.un.org/apps/news/infocus/sgspeeches/search_full.asp?statID=70.

[24] ' "Doomsday Clock" Moves Two Minutes Closer to Midnight' (Press Release of the *Bulletin of the Atomic Scientists*, 17 January 2007), www.thebulletin.org/minutes-to-midnight/board-statements.html.

[25] *Global Strategic Trends Programme 2007–2036*, 3rd edn (Swindon, Ministry of Defence, 2007).

[26] CNA, *National Security*, above n 22.

controversial, debate on global warming in the same month. British Foreign Secretary Margaret Beckett, at the time President of the Security Council, told the Council that the threat from climate change had grown 'larger in scale and sharper in outline' with consequences that 'reach to the very heart of the security agenda'.[27]

In September 2007, the London-based International Institute for Strategic Studies, which styles itself as the world's leading authority on political–military conflict, included a long discussion of climate change in its annual *Strategic Survey*, identifying climate change as a potential 'existential security threat'.[28] The Institute argued that:

> [the] security dimension will come increasingly to the forefront as countries begin to see falls in available resources and economic vitality, increased stress on their armed forces, greater instability in regions of strategic import, increases in ethnic rivalries, and a widening gap between rich and poor. Climate change is at the heart of both national and collective security.[29]

The UK Ministry of Defence demonstrated that it was also taking this concern seriously, announcing a £12 million contract with the UK Meteorological Office (the Hadley Centre) to support research that would focus on the relationship between climate change and conflict, identify countries where conflict over food and water scarcity was likely to occur, and examine the related conditions in which British troops might be deployed in the future. In October 2007, in a widely anticipated but still controversial decision, the 2007 Nobel Peace Prize was awarded jointly to the Intergovernmental Panel on Climate Change and former US Vice-President Al Gore for their work on climate change. In announcing the prize, the Norwegian Nobel Committee said that climate change was a threat to the security of humankind that might also 'induce large-scale migration' and 'increase [the] danger of violent conflicts and wars within and between states'.[30] In August 2009, just as this chapter was being finalised, UN Secretary-General Ban Ki-moon told a Global Environment Forum in Korea (at the same time that governments were meeting in Bonn for five days of informal climate negotiations) that a failure to act quickly on climate change could lead to a worsening of tensions, social unrest and even violence.[31] The Secretary-General's speech anticipated at least some of the findings of his report on climate change and its possible security implications, submitted to the UN General Assembly in September 2009.[32]

This adversarial model of climate security runs the risk of militarising climate change and its consequences, drawing attention away from its underlying causes,

[27] UNSC, 5663rd meeting (17 April 2007) UN Doc S/PV.5663, 18.

[28] International Institute for Strategic Studies, 'Strategic Policy Issues' (2007) 107 *Strategic Survey* 47.

[29] ibid, 68.

[30] Norwegian Nobel Committee, 'The Nobel Peace Prize for 2007' (Press Release, 12 October 2007), http://nobelprize.org/nobel_prizes/peace/laureates/2007/press.html.

[31] UN Secretary-General, 'Remarks to the Global Environment Forum' (Incheon, Republic of Korea, 11 August 2009), www.un.org/apps/news/infocus/sgspeeches/statments_full.asp?statID=557#.

[32] 'Climate Change and Its Possible Security Implications: Report of the Secretary-General', UN Doc, A/64/350 (11 September 2009).

and overlooking the possibilities for, and the importance of, preventive action (mitigation), cooperation, and building social resilience and enhancing adaptation within vulnerable communities. As Bilgin puts it, the supposed 'common-sense' of statism 'forclos[es] alternative non-statist conceptions of security and the constitution of alternative futures'.[33] What is missing from much of this is a human security model, an issue that becomes even clearer when we turn to consider how migration has been factored into these scenarios about security, social unrest, conflict and violence.

The genesis of the human security approach lies in ideas articulated initially by the United Nations Development Programme (UNDP). The UNDP presented human security as a universal, people-centred concern with 'human life and dignity', and as an antidote to conventional views of security that had 'for too long ... been shaped by the potential for conflict between states ... equated with ... threats to a country's borders'.[34] While environmental degradation was not the only component of human security, the UNDP nevertheless pointed to the 'basic question of human survival on an environmentally fragile planet' as a central matter of concern. The theme was also picked up by the Commission on Global Governance which reported that 'threats to the earth's life support systems [inter alia] ... challenge the security of people far more than the threat of external aggression'.[35] In his Millennium Report to the General Assembly, the UN Secretary-General identified the degradation and, in some cases, destruction of the planet's ability to provide life-sustaining services as a fundamental global challenge to the security of current and future generations.[36]

III Climate Change, Migration and 'Threats' to Security

In the face of UN estimates that there could be 'millions' of environmental migrants by the year 2020,[37] the consequences of climate-induced migration pressures have featured prominently as a key security risk and a trigger for instability, conflict and violence.[38] While 'the causal chains ... have so far rarely been substantiated with reliable evidence',[39] and while the sophistication of analysis varies, the themes take

[33] P Bilgin, 'Beyond Statism in Security Studies? Human Agency and Security in the Middle East' (2002) 2 *Review of International Affairs* 100, 100.
[34] UN Development Programme (UNDP), *Human Development Report 1994* (New York, Oxford University Press, 1994) 22.
[35] Commission on Global Governance, *Our Global Neighbourhood* (Oxford, Oxford University Press, 1995) 79.
[36] UN Secretary-General, *We the Peoples*, above n 15, 55–65.
[37] 'Statement by the President of the 62nd Session of the United Nations General Assembly at the Thematic Debate on Climate Change and the Most Vulnerable Countries' (United Nations Headquarters, New York, 8 July 2008), www.un.org/ga/president/62/statements/ccvulc080708.shtml.
[38] 'Climate Change and International Security' (Paper from the High Representative and the European Commission to the European Council, Brussels, 14 March 2008) S113/08, 4.
[39] R Nordås and NP Gleditsch, 'Climate Change and Conflict' (2007) 26 *Political Geography* 627, 627.

on a degree of repetition: that climate migration is highly probable, that the numbers involved will be in the millions, and that this will almost certainly result in, or at the very least be implicated in, conflict and instability.

In the concept paper that the UK government prepared for the Security Council debate in April 2007, it expressed concern that while migration did not of itself lead directly to conflict, it could 'alter the ethnic composition and/or population distribution within and between States, which can increase the potential for instability and conflict—particularly in situations of resource scarcity, and in already sensitive cross-border areas'.[40] The German Advisory Council on Global Change (WBGU) also argued that the conflict potential associated with the intensification of migration was 'considerable'.[41] The Center for Naval Analysis' report on climate change and US national security suggested that this 'movement of asylum seekers and refugees who, due to ecological devastation, become settlers' should be a matter of greatest concern.[42] The Center for Strategic and International Studies in Washington DC also predicted that 'perhaps the most worrisome problems associated with rising temperatures and sea levels are from large-scale migrations of people—both inside nations and across existing national borders—. . . [which] could easily trigger major security concerns and spike regional tension.'[43]

The literature draws broadly on two models to generate hypotheses (or in many cases, unsubstantiated claims) about the relationship between climate, migration and conflict. William Clark styles these 'ecological marginalisation' and 'resource capture'.[44] The expectation in much of this literature is that climate migration will result in tensions between those displaced within their own country and the communities into which they move, as well as between so-called climate 'refugees' (who cross an international border) and receiving states. The pathways are usually presented in terms of anticipated competition for scarce resources or economic support (or jobs); increased demands on social infrastructure; cultural differences based on ethnicity or nationality; and 'the fearful reactions it [migration] often receives and the inflammatory politics that often greet it'.[45] Internal and cross-border climate migration is argued to be more likely to result in social unrest, conflict and instability when it occurs in countries or regions that face other forms of social instability (or have a recent history of such instability), that possess limited social and economic capacity to adapt, and, from a human security perspective,

---

[40] 'Annex to the Letter Dated 5 April 2007 from the Permanent Representative of the United Kingdom of Great Britain and Northern Ireland to the United Nations addressed to the President of the Security Council' (5 April 2007) UN Doc S/2007/186 (5 April 2007) 3.

[41] German Advisory Council on Global Change, *World in Transition: Climate Change as a Security Risk: Summary for Policy Makers* (Berlin, WBGU Secretariat, 2007) 6.

[42] CNA, *National Security*, above n 22, 16.

[43] KM Campbell et al (eds), *The Age of Consequences: The Foreign Policy and National Security Implications of Global Climate Change* (Washington DC, Center for Strategic and International Studies, 2007) 8.

[44] Clark, *Environmentally Induced Migration and Conflict*, above n 8, 2.

[45] Smith and Vivekananda, *A Climate of Conflict*, above n 1, 3.

where migrants have inadequate 'social support mechanisms or [in]sufficient resources to assimilate or establish stable communities'.[46]

Two particular dimensions of the ways in which climate migration has been made a security issue are notable. The first relates to the rhetorical or discursive devices that are used by actors in articulating their security claims. While climate change-related people movements are more likely to be 'slow-induced migration',[47] the language—the 'speech acts' of security—in the climate security and climate migration literature conjure up the image of processes that are likely to be out of control and therefore highly threatening. Thus, the US-based Center for Strategic and International Studies worries about 'massive migrations—potentially involving hundreds of millions of people . . . dramatic movements of people . . . perhaps billions of people . . . a significant portion of humanity on the move',[48] and later of 'uncontrolled migration . . . more likely to overwhelm the traditional instruments of national security (the military in particular) and other elements of state power and authority'.[49] In its report on climate change and international security, the High Representative and European Commission talk of a 'vicious circle of degradation, migration and conflicts'.[50] In using the term 'climate refugee', governments can also invoke those labels that are often applied to others seeking refuge—illegal aliens, non-citizens, queue-jumpers—with the implication that they are both illegitimate and a source of threat.[51]

The second point of note is that the representation of the dangers and threats associated with climate migration is articulated in terms of the detrimental impacts they can have on the security interests of the US, Europe and others. The Europeans have worried that 'migratory pressure at the European Union's borders and political instability and conflicts could increase in the future'.[52] The Center for Naval Analysis' report had as one of its key findings that the predicted effects of climate change 'have the potential to disrupt *our* way of life and to force changes in the way *we* keep ourselves safe and secure by adding a new hostile and stressing factor into the national and international security environment.'[53] The UK Ministry of Defence anticipated that 'resulting risks to near neighbours' of climate-related mass migration, humanitarian crises, international crime and, potentially, international terrorism 'will demand wide-ranging defence and

---

[46] BL Preston, R Suppiah, I Macadam and J Bathols, *Climate Change in the Asia/Pacific Region: A Consultancy Report Prepared for the Climate Change and Development Roundtable* (Australia, CSIRO, 2006) 49.

[47] F Gemenne, 'Climate Change and Forced Displacement: Towards a Global Environmental Responsibility?' (47th Annual Convention of the International Studies Association (ISA), San Diego, 22–5 March 2006) 3.

[48] Campbell et al (eds), *The Age of Consequences*, above n 43, 8.

[49] ibid, 10.

[50] 'Climate Change and International Security', above n 38, 4.

[51] See also J McAdam and M Loughry, 'We Aren't Refugees', *Inside Story* (30 June 2009), http://inside.org.au/we-arent-refugees/.

[52] 'Climate Change and International Security', above n 38, 6.

[53] CNA, *National Security*, above n 22, 44 (emphasis added).

security responses' (the 'from us' is silent but pronounced).[54] Indeed, many of the reports draw attention to likely increased demands on the military capacity of the richer countries. While it worried about knee-jerk reactions that would be unsuccessful in the long run, the Oxford Research Group also raised the likelihood that 'the protection of national and maritime borders and the detention of illegal immigrants is likely to become an increasing priority' for agencies such as police, customs and (where relevant) coastguard operations.[55]

IV Climate Migration and Climate Security in the Pacific

The analysis here examines how climate-related migration from the Pacific is 'securitised' from outside the region, particularly by those within a more orthodox security environment, and how climate-related migration is 'securitised' within the region. The Pacific (rather than the 'Asia Pacific') features much less in the security debates about, and analyses of, climate-induced migration than do Africa and Asia. Yet, it is one of the parts of the world in which long-term migration might be the *only* response for some communities vulnerable to climate change. The lack of prominence of the Pacific in the literature concerning climate change and national security could reflect a number of things. It could mean that migration within the Pacific is not thought to have destabilising potential and, therefore, is unlikely to result in threats to national or international peace and security, regardless of the human security consequences for those who might have little choice but to move. Or it could be that the numbers of people are considered sufficiently small, compared with the 'millions' who might migrate within Africa or South East and North East Asia, so that they simply do not warrant as much attention.

A 'Near Neighbour': Australia

As a 'near neighbour' (recalling the UK Ministry of Defence analysis cited above)—although also as a member of the Pacific Islands Forum—Australia's approach to climate migration and security in the Pacific is worth investigating, particularly given the release in May 2009 of the Rudd Labor Government's Defence White Paper. It cautioned that Australia needed to be in a position to manage the security impacts of climate change. The authors identified climate change as one of a number of threats likely to 'increase the risk of conflict over resources, [cause] political instability in fragile states and potentially [lead to]

---

[54] *Global Strategic Trends Programme 2007–2036*, above n 25, 54.
[55] C Abbott, 'An Uncertain Future: Law Enforcement, National Security and Climate Change: Briefing Paper January 2008' (London, Oxford Research Group, 2008) 9.

destabilising mass migration flows'.[56] The White Paper did acknowledge that countries in the Pacific were particularly vulnerable to the impacts of climate change, but the authors' concerns were not with vulnerability per se (or the human security consequences thereof), but rather the possibility that weak governance and weak social and economic capacity could result in climate change engendering 'security problems of the kind to which Australia may need to respond directly with appropriate forms of humanitarian and security assistance, including by way of ADF [Australian Defence Force] deployments'.[57] The White Paper also suggested that if international cooperation on climate mitigation and economic assistance strategies was insufficient to avert climate-related stresses and strains in the region, and if precursors for conflict were exacerbated, 'the Government would possibly have to use the ADF as an instrument to deal with any threats inimical to our interests'.[58] This is somewhat reminiscent of the position taken by Australian Federal Police Commissioner Mick Keelty in 2007, when he suggested that climate change would turn border security into the country's biggest policing issue of the century. Existing cultural tensions, he argued, could be 'exacerbated as large numbers of people undertake forced migration' with 'potential security issues [that] are enormous and should not be underestimated'.[59]

It also echoes, in some measure, the position taken by the Australian Labor Party while in Opposition. In a 2006 policy discussion paper, Shadow Ministers Bob Secombe (Overseas Aid and Pacific Island Affairs) and Anthony Albanese (Environment, Heritage and Water) noted that as well as presenting a challenge to individual countries in the Pacific, the impacts of climate change 'also represent a challenge to regional stability and security' with 'the potential to . . . lead to considerable instability, disruption and conflict'.[60] This was important, they argued, because Pacific security was a precursor for Australian security.

B 'Closer than Near': The Pacific Islands

Pacific Island leaders have made climate change vulnerability a key theme at regional and international fora, recognising it as the 'great challenge of our time',[61] and calling for a robust post-2012 commitment from developed countries for financial and technological support for adaptation, and for assistance in reducing

---

[56] Australian Government Department of Defence, 'Defending Australia in the Asia Pacific Century: Force 2030: Defence White Paper 2009' (Canberra, Commonwealth of Australia, 2009) 30.

[57] ibid, 36.

[58] ibid, 40.

[59] 'Border Security Link to Climate Change: Keelty', *ABC News* (25 September 2007), www.abc.net.au/news/stories/2007/09/25/2042214.htm. It is worth noting that he was anticipating this in the context of the impacts of climate change on China's food production which could result in millions of people crossing oceans to look for new lands.

[60] Australian Labor Party, 'Our Drowning Neighbours: Labor's Policy Discussion Paper on Climate Change in the Pacific' (Canberra, Australian Labor Party, 2006) 7.

[61] 'Call to Action on Climate Change: Annex A to the Communiqué of the 40th Pacific Islands Forum' (Cairns, Pacific Islands Forum, 5–6 August 2009) 12.

reliance on fossil fuels as the bedrock of Pacific economies. The Intergovernmental Panel on Climate Change (IPCC) reports, with high and very high confidence, a worrying litany of climate-related impacts on Pacific Island states and peoples: sea-level inundation that will threaten 'vital infrastructure, settlements and facilities that support the livelihood of island communities'; increased water stress and reduction in freshwater resources; damage to coral reefs, fisheries and other marine-based resources; and negative impacts on commercial and subsistence agriculture.[62] Climate change will increase the vulnerability of Pacific Island countries and peoples to extreme weather events. The burden of diarrhoeal and other infectious diseases is likely to increase.[63]

The language of security has been used to emphasise the seriousness of climate change impacts for Pacific countries and Pacific people. The referent—security for whom—traverses somewhat seamlessly across countries and communities. The threat is to sovereignty, to statehood, to land, to communities, to society and to the very essence of 'Pacific' identity. The communiqué from the 2008 Pacific Islands Forum referred to the 'great seriousness with which [leaders] regard the growing threat posed by climate change to the economic, social, cultural and environmental well-being and security of Forum members, particularly the Forum Island Countries'.[64] The meaning and measure of 'security', and how it differs from 'well-being', is nevertheless rather vague.[65] The Pacific Plan, appended to the communiqué, does include a section on climate change, which calls for regional action on climate change (inter alia) to mainstream human security issues and to address the vulnerability of the Pacific Islands and the impacts on 'people, land, food security, infrastructure and natural resources'.[66] The long section on food security, on the other hand, makes no mention of climate change; rather, it focuses on concerns about high food prices, production and sustainable fisheries management.

The Niue Declaration on Climate Change, also adopted at this 39th Forum meeting in 2008, is more forthcoming. The leaders note their deep concern at the growing threat posed by climate change that could 'lead to significant impacts on Pacific countries' environments, their sustainable development and *future survival*'.[67] The Declaration speaks of the twin challenges of vulnerability and

---

[62] N Mimura et al, 'Small Islands' in ML Parry et al (eds), *Climate Change 2007: Impacts, Adaptation and Vulnerability Contribution of Working Group II to the Fourth Assessment Report of the Intergovernmental Panel on Climate Change* (Cambridge, Cambridge University Press, 2007) 689–70.

[63] United Nations Framework Convention on Climate Change (UNFCCC) Secretariat, 'Climate Change: Impacts, Vulnerabilities and Adaptation in Developing Countries' (Bonn, UNFCCC, 2007) 24–26.

[64] Pacific Islands Forum Secretariat, 'Final Communiqué of the 39th Pacific Leaders' Forum' (Niue, Pacific Leaders' Forum, 19–20 August 2008) para 10.

[65] The Forum Secretariat website for the Political and Security Programme refers to the 'stability and safety' of member states and the region: see Pacific Islands Forum Secretariat, 'Political & Security', www.forumsec.org.fj/pages.cfm/security/law-enforcement/. It says little about human security.

[66] Pacific Islands Forum Secretariat, 'Annex A to the Final Communiqué of the 39th Pacific Leaders' Forum' (Niue, Pacific Leaders' Forum, 19–20 August 2008).

[67] 'Niue Declaration on Climate Change: Annex B to the Final Communiqué of the 39th Pacific Leaders' Forum' (Niue, Pacific Leaders' Forum, 19–20 August 2008) (emphasis added).

building resilience. The most telling link with security (although the word is not used) comes with the recognition of the 'importance of retaining the Pacific's social and cultural identity, and the desire of Pacific peoples to continue to live in their own countries, where possible'.[68] This rather diplomatic securitisation—the Forum does, after all, include countries such as Australia and New Zealand, both substantial per capita contributors to greenhouse gas emissions—appears also in the communiqué of the 40th Pacific Islands Forum (held in Australia in August 2009). In their Call to Action on Climate Change, the Pacific leaders referred to the security of their communities, noting that 'some island States face obliteration' and calling this a 'grave threat'.[69] Regional leaders have also cast climate change as a threat to their 'inalienable rights to statehood, sovereignty and territorial integrity'.[70]

The region's environment ministers, in a joint statement to the Forum Economic Ministers Meeting in 2007, reminded the gathering that 'some in our region have raised the issue of their citizens becoming environmental refugees', noting that 'potential evacuation of island populations, raises grave concerns over sovereign rights as well as the unthinkable possibility of entire cultures being damaged or obliterated'.[71] The idea of existential threat has meaning also, in a non-physical way, for those who are displaced by the impacts of climate change. Oxfam cites a community activist from Chuuk State in the Federated States of Micronesia, who observed that 'most of the people . . . don't feel secure because [of] the water surges'. She went on to say that, with respect to those who will be displaced, 'there is really a sense of being alienated from their lands, from their culture, from their livelihoods and just a sense of who they are . . . if they are going to be displaced, they're going to feel like not belonging'.[72]

The language of grave and existential threat has been deployed in international fora as well. In a speech to the UN General Assembly in 2008, the President of the Federated States of Micronesia, Emanuel Mori, reminded his audience that 'climate change . . . impacts international peace and our own security, territorial integrity and our very existence, as inhabitants of the very small and vulnerable island nations'.[73] On the occasion of Pacific Island sponsorship of a General Assembly resolution on 'Climate change and its possible security implications', adopted on 3 June 2009, Samoa's Permanent Representative to the UN referred to 'existential threats of the adverse effects of climate change' on vulnerable Pacific countries.[74]

---

[68] ibid.

[69] 'Call to Action on Climate Change', above n 61.

[70] 'Eneko Communiqué' (9th Micronesian Presidents' Summit, Majuro, 16–17 July 2009) 2.

[71] 'Statement on the Economic Impacts of Climate Change in the Pacific Region delivered by the Honourable Fritz Koshiba, Minister of Resources, Development and Environment of Palau on behalf of the SPREP Environment Ministers Meeting at the Forum Economic Ministers Meeting (FEMM)' (Forum Economic Ministers Meeting, Palau, 10–12 July 2007) 3.

[72] Cited in Oxfam, 'The Future Is Here: Climate Change in the Pacific: Oxfam Briefing Paper' (Oxfam Australia/Oxfam New Zealand, 2009) 26.

[73] ibid, 19.

[74] Pacific Islands Forum Secretariat, 'UN Endorses Pacific Sponsored Resolution on Climate Change' (Press Statement 36/09, 11 June 2009).

Pacific leaders have not been averse to using claims about conflict in their approach to climate, security and migration. In introducing the draft resolution on climate change and security to the UN General Assembly, Nauru's representative spoke not only of the threat to the 'tiny homelands' of the Pacific and 'serious concern for the survival of whole populations and the existence of their lands', but also pointed out that 'resettlement and migration were already occurring and dangers to international peace and security would soon increase'.[75] This theme was prominent in some of the 'side-event' discussions at the Pacific Islands Forum in Cairns in August 2009. The UN Development Programme (UNDP), for example, expressed its concern that 'relocating families [might] spark social conflict due to traditional land rights' and that 'climate change will impact security dynamics in the Pacific'.[76] These concerns were behind the announcement of a new UNDP initiative—the Interface between Climate Change, Disasters and Potential for Conflict in the Pacific—which has two objectives: to map, identify and collect data about the effects that climate change and climate-related disasters could have on climate dynamics in the region, and to establish a regional mechanism to prevent conflicts sparked by climate change.

V Some Concluding Thoughts: Reclaiming Human Security in the Climate Migration Debate

The more orthodox and adversarial approaches to the securitisation of climate migration can have a number of counterproductive consequences: an emphasis on traditional security responses to the exclusion of policy options that focus on climate mitigation and adaptation, and a marginalisation of human security concerns to the extent that those who are most vulnerable are victimised. Critics of securitisation as a process (rather than of the theory itself) have also noted that it anticipates a suspension of democratic practices and a privileging of particular forms of expert knowledge that run counter to policy-making that is open, measured and allows space for debate and contestation.[77] Despite the 'tactical attractions' of securitising an issue,[78] this move from normal politics to security politics runs the risk of narrowing the policy focus to one of defence against threat, rather than one which seeks to address the causes of insecurities.

---

[75] UN Department of Public Information, 'General Assembly, Expressing Deep Concern, Invites Major United Nations Organs to Intensify Efforts in Addressing Security Implications of Climate Change' (News Release GA/10830, 3 June 2009).

[76] UNDP Pacific Centre, 'Climate Change Threatens Human Security in the Pacific Islands, Top Panel Warns' (Press Release, 6 August 2009).

[77] See, eg MC Williams, 'Words, Images, Enemies: Securitization and International Politics' (2003) 47 *International Studies Quarterly* 511; C Aradau, 'Security and the Democratic Scene: Desecuritization and Emancipation' (2004) 4 *Journal of International Relations and Development* 388.

[78] See Buzan et al (eds), *Security*, above n 4, 29.

For countries and peoples within the Pacific, it is the possibility of having to migrate that is the primary threat and pressing security issue.[79] In a report prepared for CARE International, Koko Warner and colleagues argued that 'climate-related displacement and migration should be treated, first and foremost, as a '"human security" issue' and cautioned against 'sensationalist warnings'.[80] This is not to deny that migration can be a source of tension in the Pacific. Oxfam, for example, reports 'disputes amongst the communities in Tuvalu' as coastal families seek to move inland in response to land being 'eaten away'.[81] The question is how to respond to such tensions and to the people whose lives are disrupted. A human security model, which takes people (or peoples) as the security referent, questions the 'taken for granted' assumptions and analyses within the policy community about climate change, migration, threat and (in)security. From a human security perspective, forced migration from unsustainable or uninhabitable lands is a source of insecurity for those whose lands and homes can no longer sustain them, an approach which challenges the representation of 'climate refugees' or 'climate migrants' as a potential source of pressure on, or threat to, states. Migration itself generates other human insecurities, including loss of income, loss of social capital, disruption to traditional coping mechanisms and increased vulnerability for already marginalised groups, including the poor, women and children. A human security model demands that we worry about the way that climate-related food insecurity, malnutrition and an increased disease burden destroys lives and livelihoods, and exacerbates poverty and misery for the millions of people who are affected, rather than worrying about this only as a trigger for civil unrest and potential extremism. The report of IPCC Working Group II suggests that in some parts of the world, climate-related disruptions of human populations are likely both within states and across national borders, with sudden sharp spikes in rural to urban migration in some countries, and the exacerbation of shortfalls in food production, rural poverty and urban unrest in others.[82] Yet as Preston et al point out, very little is known about how climate change will interact with other migration pressures and incentives.[83] Migration is not the only response strategy to climate change: people may, for example, choose to stay in their communities and seek to adapt to the impacts of climate change, or they may choose to stay, accept the costs of climate change and do nothing.[84] Other chapters in this volume explore the complexities of migration as a response or adaptation strategy in the

---

[79] For a report on how Pacific ambassadors to the UN resisted the idea of migration and the category of 'climate refugee', see KE McNamara and C Gibson, ' "We Do Not Want to Leave Our Land": Pacific Ambassadors at the United Nations Resist the Category of "Climate Refugees" ' (2009) 40 *Geoforum* 475.

[80] K Warner et al, *In Search Of Shelter: Mapping the Effects of Climate Change on Human Migration and Displacement* (Geneva, CARE International et al, 2009) v.

[81] Cited in Oxfam, 'The Future Is Here', above n 72, 33.

[82] RVH Cruz et al, 'Asia' in Parry et al (eds), *Climate Change 2007*, above n 62, 488.

[83] Preston et al, *Climate Change in the Asia/Pacific Region*, above n 46, 49.

[84] See, eg R Reuveny, 'Climate Change Induced Migration and Violent Conflict' (2007) 26 *Political Geography* 656 for an examination of the conditions under which people may or may not migrate in response to climate change.

face of the social, economic and environmental consequences of climate change, the factors that impel it, as well as the factors that enable individuals and communities to adapt in ways other than moving or migrating.

From a security perspective, migration need not be a destabilising factor: as the NGO International Alert points out, it is not 'the process, but the context and the political response to immigration that shape the risks of violent conflict'.[85] As well as recognising that in the Pacific, as elsewhere, it is people and their communities who are most at risk from climate change and from the instability, incapacity, social and economic stress that might occur, the human security model emphasises adaptation as a security strategy that has the potential to save lives, increase individual adaptive capacity, build societal resilience and lessen the chances of conflict. Smith and Vivekananda argue that the kinds of climate insecurities that arise from shorter growing seasons and declines in agricultural yield could be 'redressed through a redistribution of resources', rather than leading (apparently inexorably, in some analyses) to 'violent struggle for control of dwindling resources or to large scale migration'. If livelihood choices contract in low-lying coastal areas, forcing people to move, those who are affected can be 'looked after and get alternative economic opportunities' in ways that reduce the chances that they will feel 'neglected, resentful and ready to support violently overturning an unjust social order'.[86] Within the security literature, this move from a politics of security to a politics of adaptation and building resilience would be read as a process of *de-securitisation* of climate migration in the Pacific. Reading this move instead as '*human* securitisation' (or perhaps even 'counter-securitisation') has the potential not only to sustain the 'tactical attractions' of the language of security, and the urgent attention that this brings to a problem, but to redirect security policy to securing the lives, livelihoods and, wherever possible, the lands and homes of those in the Pacific who are most vulnerable and most insecure from the threats of climate change.

---

[85] Smith and Vivekananda, *A Climate of Conflict*, above n 1, 16.
[86] ibid, 8.

10

Climate-Related Displacement: Health Risks and Responses

ANTHONY J McMICHAEL, CELIA E McMICHAEL,
HELEN L BERRY AND KATHRYN BOWEN

I Introduction

This chapter examines climate change-related impacts on health occurring in association with the displacement of groups of people. This multifaceted relationship, only now evolving in some high-risk settings, has been little studied to date. Better understanding of the issue has important implications for policy responses to avert or ameliorate displacement, and the topic is therefore in need of research, documentation and the evaluation of intervention policies.

Human-induced climate change, a process that is now evidently underway, will have diverse and increasingly great impacts on the health of communities and populations around the world. Indeed, most climate change impacts on physical, ecological and social systems will have repercussions for human health.[1] The health impacts of climate change will predominantly be adverse. Early epidemiological research on this subject has focused mostly on relatively straightforward health outcomes. Prominent topics have included studies of the death toll from heatwaves, increases in diarrhoeal diseases (especially in low-income settings) from rises in temperature and rainfall intensity, and changes in geographic and seasonal patterns of mosquito-borne malaria and dengue fever occurrence. The research methods have encompassed the empirical study of relationships between recent climatic variations and health outcomes, the statistical modelling of current disease burdens attributable to climate change, and the modelling of likely future health impacts of plausible scenarios of climate change.

The relationship between climate change, health and the displacement of populations and groups is multifaceted. First, a change in actual health status, or in perceived health risks, due to changes in climatic and environmental conditions may trigger the movement of people. Secondly, the experience of displacement,

---

[1] AJ McMichael, RE Woodruff and S Hales, 'Climate Change and Human Health: Current and Future Risks' (2006) 367 *Lancet* 859.

whether because of climate change or for other reasons, typically increases the risks of various adverse health outcomes. Thirdly, the experience of living in a new physical, social and cultural environment may affect health, and may also affect the health of the receiving (or host) population.

The topic of climate change, displacement and health has attracted rather little formal research by population health researchers, whether epidemiologists, sociologists, demographers or medical anthropologists—a corollary of a more general tardiness by such disciplines in engaging with research into climate change and health.[2] Further, the health outcomes associated with the psychological, social and physical experiences of displacement are less easy to conceptualise, document and quantify than are those health risks studied in the epidemiological research examples given above. Consequently, there is not yet an empirical base of evidence that allows the scenario-based quantitative modelling of how the health impacts of climate change would be likely to trigger displacement, or of the likely future health experiences of climate-displaced groups. Hence, in relation to the above-mentioned second and third research facets, much of the initial assessment of health risks must draw on the wider literature pertaining to the documented experiences of displaced groups and communities that have been displaced for diverse reasons and in a range of settings.

The chapter reviews, briefly, the long history of human displacement or relocation for climate and/or environmental reasons, and its various consequences for well-being and health. It then provides an overview and typology of the categories of health risks from climate change, and their environmental and social manifestations. Next, after noting the main profiles of people displaced as a result of environmental and climatic changes, the predominant types of risks to health are explored in more detail, with particular reference to the general literature on displacement and its physical and mental health consequences.

The implications of these health risks, in the context of climate change, are then considered in relation to differences in vulnerability, including social resilience and coping capacities, in the exposed groups—before, during and after displacement. This has a direct bearing on social policies to reduce both vulnerability and the need for movement. It also has implications for the scope of future research and intervention evaluation that will be needed to better understand the health risks from current and (more importantly) future climate-related displacement, in its many guises and contexts, and to develop and test ways of 'adapting' so as to lessen both risks and resultant impacts. This programme of future research will need to draw on a broad spectrum of research disciplines, including epidemiology, demography, biostatistics, anthropology, sociology, psychology, and expertise in forecasting and quantitative modelling.

---

[2] H Baer and M Singer, *Global Warming and the Political Ecology of Health: Emerging Crises and Systemic Solutions* (California, Left Coast Press Inc, 2009).

II Climate Change, Migration and Health: Ancient and Modern

During the approximately 200,000 years of existence of the modern human species, *Homo sapiens*, Earth's climatic conditions have varied continuously in response to natural planetary and cosmological influences. Our species has lived through the two most recent 90,000-year glaciations, part of a quasi-cyclical series that characterises the current ice age through which Earth is passing. Exposure to variable climatic 'environments', especially shorter-term climatic fluctuations, would have often adversely affected the food supplies, nutrition, physical safety and, hence, health of human groups. This, in turn, would have often prompted relocation. At the extreme of climate fluctuation, DNA evidence suggests that the great global cooling (a rapid 5°C drop for a half-decade) that occurred 73,000 years ago following the mighty volcanic eruption of Mount Toba (in today's Indonesia) reduced the then African-Eurasian population of *Homo sapiens* to regional remnants with a combined total of 5,000–20,000 people.[3] In contrast, the past 400 generations have lived through an unusually stable inter-glacial climate over the last 10,000 years.

Throughout the long process of worldwide human dispersal out of north-east Africa, which began around 80,000 years ago, climatic changes have provided a recurring stimulus to move. Some of this movement would have resulted from displacement due to crises, including severe overcrowding, physical disasters or climate-induced shortages of food and water. Along the ancient lower Nile Valley, from around 12,000 years ago, when the world had begun to warm as the last cold-cycle glaciation receded, the palaeo-record indicates that the number of settlements fluctuated dramatically.[4] There is evidence of widespread conflict (shattered skulls) and abandoned settlements, mirroring sudden major changes in river flows, vegetation and fish stocks.

The collapse of the Mayan civilisation in Central America around 1,100 years ago, and that of the smaller West Viking civilisation in south-western Greenland around 650 years ago, were each attributable to natural climatic changes occurring over the course of a century or two—the former due to a long-term drying cycle, the latter due to a progressive cooling that led into the Little Ice Age in Europe.[5] Each such regional climate change would have caused some increases in rates of

---

[3] D Cocks, *Deep Futures: Our Prospects for Survival* (Sydney, UNSW Press, 2003) 151; SH Ambrose, 'Did the Super-Eruption of Toba Cause a Human Population Bottleneck? Reply to Gathorne-Hardy and Harcourt Smith' (2003) 45 *Journal of Human Evolution* 231.

[4] LG Straus, BG Eriksen, JM Erlandsen and DR Yesner, *Humans at the End of the Ice Age: The Archaeology of the Pleistocene-Holocene* (New York, Plenum Press, 1996) 50.

[5] AJ McMichael, *Human Frontiers, Environments and Disease: Past Patterns, Uncertain Futures* (Cambridge, Cambridge University Press, 2001) 9; J Diamond, *Collapse: How Societies Choose to Fail or Succeed* (New York, Viking Books, 2005) 172, 266.

death, disabling disease and out-migration, often as food shortages and hence under nutrition became severe.

A Human-Driven Climate Change

Today there exists, for the first time, significant *human-driven* (or anthropogenic) global climate change. This momentous process is mainly due to on-going increases in the emission of 'heat-trapping' greenhouse gas into the lower atmosphere (troposphere). The build-up of excessive concentrations of these gases in the troposphere reflects the unprecedented scale and intensity of economic activity in the industrial era, as well as the accompanying surge in human numbers over the past century. Fossil fuel combustion, land clearing, paddy rice production and intensified livestock production are the major sources of 'greenhouse' emissions.

This human-driven climate change is occurring much faster than the ever-present 'natural' climate changes that have long been experienced by human societies. Indeed, recent research indicates that this human-generated change is proceeding faster than was projected just a decade ago.[6] On current trajectories, global warming and its associated changes in rainfall and weather patterns could, within the next half-century, reach a critical stage that is dangerous to the stability and function of many of nature's systems. There are, almost certainly, some climatic-environmental surprises in store as our actions push the world's climate system into a range beyond previous human experience.

Climatic conditions are fundamental to life on Earth, as we know it. Substantial changes in climate will alter and disrupt many aspects of the natural and social environments upon which we depend for well-being, health and survival. Geophysical systems, biological processes and ecological relationships will be altered; ecosystems (including food-producing systems) will be changed and often disrupted; monsoon systems will shift and may weaken.[7] The food sources, life cycles, annual rhythms and geographic ranges of many non-human species have already been affected.[8] Inevitably, those changes portend risks to human health and survival, both from direct-acting exposures (such as temperature extremes and weather disasters) and from a diversity of less direct influences mediated by disruptions to environmental, ecological and social systems.

---

[6] TM Lenton et al, 'Tipping Elements in the Earth's Climate System' (2008) 10 *Proceedings of the National Academy of Sciences USA* 1783; JB Smith et al, 'Assessing Dangerous Climate Change through an Update of the Intergovernmental Panel on Climate Change (IPCC) "Reasons for Concern"' (2009) 106 *Proceedings of the National Academy of Sciences USA* 4133; J Rockström et al, 'A Safe Operating Space for Humanity' (2009) 461 *Nature* 472.

[7] AB Pittock, *Climate Change: The Science, Impacts and Solutions*, 2nd edn (Melbourne, CSIRO Publishing, 2009); M Ashfaq et al, 'Suppression of South Asian Summer Monsoon Precipitation in the 21st Century' (2009) 36 *Geophysical Research Letter*.

[8] Intergovernmental Panel on Climate Change (IPCC), *Climate Change 2007: Impacts, Adaptation, and Vulnerability Contribution of Working Group II to the Fourth Assessment Report of the Intergovernmental Panel on Climate Change* (Cambridge, Cambridge University Press, 2008) 214–39; TL Root et al, 'Fingerprints of Global Warming on Wild Animals and Plants' (2003) 421 *Nature* 57.

These current and projected changes in climatic conditions, accompanied by an increase in extreme weather events, augment the likelihood of displacement of people. Further, changes in climate will often intensify the stresses, privations and health risks that displacement entails, and may erode environmental resources at the site of resettlement. Hence the profile, if not the type, of risks to health among displaced people will often differ from those encountered in circumstances of political or economic displacement.

This topic of health risks in relation to climate-related displacement takes on a greater significance in a world that already faces considerable and persistent health inequities. The absolute number of undernourished people increased by over 10 per cent during the last decade, and it has become clear that, at the global level, the Millennium Development Goals for reducing disease, preventing deaths, alleviating poverty, curtailing gender inequities and creating a safer and hygienic physical environment cannot be met by 2015.[9] Rates of undernutrition, stunted child development, maternal mortality and serious infections (diarrhoeal disease, malaria, tuberculosis, HIV/AIDS and others) are either not declining or are doing so more slowly than anticipated, while access to clean drinking water remains very poor in some parts of the world. Given that climate change acts predominantly as an amplifier of many existing public health problems, its impact will be of greater absolute magnitude if the numbers of vulnerable and displaced people increase.

III Climate-Related Risks to Human Health: Overview

Changes in the prevailing climatic conditions and in weather variability affect human well-being, safety, health and survival in many ways. These various types of health impacts may, in turn, influence decisions to relocate, and may affect people during the process of displacement and resettlement. Some impacts, such as those of heatwaves and weather disasters, are direct, immediate and easily understood. Other health effects are less immediate, less direct, and typically occur via more complex causal pathways involving changes in or disruptions to various types of natural environmental and social systems.

The main categories of health risks from climate change are listed in Table 1. All the health outcome categories are familiar, since climate change is not a distinct and separate category of health hazard—and climate change therefore does not loom as a cause of novel types of disease or disorder.[10] Rather, climate change, both via direct meteorological extremes and via impacts on physical, ecological

---

[9] D Gil-Gonzalez, MT Ruiz-Cantero and C Alvarez-Dardet, 'How Political Epidemiology Research Can Address Why the Millennium Development Goals Have Not Been Achieved: Developing a Research Agenda' (2009) 63 *Journal of Epidemiology and Community Health* 278.

[10] That said, climate change may plausibly contribute to the emergence of some new infectious diseases in humans, for example by influencing the flight paths and numbers of wild birds and the passage of their avian influenza viruses to domesticated birds.

and social conditions, can amplify or extend a range of existing population health problems. For example, if rainfall events become more intense, then flooding of local sanitation systems and consequent faecal contamination of drinking water becomes much more likely. If average temperatures rise and short-term climate variability also increases, then the death toll from more frequent and more extreme heatwaves will increase.

Many of these climate-related risks to health and physical safety will impinge on displaced people before, during or after that displacement. Meanwhile, for some more fortunate groups, the displacement may result in health gains—for example, if the move to a new location alleviates antecedent health deficits from undernutrition or freshwater shortages.

Table 1: Summary of major categories of health risks from climate change

---

Direct-acting risks

- Increased risk of injury or death from extreme weather events such as floods, fires or storms.
- Increased illness and death associated with more frequent and intense heatwaves.
- Increased risk of respiratory illnesses from higher ground-level ozone and some other air pollutants.
- Exacerbation of asthma and other respiratory allergic conditions from increases in airborne pollens and spores.

More complex, indirect, risk pathways

- Increased risk of malnutrition from impaired/failed agriculture (and from associated impoverishment from loss of rural livelihoods).
- Increased risk of gastroenteritis (for example, from salmonella, campylobacter and temperature-sensitive vibrios).
- Change in the range and seasonality of outbreaks of mosquito-borne infections such as malaria, dengue fever or Ross River virus.
- Health risks in displaced people/groups, and possible risks to their host populations.
- Increased mental health risks such as post-traumatic stress disorder associated with extreme weather events, or depression/suicide associated with impoverishment or lost livelihood (for example, long-term drying in rural regions) or displacement.

Some aspects of health in some populations have been affected by the initial phase of human-driven climate change—that is, by the 0.7°C rise in global average temperature that has occurred since 1950, mostly due to human actions.[11] For example, in recent decades the annual numbers of people affected by heatwaves and weather disasters in various countries has risen in association with an upward trend in the annual number of very hot days. Food shortages and undernutrition are increasing in some regions where warming and drying has occurred, including in parts of Sahelian Africa.[12] Some infectious diseases have changed their

---

[11] IPCC, *Climate Change 2007*, above n 8.
[12] B Walker et al, 'Looming Global-Scale Failures and Missing Institutions' (2009) 325 *Science* 1345.

geographic range and seasonal duration, in association with regional warming—as indicated by the northwards extensions in Sweden of tick-borne encephalitis (and its tick vector) and, in China, of the critical winter survival zone for water snails that transmit schistosomiasis.[13]

Health risks will increase, often in accelerated non-linear fashion, as climate change proceeds and physiological, psychological or social coping thresholds are exceeded. As indicated in Table 1, risks will arise from changes in levels of thermal stress, the availability and nutrient quality of food, the range and activity of infectious diseases, the frequency and severity of extreme weather events, and the viability of livelihoods (especially in the rural sector).

The health ramifications of climate change will extend yet further. The environmental, social and economic consequences of climate change will cause strains and disruptions that can affect health risks, as indicated in Figure 1. For example, a decline in farm and fishery yields will jeopardise livelihoods and family incomes, mental health and, by exacerbating various health-endangering personal behaviours (such as alcohol consumption and self-medication), will impair physical health. Climate-related resource depletion (especially of transboundary

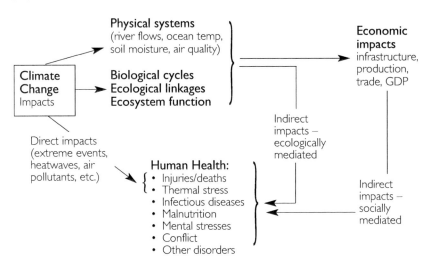

Figure 1: Diagrammatic representation of direct and indirect paths by which climate change affects human health. Most of the impacts are mediated by climate-induced changes in environmental, ecological or socio-economic conditions.

---

[13] E Lindgren, L Tälleklint and T Polfeldt, 'Impact of Climatic Change on the Northern Latitude Limit and Population Density of the Disease-Transmitting European Tick Ixodes Ricinus' (2000) 108 *Environmental Health Perspectives* 199; E Lindgren and R Gustafson, 'Tick-Borne Encephalitis in Sweden and Climate Change' (2001) 358 *Lancet* 16; XN Zhou et al, 'Potential Impact of Climate Change on Schistosomiasis Transmission in China' (2008) 78 *American Journal of Tropical Medicine and Hygiene* 188.

'commons', such as water supplies from river systems) is likely to become an increasing source of tension and conflict, resulting in injury, deaths, food shortages and mental depression.[14] Climate change, as an amplifier and modulator of many existing health risks, will affect malnutrition, diarrhoeal diseases, mosquito-borne infections, exposure to extreme weather, exacerbation of urban air pollution, and mental health and trauma. An important point is that populations with high pre-existing rates of health problems will therefore tend, in absolute terms, to be those most affected. Hence, climate change will often magnify existing persistent health inequalities.

IV Health Risks of Climate-Related Displacement

Climate-related health impacts may initiate, accompany and follow the displacement of groups of people. Given the recent advent of climate change, the reluctance of most settled groups to abandon home and local culture, and the complexity of the social, environmental and biomedical processes involved, there are as yet rather few formal empirical research findings on this specific set of relationships. Extrapolation from the documented experience of other categories of displaced people is therefore a necessary resource for much of the ensuing discussion.

A reasonable assumption is that when the adverse health consequences of climate change become serious or widespread within a community, then the inclination or need to move away will often increase. However, as yet, few such recorded moves can be attributed to the initial phase of human-driven climate change. Suggestive examples include the recent displacement of people from the Carteret Islands to nearby mainland Bougainville in Papua New Guinea, contributed to by rising sea level, coastal inundation, consequent food insecurity and associated health risks,[15] and recent migrations in the chronically drying and increasingly food insecure eastern Sahelian region (including people moving westwards from southern Sudan and Darfur).[16]

The health experiences of people displaced partly or largely as a result of climate change over the coming decades will span the full range of health risks that displaced groups frequently encounter, discussed more fully below. Furthermore, they may incur additional risks to health and safety, since their displacement is likely to occur in a world in which, on some current indications, national borders may be more strictly policed, natural resource supplies may be declining in intended host countries or communities, and popular concerns about geopolitical

---

[14] CD Butler and AJ McMichael, 'Environmental Health' in BS Levy and VW Sidel (eds), *Social Injustice and Public Health* (New York, Oxford University Press, 2005) 318–36.

[15] See J Campbell, 'Climate-Induced Community Relocation in the Pacific: The Meaning and Importance of Land', in the present volume.

[16] United Nations Environment Programme (UNEP), *Sudan: Post-Conflict Environmental Assessment* (Nairobi, UNEP, 2007) 100–17.

destabilisation and risks of violence and terrorism may affect the reception, conditions and resources afforded to incoming migrant groups.[17] These more stringent, less supportive, conditions of 'receptivity' may thus further exacerbate some risks to health, including via the processes of hostile confrontation, alienation, depression, impoverishment and, perhaps, detention.

In the longer term, climate change and its many environmental, ecological and social ramifications will affect the health of populations everywhere. That, in turn, will add further layers of complexity to the relationship between those who move and the communities in which they settle.

A Circumstances of Displacement and Types of Health Risks

Relationships between the climate-related circumstances of displacement, the conditions and experiences of resettlement, and the resultant health impacts on displaced people are complex. The social and health impacts will differ between localities and regions because of geophysical context, regional patterns of climate change, and differences in resilience and adaptive capacities of the local social, political and economic structures.[18] Further, the continuum of migration decisions ranges from voluntary movement to forced displacement.[19] These multiple causes, motivations and pathways will have variable impacts on health. For example, the health risks for populations caught up in sudden and large-scale movements due to climate-driven disaster will differ significantly from those in groups which leave risk areas via formally negotiated intergovernmental resettlement programmes.

As human-induced climate and resultant (or accompanying) environmental changes increase, allied with the likely widespread persistence of poverty, the need to move away from situations of danger, disease or despair will increase.[20] The number of climate change-related 'refugees'[21] in coming decades cannot be

---

[17] E Voutira and G Dona, 'Refugee Research Methodologies: Consolidation and Transformation of a Field' (2007) 20 *Journal of Refugee Studies* 163.

[18] C Boano, R Zetter and T Morris, 'Environmentally Displaced People: Understanding the Linkages between Environmental Change, Livelihoods and Forced Migration', Forced Migration Policy Briefing No 1 (Oxford, Refugee Studies Centre, 2008).

[19] J Barnett and M Webber, 'Accommodating Migration to Promote Adaptation to Climate Change' (Stockholm, Commission on Climate Change and Development, 2009); F Renaud, JJ Bogardi, O Dun and K Warner, *Control, Adapt or Flee: How to Face Environmental Migration?* (UNU-EHS, InterSecTions No 5/2007, 2007).

[20] J Borger, 'Conflicts Fuelled by Climate Change Causing New Refugee Crisis, Warns UN', *The Guardian* (London, 17 June 2008), www.guardian.co.uk/environment/2008/jun/17/climatechange.food.

[21] People who are displaced because of the threat and impacts of environmental hazard or change are often referred to as 'environmental refugees': E El-Hinnawi, *Environmental Refugees* (Nairobi, UNEP, 1985). However, this term is widely contested and is rejected by many to whom it is applied; there is much scholarly debate about terminology and definitions: R Black, 'Environmental Refugees: Myth or Reality', *New Issues in Refugee Research*, Working Paper No 34 (Geneva, UNHCR, 2001); S Castles, 'Environmental Change and Forced Migration: Making Sense of the Debate', *New Issues in Refugee Research*, Working Paper No 70 (Geneva, UNHCR 2002); WB Wood, 'Ecomigration: Linkages between Environmental Change and Migration' in AR Zolberg and P Benda (eds), *Global Migrants, Global Refugees: Problems and Solutions* (New York, Berghahn Books, 2001).

reliably foreseen, although some estimates suggest that the figure may be in the hundreds of millions by mid-century.[22]

The three major environmental consequences of climate change that particularly predispose people to displacement are: (i) loss of ecosystem services through environmental degradation, desertification and flooding; (ii) loss of land due to sea-level rise, shoreline erosion and coastal flooding; and (iii) increased severity and frequency of climate-related natural disasters.[23] These environmental losses will weaken local socio-ecological systems and lessen people's ability to subsist in some regions.[24] This will jeopardise health status (for example, causing under-nutrition, immune depression and mental health problems) which, in turn, may reinforce the motivation to move. Those health deficits will also heighten people's vulnerability, both during and after displacement, to additional health problems such as infection.

Populations in many low-income countries in tropical and sub-tropical regions, especially coastal-dwelling communities and impoverished slum-dwelling people, are at particular risk of adverse health impacts from climate change, which may be exacerbated by displacement.[25] Bangladesh, for example, is vulnerable on many existing counts: widespread poverty, crowding and food insecurity; high rates of tropical infectious diseases; low-lying exposed coastal populations; and threats to river water flows (due to Himalayan glacier retreat and possible upstream diversion by China and India). Heightened vulnerabilities also occur within higher-income countries. In the United States, for example, the impacts of the 1995 heatwave in Chicago differed greatly between socio-economic and racial groups, affecting the poorer, less well-housed, non-white segments of those urban populations.[26]

The health outcomes of migration due to climate change, as for all migrating and displaced groups, will also reflect the social, political, cultural, economic and ecological contexts from and into which people move. Although the literature on the likely geographical and temporal distribution of climate change-related movement is still rudimentary, it is likely that climate change will generally exacerbate existing migration patterns, rather than create entirely new patterns of movement.[27] Currently, most hosting of displaced people is by developing countries (such as Pakistan, Syria and Iran), which currently host four-fifths of the world's

---

[22] O Brown, 'Climate Change and Forced Migration: Observations, Projections and Implications', Human Development Report Office Occasional Paper (Geneva, UNDP, 2007); N Myers, 'Environmental Refugees: An Emergent Security Issue' (Paper presented to the 13th Economic Forum, Prague, 23–27 May 2005). The difficulties in defining this category of person, and in estimating future numbers, are discussed in W Kälin, 'Conceptualising Climate-Induced Displacement' and R Zetter, 'Protecting People Displaced by Climate Change: Some Conceptual Challenges', both in the present volume.

[23] A Oliver-Smith, 'Climate Change and Population Displacement: Disasters and Diasporas in the Twenty-First Century' in S Crate and M Nuttall (eds), *Anthropology and Climate Change* (California, Left Coast Press Inc, 2009).

[24] Renaud et al, *Control, Adapt or Flee*, above n 19.

[25] IPCC, *Climate Change 2007*, above n 8, 324–36.

[26] JC Semenza et al, 'Heat-Related Deaths during the July 1995 Heat Wave in Chicago' (1996) 335 *New England Journal of Medicine* 84.

[27] Barnett and Webber, 'Accommodating Migration', above n 19.

refugees, as well as groups of internally displaced persons (IDPs).[28] Much climate change-related displacement is therefore likely to occur in developing regions, where public health resources are lacking or inadequate.[29] Increased flooding, water shortages and drought are likely to amplify rural-to-urban migration in many such countries, yet many urban poor communities are situated in parts of cities that are themselves at high risk of climate change impacts. Hence, people migrating into these settings may face continued environmental and health threats.[30]

B Health Consequences of Displacement: What Do We Know?

> Migration is not stoppable. Neither is it always negative—in fact, migration is a legitimate way that people have used through the ages to cope with lands and lives that have for one reason or another become unsustainable. But the main impacts of sudden mass migration are invariably, overwhelmingly and profoundly damaging.[31]

The health profile of displaced people and refugees reflects both the illnesses that are endemic in their countries of origin and the health hazards they encounter during flight and resettlement. In addition, specific physical and mental health problems can result from the particular circumstances and events that spur and accompany migration—including the upheaval of migration and resettlement, and the civil tensions and conflict often associated with the large-scale movement of people.[32]

There is currently little scholarly literature or research data that specifically addresses the health consequences of displacement related to climate change. However, the health risks confronting displaced people and refugees, in general, provide a clear pointer to the main health risks likely to be encountered by climate-displaced people.

There is a considerable literature on the risks to physical and mental health, and socio-cultural well-being, faced by refugees and IDPs.[33] That research has focused on two main aspects. First, in large-scale population movements associated with humanitarian emergencies due to natural disasters and conflict, the key health

---

[28] United Nations High Commissioner for Refugees (UNHCR), *2008 Global Trends: Refugees, Asylum-Seekers, Returnees, Internally Displaced and Stateless Persons* (Geneva, UNHCR, 2009) 2.

[29] M Carballo, C Smith and K Pettersson, 'Climate Change and Displacement: Health Challenges' (2008) 31 *Forced Migration Review* 32.

[30] J Sward, *Migration and Climate Change: How Will Climate Shifts Affect Migration Trends?* (Brighton, Development Research Centre on Migration, Globalisation and Poverty, 2008).

[31] Oxfam International, *Suffering the Science: Climate Change, People, and Poverty* (London, Oxfam, 2009) 48.

[32] P Allotey, 'Refugee Health' in CR Ember and M Ember (eds), *Encyclopedia of Medical Anthropology: Health and Illness in the World's Cultures* (New York, Kluwer Academic /Plenum Publishers, 2004) 191.

[33] See, eg MM Cernea, 'The Risks and Reconstruction Model for Resettling Displaced Populations' (1997) 25 *World Development* 1569; MM Cernea and C McDowell (eds), *Risks and Reconstruction: Experiences of Resettlers and Refugees* (Washington DC, World Bank Group, 2000); Oliver-Smith, 'Climate Change and Population Displacement', above n 23.

risks stem from infectious disease and nutritional impairment. The relevant literature is primarily concerned with the health risks in people living in refugee camps for periods of weeks, months or several years.[34] The second research focus is on the (usually longer-term) psychological consequences of displacement and violence.[35] There has, however, been relatively little research into the physical health outcomes in longer-term refugees and forced migrants.[36]

In addition to this generalised evidence of health risks in displaced people, some of the particular circumstances relating to climate change and the resultant displacement experience itself may have distinctive impacts on health. Relevant known or likely influences include the following:

(i)   greater biomedical vulnerability of displaced groups if their movement arises against a background experience of chronic food deprivation and attendant undernutrition;

(ii)   the additional risks to physical safety and health that could result from greater background apprehensions (including in potential host populations), however unfounded, about the prospects for destabilisation, violence and even terrorism that an influx of migrants from diverse backgrounds might bring;

(iii) by extension of the above, a reduced willingness among potential host populations to take in displaced people and share resources;

(iv)   once the serious global and unavoidable nature of climate change is finally accepted by states and international institutions, the (more positive) prospect of creative new international agreements, extending to climate-vulnerable populations funding, technical assistance and, potentially, rights relating to movement.

Those context-specific considerations will help shape new research initiatives and intervention studies as the climate change topic commands rapidly increasing attention. Meanwhile, the main categories of health risks in displaced people, in general, are discussed below, noting particular links that may apply to climate-related displacement.

i Infectious Disease

Large-scale displacement is often accompanied by infectious disease outbreaks.[37] These occur particularly in camps or settlements that are insanitary, crowded,

---

[34] P Loizos and C Constantinou, 'Hearts, as Well as Minds: Wellbeing and Illness among Greek Cypriot Refugees' (2007) 20 *Journal of Refugee Studies* 86.

[35] C Watters, 'Emerging Paradigms in the Mental Health Care of Refugees' (2001) 52 *Social Science and Medicine* 1709; M Loughry, 'Climate Change, Human Movement and the Promotion of Mental Health: What Have We Learnt from Earlier Global Stressors?', in the present volume.

[36] Loizos and Constantinou, 'Hearts, as Well as Minds', above n 34.

[37] International Federation of Red Cross and Red Crescent Societies, *The Johns Hopkins and Red Cross and Red Crescent Public Health Guide in Emergencies* (Geneva, International Federation of Red Cross and Red Crescent Societies, 2007).

poorly ventilated and which provide inadequate shelter and access to health care facilities.[38] Since many climate-driven disasters are likely to lead to large-scale and prolonged population displacement, infectious disease is likely to be a significant recurring health problem. Historical studies of flooding in the Madras Presidency in southern India during the first half of the twentieth century show a strong positive correlation between local population displacement, crowding and social disorder, and outbreaks of cholera.[39]

Refugees and IDPs typically have elevated death rates during the period immediately after flight and migration. The most common causes of death are infectious diseases, particularly diarrhoeal disease, measles, acute respiratory infections and malaria.[40] Malaria-specific mortality rates are especially high when refugees from regions of low-malaria endemicity flee through or into areas of high endemicity (such as highland Ethiopians fleeing into eastern Sudan in 1985, and highland Rwandans moving to Zaire in 1994).[41] The high prevalence of acute undernutrition contributes to elevated mortality rates from some infectious diseases. Many such deaths occur among children under five years of age.[42]

Tuberculosis is a serious health problem among refugee and displaced populations.[43] Because of the disruptive effects of displacement, including reduced contact with health care facilities, individuals with active tuberculosis may not complete their treatment, thereby increasing the risk of transmission within displaced populations. Crowded living conditions and poor nutritional status may further increase the spread of the disease. Among adult refugees in eastern Sudan in 1985, 38 per cent of deaths were attributed to tuberculosis.[44]

Studies have identified that sexually transmissible infections (STIs) and HIV/AIDS spread most rapidly where there is poverty, powerlessness and social instability.[45] However, vulnerability to STIs and HIV/AIDS will depend in multivariate fashion on the prevalence within displaced populations and the surrounding or host community after displacement, the level of interaction between

---

[38] A Rajabali, O Moin, AS Ansari, MR Khanani and S Ali, 'Communicable Disease among Displaced Afghans: Refuge without Shelter' (2009) 7 *Nature Reviews Microbiology* 609.

[39] D Ruiz-Moreno, M Pascual and M Bouma, 'Cholera Seasonality in Madras (1901–1940): Dual Role for Rainfall in Endemic and Epidemic Regions' (2007) 4 *EcoHealth* 52.

[40] B de Bruijn, *The Living Conditions and Well-Being of Refugees* (Geneva, UNDP, 2009); MJ Toole, 'The Health of Refugees: An International Public Health Problem' in P Allotey (ed), *The Health of Refugees: Public Health Perspectives from Crisis to Settlement* (Melbourne, Oxford University Press, 2003).

[41] MJ Toole and RJ Waldman, 'The Public Health Aspects of Complex Emergencies and Refugee Situations' (1997) 18 *Annual Review of Public Health* 283.

[42] Toole, 'The Health of Refugees', above n 39.

[43] RJ Murray, JS Davis and DP Burgner, 'The Australasian Society for Infectious Diseases Guidelines for the Diagnosis, Management and Prevention of Infections in Recently Arrived Refugees: An Abridged Outline' (2009) 190 *Medical Journal of Australia* 421.

[44] Toole and Waldman, 'The Public Health Aspects of Complex Emergencies', above n 40, 296; Centre for Disease Control Prevention, 'Famine Affected Refugee and Displaced Populations: Recommendations for Public Health Issues' (1992) 41 *Morbidity and Mortality Weekly Report* 9.

[45] International Federation of Red Cross and Red Crescent Societies, *Public Health Guide in Emergencies*, above n 36.

displaced populations and host communities, the duration of displacement, and the length of time a displaced population has lived in camp settings.

As noted above, the impacts of climate change displacement are likely to be felt particularly in developing countries. The rates of infectious disease transmission in low-income countries are typically high and are a major cause of child mortality. Developed countries will also experience some changes in risks of infectious disease due to in-migration, since displaced populations often carry certain diseases to places where they have previously been uncommon.[46] Malaria, dengue and chikungunya are mosquito-borne diseases that can move with people, and population displacement from endemic areas can thus increase the spread of these diseases. Schistosomiasis (for which water snails are the intermediate host organism) is also readily spread by population movement, and this may be of particular concern with changes in water distribution patterns, especially in areas of increased rainfall and flooding.[47]

Identifying infectious disease is of primary concern in refugee health screening, assessment and treatment during the processes of resettlement to third countries.[48] Nonetheless, refugees arrive in countries of resettlement with high rates of tuberculosis, malaria, hepatitis and HIV.[49] For example, people born in sub-Saharan Africa are over-represented among new diagnoses of HIV infection in Australia, and 60 per cent of those with HIV infection are diagnosed late in the illness when it is more complex to treat and major symptoms have begun to appear.[50] It is important, however, that risk of infectious disease transmission is not mobilised as a way of controlling population movement, given that providing protection to refugees is an obligation of states under international law.[51]

ii Nutritional Deficits

Food shortage is a recurring, often critical, problem for displaced people. A joint UNHCR and World Food Programme review found in 2006 that acute malnutrition was present in many protracted refugee camp situations (where people had

---

[46] Carballo et al, 'Climate Change and Displacement', above n 29; LA Palinkas et al, 'The Journey to Wellness: Stages of Refugee Health Promotion and Disease Prevention' (2003) 5 *Journal of Immigrant Health* 19.

[47] Carballo et al, 'Climate Change and Displacement', above n 29.

[48] P Allotey, 'Introduction' in P Allotey (ed), *The Health of Refugees: Public Health Perspectives from Crisis to Settlement* (Melbourne, Oxford University Press, 2003). In Australia, refugees, like other migrants, must meet certain health criteria prior to being awarded a permanent visa. Most refugees also undergo an additional pre-departure medical screening 72 hours before their departure for Australia. In certain regions, this includes a malaria test, empirical treatment for intestinal parasites, and administration of the MMR vaccine for those younger than 30 years of age: Department of Immigration and Citizenship, 'Fact Sheet 22: The Health Requirement' (2009), www.immi.gov.au/media/fact-sheets/22health.htm.

[49] Palinkas et al, 'The Journey to Wellness', above n 46.

[50] B Biggs, M Hellard, A Street and C Lemoh, *Reducing the Risk of Transmission of HIV/AIDS in African and Arabic-Speaking Communities in Victoria* (Melbourne, University of Melbourne Department of Medicine, 2006).

[51] Allotey, 'Introduction', above n 48.

sought refuge in a host nation for five years or more).[52] Most notably, it exceeded 15 per cent in Kenya, Ethiopia, Sudan and some camps in Sierra Leone and Chad. The prevalence of acute malnutrition in children under five in refugee populations is usually high: earlier reports noted, for example, a prevalence of 50 per cent among Ethiopian refugees in eastern Sudan (1985), 45 per cent among Sudanese refugees in Ethiopia (1990) and 48 per cent among Mozambicans in Zimbabwe (1992).[53] In some settings, children develop acute malnutrition from food deprivation or severe diarrhoeal disease. A high incidence of micronutrient deficiency diseases has been reported in refugee camps, particularly in Africa, including pellagra (niacin deficiency), scurvy (vitamin C deficiency) and anaemia (iron deficiency).[54] Malnutrition and food insecurity are amplified where host governments apply encampment policies and prohibit income-generating and agricultural activities.[55]

The yields from plant foods depend critically on photosynthetic activity, which is finely tuned to prevailing temperature and soil moisture. For example, an increase in night-time temperature of 1°C reduces rice crop yields by approximately a tenth.[56] Animal health and bodily growth, also, are attuned to a particular climatic range. Both plants and animals are subject to infectious diseases which, as for those in humans, are sensitive to climatic conditions, and both are liable to extensive damage and losses from extreme weather events.

Climate change will entail long-term shifts both in average climatic conditions and increased adverse weather events. Sub-tropical regions will experience drier conditions and more severe droughts, in part because of the polewards shift of seasonal rainfall systems as the world warms. These changes, along with disruptive effects of related changes in infectious diseases and infestations in plant and animal food sources, will affect food yields, costs and accessibility. A preliminary estimation of the burden of disease attributable to the initial phase of climate change, as at the year 2000, indicated that already half of the attributable deaths (occurring predominantly in children) were due to undernutrition.[57] In fact, the risks to health arise not only from food shortages and undernutrition, but also as indirect consequences of the loss of livelihoods and family incomes.

A further potentially large category of displaced people may arise from the many coastal communities whose livelihoods and major protein sources depend on local

---

[52] de Bruijn, *The Living Conditions and Well-Being of Refugees*, above n 40, 22; UNHCR and United Nations World Food Programme (WFP), *Acute Malnutrition in Protracted Refugee Situations: A Global Strategy* (Geneva, UNHCR and WFP, 2006) 6.

[53] Toole and Waldman, 'The Public Health Aspects of Complex Emergencies', above n 41, 297. See also UNHCR and WFP, *Acute Malnutrition in Protracted Refugee Situations*, above n 52.

[54] UNHCR and WFP, *Acute Malnutrition in Protracted Refugee Situations*, above n 52.

[55] de Bruijn, *The Living Conditions and Well-Being of Refugees*, above n 40.

[56] S Peng et al, 'Rice Yields Decline with Higher Night Temperature from Global Warming' (2004) 101 *Proceedings of the National Academy of Science USA* 9971.

[57] AJ McMichael et al, 'Global Climate Change' in M Ezzati, AD Lopez, A Rodgers and CJL Murray (eds), *Comparative Quantification of Health Risks: The Global and Regional Burden of Disease Attributable to Selected Major Risk Factors* (Geneva, World Health Organization, 2004).

fisheries[58]—a total of around 2.6 billion people, including the poorer segments of many low-income countries.[59] Ocean warming, changes in currents and ocean acidification are beginning to affect marine ecosystems and productivity. The world's oceans have undergone an estimated 30 per cent increase in acidity since the beginning of the industrial revolution, including a documented decline in pH in recent decades.[60] This acidity threatens several critical biological processes, especially calcification (exoskeletons and so on) in zooplankton, crustaceans and corals—creatures that support the marine food web.

Overall, it is likely that many people and groups displaced as a result of climate change will come from increasingly food-insecure regions—and many of them will be nutritionally compromised at the outset.

iii Reproductive Health

It has been well documented that women living in refugee camps and countries of first asylum face additional health risks. These include elevated risks of maternal mortality, unmet needs for family planning, limited access to clinical health services, complications following unsafe abortions, gender-based violence, as well as sexually transmitted infections, including HIV/AIDS.[61] Among refugee women of childbearing age, complications related to pregnancy and childbirth are leading causes of death.[62] Though relief and development agencies and UN bodies have made positive policy changes specific to crisis settings and are working to provide better reproductive health care, considerable problems persist.[63]

Other than studies focusing on HIV/AIDS, there is limited research that addresses the sexual and reproductive health of refugees and displaced people living in countries of resettlement.[64] However, resettled refugees may have particular sexual and reproductive health needs due to pre-arrival experiences characterised by violence and insecurity, and to disrupted schooling and education, limited access to health care and health information, and fragmentation of family and social networks.[65]

---

[58] EH Allison et al, 'Vulnerability of National Economies to the Impacts of Climate Change on Fisheries' (2009) 10 *Fish and Fisheries* 173.

[59] WFP, 'UN Food Agencies Urge Climate Change Action to Avert Hunger' (News Release, Rome, 2007), www.wfp.org/news/news-release/un-food-agencies-urge-climate-change-action-avert-hunger.

[60] RA Feely et al, 'Evidence for Upwelling of Corrosive "Acidified" Water onto the Continental Shelf' (2008) 320 *Science* 1490.

[61] J Austin et al, 'Reproductive Health: A Right for Refugees and Internally Displaced Persons' (2008) 16 *Reproductive Health Matters* 10; RK Jones, 'Reproductive Health for Adolescent Refugees' (1999) 27 *Siecus Report* 15; J Matthews and S Ritsema, 'Addressing the Reproductive Health Needs of Conflict-Affected Young People' (2004) 19 *Forced Migration Review* 6; R Petchesky, 'Conflict and Crisis Settings: Promoting Sexual and Reproductive Rights (Editorial)' (2008) 16 *Reproductive Health Matters* 4.

[62] de Bruijn, *The Living Conditions and Well-Being of Refugees*, above n 40.

[63] Austin et al, 'Reproductive Health', above n 61.

[64] N Ascoly, I Van Halsema and L Keysers, 'Refugee Women, Pregnancy and Reproductive Health Care in the Netherlands' (2001) 14 *Journal of Refugee Studies* 371; L Straus, A McEwan and FM Hussein, 'Somali Women's Experience of Childbirth in the UK: Perspectives from Somali Health Workers' (2009) 25 *Midwifery* 181.

[65] C McMichael and SM Gifford, 'It Is Good to Know Now . . . Before It's Too Late: Promoting Sexual Health Literacy Amongst Resettled Young People With Refugee Backgrounds' (2009) 13 *Sexuality & Culture* 218.

iv Chronic Disease

There is accruing evidence that displacement and resettlement lead to increases in non-communicable diseases, such as cancer, hypertension, cardiovascular disease and Type II diabetes.[66] Displaced populations are at higher risk of developing these chronic diseases and their subsequent health outcomes are worse than those of non-migrants.[67] The causal link between migration and these chronic diseases has been attributed to adverse changes in diet,[68] acculturative stress,[69] and increases in health risk behaviours, such as tobacco smoking[70] and hazardous use of alcohol.[71] Poor chronic disease outcomes are also due to lack of access to health care services, including preventative health care and early diagnosis.[72] Social isolation, exacerbated by language difficulties and lack of transport, also means that chronic disease may be inadequately treated. Physical inactivity is common in a number of different migrant groups, contributing substantially to elevated chronic disease rates and poor outcomes.[73]

Recent studies of immigrant and refugee populations in Australia, for example, have identified a high prevalence of obesity among African groups.[74] A study of dietary changes among Somali women who migrated to Australia found that, while the structure of the diet from Somalia persisted, energy intake increased through consumption of processed foods. For example, ready-baked bread was often substituted for traditional bread, lamb was eaten instead of camel meat, and breakfast cereals were included as part of the everyday diet. Sixty per cent of the Somali women were overweight or obese (as assessed in relation to body mass index (BMI)).[75]

v Mental Health and Psychosocial Impacts[76]

Previous research on the mental health of refugees and displaced people has focused primarily on post-traumatic stress disorder and depression. Many such studies have

[66] Palinkas et al, 'The Journey to Wellness', above n 46.

[67] Carballo et al, 'Climate Change and Displacement', above n 29.

[68] C Burns, 'Effect of Migration on Food Habits of Somali Women Living as Refugees in Australia', (2004) 43 *Ecology of Food and Nutrition* 213; Palinkas et al, 'The Journey to Wellness', above n 46.

[69] LA Palinkas, 'Health under Stress: Asian and Central American Refugees and Those Left Behind: Introduction' (1995) 40 *Social Science & Medicine* 1591.

[70] M Bermingham et al, 'Smoking and Lipid Cardiovascular Risk Factors in Vietnamese Refugees in Australia' (1999) 28 *Preventative Medicine* 378.

[71] J Westermeyer, 'Substance Use Disorders among Young Minority Refugees: Common Themes in a Clinical Sample' (1993) 130 *NIDA Research Monograph* 308.

[72] McMichael and Gifford, 'It Is Good to Know Now', above n 65; L Uba, 'Cultural Barriers to Health Care for Southeast Asian Refugees' (1992) 107 *Public Health Report* 544.

[73] C Caperchione, GS Kolt and WK Mummery, 'Physical Activity in Culturally and Linguistically Diverse Migrant Groups to Western Society: A Review of Barriers, Enablers and Experiences' (2009) 39 *Sports Medicine* 167.

[74] Burns, 'Effect of Migration on Food Habits', above n 68; AM Renzaho et al, 'Obesity and Undernutrition in Sub-Saharan African Immigrant and Refugee Children in Victoria, Australia' (2006) 15 *Asia-Pacific Journal of Clinical Nutrition* 482.

[75] Burns, 'Effect of Migration on Food Habits', above n 68.

[76] See also Loughry, 'Climate Change', above n 35.

shown significantly elevated rates of these common mental health problems. While this research has frequently implicated the role of pre-displacement violence and trauma, there is clear evidence that post-displacement stressors also create mental health risks.[77]

The depression and trauma that displaced people experience are often associated with loss of home and material resources, fragmented social networks, economic deprivation and loss of power.[78] A wide range of material resources can be lost through disasters and displacement, including housing, personal possessions, infrastructure services, health care, transportation and communication. The combination of the loss of these resources, plus the process of displacement itself, affects the economic, social and cultural domains of life, stripping away the familiar social context in which people find meaning.[79] This, in turn, erodes psychosocial well-being; indeed, refugees' diminished sense of belonging (a sense which is strongly and protectively related to mental health, especially for people facing disadvantage),[80] is a significant source of distress and tension for newcomers and, therefore, also potentially stressful for their host community.[81] This is particularly the case in countries where displaced people find themselves in inadequate housing and poorly serviced areas, with little educational and job security.[82]

'Social disarticulation' resulting from displacement and relocation, which includes separation from and fragmentation of family and community networks,[83] is particularly damaging to the sense of belonging. Clinical and field studies have documented substantial psychosocial distress in refugee populations separated from family, and this distress, and associated impaired mood and behaviour, can create long-term psychosocial disadvantage, including in relation to engagement with the host community and participation in the workforce.[84] Further, as psychosocial dis-

---

[77] Palinkas 'Health under Stress', above n 69; C McMichael and L Manderson, 'Somali Women and Well-Being: Social Capital and Social Networks among Immigrant Women in Australia' (2004) 63 *Human Organization* 88; N Warfa et al, 'Post-Migration Geographical Mobility, Mental Health and Health Service Utilisation among Somali Refugees in the UK: A Qualitative Study' (2006) 12 *Health & Place* 503. There is also significant psychological literature on the mental health impacts of detention and the temporary protection visa regime on asylum seekers and refugees in Australia: see, eg Z Steel et al, 'Psychiatric Status of Asylum Seeker Families Held for a Protracted Period in a Remote Detention Centre in Australia' (2004) 28 *Australian and New Zealand Journal of Public Health* 527.

[78] T Scudder and E Colson, 'From Welfare to Development: A Conceptual Framework for the Analysis of Dislocated People' in A Hansen and A Oliver-Smith (eds), *Involuntary Migration and Resettlement* (Boulder, Westview Press, 1982).

[79] Oliver-Smith, 'Climate Change and Population Displacement', above n 23, 123.

[80] HL Berry, 'Social Capital Elite, Excluded Participators, Busy Working Parents and Aging, Participating Less: Types of Community Participators and their Mental Health' (2008) 43 *Social Psychiatry and Psychiatric Epidemiology* 527.

[81] D Bhugra, 'Migration and Mental Health' (2004) 109 *Acta Psychiatrica Scandinavica* 243; RD Putnam, *Bowling Alone: The Collapse and Revival of American Community* (New York, Simon and Schuster, 2000); RD Putnam, 'E Pluribus Unum: Diversity and Community in the Twenty-first Century: The 2006 Johan Skytte Prize Lecture (2007) 30 *Scandinavian Political Studies* 137.

[82] Carballo et al, 'Climate Change and Displacement', above n 29.

[83] Cernea and McDowell (eds), *Risks and Reconstruction*, above n 33.

[84] L Manderson, 'A Woman without a Man is a Woman at Risk: Women at Risk in Australian Humanitarian Programs' (1998) 11 *Journal of Refugee Studies* 267; McMichael and Manderson, 'Somali Women and Well-Being', above n 77.

advantage in one generation is associated with continuing disadvantage in the next,[85] displacement may initiate a damaging cycle of inter-generational disadvantage. Family support is thus very important throughout the process of displacement and relocation: it can buffer pre-migration trauma as well as post-migration stresses,[86] and is crucial to overcoming barriers in the host community—from improving educational adaptation and psychosocial adjustment, to managing the physical and mental health impacts of migration.[87]

vi Conflict[88]

The relationship between climate change, migration and conflict is contentious. While climate change alone will rarely lead to migration or violence, it is more likely to do so in conjunction with high population densities and growth, inequality, other environmental stresses, under-development and poor governance.[89] Forced migration may be triggered in part by environmental conflicts. For example, degradation of freshwater resources can trigger competition and conflict leading to flight and displacement.[90] Indeed, forced migration can itself contribute to environmental conflicts. Such a link has been observed, for example, in southern Sudan. In the background to that catastrophic conflict situation, average rainfall in southern-western Sudan fell dramatically in recent decades. An assessment by the UN Environment Programme concluded that climate change and desertification may have created additional population stressors and increased migration southwards, thus contributing to initiation of the conflict.[91]

Where climate change is associated with conflict, the health impacts on displaced people will include increased mortality, injuries, gender-based violence,

[85] HL Berry et al, 'Intergenerational Transmission of Reliance on Income Support: Psychosocial Factors and their Measurement', Department of Family and Community Services and Indigenous Affairs Academic Series, Social Policy Research Paper No 31 (Canberra, 2007).

[86] E Montgomery, 'Traumatised Refugee Families: The Child's Perspective' in P Perliner, J Arenas and JO Haagensen (eds), *Torture and Organised Violence: Contributions to a Professional Human Rights Response* (Copenhagen, Dansk Psykologisk Forlag, 2005).

[87] M Drukker et al, 'Social Capital and Young Adolescents: Perceived Health in Different Sociocultural Settings' (2005) 61 *Social Science and Medicine* 185; A Fuligni, 'Authority, Autonomy, and Parent–Adolescent Conflict and Cohesion: A Study of Adolescents from Mexican, Chinese, Filipino and European Backgrounds' (1998) 34 *Developmental Psychology* 782; A Portes and R Rumbaut, *Legacies: The Story of the Second Generation* (Berkeley, University of California Press, 2001); DB Qin, 'Gendered Processes of Adaptation: Understanding Parent–Child Relations in Chinese Immigrant Families' (2009) 60 *Sex Roles* 467.

[88] See L Elliott, 'Climate Migration and Climate Migrants: What Threat, Whose Security?', in the present volume.

[89] J Barnett and WN Adger, 'Climate Change, Human Security and Violent Conflict' (2007) 26 *Political Geography* 627; VO Kolmannskog, *Future Floods of Refugees: A Comment on Climate Change, Conflict and Forced Migration* (Oslo, Norwegian Refugee Council, 2008); DA McDonald, 'Lest the Rhetoric Begin: Migration, Population and the Environment in Southern Africa' (1999) 31 *Geoforum* 13; R Reuveny, 'Climate Change-Induced Migration and Violent Conflict' (2007) 26 *Political Geography* 656.

[90] Kolmannskog, *Future Floods of Refugees*, above n 89.

[91] UNEP, *UNEP Annual Report 2007* (Geneva, UNEP, 2008). But see also UNEP, 'From Conflict to Peacebuilding: Introduction', *The Encyclopedia of Earth* (2009), www.eoearth.org/article/From_ Conflict_to_Peacebuilding~_Introduction.

physical and psychological trauma. The secondary public health effects of conflict include food shortages, malnutrition and micro-nutrient deficiencies, and collapsed primary health care services, including prevention programmes such as child immunisation and antenatal care.

vii Urbanisation and Health Issues

The adverse environmental and economic effects of climate change (especially via declines in farm yields and consequent damage to local livelihoods and community life due to droughts and long-term water shortages in rural areas) have begun to increase the volume of migration into cities in many regions.[92] This is accelerating the rates of city population growth, placing stress on urban socio-economic conditions and facilities. This, in turn, has health consequences.

The urban poor, particularly those living in slums with poor water and sanitation facilities, are especially prone to ill-health. ActionAid carried out analyses of slum dwellers in six African cities and found that intra-city flooding and the impact on hygiene and sanitation were a major risk to health.[93] Further, rural-to-urban migration is associated with increased transmission of certain infectious diseases. For example, the malaria and dengue pathogens often move with people and can either initiate outbreaks or increase the level of endemic transmission in the site of settlement.[94]

Rural-to-urban movement can also affect mental health, reflecting the burdens of socio-economic disadvantage in poor parts of cities and the impact of loss of community and, often, social hostilities.[95] These conditions drive a number of psychosocial stressors that, in turn, adversely affect mental health. In the reverse direction, social drift—in which those with (especially, chronic and severe) psychiatric disorders 'drift' over their life-course into ever poorer economic and social circumstances—contributes to the disproportionate prevalence of mental health problems in disadvantaged parts of cities. It is probable that migration to cities, driven at least in part by climate change, will compound both of these pernicious mental health-related dynamics.

viii Health Impacts on Those Who Are Left Behind

In the face of climate risks, not everyone will respond by migrating. Some may draw (successfully, even) upon adaptive strategies without recourse to migration. But, on balance, climate change is likely to exacerbate an already existing trend towards depopulation and ageing in many rural areas. Environmental migrants

---

[92] IPCC, *Climate Change 2007*, above n 8.

[93] ActionAid International, *Unjust Waters: Climate Change, Flooding and the Protection of Poor Urban Communities: Experiences from Six African Cities* (Johannesburg, ActionAid International, 2007), www.actionaid.org.uk/doc_lib/unjust_waters.pdf.

[94] Carballo et al, 'Climate Change and Displacement', above n 29.

[95] HL Berry, ' "Crowded Suburbs" and "Killer Cities": A Brief Review of the Relationship between the Built Environment and Mental Health' (2007) 18 *NSW Bulletin of Public Health* 222; Loughry, 'Climate Change', above n 35.

often leave behind barely enough labour to address on-going land degradation processes.[96] Despite this, it may be that, overall, the numbers of people who cannot migrate in response to climate change (for example, because of poverty, geography, ill-health or age) may be far greater than those who can.[97] The problem is not so much the absolute number of those who are left behind, but that these people are likely to be the least able to cope. Thus, those who cannot adapt or who do not migrate may experience livelihood decline, increased health problems and declining life expectancy.[98]

C Concluding Comment

There is, as ever for refugees and other displaced people, a diversity of health risks facing climate-related displaced people. The health risks are linked more to the experiences of displacement and resettlement than to exposure to the actual environmental and social consequences of climate change. However, the impacts of climate change on food yields, water supplies, damage to property (homes and possessions), and risks of various infectious diseases at the point of origin, along with the psychological, political and perhaps physical impacts of climate change on the host populations and their environs, all add an extra dimension of health risk for climate-displaced people.

[handwritten margin note: climate change adds another dimension of health risk]

V Vulnerability, Resilience and Adaptive Capacity

A Understanding 'Vulnerability'

The advent of climate change as a threat to human communities has fostered a more analytic and integrated view of 'vulnerability'. Groups of displaced people will differ in their vulnerability to (or likelihood of) experiencing adverse health impacts. This differential vulnerability reflects three factors: (i) the external environmental conditions that impinge on them; (ii) their constitutive characteristics (which determine their sensitivity to those external exposures); and (iii) their potential and capacity to apply adaptive responses to lessen the resultant potential risks to health.

The Intergovernmental Panel on Climate Change defines vulnerability to climate change as 'the degree to which a system is susceptible to, or unable to cope with, adverse effects of climate change, including climate variability and extremes'.[99] By referring to coping capacity, this definition also recognises the social dimensions of vulnerability. Few proposes that both vulnerability to—and coping capacity for managing—the health impacts of climate hazards reflect

---

[96] Boano, Zetter and Morris, 'Environmentally Displaced People', above n 18.
[97] Barnett and Webber, 'Accommodating Migration', above n 19.
[98] U Kothari, 'Staying Put and Staying Poor?' (2003) 15 *Journal of International Development* 645.
[99] IPCC, *Climate Change 2007*, above n 8, 883.

physiological and psychological states, the conditions of the physical and social environments and human agency.[100]

Forced migrants and displaced people are not a homogeneous group, even when fleeing the same hardships and circumstances. Therefore, vulnerability and resilience among people fleeing the effects of climate change will differ greatly, reflecting both community and individual-level characteristics (such as class, race, ethnicity, sex and age) that place people at different levels of risk from the same hazard.[101] Certain generic, contextual and community characteristics may also influence the vulnerability profile of a displaced group, such as the community's overall level of health, poverty and economic inequality, and local and national governance.[102]

Interacting with these community-level characteristics are diverse individual factors—socio-economic, biomedical, behavioural, life-stage and life events.[103] In developing countries, where people have fewer resources to manage threats or recover from their impacts,[104] contextual, place-based and individual vulnerabilities may be extreme. Hence, some refugees are much more vulnerable than others in the same community or circumstances to the succession of health risks associated with displacement—from pre-displacement trauma to long-term inter-generational post-displacement consequences.

We do not have the scope, here, to address the role and needs of indigenous peoples adequately. Indigenous peoples are particularly vulnerable to the adverse effects of climate change, not just because of their poverty and poor health in absolute terms but because of their relative disadvantage. Migration away from climate impacts (with sea-level rise a notable threat[105]) might have different and/or worse impacts on the health of indigenous peoples than on other populations.[106] Meanwhile, indigenous peoples can often draw on certain strengths: they are accustomed to dealing with tragically difficult circumstances (often imposed by human actions); they are the keepers of traditional ecological knowledge, which will often be valuable in responding to aspects of climate change (though perhaps not to the challenges of sea-level rise); and they have a strong tradition of inter-generational stewardship of and responsibility for the land.[107] While there is a

---

[100] R Few, 'Health and Climatic Hazards: Framing Social Research on Vulnerability, Response and Adaptation' (2007) 17 *Global Environmental Change* 281.

[101] Oliver-Smith, 'Climate Change and Population Displacement', above n 23.

[102] N Brooks, NW Adger and PM Kelly, 'The Determinants of Vulnerability and Adaptive Capacity at the National Level and the Implications for Adaptation' (2005) 15 *Global Environmental Change* 151.

[103] TS Brugha and D Cragg, 'The List of Threatening Experiences: The Reliability and Validity of a Brief Life Events Questionnaire' (1990) 82 *Acta Psychiatrica Scandinavica* 77.

[104] Oliver-Smith, 'Climate Change and Population Displacement', above n 23.

[105] See J McAdam, ' "Disappearing States", Statelessness and the Boundaries of International Law', in the present volume.

[106] D Green, 'Climate Impacts on the Health of Northern Australian Indigenous Communities', Commissioned Background Paper for the Garnaut Climate Change Review (Sydney, 2008).

[107] HL Berry et al, 'Climate Change and Mental Health: Creating Opportunity in Rural and Remote Aboriginal Communities', *Australian and New Zealand Journal of Public Health* (forthcoming); ML Martello, 'Arctic Indigenous Peoples as Representations and Representatives of Climate Change' (2008) 38 *Social Studies of Science* 351.

need for sensitivity to special considerations relating to indigenous peoples' continuing loss of place and culture, it is also appropriate to emphasise their important strengths—and the resultant opportunities for future development.[108]

B Adaptive Capacity and Resilience

Reducing vulnerability to health impairment works best when action is guided by appropriate theory and strategy.[109] Adaptive interventions, whether in stable or displaced communities, can confer long-term gains in underlying community capacity. An 'adaptive capacity' approach is therefore attractive to development workers and agencies concerned to lessen the risks to countries and communities at greatest risk of adverse climate change impacts.

Basic features of communities or regions that influence adaptive capacity are economic wealth, technology, infrastructure, information and skills, institutions and equity.[110] Public health resources and programmes and pre-existing disease burdens are also important.[111] Less tangible factors, such as community cohesion, governance structures and social inclusion, are more difficult to conceptualise and measure, even though studies indicate that such factors are consistently related to stronger communities and better outcomes in health and well-being.[112]

Most adaptation to the risk of climate-related stressors and disasters needs to occur at the community level.[113] Therefore, the public health system, with its typical whole-of-population focus, is well placed to take a leadership role in building community resilience to climate-related stressors and disasters. Such community strengthening may help to reduce the need for relocation if appropriate, and effective public health measures can strengthen community adaptive capacity. However, there has been little research done to evaluate the actual relationship between adaptive capacity and health outcomes in particular settings, perhaps because of insufficient awareness of the important mediating role, and nature, of the community's resilience.

---

[108] HL Berry, 'Pearl in the Oyster: Climate Change as a Mental Health Opportunity' (2009) 17 *Australasian Psychiatry* 453; Martello, 'Arctic Indigenous Peoples', above n 107.

[109] BL Preston and M Stafford-Smith, 'Framing Vulnerability and Adaptive Capacity Assessment: Discussion Paper', Climate Adaptation National Research Flagship, Working Paper No 2 (Melbourne, CSIRO, 2008).

[110] IPCC, *Climate Change 2001: Impact, Adaptation and Vulnerability Contribution of Working Group II to the Third Assessment Report of the Intergovernmental Panel on Climate Change* (New York, Cambridge University Press, 2001).

[111] A Grambsch and B Menne, 'Adaptation and Adaptive Capacity in the Public Health Context' in AJ McMichael et al (eds), *Climate Change and Human Health: Risks and Responses* (Geneva, World Health Organization, 2003).

[112] I Kawachi, SV Subramanian and D Kim, 'Social Capital and Health: A Decade of Progress and Beyond' in I Kawachi, SV Subramanian and D Kim (eds), *Social Capital and Health* (New York, Springer, 2008).

[113] ME Keim, 'Building Human Resilience' (2008) 35 *American Journal of Preventive Medicine* 508; SG Zakowski, MH Hall, LC Klein and A Baum, 'Appraised Control, Coping and Stress in a Community Sample: A Test of the Goodness-of-Fit Hypothesis' (2001) 23 *Annals of Behavioral Medicine* 158.

Both vulnerability and adaptive capacity are shaped by differential access to economic, political and social resources.[114] Low levels of wealth tend to restrict adaptive capacity; hence, developing nations are often regarded as necessarily having low adaptive capacity.[115] In fact, some communities with fewer economic and material resources may be quite resilient because they have had to rely on their own resources to develop innovative ways to cope with challenges. This collective experience alone can be protective for health, especially for mental health;[116] working together to resolve shared problems builds social capital. Communities rich in social capital display dense networks with high levels of social interaction, connectedness and cohesion, all of which are related to better health,[117] including via the sharing and uptake of health-related information.[118]

Social capital has been suggested as a necessary 'glue'[119] for adaptive capacity, particularly when dealing with hazardous events (climatic and other). This is especially so in disadvantaged (including indigenous) communities.[120] Three factors influence the effectiveness of strategies for adapting to the health (and other) risks of climate change: the social acceptability of options for adaptation, the institutional constraints on adaptation, and the architecture of economic development and social evolution.[121] These can be broadly framed as issues of community agreement, governance and contextual priorities. To the extent that displaced people cohere as communities during and after displacement, or subsequently re-form as new communities, these factors will affect their health risk profile and disease burden.

On the positive side, displacement and resettlement can have beneficial health impacts by removing people from the physical dangers of extreme weather events or degraded physical environments to places with better living conditions. In the case of Hurricane Katrina, for example, pre-hurricane Louisiana was one of the poorest areas in the United States with respect to critical health indicators. Climate disaster-forced movement from an environment with pre-existing multiple stressors, violence and sub-standard medical care can thus actually produce positive long-term health effects.[122]

---

[114] M Pelling, 'Natural Disasters?' in N Castree and B Braun (eds), *Social Nature: Theory, Practice and Politics* (Malden, Blackwell, 2001); B Wisner, P Blaikie, T Cannon and I Davis, *At Risk: Natural Hazards, People's Vulnerability and Disasters*, 2nd edn (London, Routledge, 2004).

[115] Preston and Stafford-Smith, 'Framing Vulnerability, above n 109.

[116] Berry, 'Social Capital Elite', above n 80; HL Berry, 'Social Capital and Mental Health among Indigenous Australians, New Australians and Other Australians in a Coastal Region' (2009) 8 *Australian e-Journal for the Advancement of Mental Health* <http://www.auseinet.com/journal/vol8iss2/berry.pdf>.

[117] AM Almedon, 'Social Capital and Mental Health: An Interdisciplinary Review of Primary Evidence' (2005) 61 *Social Science and Medicine* 943; MJ de Silva, SR Huttley, T Harpham and MG Kenward, 'Social Capital and Mental Health: A Comparative Analysis of Four Low Income Countries' (2007) 64 *Social Science and Medicine* 5.

[118] N Sartorius, 'Social Capital and Mental Health' (2003) 16 *Current Opinion in Psychiatry* S101.

[119] NW Adger, 'Social Capital, Collective Action, and Adaptation to Climate Change' (2003) 79 *Economic Geography* 387, 392.

[120] Berry, 'Social Capital Elite', above n 80 and 'Social Capital and Mental Health', above n 116.

[121] Adger, 'Social Capital', above n 119.

[122] L Uscher-Pines, 'Health Effects of Relocation Following Disaster: A Systematic Review of the Literature' (2009) 33 *Disasters* 1.

C Role of the Health Sector in Lessening Health Risks; Collaboration with Other Sectors

As discussed in relation to Figure 1 above, climate change affects human health both directly and indirectly. In anticipation, adaptive strategies to lessen risks, plus general public health preparedness and response capacity, can help build community resilience and reduce human vulnerability, including in relation to climate change.[123] Vulnerable populations—including many of those that are prone to displacement—are typically described at the sub-national and local levels.[124]

The complex paths by which climate change impinges on communities and groups, and the modulating influences of diverse cultural, social and economic factors, means that health-protecting (and health-restoring) adaptation strategies must embrace policies across multiple sectors, including health, water, agriculture, energy and transport. Indeed, there is a need for multilevel, interdisciplinary and integrated adaptation measures and emergency responses. Sometimes the public health sector will take a lead role in driving effective inter-sectoral collaboration; sometimes it will be a more minor contributor.

Effective adaptation can result in developmental, environmental and health co-benefits as a consequence of the building of trust and cooperation—two central components of social capital[125]—between parties in the state and in civil society.[126] First, high levels of trust (and social capital generally) are directly related to gains in health, especially where inequality is high.[127] This is especially so for mental health.[128] Secondly, inclusive decision-making promotes the sustainability and legitimacy of an adaptation strategy. Finally, adaptation processes initiated within communities, and building on existing social capital, can shift climate change from being seen as a global (that is, international governments') problem, to a local problem with which local communities can engage. This process, though, is often not 'bottom up' or egalitarian, since social capital tends to be created and controlled by elites,[129] with health gains accruing preferentially to those same privileged people.[130]

---

[123] Keim, 'Building Human Resilience', above n 113.

[124] H Frumkin, J Hess, G Luber, J Malilay and M McGeehin, 'Climate Change: The Public Health Response' (2008) 98 *American Journal of Public Health* 435.

[125] Putnam *Bowling Alone*, above n 81.

[126] Adger, 'Social Capital', above n 119.

[127] MK Islam, J Merlo, I Kawachi, M Lindström and UG Gerdtham, 'Social Capital and Health: Does Egalitarianism Matter? A Literature Review' (2006) 5 *International Journal for Equity in Health* 1.

[128] HL Berry and JA Welsh, 'Social Capital and Health in Australia: An Overview from the Household Income and Labour Dynamics in Australia Survey', (2010) 70 *Social Science and Medicine* 588.

[129] CH Heying, 'Civic Elites and Corporate Dislocation: An Alternative Explanation for Declining Civic Engagement' (1997) 40 *American Behavioral Scientist* 657; P Rich, 'American Voluntarism, Social Capital, and Political Culture' (1999) 565 *The Annals of the American Academy of Political and Social Science* 15.

[130] Berry, 'Social Capital Elite', above n 80.

VI Implications for Research

This chapter has noted the current dearth of published research on the health risks that confront people displaced because of climate change. This reflects at least three circumstances. First, manifestly human-driven climate change has only been recognised over the past decade. To date, the resultant changes in climate have been relatively modest—in other words, there has not yet been very much 'exposure' to climate change. Secondly, most displacement has multivariate causation, meaning that there will be relatively few examples of people movement that are exclusively and obviously due to a change in climatic conditions[131]—at least in this still initial phase of the process. Thirdly, the research community in general is not yet very attuned to the need for research in this domain, nor does it have fluency in the types of methods that will be required.[132]

However, research into the effects of climate change is increasingly emphasising human experience, agency, interactions with environments, social and cultural change, and local knowledge.[133] Descriptive studies will become increasingly possible if people start to move from their homes (as has been anticipated with respect to some small, low-lying island states). However, the experiences and contexts of displacement will differ, and so, too, will some of the described health consequences. A key research challenge will be to find opportunities to make informative comparisons of two or more groupings or categories of displaced people, to better understand the (complex of) determinants of health outcomes.

A Research Concepts and Methods

If climate change continues on its current and likely trajectory and disrupts many communities, then an increase is likely in the numbers of people moving in response to these disruptions over the coming decades. The need for research, understanding and appropriate policy responses will therefore be heightened. In principle, the main directions of research in relation to climate-related displacement and health should include: (i) finding ways of best assisting threatened or stressed communities so that (in at least some circumstances) relocation is not necessary and good health is maintained; (ii) understanding the circumstances and personal or group characteristics that entail the greatest risks to health in groups on the move; (iii) understanding the key determinants of health outcomes after resettlement; and (iv) identifying and evaluating intervention strategies and supportive policies that will lessen the impost of poor health, disease and risk of death in those who move.

---

[131] Kälin, 'Conceptualising Climate-Induced Displacement', above n 22; Zetter, 'Protecting People Displaced by Climate Change: Some Conceptual Challenges', above n 22.

[132] Baer and Singer, *Global Warming*, above n 3.

[133] Martello, 'Arctic Indigenous Peoples', above n 107.

In practice, such research will be very demanding. Due to heightened mobility, displaced populations can be difficult to reach as people move across multiple geographic borders and through formal and informal 'bureaucratic' regimes.[134] Indeed, it may be even harder to access those who move internally, within countries, because they are not monitored (or even counted) in the same way. The interplay of socio-cultural and geographic circumstances, factors associated with movement, unfavourable climatic–environmental conditions and so on will put a premium on integrated, perhaps systems-based, thinking, modelling and analysis and multidisciplinary research.

There is a need for differentiated types of analyses that explore particular configurations of environmental risks and behavioural responses.[135] People who are accustomed to living with an on-going hazard, such as drought or seasonal flooding, may respond differently to the advent of an acute climate-related health risk than other groups. People who move away from a disaster situation or are displaced because of it may undergo a reduction in their hazard-related coping mechanisms, compared to those who coexist. Such analyses may benefit further from focusing on specific hazard types and health outcomes.

Where the displacement is between countries, bilateral or multilateral research collaborations will be needed between research groups and relevant organisations, services and government agencies in the countries of origin, passage and reception. In general, the research should be participatory, involving, as appropriate, those who have been, or are likely to be, displaced.[136] Further, research into the experiences and health outcomes of this particular category of displaced people will face some unusual time pressures, since the research is likely to be done against a background of increasing environmental and social disruption and consequent displacement—that is, a background that emphasises the need for early understanding and effective intervention.

VII Conclusion

The topic of this chapter is important and timely. Yet, there is as yet a sparse research base from which to characterise the types, mixes and levels of health risks faced by, specifically, climate-related displaced people. This is not surprising, since climate-related displacement has, to date, not been substantial—or, where it has occurred (perhaps more within, than between, countries), it has not been easy to differentiate from displacement due to other coexistent social, economic and physical factors.

---

[134] B Harrell-Bond and E Voutira, 'In Search of "Invisible" Actors: Barriers to Access in Refugee Research' (2007) 20 *Journal of Refugee Studies* 281; Voutira and Dona, 'Refugee Research Methodologies', above n 17.

[135] Few, 'Health and Climatic Hazards', above n 100.

[136] Voutira and Dona, 'Refugee Research Methodologies', above n 17.

It is in the nature of climate-related health risks that simple itemisation is not possible. Many of the health risks are not of a discrete and causally transparent kind: the context is complex, and a systems-based approach to research may be needed to elucidate the coexisting, often interacting, causal influences and feedback processes, in order to more clearly understand the sources of risks to health and the likely optimal intervention points. Further, context varies between regions and cultures, and will change over the coming decades. Each displacement event will have distinctive characteristics, reflecting the number of people involved, the process and duration of the displacement, and the cultural context and pre-displacement condition of affected populations. Nevertheless, the main health risks bearing on displaced people in the context of climate change are those of anxiety and mental health stressors, food shortages and possible nutritional deficits, increased risks of infectious diseases and exposures to physical hazards.

Much of the 'climate proofing' of likely regions of origin and the reception of displaced people will require a broad and coordinated spectrum of inputs from many different sectors of government and other parties. There are limits to what the health sector can do on its own; indeed, it is important to recognise that health is rarely a matter for health policy alone. At the international level, there is a clear challenge for the World Health Organization to act in concert with other UN agencies and international non-governmental organisations. It will also be critical to involve national governments and community-based organisations in understanding and addressing issues associated with climate change, displacement and health.

Displacement also raises a major moral challenge.[137] Climate change will bring (at least temporary) opportunities and improved conditions to some parts of the world.[138] For example, parts of coastal Australia have recently experienced warmer temperatures and more rainfall, which, if sustained, may translate into substantial agricultural and economic advantages. At the same time, these apparently fortunate places may have to adapt to the impact of an increasing flow of people leaving less favourable conditions to seek the security afforded by such places. How can these (for the moment, lucky) people help others, and what help will they need if they are, ultimately, unable to adapt to the inclusion in their communities of large numbers of displaced persons? There are moral challenges in this, of course, but also economic and other opportunities. If appeals to moral sensibility fail, what other strategies or criteria might persuade (and support) the more fortunate to assist in practical ways *en masse*? We will need to be creative, to think collectively and to seek (perhaps counter-intuitive) opportunities among the challenges that present themselves.

Climate change will be a factor, sometimes a major factor, in the future displacement of people. As ever, each such displacement will entail particular circumstances

---

[137] See P Penz, 'International Ethical Responsibilities to "Climate Change Refugees"', in the present volume.

[138] See J Barnett and M Webber, 'Migration as Adaptation: Opportunities and Limits', in the present volume, who argue that climate impacts are felt differentially.

and hardships, including increased risks to well-being, health, physical safety and survival. This constitutes a clear mandate for, first, well-pitched participatory research that includes health risk assessment and evaluation of risk-reduction strategies, and secondly, a moral imperative to strive for a more compassionate world—one that is capable of far-sighted policy-making that curbs today's burgeoning but unsustainable production and consumption practices, the root cause of systemic environmental changes and the attendant social disruption and stress.

11

Climate Change, Human Movement and the Promotion of Mental Health: What Have We Learnt from Earlier Global Stressors?

MARYANNE LOUGHRY

Climate change is but one of the many factors impacting millions of people's psychological and social well-being today: unemployment, urbanisation, overcrowding, water scarcity, pollution and poverty, to name a few, are the present-day stressors in their lives, and yet little is known about the interaction of any of these factors on their mental health. Far less is known of the anticipatory effects of future displacement resulting from climate change and environmental degradation, a prospect facing up to 200 million people in the next few decades.[1]

While there is now an increasing understanding of the role of social, economic and environmental determinants in promoting mental health, this knowledge has not yet been used to shed light on communities vulnerable to climate change. Many of these communities are currently experiencing the disruption of these determinants, putting them at risk of poor mental health outcomes.[2] This chapter will describe psychological frameworks that can be used to assess the well-being and mental health prospects of populations who face natural hazards, an uncertain future and possible forced displacement on account of climate change. It will also explore how these models might best be used to inform climate adaptation programmes so as to minimise the impact of climate change on people's well-being.

---

[1] In 2009, it was estimated that between 50 million and 200 million people would be forced to move on a temporary or permanent basis by the middle of this century: see International Organization for Migration (IOM), United Nations High Commissioner for Refugees (UNHCR), United Nations University, Norwegian Refugee Council and the Representative of the Secretary-General on the Human Rights of Internally Displaced Persons, 'Climate Change, Migration, and Displacement: Impacts, Vulnerability, and Adaptation Options' (Joint Submission for the 5th Session of the Ad Hoc Working Group on Long-Term Cooperative Action under the Convention, Bonn, 29 March–8 April 2009), www.humanitarianinfo.org/iasc/downloaddox.aspx?docID=4878.

[2] JG Fritze, GA Blashki, S Burke and J Wiseman, 'Hope, Despair and Transformation: Climate Change and the Promotion of Mental Health and Wellbeing' (2008) 2 *International Journal of Mental Health Systems* 13.

I Introduction

On a 2007 visit to the small island developing state of Kiribati, the author participated in a two-week workshop with I-Kiribati youth, who shared their hopes and
concerns about their country's future. This workshop had two clear aims: first, to
prepare the I-Kiribati youth delegates for their participation in the United Nations
Climate Change Conference in Bali in December 2007, and secondly, to expose the
Australian visitors to the experience of climate change in Kiribati. Kiribati and its
neighbour, Tuvalu, have been identified as countries that are particularly vulnerable to the effects of climate change. In 2007, the influential Intergovernmental
Panel on Climate Change (IPCC), established by the World Meteorological
Organization (WMO) and United Nations Environment Programme (UNEP),
stated 'with very high confidence' that by 2080 many millions of people are likely
to experience floods every year due to sea-level rise. Further, it highlighted that
while the majority of affected people will be from the low-lying mega-deltas of
Africa and Asia, small island states are also especially vulnerable.[3]

In a recent research proposal to the New Zealand National Institute of Water
and Atmospheric Research (NIWA), the government of Kiribati acknowledged
that Kiribati was one of the most vulnerable countries in the world due to the
effects of climate change and sea-level rise. Focusing on its most densely populated
atoll, Tarawa, home to the majority of I-Kiribati people, the Kiribati government
stressed that most of the land on this atoll was less than three metres above sea
level. With its average width of only 450 metres, the government acknowledged
that retreat from floods or an inundation of sea water would be impossible.[4]

Unless there are very significant changes in greenhouse gas emissions by the
major nations of the world, it is anticipated that Kiribati and Tuvalu could be the
first of many nations to become uninhabitable, forcing their populations to relocate to larger and more resilient settings. The prospect of dislocation looms large
in the minds of these nations' governments and their neighbours.[5] What are the
psychological and social impacts of climate change on these populations? Is the
anticipation of forced displacement eroding the community's mental health,
and how might this be best conceptualised and addressed in the light of previous
studies of displacement and mental health?

---

[3] Intergovernmental Panel on Climate Change (IPCC), *Climate Change 2007: Synthesis Report:
Contribution of Working Groups I, II and III to the Fourth Assessment Report of the Intergovernmental Panel
on Climate Change* (Geneva, IPCC, 2008) 48.

[4] National Institute of Water and Atmospheric Research (NIWA), *Kiribati Adaptation Program:
Phase II: Information for Climate Risk Management: High Intensity Rainfall and Drought* (Auckland,
NIWA, 2008).

[5] The issue of possible relocation of populations was recently raised at the Pacific Islands Forum,
Cairns, Australia (5 August 2009): Transcript of Joint Press Conference with Australian Climate Change
Minister, Penny Wong; Prime Minister of Vanuatu, Edward Natapei; and Secretary for Foreign Affairs
and Immigration in Kiribati, Tessie Lambourne, http://parlinfo.aph.gov.au/parlInfo/download/
media/pressrel/PLBU6/upload_binary/plbu61.pdf%3BfileType%3Dapplication/pdf.

Global sea-levels rose by 1.2 to 2.2 mm per year over the twentieth century. In Kiribati, the average sea-level rise has been 2.1 mm per year since 1974, but between 1993 and 2007 the average sea-level rise was 5.3 mm per year. This increased rate is likely to be predominantly due to natural climate variations, rather than a long-term increase in the rate of sea-level rise.[6] Similarly, Tuvalu has reported annual sea-level rises of 1 to 2 mm each year, consistent with the IPCC's 2007 predictions.

There have been earlier studies investigating the attitudes of populations to climate change,[7] many of which were conducted within the context of climate adaptation programmes with a view to assessing the coping range and social resilience of populations in the face of expected climate stresses. However, there are still very few social science studies of the impact of climate change: the vast majority of climate change studies have been conducted by meteorologists, biologists, chemists, geologists and oceanographers, who have concentrated on greenhouse gas emissions, water quality, sea-levels, coastal erosion and related aspects of the natural environment.

The United Nations Framework Convention on Climate Change (UNFCCC) defines 'climate change' as: 'a change of climate which is attributed directly or indirectly to human activity that alters the composition of the global atmosphere and which is in addition to natural climate variability observed over comparable time periods'.[8] Its focus is clearly on the anthropogenic effects on the environment—in other words, gases or materials that stem from human activities, as opposed to those occurring in natural environments without human influence.

It is this emphasis on human activity in the UNFCCC definition that highlights why it is equally important to bring the social sciences into research on climate change. If humans are going to be helped to understand how their activities in the past and present are contributing to climate change, and if they are going to be compelled to change these activities through adaptation and mitigation programmes, then attention needs to be paid to how populations understand what is happening and what is required of them. Research needs to explore particular populations' beliefs about climate change, their ranges of coping mechanisms for change, as well as their adaptive capacity. In settings where the effects of climate change have already reached such a point that migration is being considered as one of the most likely adaptive strategies, social science research can address how migration—and the anticipation of it—will affect individuals and their families, communities and, in some instances, whole populations. An examination of human activity and climate change in an affected setting, community belief systems and coping mechanisms, and possible ways in which particular communities

[6] NIWA, *Kiribati Adaptation Program*, above n 4, 1.
[7] N Kuruppu, 'Mental Preparation for Climate Adaptation: The Role of Cognition in Enhancing Capacity of Water Management in Kiribati' (Third International Conference on Climate and Water, Helsinki, 3–6 September 2007).
[8] United Nations Framework Convention on Climate Change (adopted 9 May 1992, entered into force 21 March 1993) 1771 UNTS 107, Art 1(2).

may adapt to such changes is essential to obtain a full sense of the human activities contributing to climate change, and, more significantly, the issues that need to be addressed. A failure to do this will result in a limited picture of the effects of climate change and how they might be addressed.

II Why Engage the Discipline of Psychology in Addressing the Impacts of Climate Change?

Simply put, psychology is the study of mind and behaviour,[9] which focuses on explaining human activity. As a discipline, psychology engages in the scientific study of the nature, function and development of the human mind, including the faculties of reason, emotion, perception and communication. It is a branch of science that deals with the mind as an entity, and its relationship to the body and the environmental or social context, based on observation of the behaviour of individuals or groups in particular (ordinary or experimentally controlled) circumstances.

Overall, the goals of psychology are to describe, explain and predict human behaviour and to assist people to control it.[10] Psychology is therefore also concerned with people's mental health and helping them to improve it. If a person's range of psychological functioning is considered unhealthy or abnormal, this is often referred to as 'psychopathology' or 'psychological disorder'.[11]

In the grand scheme of things, psychology is a relatively new discipline. Psychological studies were introduced as part of the 'science of life', or biology, from 1879.[12] Preoccupied with explaining human behaviour, psychology has developed many theories over the past century, which have either elaborated on or emerged from older theories, or have been developed in reaction to these. In recent times, a dominant understanding in psychology of the complex relationship between mind and body has resulted in the elaboration of the bio-psychosocial approach, which posits that human behaviour is explained by the dynamic interplay of biological factors, such as brain development, genes and the body's chemistry with emotional and cognitive factors within critical social and cultural environments. Consistently, psychology has been concerned with behaviour across the lifespan. Present-day psychologists are particularly interested in two critical relationships: one between brain function and behaviour, and one between environment and behaviour.[13]

---

[9] See generally American Psychological Association (APA), www.apa.org.

[10] Definition, 'psychology, *n*.', *The Oxford English Dictionary Online* (Oxford, Oxford University Press, 2009).

[11] PG Zimbardo and AL Weber, *Psychology*, 2nd edn (New York, Longman, 1997) 5.

[12] *The Oxford English Dictionary Online*, above n 10.

[13] APA, above n 9.

It is surprising, then, that while psychology (and arguably social science generally) is clearly concerned with humans, their behaviour and the environment, it has played a very limited role in contemporary discussions about climate change. Some suggest that psychology has been left out because major governmental and institutional players are unsure of the role that it might play, or perceive its contribution to be too 'fluffy'.[14] Yet the omission of the discipline of psychology, and the related topic of mental health, from climate change discussions could be to the detriment of policy formation, as well as to those seeking to work with affected communities. Recently, the American Psychological Association (APA) commissioned a task force on the interface between psychology and global climate change with the stated aim of engaging members of the psychological community in the issue of climate change.[15] The report demonstrates that there is already a significant body of knowledge on determinants that promote individual and community well-being in the face of adversity and that much of this knowledge might now be applied to studies of the impact of climate change. Similarly, there are applied studies on the subject of forced migration, mental health and psychosocial support. The learning from these could also constructively inform policy and practice with respect to climate change and displacement. It is therefore timely to bring together what psychologists know about human behaviour, the impacts of environment and climate on it, and what happens when people have to adapt, and even move, because of these impacts. Psychology can assist here in two key ways: first, by enhancing understanding of how to change human activity to reduce future climate change; and secondly, by providing insight into how to address the inevitable impacts of climate change, particularly on vulnerable communities.

III Psychology and Today's Global Challenges

Psychology is being used more and more to shed light on today's major global challenges, of which climate change is one. At the 2007 APA annual convention, Professor Thomas W Miller received the Award for Distinguished Professorial Contributions to Practice in the Public Sector. In his award address, delivered at the 115th annual meeting of the APA, he addressed the topic 'Trauma, Change, and Psychological Health in the 21st Century'.[16] Professor Miller focused on the relationship between various life stressors in the twenty-first century— social stressors, political stressors and environmental stressors—and critical

---

[14] R Gifford, 'Psychology's Essential Role in Alleviating the Impacts of Climate Change' (2008) 49 *Canadian Psychology* 273.

[15] APA Task Force on the Interface between Psychology and Global Climate Change, 'Psychology and Global Climate Change: Addressing a Multi-faceted Phenomenon and Set of Challenges', Task Force Report (Washington DC, APA, 2009) 6.

[16] TW Miller, 'Trauma, Change, and Psychological Health in the 21st Century' (2007) 62 *American Psychologist* 887.

health-related issues. Surveying the impact of these stressors over the past century, Miller found that many had a profound effect on the health and well-being of the global population. He posited that stressors in the first decade of the twenty-first century such as war, famine and climatic changes have traumatised many people, often as a result of exposure to violence. Among these he listed traumatic events such as the 9/11 terrorist attacks, and natural disasters such as Cyclone Katrina. Miller called upon his audience to think about environmental, social and political trauma from a psychological perspective, recognising that there has been increasing awareness of the interaction between individuals and their social environments during the twentieth century.

Looking at contemporary stressors, Miller singled out climate change as an element of environmental stressors and psychological health, and urged that if the projections of climate change prove correct, there will be a significant impact on all systems on which human life depends. He spoke of the need to engage with psychology to address the present-day challenges facing 'globalised society', claiming that psychology has the tools and expertise to partner with other disciplines to formulate both a model for prevention of physical and mental illness, as well as a model for health promotion.

In spite of such recognition, psychology has been given very limited attention in public policy on climate change and in the programmes being developed to address its effects.

IV Climate and Mental Health

Investigations into the effects of climate on individuals are not entirely new to psychologists and psychiatrists. Earlier psychological studies investigated the role that climate and climate events have played with respect to mental health.[17] One such body of knowledge concerns seasonal climate variation and mental health. Studies in this field have looked into the effect that climate variation has had on individuals' levels of depression and mania. Known more formally as 'seasonal affective disorder' (SAD) in the Diagnostic and Statistical Manual (DSM-IV) published by the American Psychiatric Association, SAD is a mental health diagnosis for a mood disorder that is related to increased symptoms of depression in winter when there are fewer hours of sunlight.[18] Similarly, SAD is also used to explain increased mania in spring. It is thought that this disorder explains why there are increased rates of suicide in some countries, particularly in the northern hemisphere, at certain times of the year. In countries that have very few daylight hours in winter, bright light therapy has been introduced to help address this problem.

[17] See, eg reference to such studies in PK Chand and P Murthy, 'Climate Change and Mental Health' (2008) 12 *Regional Mental Health Forum* 1, 43.

[18] American Psychiatric Association, 'Quick Reference to the Diagnostic Criteria from DSM-IV-TR (Washington DC, American Psychiatric Association, 2000) 207.

Of greater relevance to climate change and mental health are studies investigating the effects of extreme weather events and mental health.[19] The IPCC noted that some extreme weather events have changed in frequency and intensity over the last 50 years,[20] with many 'likely' or 'very likely'[21] to become more frequent or more intense in the future.[22] These alterations, along with sea-level rise, are expected to have mostly adverse effects on natural and human systems. Past psychiatric and psychological studies have investigated the effects of prolonged high temperatures, flooding, droughts and storms on human behaviour and have found that such events can place populations at heightened risk of psychological distress.[23] A third area of climate study familiar to psychologists and psychiatrists is on the psychological effects of specific climatic disasters, such as the 2004 Tsunami in South Asia and Hurricanes Mitch (1998) and Katrina (2005) in the United States. These studies reveal increased levels of post-traumatic stress disorder, depression and anxiety in the affected populations (many displaced from their homes), particularly in the first months after the event.[24]

The enormous global debate that has been generated by climate change over the past decade has in part arisen because the science of climate change has been complex and controversial, with experts disagreeing on what exactly is causing climate change and the extent of its effects.[25] However, in spite of this debate, it has now been concluded through processes such as the expert reports to the IPCC that some degree of future climate change will continue to occur, regardless of future greenhouse gas emissions.[26] What is not agreed is the degree of this change and its resulting timeline. However, of increasing concern are the predictions that the pace of climate change is likely to be much faster than previous estimates of only a few years ago.[27] Observed changes include increased sea-level rise, heavy precipitation, droughts, temperature rise and more frequent extreme weather incidents such as cyclones. It is also now agreed that in most settings, poorer people will be the most susceptible to the effects of climate change because of their location, the impact on their livelihoods and their

---

[19] Chand and Murthy, 'Climate Change and Mental Health', above n 17, 44.

[20] IPCC, *Climate Change 2007*, above n 3, 30.

[21] ibid, 27 where 'very likely' refers to a probability greater than 90 per cent and 'likely' refers to a probability greater than 66 per cent.

[22] ibid, 53.

[23] M Reacher et al, 'Health Impacts of Flooding in Lewes: A Comparison of Reported Gastrointestinal and Other Illness and Mental Health in Flooded and Non-Flooded Households'(2004) 1 *Communicable Disease and Public Health* 39.

[24] See, eg F Van Griensven et al, 'Mental Health Problems among Adults in Tsunami-Affected Areas in Southern Thailand' (2006) 296 *Journal of the American Medical Association* 537.

[25] See, eg IR Plimer, *Heaven + Earth: Global Warming: The Missing Science* (Ballan, Connor Court Publishing, 2009) where the author, a geologist, argues that climate change is cyclical and not driven by increasing carbon emissions. See also United States Senate Committee on Environment and Public Works, 'Senate Minority Report on Climate Change' (2009) where the Committee reports the work of hundreds of US scientists who reject the notion of anthropogenic climate change.

[26] United States Environmental Protection Agency website (2009), www.epa.org.

[27] K Richardson et al, *Synthesis Report from Climate Change: Global Risks, Challenges and Decisions*, 2nd edn (Copenhagen, 10–12 March 2009), www.pik-potsdam.de/news/press-releases/files/synthesis-report-web.pdf.

reduced capacity to respond to emergencies.[28] The language that is frequently used to refer to this emerging problem is that of 'vulnerability' and 'resilience'.

It is in this terminology that the social dimension of climate change can be explored using a framework more familiar to social scientists and development theorists. This language and framework is evident in reports such as the World Bank's 'Climate Resilient Cities: A Primer on Reducing Vulnerabilities to Climate Change Impacts and Strengthening Disaster Risk Management in East Asian Cities'.[29] With the recognition that climate change is inevitable, even if solely because of earlier greenhouse gas emissions, nation states have started to put in place adaptation and mitigation measures to address these changes and redress nations' vulnerabilities so as to increase their adaptive capacity.

V Psychology and Human Insecurity

Given the dire predictions of how populations may be impacted by climate change in the future, one theory of psychology that may have immediate application to addressing climate change is humanistic psychology. While not without critics, this theory has had immense influence on medical and emergency settings and on the determination of how best to address human needs in humanitarian settings. This theory/school of psychology was founded by Abraham Maslow in the 1940s. Much of its popularity derives from the fact that it differed markedly from earlier schools of psychology in its focus on individuals with good mental health and human potential, rather than mental illness. Maslow theorised that human beings were not just subjects reacting blindly to the various situations in which they found themselves, but rather responded to their many needs. He believed that healthy human beings had peak experiences in their lives and that these experiences put individuals in harmony with themselves and their surroundings.

To explain his theories Maslow developed a theory of human motivation that posited that humans had a hierarchy of needs.[30] He proposed that there were five levels of human need—physiological needs, safety needs, love needs, esteem needs and self-actualisation needs—and he posited that these needs were hierarchical. He said that each level needed to be satisfied, or else the individual would become temporarily preoccupied with unmet needs and would not be motivated to move forward. Maslow categorised the first four sets of needs as 'deficiency needs'. Once these 'deficiency needs' were met, the individual could seek to satisfy 'being needs', such as self-actualisation, that focused on identity and purpose.

---

[28] See especially World Bank, 'Climate Change' (2009), www.worldbank.org/climatechange.
[29] World Bank, *Climate Resilient Cities 2008: A Primer on Reducing Vulnerabilities to Climate Change Impacts and Strengthening Disaster Risk Management in East Asian Cities* (Washington DC, World Bank Group, 2008).
[30] AH Maslow, 'A Theory of Human Motivation' (1943) 50 *Psychological Review* 370.

While Maslow's theory has had its detractors, and has been criticised by cross-cultural researchers,[31] it has persisted as a popular psychological theory and has a lot of prominence in marketing theory as well as disaster and 'first aid' psychology.

The influence of Maslow's work arguably can be seen today in how human needs are conceptualised, especially in humanitarian work. A powerful example is the way the United Nations Development Programme in 1994 described 'human security' as 'first, safety from such chronic threats as hunger, disease and repression. And second, it means protection from sudden and hurtful disruptions in the patterns of daily life—whether in homes, in jobs or in communities.' It also described human security as 'people-centred', that is, 'concerned with how people live and breathe in a society, how freely they exercise their many choices, how much access they have to market and social opportunities—and whether they live in conflict or in peace.'[32] Climate change threatens millions of people with such 'insecurity', and humanistic psychology presents a framework for understanding and addressing the needs of people in insecure settings.

VI Environmental Psychology

With the evolution of the dominant bio-psychosocial approach of psychology in recent decades, there has been increased acknowledgement of the major role that the physical environment plays in shaping an individual's thoughts, feelings and behaviour.

In the 1970s, a new field of psychology was founded: environmental psychology. One of its early proponents, Harold Proshansky, defined it as 'the attempt to establish empirical and theoretical relationships between the behaviour and experience of the person and his built environment'.[33] Proshansky argued that psychology needed to move away from studies of human behaviour in laboratories (a setting where much psychological research was conducted) into the real world, out of a growing recognition of the integrity of people and physical-setting events. In its early days, environmental psychology focused on the physical world of rooms, buildings, hospital wards and streets. However, Proshansky also recognised that this field was not to be limited to these constructions.[34] Environmental psychology began to empirically examine the contribution of physical settings in explaining human behaviour. Since its inception, environmental psychology has researched environmental problems and now has an extensive toolbox of ideas

---

[31] EM Pearson and RL Podeschi, 'Humanism and Individualism: Maslow and His Critics' (1999) 50 *Adult Education Quarterly* 41.

[32] United Nations Development Programme, *Human Development Report 1994* (New York, Oxford University Press, 1994) 23.

[33] H Proshansky, 'Environmental Psychology and the Real World' (1976) 31 *American Psychologist* 303.

[34] ibid, 305.

and techniques for addressing them. Arguably, many of these could be brought to an examination of the impacts of climate change on human society.[35]

VII The Realities of Climate Change and International Responses: Adaptation and Mitigation

A Adaptation

At present the two dominant approaches to addressing climate change are adaptation and mitigation. These concepts have much resonance in the discipline of psychology. Equally, the concepts of resilience and vulnerability, terms used to describe both affected populations and natural settings in climate change settings, are concepts that have been researched at length by psychologists. The IPCC defines adaptation as the 'adjustment in natural or human systems in response to actual or expected climatic stimuli or their effects, which moderates harm or exploits beneficial opportunity'.[36] This adaptation usually refers to a process or action in a system that helps the system better cope with, or manage, changing conditions, stress, risks and opportunities.[37] There are multiple concepts surrounding this adaptation process, including adaptive capacity, exposure, sensitivity, vulnerability, risk and resilience. In much of the scholarship on climate change these terms are used to examine adaptation in ecological systems.

In 2006, Smit and Wandel reviewed the concept of adaptation of *human communities* to global environmental changes. In particular, they focused on the scholarship that has contributed to practical implementation at the community level.[38] They described how the concept of adaptation has been used explicitly and implicitly in social science, including in research on natural hazards, political ecology and food security. When examining natural hazards akin to those resulting from climate change, Smit and Wandel focused on people's perception and management of the hazard. Other scholars have also investigated such perception and management in relation to environmental disasters such as hurricanes, earthquakes and floods.[39]

The term adaptation is also familiar to anthropological studies on 'cultural adaptation'. These have looked at the adaptive capacity of different cultures to

[35] Gifford, 'Psychology's Essential Role', above n 14, 273.

[36] IPCC, *Climate Change 2007: Impacts, Adaptation and Vulnerability: Contribution of Working Group II to the Fourth Assessment Report of the Intergovernmental Panel on Climate Change* (Cambridge, Cambridge University Press, 2008) 869.

[37] B Smit and J Wandel, 'Adaptation, Adaptive Capacity and Vulnerability' (2006) 16 *Global Environmental Change* 282, 282.

[38] ibid.

[39] See, eg DA Lytle and NL Poff, 'Adaptation to Natural Flow Regimes' (2003) 19 *Trends in Ecology and Evolution* 94.

survive, and how such cultures have adapted to the challenges of modern times. Archaeologists have examined (primarily from a 'Darwinian' perspective) how humans have coped over time, adapting to new stressors and acquiring additional 'adaptive features'.[40]

Similarly, scholarship has emerged in development studies on the adaptive capacity and vulnerability of human systems to global changes. As climate change has become increasingly recognised as one of the multiple stressors in poor people's lives, there has been increased scholarship attempting to map communities' adaptive capacity and vulnerability to climate change.[41]

In 2009, the peak scientific research body in Australia, the Commonwealth Scientific and Industrial Research Organization (CSIRO), completed such a study for the Australian Government's overseas aid programme (AusAID).[42] Investigating the impact of climate change on livelihoods in the Pacific, this study employed various measures to assess the vulnerability of small Pacific island states. It focused on indicators in the following areas of capital: human, social, natural, physical and financial. It concluded that Nauru, the Federated States of Micronesia, Tuvalu, the Marshall Islands and Kiribati were the five Pacific nations most vulnerable to climate change. Of significance, for the purposes of this chapter, were the reports that focused on migration as a measure of adaptability.[43] Migration, both internal (from outer islands to more urban settings), as well as abroad, was considered to be an indicator of an island population's ability to provide agricultural products for their local people, as well as their capacity to access support from outside the country, including through remittances. Overall, migration was thought to have potentially positive and negative impacts on the ability of each country to adapt to climate change and sea-level rise. When the CSIRO researchers asked Pacific islanders how they viewed migration, they were informed that generally they thought that population pressures were negatively impacting on the agricultural and natural resource base of countries, forcing many people to consider migration.[44]

B Mitigation

According to the IPCC, mitigation is 'technical change and substitution that reduce resource inputs and emissions per unit of output'. It is about the implementation of policies that reduce greenhouse gas emissions and enhance natural and purpose-built 'sinks' that can store carbon-containing compounds for indefinite periods of

---

[40] See especially the reference to these studies in Smit and Wandel, 'Adaptation', above n 37, 283.

[41] See, eg the study undertaken in India: K O'Brien et al, 'Mapping Vulnerability in Climate Change and Globalization in India' (2004) 14 *Global Environmental Change* 303.

[42] S Park et al, *Assessing the Vulnerability of Rural Livelihoods in the Pacific to Climate Change* (Canberra, CSIRO Sustainable Ecosystems, 2009).

[43] ibid, 22.

[44] ibid, 29; J Barnett and M Webber, 'Migration as Adaptation: Opportunities and Limits', in the present volume.

time.[45] The capacity of each country to do this depends on the skills and competencies within its institutions and infrastructure. While small island states in the Pacific are generally not big greenhouse gas emitters relative to other nations,[46] they have a very limited capacity to engage in mitigation strategies.

For this reason, major international institutions like the World Bank sponsor and support vast adaptation and mitigation programmes in the Pacific region. These programmes include:

- improving weather data collection and forecasts (for farmers and insurers);
- providing technical assistance (such as extension services on new crop varieties; help for health systems addressing new diseases);
- developing and sharing knowledge on options in land use, forestry and agriculture;
- assessing risk and vulnerability;
- prioritising investment through better understanding of options and costs;
- helping develop drought and saline-resistant crops.[47]

What is not so evident are adaptation programmes and interventions that target the behaviour of individuals and communities, beyond measuring their attitudes towards and knowledge of climate change, and this work is happening on a very limited scale. Programmes that strengthen the adaptive capacity of communities through social support, knowledge and professional mental health services are necessary and, indeed, essential if the effects of climate change are to be addressed and adaptation programmes made sustainable.

VIII Migration as a Response to Climate Change

As has already been noted, migration in itself is seen as an adaptive measure to manage the impact of climate change, and there is a significant body of knowledge about the effects of migration on individuals, communities and populations.[48] Within this body of knowledge, considerable literature exists about the psychosocial impacts of forced migration. As more and more people are either displaced, or anticipate displacement, at least in part because of changes to the climate, this knowledge can be drawn upon to conceptualise the issue and assist in the

---

[45] IPCC, *Climate Change 2007: Mitigation of Climate Change: Contribution of Working Group III to the Fourth Assessment Report of the Intergovernmental Panel on Climate Change* (Cambridge, Cambridge University Press, 2008) 818.

[46] US Energy Information Administration Independent Statistics and Analysis, 'International Energy Statistics', http://tonto.eia.doe.gov/cfapps/ipdbproject/IEDIndex3.cfm?tid=90&pid=44&aid=8.

[47] World Bank, 'Climate Change', above n 28.

[48] See, eg S Castles and M Miller, *The Age of Migration: International Population Movements in the Modern World*, 4th edn (Basingstoke, Palgrave Macmillan, 2009); R Zetter, 'Legal and Normative Frameworks' (2008) 31 *Forced Migration Review* 62 .

development of appropriate programme responses—measures that will contribute to the reduction of the impact of climate change.

By way of an introduction to this knowledge, it is useful to draw upon the case study of Kiribati and Tuvalu. Both of these small Pacific island nations have a significant history of migration. The Pacific has always been a place of migration, and in recent years many Pacific islanders have used migration as a medium for economic growth.[49] Under British colonisation, these two nations, though different in ethnic origins, comprised the British protectorate of the Gilbert and Ellice Islands. During this period there was considerable migration between the islands and also to other nations for education and training. From colonial times, the men of Kiribati and Tuvalu have developed a strong reputation as seafarers. However, it now seems that demographic pressures and climate change impacts are forcing I-Kiribati and Tuvaluans to consider migration not just as an option, but as a necessity. The question here is whether the forced nature of this migration will have new and different psychological and social impacts for Pacific communities compared to what they have experienced in the past.

In 2004, at the Pacific Churches' consultation (convened by the World Council of Churches), the people of Kiribati described their present experience of climate change as:

• Loss of coastal land and infrastructure due to erosion, inundation and storm surges.
• Increase in frequency and severity of cyclones with risks to human life, health, homes and communities.
• Loss of coral reefs, with implications for the sea ecosystems on which the livelihood of many islanders depends.
• Changes in rainfall patterns, with increased droughts in some areas and more rainfall with flooding in other areas.
• Threats to drinking water supplies due to changes in rainfall, sea-level rise and inundation.
• Loss of sugarcane, yams, taro and cassava due to extreme temperatures and rainfall changes.
• Human health impacts, with an increase in the incidence of dengue fever and diarrhoea.[50]

Clearly, the people of Kiribati were able to describe the effects of climate change on their land, fishing patterns and crops. At the 2007 workshop, I-Kiribati youth and guest speakers from the Kiribati government and non-government sector expressed grave and pressing concerns for their nation's future. Their dominant

[49] CW Stahl and RT Appleyard, *Migration and Development in the Pacific Islands: Lessons from the New Zealand Experience* (Canberra, AusAID, 2007).

[50] Otin Tai Declaration (A Statement and Recommendations from the Pacific Churches' Consultation on Climate Change, 6–11 March 2004, Tarawa, Kiribati), www.oikoumene.org/en/resources/documents/wcc-programmes/justice-diakonia-and-responsibility-for-creation/climate-change-water/11-03-04-otin-tai-declaration.html.

concern was that, in time, their nation would be covered with sea water, resulting in a loss of their country and, with it, their culture. They were concerned that even if they were able to migrate to other countries in large numbers, it would be difficult to maintain their cultural practices in these new lands. Significantly, they also spoke of the widespread belief in Kiribati that the changes they were witnessing in their climate and on their land were attributed to the work of God, and not human activity. This hindered many people from taking preventative action or believing that they could make a difference. They also talked about Kiribati's other, sometimes more immediate, problems, such as overcrowding, youth unemployment and poverty. Frequently when these discussions took place there was great sadness, tears and descriptions of helplessness. Migration was portrayed more as a necessary evil than as an opportunity.

IX Displacement from Climate Change and Mental Health: What Do We Know from Earlier Work?

While it has been argued earlier in this chapter and elsewhere[51] that Pacific islanders who are forced to migrate because of the impacts of climate change are not considered refugees under the 1951 Refugee Convention,[52] many clearly face and fear displacement. Recent scholarship on forced migration has sought to address displacement arising from development projects, trafficking across borders for sexual or labour exploitation, and internal displacement (within the borders of one's own country) due to conflict or natural disasters.[53] Climate-induced displacement is now a new concern and potentially encompasses the largest group of displaced people ever considered.[54] How is this fear of displacement affecting communities?

First, we know that relocation of any sort is stressful and can impact on people's mental and physical health.[55] An early psychiatric study by Rahe and others established that a cluster of social events requiring change in life adjustment was

[51] J McAdam and M Loughry, 'We Aren't Refugees', *Inside Story* (30 June 2009), http://inside.org.au/we-arent-refugees/.

[52] Convention relating to the Status of Refugees (adopted 28 July 1951, entered into force 22 April 1954) 189 UNTS 137, read in conjunction with the Protocol relating to the Status of Refugees (adopted 31 January 1967, entered into force 4 October 1967) 606 UNTS 267.

[53] See WC Robinson, 'Risks and Rights: The Causes, Consequences, and Challenges of Development-Induced Displacement', SAIS Project on Internal Displacement (Washington DC, The Brookings Institution, 2003), www.brookings.edu/fp/projects/idp/articles/didreport.htm; C Phuong, *The International Protection of Internally Displaced Persons* (Cambridge, Cambridge University Press, 2004) for examples of scholarship in some of these wider areas of forced migration.

[54] IOM et al, 'Climate Change', above n 1.

[55] AJ McMichael, CE McMichael, HL Berry and K Bowen, 'Climate-Related Displacement: Health Risks and Responses', in the present volume.

significantly associated with the time of illness onset.[56] Holmes and Rahe went on to develop the Social Readjustment Rating Scale,[57] which included items related to change in residence and major change in living conditions. Through the use of this scale and other instruments, psychologists went on to establish that social, political and environmental factors had a profound impact on the health and well-being of individuals. Similarly, factors that were thought to be stressful to humans were examined for their impact on individuals' physical and mental health, including by significant researchers like Dohrenwend and Dohrenwend.[58] They explored how stressful life events affect human health and illness, and the nature and relationship between stressors and distress. They also discovered what factors helped to ameliorate the effects of these stressors. However, the examples of relocation, i.e. moving home or relocating to another neighbourhood in these studies did not involve impacts of a comparable magnitude to those faced by people whose very homes are threatened by climate change, given that they may lose property, livelihoods and even identity if their nation ultimately disappears.

Climate change has been characterised as one of the most significant stressors facing humans in the twenty-first century. In 2003, the then Prime Minister of Tuvalu, Mr Saufatu Sopoanga, in an address to the 58th session of the United Nations General Assembly in New York, likened the threat of climate change to terrorism:

> We live in constant fear of the adverse impacts of climate change. For a coral atoll nation, sea level rise and more severe weather events loom as a growing threat to our entire population. The threat is real and serious, and is of no difference to a slow and insidious form of terrorism against us.[59]

The participants at the 2007 workshop in Kiribati highlighted that climate change is a source of fear and worry for these nations' populations, and there is a concern that people will be forced to migrate because of climate change and other related and compounding factors.

During the twentieth century, considerable research was undertaken into the human cost of conflict-induced displacement.[60] Early studies of displacement and mental health emerged from research on those displaced by conflict in the Second

---

[56] RH Rahe, M Meyer, M Smith, G Kjaer and TH Holmes, 'Social Stress and Illness Onset' (1964) 8 *Journal of Psychosomatic Research* 35.

[57] TH Holmes and RH Rahe, 'The Social Readjustment Scale' (1967) 11 *Journal of Psychosomatic Research* 213.

[58] BS Dohrenwend and BP Dohrenwend (eds), *Stressful Life Events: Their Nature and Effects* (New York, Wiley, 1974).

[59] Statement by the Hon Saufatu Sopoanga OBE, Prime Minister and Minister of Foreign Affairs of Tuvalu, 58th Session of the United Nations General Assembly (24 September 2003), www.un.org/webcast/ga/58/statements/tuvaeng030924.htm.

[60] See, eg AJ Marsella, T Bornemann, S Ekblad and J Orley (eds), *Amidst Peril and Pain: The Mental Health and Well-Being of the World's Refugees* (Washington DC, American Psychological Association, 1994); PJ Bracken and C Petty (eds), *Rethinking the Trauma of War* (London, Free Association Books, 1998). See also the journal *Intervention: International Journal of Mental Health, Psychosocial Work, and Counselling in Areas of Armed Conflict*, which began in 2003.

World War, but it was arguably the recognition of the emotional origins of shell shock in the First World War that first introduced the distinct disciplines of psychology and psychiatry into Britain. Previously, shell shock had been thought to be a response to the physical effects of war, and the recognition that it was in fact a psychological disorder, treatable by psychotherapy, resulted in the introduction of psychological 'medicine'.[61] In the first half of the twentieth century, much of the body of knowledge about the psychological and social effects of conflict and displacement developed out of observations from psychotherapy. These included the famous studies of Sigmund Freud's daughter, Anna Freud, and Dorothy Burlingham on the deprivation experienced by children separated from their families in wartime.[62]

Displacement arising from the Indochinese war led to the next substantial input on displacement and mental health. By this time, psychology and psychiatry had made huge advances and there was now research based not only on insights from observation and psychotherapy, but also from clinical research. The Indochinese war was also significant in our understanding of the phenomenon of trauma, a concept that has played a major role in studies of displacement and mental health. While the phenomenon of trauma had been around since the recognition of shell shock as a psychiatric disorder, it was not until 1980 that the American Psychiatric Association classified Post-Traumatic Stress Disorder (PTSD) as an illness—a diagnosis that was used to explain the behaviour of vast numbers of US servicemen who were returning from Vietnam with profound symptoms of stress and anxiety. Because the refugees fleeing the Indochinese war had also been subjected to similar experiences as the servicemen, it was not long before much of the research into displacement and mental health focused on trauma symptomatology and psychopathology—or signs of mental illness explained by exposure to extreme events.

The development of questionnaires and access to mental health clinics in countries of resettlement also afforded the opportunity to measure the mental health status of refugees.[63] A criticism of this approach at the time was that it reduced refugee health to disease and pathology.[64]

Possibly in reaction to this dominance of psychopathology, but also partly because many refugees and displaced people have not had access to psychologists and psychiatric services, more recent studies have tended to move away from look-

---

[61] T Loughran, 'Shell Shock and Psychological Medicine in First World War' (2009) 22 *Social History of Medicine* 79.

[62] A Freud and DT Burlingham, *War and Children* (New York, Medical War Books, 1943).

[63] See, eg RF Mollica, G Wyshak and J Lavelle, 'The Psychosocial Impact of War Trauma and Torture on Southeast Asian Refugees' (1987) 144 *American Journal of Psychiatry* 1567; RF Mollica et al, 'The Harvard Trauma Questionnaire: Validating a Cross-Cultural Instrument for Measuring Torture, Trauma, and Posttraumatic Stress Disorder in Indochinese Refugees' (1992) 180 *Journal of Nervous Mental Disorder* 111; JD Kinzie and SM Manson, 'The Use of Self-Rating Scales in Cross-Cultural Psychiatry' (1987) 38 *Hospital and Community Psychiatry* 190.

[64] M Meucke, 'New Paradigms for Refugee Health Problems' (1992) 35 *Social Science and Medicine* 515.

ing at the psychopathology of the displaced to instead focus on their psychosocial needs and resilience in extraordinary settings. This emphasis can be seen in the 2007 Guidelines on Mental Health and Psychosocial Support in Emergency Settings by the Inter-Agency Standing Committee (the primary mechanism for inter-agency coordination of humanitarian assistance involving key UN and non-UN humanitarian partners). The guidelines recognise that conflict and disasters cause human suffering and that the psychological and social impact of such emergencies can undermine people's mental health.[65] However, their focus is on the resources and resourcefulness of the affected people, not their deficits.

X Mental Health and Extreme Climate Events

A further body of knowledge that can shed light on the impact of climate change on mental health is the scholarship on natural disasters. Like the forced displacement studies, this research has focused significantly on trauma symptomatology. Studies of the impact of Hurricane Katrina in the US have meant that psychologists and psychiatrists have had access to affected populations over time, something that is not always possible in developing countries where there are few mental health professionals, and also have been able to use measures of psychological distress that have been developed for use with US populations.[66] Recent research into the South Asian Tsunami of 2004 has also produced large studies focusing on the symptomatology of the affected population.[67] While such studies may provide insights relevant to climate-affected populations, there is a marked difference: many climate change impacts are likely to be slow onset, as opposed to rapid and unexpected events. In Kiribati, the workshop participants reported that extreme climatic events in other countries contributed to their own fears, because were such events to happen in Kiribati, they would have nowhere to flee to.

So, is it best to understand the possible mental health implications of climate change through the lens of psychological distress, psychopathology and trauma, through an examination of stress and stressors—or psychosocial responses—coupled with mental health, or all of the above? In assessing this, it is important to bear in mind that unlike many earlier events resulting in displacement, climate change processes are slow onset. Movement can be anticipated for many years. In addition, the reasons for moving are obviously compounded by other factors, such

---

[65] Inter-Agency Standing Committee (IASC), *Guidelines on Mental Health and Psychosocial Support in Emergency Settings* (Geneva, IASC, 2007).

[66] See generally JR Elliot and J Pais, 'Race, Class, and Hurricane Katrina: Social Difference in Human Responses to Disaster' (2006) 35 *Social Science Research* 295; S LaJoie, 'Exposure, Avoidance, and PTSD among Hurricane Katrina Evacuees'(2009) 15 *Traumatology* 10 for examples of such research.

[67] R Souza, S Bernatsky, R Reyes and K de Jong, 'Mental Health Status of Vulnerable Tsunami-Affected Communities: A Survey in Aceh Province, Indonesia' (2007) 20 *Journal of Traumatic Stress* 263.

as unemployment, overcrowding and lack of educational opportunities. Though significant, environmental or climate-related factors are more likely to be part of a complex pattern of multiple causality.[68] People have always moved for many reasons, and in the Pacific islands, climate change factors are inextricably linked with economic, social and political ones.

From the interviews conducted in Kiribati, and drawing on the displacement literature more broadly, there is an imperative to establish culturally appropriate mental health measures as well as mental health services among affected populations. The psychological and social models that are used to explain the behaviour, thoughts and emotions of the community need to be compatible with their own cultural epistemologies. Similarly, mental health services, while reflecting good practice, need to be compatible and in harmony with local health and welfare services. Potential barriers to mental health services, including stigmatisation, finance, and knowledge, need to be addressed.

Climate change, similar to the impact of disasters and displacement, results in a great deal of social upheaval characterised by separation from loved ones, loss of livelihood, lack of shelter, poverty and uncertainty. Many times it is these social issues that need to be addressed to promote good mental health outcomes. To neglect to do this is to place the communities at heightened risk of domestic violence, alcoholism and public violence. From resilience studies, it is known that resilience, and thereby increased adaptive capacity, can be fostered by increased social support and good community education.

Many of these interventions are within reach of the communities now facing the impact of climate change in their daily lives. In addition to the existing adaptation and mitigation programmes, these psychosocial interventions need to be given due recognition, incorporated into climate change policy and adequately funded if the full impact of climate change on communities' mental health is to be addressed. In Kiribati, there is only one psychiatrist working with the mentally ill, and very few community mental health programmes. In Tuvalu, the only mental health worker is on a youth ambassador abroad programme for a year. Psychosocial interventions need to be introduced now so that the fears presently expressed by the community about their future do not overwhelm their traditional capacity to cope with adversity, and the limited professional services currently available to them. The future impact of climate change has the prospect of overwhelming even the most resourced country and the most established mental health system, and given the very limited resources in two of the countries likely to be among the hardest hit, the prospects are not good. It is in poorer countries, where mental health services are found most wanting, that nations have frequently failed to protect people with mental illness.[69] History has shown that if mental health is to be promoted in the face of future adversity, the time to prepare is now.

---

[68] S Castles, 'Environmental Change and Forced Migration: Making Sense of the Debate', *New Issues in Refugee Research*, Working Paper No 70 (Geneva, UNHCR, 2002).

[69] A Kleinman, 'The Art of Medicine: Global Mental Health: A Failure of Humanity' (2009) 374 *The Lancet* 603.

12

Afterword: What Now?
Climate-Induced Displacement
after Copenhagen

STEPHEN CASTLES

I Introduction

The contributions to this book were mainly written during the period of cautious hope in the run-up to the UN Climate Conference in Copenhagen. But by 19 December 2009, any expectations that the world's political leaders would work together to find solutions to the pressing problems of anthropogenic (human-induced) climate change were dashed. The key hope was that leaders would unite to introduce measures to keep global warming at or below an average of 2°C—still a level that would provoke massive changes, but that might give opportunities and time for protective measures. In fact, no binding agreement was reached, and the voluntary commitments which formed the basis of a last-minute face-saving deal seem unlikely to have much effect on global warming. The failure of international action on climate change provides a new and grim context for assessing the complex issues of climate change and displacement addressed in differing ways in this book.

The debate on climate-induced displacement has been a relatively small—if sometimes heated—part of the wider debate on how states, civil society and affected communities should respond to global warming. Advocacy groups sought in vain to include displacement issues in the final agreement of the Copenhagen summit (which never materialised).[1] The wider debate on global warming since the 1990s has revolved around two response paradigms: mitigation and adaptation. *Mitigation* means addressing the causes of global warming—especially the carbon-based economies which produce vast quantities of greenhouse gases. Limiting production of such gases requires major shifts in industrial technologies and lifestyles—not only for existing industrial nations, but also for emerging ones.

---

[1] C Lawton, 'What about Climate Refugees? Efforts to Help the Displaced Bog Down in Copenhagen', *Spiegel Online* (17 December 2009), www.spiegel.de/international/europe/0,1518,druck-667256,00.html.

By 2009, it was already too late to prevent massive climatic changes, but the process could have been slowed. That possibility now appears to be closed off—at least for a period which may well prove decisive.

Adaptation means designing and implementing measures to help communities affected by climatic change to modify the ways they work and live to be able to cope with new environmental conditions. For a long time, adaptation was a strategy treated with suspicion by environmentalists, because it meant conceding that global warming could not be halted. The tension between mitigation and adaptation was also a major factor in the debate between environmentalists, on the one hand, and scholars and advocacy groups concerned with refugees and migration, on the other. The environmentalists tended to portray migration as an inevitable but undesirable form of adaptation for people affected by sea-level rise and other effects of global warming; the migration specialists saw migration as one possible form of adaptation among others, and as a strategy that could often bring considerable benefits.

The failure of Copenhagen was admittedly not an unexpected result, and the authors of this book provide in-depth analyses from a range of perspectives that go beyond the day-to-day politics of international agreements (or rather, disagreements). Nonetheless, the context for assessing climate-induced displacement is different in 2010 than it was in 2009: adaptation is now the only game in town. Mitigation is off the agenda, and if it ever does come back, it may well be too late. This changes the terms of the debate on climate-induced displacement. The aim of this Afterword is, first, to discuss how the politics of climate change displacement have evolved over the last 20 years, and how the frame of reference for this debate has been changed by the Copenhagen debacle. Secondly, it seeks to sum up some key aspects of the current state of knowledge about the causes and consequences of climate-induced displacement. This will allow me to draw attention to some of the important ideas emerging from the various chapters of this book.

II The Politics of Climate Change Displacement

The old debate between environmentalists and migration specialists about the existence of 'environmental refugees' and the extent of climate change-induced displacement does not seem worth warming up yet again. It has been analysed repeatedly in the literature, and is covered in some of the contributions to this book.[2] But the key elements of the politicisation of the issue do need to be mentioned briefly before we can move on.

---

[2] Possibly the best account of the politicisation of climate change migration is to be found in F Gemenne, 'Environmental Changes and Migration Flows: Normative Frameworks and Policy Responses' (unpublished PhD thesis, Institut d'Etudes Politiques de Paris and University of Liège, 2009).

The controversy about the characteristics and the likely extent of climate-induced displacement goes back at least to the mid-1980s. A much-cited paper published by the United Nations Environment Programme (UNEP) argued that large numbers of people, especially in poor countries, would be displaced by environmental change. The author coined (or at least popularised) a term which was to become a core theme of contention: 'environmental refugees'.[3] There were two reasons why this concept was so controversial.

The main one was the use of the label 'refugees' for people who moved because of environmental factors. As refugee scholars pointed out, this was a misnomer: in international law, the term 'refugee' refers only to people who have crossed an international border to seek protection from persecution based on a range of factors that are clearly defined in the 1951 Refugee Convention.[4] Environmental or climate change was not included in the 1951 Convention. This was not hair-splitting: since the 1990s, refugee lawyers and non-governmental organisations have been struggling to ward off restrictions to the right to international protection, especially on the part of European states. Any watering down of the 1951 Convention was seen as a potential threat, since states might use it to reinforce their efforts to keep out asylum seekers. In any case, most people affected by environmental factors such as drought or floods were likely to move internally, not internationally. If they were forced to move, they should be seen as internally displaced persons (IDPs), not refugees.

The second problem with the term 'environmental refugee' related to the environmental part. Migration scholars pointed out that people have migrated for environmental reasons throughout history, and that environmental changes, or livelihood opportunities resulting from environmental differences, could be both negative and positive. In many cases, migration related to environmental change should not be equated with forced displacement. The issue therefore was not migration caused by the very broad range of environmental changes, but much more specifically, migration related to current climate change processes. As migration scholars pointed out, climate change should not be seen in isolation: in the great majority of cases, people's decisions to migrate or not to migrate are based on a wide range of economic, social, political and cultural factors. Climatic changes which affect the environmental conditions for work and life should be seen as a factor in migration, but hardly ever the only or even the predominant cause. Migration scholars emphasised the *multi-causality* of migration decisions, and accused environmentalists of postulating environmental *mono-causality* for political reasons.

This critique was well-placed, but environmentalists could counter it by arguing that their emphasis on climate change had a very good purpose: namely that of awakening the world to the dangers of global warming by making politicians and

---

[3] E El-Hinnawi, *Environmental Refugees* (Nairobi, UNEP, 1985).
[4] Convention relating to the Status of Refugees (adopted 28 July 1951, entered into force 22 April 1954) 189 UNTS 137, read in conjunction with the Protocol relating to the Status of Refugees (adopted 31 January 1967, entered into force 4 October 1967) 606 UNTS 267.

the public think about the consequences of large-scale human displacement. Leading proponents of this approach warned of tens or even hundreds of millions of displaced persons in the future, and put forward apocalyptic visions of third world poverty and disease sweeping over the rich parts of the world.[5] Others put forward scenarios of mass displacement as a cause of future global insecurity,[6] while certain non-governmental relief agencies (sometimes as part of their fundraising efforts) were happy to escalate forecasts of vast population movements, up to one billion by 2050.[7]

But, however well-intentioned, these shock tactics were risky. Not only did they present questionable data, which might undermine public trust in environmental predictions, but more seriously they tended to reinforce existing negative images of refugees as a threat to the security, prosperity and public health of rich countries in the global North. Headlines like 'millions will flee degradation', coupled with the assertion that 'there will be as many as 50 million environmental refugees in the world in five years' time'[8] were likely to fuel widespread fears of uncontrollable migration flows.[9] Migration was constructed as intrinsically bad and as something to be stopped: part of the 'sedentary bias' which has become so dominant in discourses on migration.[10] Thus the doomsday prophecies of environmentalists may have done more to stigmatise refugees and migrants, and to support repressive state measures against them, than to raise environmental awareness.

In response, refugee and migration scholars argued that such neo-Malthusian visions were based on dubious assumptions and that it was virtually impossible to identify individuals or groups forced to move by environmental factors alone.[11] Part of this critique was methodological: it was argued that some environmentalists were simply mapping forecasts of climatic changes, such as sea-level rise or drought, on to existing global population patterns, and assuming that everyone in the affected regions would have to leave. By contrast, migration scholars argued that mobility was just one of a range of possible strategies, and called for micro-level studies to find out how individuals and communities affected by climate change actually reacted.

---

[5] N Myers, 'Environmental Refugees' (1997) 19 *Population and Environment* 167; N Myers and J Kent, *Environmental Exodus: An Emergent Crisis in the Global Arena* (Washington DC, Climate Institute, 1995).

[6] T Homer-Dixon and V Percival, *Environmental Scarcity and Violent Conflict: Briefing Book* (Toronto, University of Toronto and the American Association for the Advancement of Science, 1996).

[7] Christian Aid, *Human Tide: The Real Migration Crisis* (May 2007) 5–6.

[8] 'Millions "Will Flee Degradation"', BBC News (11 October 2005), http://news.bbc.co.uk/2/hi/science/nature/4326666.stm.

[9] A web search for the term 'climate refugees' brings up over 700,000 items, many of which seek to outbid each other with claims on the many millions of expected displacees.

[10] O Bakewell, 'Keeping Them in Their Place: The Ambivalent Relationship between Development and Migration in Africa' (2008) 29 *Third World Quarterly* 1341.

[11] See, eg R Black, *Refugees, Environment and Development* (Harlow, Longman, 1998); R Black, 'Environmental Refugees: Myth or Reality?', *New Issues in Refugee Research*, Working Paper No 34 (Geneva, UNHCR, 2001); WB Wood, 'Ecomigration: Linkages between Environmental Change and Migration' in AR Zolberg and P Benda (eds), *Global Migrants, Global Refugees: Problems and Solutions* (New York, Berghahn Books, 2001).

In retrospect, it seems clear that the politicisation and polarisation of the debate on migration and the environment had quite negative consequences. Environmentalists may have been misguided in using misleading and threatening images of mass displacement to raise public awareness of climate change, but the defensive postures adopted by refugee and migration scholars also held back scientific analysis and thus probably the development of appropriate strategies to respond to the challenges of climate-induced displacement.

The failure of the Copenhagen talks means that affected communities and states are largely going to be left alone with climate-induced migration and its consequences. At least for the foreseeable future, there will be no concerted international response, and no large-scale programmes by powerful states to provide support for adaptive responses in the poor and vulnerable regions most affected by anthropogenic climate change. We are entering a dangerous new phase, in which polarised positions on the causes and consequences of migration have become distinctly unhelpful. Migration scholars must recognise the potential of climate change to bring about fundamental changes in the nature of human mobility, just as environmentalists need to recognise the complex factors that lead some people to adopt migration as a part of their survival strategies. This situation makes many parts of the book even more relevant, especially those that deal directly with strategies of groups affected by climate change, and the legal and institutional responses of states and intergovernmental organisations.

III The State of Knowledge

After more than 20 years of debate on climate-induced displacement, we still lack a body of agreed knowledge on the topic. In view of the complex characteristics of the phenomenon, such knowledge would have to be based on the contributions of natural and social scientists working in a range of disciplines—in other words, broad interdisciplinary collaboration is crucial, and old barriers must be broken down. As Jane McAdam points out in her Introduction to this volume, we are still far from true *inter*disciplinary approaches, so that the *multi*disciplinarity aimed for in this book represents a step forward, but one that needs to be taken further.

Despite a great growth in interest by both environmental and social scientists, especially since about 2005, there is a surprising lack of sound empirical evidence. The most ambitious effort so far has been the Environmental Change and Forced Migration Scenarios (EACH-FOR) Programme funded by the European Union under its Sixth Framework Research mechanism. Twenty-three research projects were carried out all over the world from 2007 to 2009.[12] I have not had an opportunity to review the findings of these projects in detail, but some concern has been

---

[12] See Environmental Change and Forced Migration Scenarios (EACH-FOR) project, which concluded in May 2009: www.each-for.eu/index.php?module=main.

expressed over the rather short-term nature of the research and about the rather narrow focus of some projects on perceived environmental push factors, as opposed to long-term analyses of a much wider range of factors and responses.[13] For a full understanding, such long-term multifactorial analyses are crucial, but have been rather neglected so far.[14] This makes the debate on definitions and methodology for research in this field all the more important.[15]

The current state of debate does represent a considerable advance in knowledge compared with, say, 10 years ago, but still only represents a half-way house. A great deal needs still to be done by researchers (and indeed by the governments and foundations that commission and fund research), before we can speak of an adequate knowledge base for policy formation and civil society action. It is probably too early to speak of any meaningful scientific consensus at present, but it appears that the following ideas are gaining increasing recognition as pointers for further research and intervention.

First, there is very little evidence that climate change has caused much migration so far. Despite worrying prognoses put forward in the past, it is virtually impossible to identify groups of people already displaced by climate change alone. There are certainly groups which have been affected by climatic (or broader environmental) factors, but economic, political, social and cultural factors are also at work.

Secondly, this should not be taken as a reason to ignore the issue. It seems probable that the predicted acceleration of climate change over the next few decades will have major effects on production, livelihoods and human security. The predictions of 'submerging islands', discussed in this volume by McAdam and Loughry (among others), are the most obvious form, although the affected numbers will be relatively small.[16] As Hugo's chapter shows, it is already possible to identify the 'hot spots'. This does not mean that we should adopt a mono-causal approach: the complex interlinkages with other factors will remain operative, but the climate change component is likely to become increasingly significant.

Thirdly, as the contribution by Barnett and Webber shows so clearly, migration is not an inevitable result of climate change, but one possible adaptation strategy out of many. It is crucial to understand the factors that lead to differing strategies

---

[13] For a discussion of EACH-FOR's African research, and of other research findings on environmental factors in African migration dynamics, see G Jonsson, *The Environmental Factor in Migration Dynamics: A Review of African Case Studies* (Oxford, International Migration Institute, University of Oxford, Working Paper 21, 2010).

[14] For an example of such a study using comprehensive data and sophisticated methods of analysis, see P Bohra and DS Massey, 'Processes of Internal and International Migration from Chitwan, Nepal' (2009) 43 *International Migration Review* 621.

[15] See D Kniveton, K Schmidt-Verkerk, C Smith and R Black, *Climate Change and Migration: Improving Methodologies to Estimate Flows* (Geneva, IOM Migration Research Series No 33, 2008).

[16] As Professor Richard Bedford of the University of Waikato, New Zealand, has pointed out, 68 per cent of the population of the Pacific region lives in Papua New Guinea (PNG). Most of PNG's population lives inland and will be affected not by sea-level rise, but by changes in temperature, rainfall and wind patterns. The possible severe impacts on livelihoods are not likely to lead to significant international migration.

and varying degrees of vulnerability and resilience in individuals and communities. Moreover, migration should not generally be seen as negative: people have always moved in search of better livelihoods, and this can bring benefits both for origin and destination areas. As Zetter points out in his contribution, migrants have some degree of agency, even under the most difficult conditions. Strategies that treat them as passive victims are counterproductive, and protection of rights should also be about giving people the chance to deploy their agency. The objective of public policy should not be to prevent migration, but rather to ensure that it can take place in appropriate ways and under conditions of safety, security and legality.

Fourthly, this makes it all the more urgent to carry out in-depth micro-level empirical research to understand the changes that are taking place, how they affect various groups, and what response strategies these groups adopt. Such empirical studies are now being done, and their findings are beginning to become available. However, short-term studies focusing only on displacement as a problem may be misleading. It is important to link newer research with the findings of existing studies on environmental and developmental issues in various regions, and to build on the considerable existing expertise of development sociologists, human geographers, anthropologists and area studies specialists.

Fifthly, climate change is experienced at the local level, but it has global causes. The ability of individuals, communities and states to respond to such changes is very strongly linked to political and economic factors. The causes of climate change lie in the production systems and the consumer-oriented lifestyles of rich countries of the global North—although newly industrialising economies of the South are also beginning to play a major part. It is people in the poorest parts of the world who are most affected by climate change, yet who lack the resources for effective coping and adaptation strategies. Weak states are not a fact of nature, but a result of inequality based historically on colonialism and, today, on neo-liberal globalisation. Decrying potential climate change migration as a threat to the security of developed countries misses the point—analysed so well in Elliott's chapter—that climate-induced displacement is a result of the human insecurity imposed on the South in the current global order.

Sixthly, this understanding of the inequality that underpins climate-induced migration can be an important starting point for normative debates concerned with the responsibility of rich nations and the 'international community'. These are addressed in detail by Zetter and Penz in their contributions. Zetter, in particular, makes the important point that not only the rights of migrants, but also those of the much larger numbers of people who do *not* move in response to climate change, need protection. Penz concludes with the hope that a just climate regime will not be seen as just an 'ethical fantasy'. However, after the Copenhagen debacle, it seems doubtful whether moral arguments carry much weight with powerful states. Strategies based on hoping that those in control will do the right thing give little cause for optimism. That is why it is so crucial to explore what action is possible now.

Seventhly, a key locus of practical action is to be found at the macro-level of international and national law. It is of utmost importance to determine the legal status of people induced to migrate by changes in their living conditions linked to climate change (generally along with other factors). Clearly, there is a broad spectrum of migration motivations, ranging from forced migrants who have to leave unviable locations, through to migrants who can exercise various levels of agency. It is also crucial to find ways of using legal frameworks to protect and enhance the rights of both migrants and non-migrants. Walter Kälin presents a definitive overview of the legal instruments involved, while Jane McAdam focuses on the potential for statelessness in the case of people displaced from small Pacific island states. Debates on refugee and asylum issues over the last 20 years show the increasing unwillingness of governments and bureaucracies in developed countries to enhance protection of displaced people, but law can be a potent instrument to make states face up to their responsibilities.

Eighthly, practical interventions to support people affected by climate change are needed in many areas of social action: employment, housing, welfare and education all spring to mind. Health is clearly a crucial area. The contribution by McMichael, McMichael, Berry and Bowen presents a valuable overview of the types of health risk involved, and of possible responses at the political and professional levels. Loughry, in a study enriched by fieldwork in the Pacific island of Kiribati, focuses on the consequences of displacement for mental health. Far more work of this kind is needed for all the areas of social action mentioned above as well as for health. Interestingly, in both these contributions, research findings derived from studies of people affected by war and violence are used as a basis for analogies with people affected by climate change. This procedure is necessary and productive at present, but also reveals the lack of adequate research on the newer phenomenon: we do not know for sure that people affected by climate change will follow the same patterns as soldiers or refugees affected by violence. Moreover, the slow onset of climate change processes may have substantially different effects compared with warfare, persecution or even natural disasters.

Finally, we need to listen to the cautionary tales of those who study the microdynamics of human behaviour in cultural groups affected by climate change. Campbell's account of the dilemmas of past attempts at relocating Pacific peoples make it clear that there will be no one-size-fits-all solution to the problem of displacement. Top-down bureaucratic rationality may not achieve much when it comes up against very different ways of thinking and living. This is all the more reason why we need far more local-level research, to inform strategies for responding to climate-induced displacement.

INDEX